# The Reinvention of Development Banking in the European Union

# The Reinvention of Development Banking in the European Union

## *Industrial Policy in the Single Market and the Emergence of a Field*

*Edited by*

DANIEL MERTENS, MATTHIAS THIEMANN,

*and*

PETER VOLBERDING

OXFORD
UNIVERSITY PRESS

**OXFORD**
UNIVERSITY PRESS

Great Clarendon Street, Oxford, OX2 6DP,
United Kingdom

Oxford University Press is a department of the University of Oxford.
It furthers the University's objective of excellence in research, scholarship,
and education by publishing worldwide. Oxford is a registered trade mark of
Oxford University Press in the UK and in certain other countries



First Edition published in 2021

Impression: 1



Published in the United States of America by Oxford University Press
198 Madison Avenue, New York, NY 10016, United States of America

British Library Cataloguing in Publication Data
Data available

Library of Congress Control Number: 2020951688

ISBN 978-0-19-885970-3

DOI: 10.1093/oso/9780198859703.001.0001

Printed and bound in the UK by
TJ Books Limited

# Preface

In 2010, in the shadow of the global financial crisis, and in the midst of the still-unfolding crisis of Fannie Mae and Freddie Mac, two of this volume's editors met for the first time at the Max Planck Institute for the Study of Societies in Cologne to discuss state involvement in private financial markets. Both of them puzzled by the question of whether European economies would have a similar set of risk-absorbing, market-creating public institutions, they began a casual exchange over the role of public development banks. When they met again, a few years later, at Goethe University in Frankfurt, this exchange morphed into a fruitful research collaboration on their expanding role. Enriched by discussions with the third editor of this book, who came as a visiting PhD researcher from Harvard to Frankfurt, the academic reflection of what was evolving in real time after the election of Jean-Claude Juncker as Commission President triggered a set of questions that this joint volume is now seeking to answer. Where did recent initiatives to expand public development banks' activities—crowding in private money through financial instruments—come from in a longer-term historical perspective and whose interests were being served by them? Could new tools and an emerging network of European development banks empower the EU to pursue a common investment policy?

Just as this book is going to press, this question has taken on a new urgency with Covid-19 and the looming recession in the European Union. In line with the main findings of this book, the European Commission has drawn upon the European Investment Bank to craft a crisis response, as national development banks have been steadfast pillars of national crisis responses. Nowhere is this more visible than in the case of Germany; where the national development bank KfW has been used to enact an unlimited credit guarantee for companies impacted by the pandemic. As countries in the European Union are emerging from the short-term shock and face the long-term consequences, development banks across Europe are preparing to expand both their loan volumes as well as their equity support for start-ups and strategic sectors, taking up their countercyclical lending function in light of a retreating private banking sector. As one seeks to understand the current dynamics, we believe this volume provides important insights based on the unfolding of the last crisis response post-2008.

Keen on exploring both the supranational and national dimensions of European development banking after this prior crisis, the editors were fortunate to receive funding for this research endeavor from three institutions, whose financial and organizational support is gratefully acknowledged. The first is the Foundation of

European Progressive Studies (FEPS) in Brussels, who generously hosted this project and one of the workshops for this book. In addition, Sciences Po Paris and the Center for "Sustainable Architecture for Finance in Europe" (SAFE) in Frankfurt provided both organizational and financial support to further realize the project which began as "The Rise of Promotional/Development Banks in Europe – Potentials and Pitfalls" (2018–2019). Together, these institutions allowed us to bring together a wonderful group of researchers from across Europe, all of whom share the rare interest in the political economy of development banks and form the backbone of this edited volume.

Throughout the research process, many colleagues have supported us in bringing this book to fruition. This volume has enormously benefitted from the insightful critiques and comments of Cornel Ban, Adam Dixon, Timur Ergen, Helen Kavvadia, Elsa Massoc, Marek Naczyk, Andreas Nölke, and Cornelia Woll, as well as three anonymous reviewers. We are grateful to them, and to all the development bankers, policymakers, and fellow academics who have shared their thoughts with us and our contributors. Finally, we would like to thank Oxford University Press for realizing this publication with us.

We believe that this edited volume can advance our understanding of not only what development banking in Europe is, but also when, where, and how it takes place and expands. As development banking has come to the forefront of European public policy, be it in its attempt to respond to the Covid-19 pandemic, tackle climate change, or the thorough digitization of the European economy, we believe that investigating its consequences, its promises, as well as its problems, requires a thoughtful interdisciplinary effort, to which this volume is but the first step. We hope that many other social science researchers will engage with us in this endeavor to critically, but benevolently supervise these activities and their intended and unintended consequences.

D.M., M.T., P.V.

*Frankfurt, Paris, New York,*
*May 2020*

# Table of Contents

# List of Illustrations

# List of Tables

# List of Contributors

**Jens Bastian** is an independent economic consultant and financial sector analyst based in Athens, Greece. His main areas of expertise concern China's expanding investment and bank lending footprint in Europe. From September 2011 to September 2013 Dr. Jens Bastian was appointed by the European Commission as a member of the Task Force for Greece in Athens, Greece. His previous professional experience includes working as Lead Economist / Institution Building for the European Agency for Reconstruction, Thessaloniki, Greece, at Alpha Bank in Athens, Greece, as well as various academic positions held at St. Antony's College, Oxford, Nuffield College, Oxford and the London School of Economics. He serves as a Senior Policy Advisor at ELIAMEP (Hellenic Foundation for European and Foreign Policy) in Athens, Greece. Jens Bastian received his Ph.D. from the European University Institute in Florence, Italy in 1993.

**Fabio Bulfone** is a postdoctoral researcher at the Max Planck Institute for the Study of Societies in Cologne. His research focuses on industrial policy, labor market, industrial relations and Southern European capitalism. He has published in the *Socio-economic Review, Journal of European Public Policy, Governance* and *Comparative Political Studies* among others.

**Judith Clifton** is Professor and Jean Monnet Chair at the Faculty of Business and Economic Sciences, University of Cantabria. She is Editor-in-Chief of *Journal of Economic Policy Reform*, and Co-Editor of *Cambridge Journal of Regions, Economy & Society* and *Cambridge Elements in Public Policy*. She has published around 100 papers in major international journals. Judith received her D.Phil. in Political Economy from the University of Oxford and has been Visiting Scholar at CSIC, Colmex, Cornell University, European Institute and, most recently, Cambridge University. She is currently Principal Investigator for Spain for the major H2020 TOKEN project on disruptive technologies and the public sector.

**Donato Di Carlo** is a post-doctoral researcher at the Max Planck Institute for the Study of Societies in Cologne. He has obtained his Ph.D. in Political Economy and European Integration from the same institute. His research interests cover comparative political economy, industrial relations, public policy and the state. His research work has mostly analyzed the role of public sector wage setting as an instrument of states' economic governance in the EMU.

**Daniel Díaz Fuentes** is full Professor of Economics at the University of Cantabria and has been visiting research fellow at various universities, including Michigan, Oxford, London School of Economics, Manchester, and European University Institute. At the University of Cantabria, he is responsible for running the MSc and PhD in Economics. His main research and teaching interests are Public Service Economics and Multilateral Financial Institutions. He has published over 100 referred articles in leading international journals.

He has worked as a consultant for the United Nations, OECD and European Commission, European Investment Bank, and so on. He received his Ph.D. in Economics from the Universidad de Alcalá–Madrid and is currently Visiting Fellow at Oxford University's Department of International Development.

**Clara García Fernández-Muro** holds a Ph.D. in Economics from Complutense University of Madrid (UCM). She is Professor of Applied Economics and Political Economy at that same university, and member of the Complutense Institute for International Studies (ICEI). Previously, she was Associate Professor at University of Huelva; and visiting researcher at University of California-Berkeley and University of Massachusetts-Amherst. Her research deals with the political economy of productive and financial development. More specifically, she has worked on productive upgrading, energy transitions, and financial fragilities and crises; all this with a double geographical specialization, having done empirical work on East Asia and more recently on Spain. On these issues she has published extensively in journals and books (as in, for example, *Cambridge Journal of Economics*, *Energy Policy*, *Governance*, and *Routledge*). She is member of the Academic Committee of the Doctorate program in Economics of the UCM and independent member of the General Board of the Spanish Official Credit Institute (ICO).

**Ana Lara Gómez** is a Lecturer at the University of Cantabria and postdoctoral researcher. After completing her Ph.D. she obtained a postdoctoral fellowship funded by the Government of Cantabria. She has been working on the Santander Financial Institute project entitled *Origin and historical evolution of financial and banking globalization: Latin America and Spain in a comparative perspective.* Previously, Ana was awarded a Ph.D. scholarship by the Lombardy Advanced School of Economic Research after completing her second Masters in Economic Analysis. She has also been Junior Researcher for the European Investment Bank Project, The History of European Infrastructure Finance, (EIBURS Competitive Programme). Additional experience includes working for the Economic and Foreign Trade Department of the Spanish Embassy in Morocco and the French journal of economics, *Futuribles.*

**Stephany Griffith-Jones** is Financial Markets Director at the Initiative for Policy Dialogue, Columbia University; Emeritus Professorial Fellow at the Institute of Development Studies, Sussex University; Senior Research Associate at the Overseas Development Institute; and Non-Resident Fellow at the Center for Global Development. She is researching and providing policy advice on reforming the international and national financial architecture, especially the role of regional and national development banks, with a focus on the European Investment Bank. Published widely, Stephany Griffith-Jones has written or edited 25 books and numerous articles. A 2010 book, co-edited with Joseph Stiglitz and Jose Antonio Ocampo, *Time for a Visible Hand*, dealt with financial regulation. Her most recent book, co-edited with J.A. Ocampo, *is The Future of National Development Banks.* She also advised international organizations, including the European Commission, European Parliament, World Bank, IADB, various UN agencies and several governments.

**Egert Juuse** is a Research Fellow at the Ragnar Nurkse School of Innovation and Governance, Tallinn University of Technology. His main research interests include financial policy, economic development and innovation policy. Egert published in the *Journal of Post Keynesian Economics* and the *Journal of Baltic Studies.*

**Katalin Mérő** is Associate Professor at the Department of Finance, Budapest Business School. Since 2011 she has been a member of the Joint Board of Appeal of the European Supervisory Authorities. Prior to her academic carrier, between 2005 and 2010, she was the director of Hungarian Financial Supervisory Authority's Economics, Risk Assessment and Regulatory directorate. Before that, she was the deputy head of the Financial Stability Department of the Hungarian central bank. From 1990 to 1997, she was director of Strategy and Economic Analysis at K&H, a large Hungarian commercial bank. She holds a Ph.D. from Budapest University of Technology and Economics.

**Daniel Mertens** is Professor of International Political Economy at the University of Osnabrück. Prior to that, he was an assistant professor (*Habilitand*) at Goethe University Frankfurt and a visiting scholar at Northwestern University. He received his Ph.D. from the Max Planck Institute for the Study of Societies and the University of Cologne. His work ranges from the politics of credit markets and banking to analyses of the modern tax state and has been published in outlets such as the *Journal of European Public Policy*, *New Political Economy*, and *Socio-Economic Review*. He is also one of the editors of the *International Handbook of Financialization* (Routledge 2020).

**Olga Mikheeva** is a Marie Curie Research Fellow at the Institute for Innovation and Public Purpose, University College London. She received her Ph.D. from the Ragnar Nurkse School of Innovation and Governance, Tallinn University of Technology. Olga works on the financing of innovation and development, development banks, innovation policies, governance of STI policies, and the political economy of financing development. She published in the *Journal of Post Keynesian Economics*, the *Journal of Baltic Studies*, and *Administrative Culture*.

**Natalya Naqvi** is an assistant professor in international political economy at the London School of Economics. Her research focuses on the role of the state and the financial sector in economic development, as well as the amount of policy space developing countries have to conduct selective industrial policy. She is also interested in the role of public ownership of large firms, and the consequences of privatisation in developing and industrialised economies. She holds a PhD from the Centre of Development Studies at the University of Cambridge.

**Dóra Piroska** is Visiting Professor at the Department of International Relations, Central European University (CEU) and Associate Professor at the Department of Economic Policy, Corvinus University of Budapest. She is a political economist with research and teaching interests in international and comparative political economy, politics of finance, and institutional theories. Her research focuses on the European Union and the Central and Eastern European region. Her latest research deals with development finance both at the national and international levels. Recently, she has published on the macroprudential turn, non-Eurozone Member States' take on the Banking Union, and Troika institutions' different kinds of crisis management. She has published in *Competition and Change*, *Europe-Asia Studies*, *Third World Thematics*, *Journal of Economic Policy Reform*, *Policy and Society*, and *New Political Economy*.

**Eulalia Rubio Barcelo** is Senior Research Fellow at the Jacques Delors Institute in Paris and Associate Professor at the European School of Political and Social Sciences of the Catholic University of Lille (ESPOL). She holds a Ph.D. in Political Sciences from the

European University Institute of Florence (EUI). Her work centres on the European Union's economic policies, with particular emphasis on the EU budget and the role of the EIB and other promotional institutions in the implementation of EU financial instruments and guarantees.

**Matthias Thiemann** is an Assistant Professor of European Public Policy at Sciences Po Paris. His work focuses on the regulation of financial markets pre- and post-crises as well as the role development banks play in the reconfiguration of these markets post-crises. His work has appeared in the *Journal of European Public Policy*, *American Journal of Sociology*, *Review of International Political Economy* and *New Political Economy*, among others.

**Peter Volberding** holds a Ph.D. from the Government Department at Harvard University. His work centers on the intersection between public institutions and private finance, particularly as it relates to economic development (e.g. *Leveraging Financial Markets for Development: How KfW Revolutionized Development Finance*, Palgrave Macmillan, 2020). He has also published work relating to public-private partnerships (PPPs), economic development policy, and natural resources in economic development. He is currently based in New York and works in consulting.

# 1

# Introduction

## The Making of the European Field of Development Banking

*Daniel Mertens, Matthias Thiemann, and Peter Volberding*

### 1.1 Introduction

On July 22, 2015, in the context of Jean-Claude Juncker's Investment Plan for Europe, the European Commission (EC) formally published a communication on the role of national development banks (NDBs)[1] in Europe. In it, the EC declared that NDBs could serve as important financial partners to EU institutions and investment platforms to coordinate growth-promoting investments, and that states without an NDB should consider establishing one. Over time, this could even evolve into "an integrated system of [NDBs], which would be able to apply proven products and best practices across Member States" (European Commission, 2015a, p. 13). Pierre Moscovici, then Commissioner for Economic and Financial Affairs, Taxation, and Customs, echoed the sentiment: "The synergy between European and national tools will be essential to start rapidly closing the investment gap that our economies face. In order to make this happen, we're convinced that a well-structured network of [NDBs] can play a key role and complement the European Investment Bank."[2]

This announcement marked a turning point for European NDBs. Even just a few years earlier, the EC had looked suspiciously at NDBs, viewing them as relics of a bygone era of national industrial policy that could imperil the single market project. After all, NDBs were precisely that—national financial institutions. The primary concern was that NDBs could unfairly tilt the scales towards those firms or sectors that Member States prioritized, leading to a beggar-thy-neighbor dynamic and inhibiting further integration. However, as is evidenced by the

[1] The EU normally uses the label national promotional banks and institution (NPBIs). We elaborate on the political context of this terminology in section 2.1 below.

[2] Press Release by the European Commission on 22 July 2015. Available at http://europa.eu/rapid/press-release_IP-15-5420_en.htm; last accessed on June 17, 2019.

Daniel Mertens, Matthias Thiemann, and Peter Volberding, *Introduction: The Making of the European Field of Development Banking* In: *The Reinvention of Development Banking in the European Union: Industrial Policy in the Single Market and the Emergence of a Field.* Edited by: Daniel Mertens, Matthias Thiemann, and Peter Volberding, Oxford University Press (2021).
 DOI: 10.1093/oso/9780198859703.003.0001

communications, NDBs have secured a role in the pantheon of European economic institutions. The growing support for NDBs was mirrored in their expansion in size, number, and scope. This trend, which accelerated after the financial crisis of 2008, went hand in hand with an expansion of development banking activities at the European level, driven by the European Investment Bank (EIB) and the Juncker Plan from 2015 onwards.

Yet this turn towards discretionary public intervention in markets and the form it is taking are surprising. European integration has usually meant that Member States lost autonomy in economic policy making (cf Pierson, 1996). The strengthening of competition law, restrictions on fiscal deficit spending, heightened regulations across sectors, and a loss of independent monetary policy, among others, have significantly circumscribed policy choices and appear to be in contradiction with steered investment. State banking in particular came under pressure from European financial liberalization (Seikel, 2014; Epstein, 2017; Verdier, 2000) and one might have expected the role of NDBs to shrink as a result of expanding EU market governance. Instead, NDBs have done precisely the opposite, allowing Member States to directly finance activities within their borders. Moreover, not only are NDBs tolerated by the EC, they are now encouraged by it to expand in size and scope and to act as intermediaries for European-level financial resources, a fact that after the financial crisis has led to the emergence of an entire ecosystem of NDBs. Today, NDBs are participating in an ever-growing list of sectors, financial instruments, risk-sharing techniques, and branch networks. This book is therefore driven by this central puzzle—why have NDBs not only expanded their balance sheets, but also ventured into new economic activities during a time of deepening EU integration?

The puzzle of strengthening NDBs is more complex than a simple growth story. Of particular note is that, in addition to expanding operations, NDBs have also increasingly integrated their activities both with each other—via associations and through joint ventures[3]—and with EU-wide development-banking institutions and investment platforms.[4] NDBs have exerted concerted efforts to join together in associations to directly lobby the EU, as well as to promote financial tools within their respective Member State governments. Therefore, our second question is: why have NDBs not only coalesced with other NDBs, but also developed strong linkages with supranational institutions

[3] E.g. the joint investment into venture capital by Bpifrance and KfW, started in fall 2017 (s. https://www.kfw.de/KfW-Group/Newsroom/Press-Material/Themen-kompakt/Europa/Kooperation, last accessed on 29 August 2019.

[4] A trend initiated by the Margueritte Fund in 2010, which was a joint investment by the five large NDBs in Europe (CDC, CDP, KfW, ICO, BGK), the EIB and the European Commission (http://www.marguerite.com/about-us/background), which was renewed in 2016, and was continued through the European Fund for Strategic Investment (EFSI) and its successor InvestEU.

and investment vehicles, most notably the European Investment Bank and the European Investment Fund?

This edited volume tries to make sense of this transformation and, more importantly, the dynamics that now govern the political and economic array of NDBs. In particular, we seek to explain the surprising presence of NDBs within the EU and its implications for broader state-market relations, as the integration of markets and the harmonization of competition policy continue to leave space for innovation in industrial and regulatory policy. The forms of NDBs, however, can vary profoundly in the single market and also be very different from "old school" state-centered development banking for economic catch-up processes (Evans, 1995; Thurbon, 2016). NDBs in the EU are certainly far from being uniform entities, and given European incentives and constraints, they maintain a remarkable variety of organizational and political-economic characteristics. The third aim of this book is, therefore, to gain an understanding of national trajectories in development banking across the EU and how persistent diversity relates to the cross- and supranational dynamics of European development banking.

In order to do so, we identify a new field of development banking around an innovative conceptualization of state-backed financing for the purposes of policy implementation. Rather than focusing solely on national development *banks*, we broaden the focus to the entire ecosystem of the field of development *banking*. This not only includes state-owned banks, but also the European multilateral development bank (EIB) and other actors that directly shape development banking, including political institutions and policy makers (both in Brussels and in Member States), European financial instruments and financing programs (such as the Juncker Plan), regulatory bodies (DG Competition, DG ECFIN), and commercial actors. We contend that only when all of these actors—which collectively constitute the field of European development banking—are considered can we understand the evolution, development, and dynamics of NDBs. Therefore, this edited volume is dedicated to documenting and then theorizing the dynamics of this development banking field and its implications for national and European economic policies. By doing so, we are also able to understand when, where, and how development banking occurs in the EU, the differences between EU NDBs, as well as identify how these trends have contributed to a broadly perceived revival of national and—critically—EU-wide industrial policy (see e.g. Wade, 2012; IMF, 2019). In this introduction, we therefore begin with an effort to examine the landscape of NDBs in the European Union (section 1.2) before we present our theoretical framework (section 1.3). Section 1.4 then presents our field-theoretical argument about European development banking, which involves as much a *reinvention of development banking* in terms of its properties as it is ridden by inequalities across the Union. The introduction concludes with a key summary of the chapters.

## 1.2 National Development Banks in an Integrated Europe

National development banks (NDBs) are far from being a new institution in European political economy. The progenitors to modern NDBs have origins in parastatal finance institutions in the early- to mid-nineteenth century (Armendáriz de Aghion, 1999; Cameron, 1953) and, since then, state-backed banks have waxed and waned with trends in both ideology and political economy. However, the modern manifestation has taken on new importance in the last decade, as NDBs have become more integrated with European industrial policy objectives and it is this newly gained importance, its origins and articulations, that have largely escaped the literature and that this book seek to capture.

To be certain, there is a rapidly growing corpus of literature on NDBs. Three recent pieces of scholarship—World Bank economists de Luna-Martínez et al.'s (2018) global survey of NDBs, Griffith-Jones and Ocampo's (2018) edited volume on NDBs, and Chandrasekhar's (2016) comparison of NDBs—stand out as the most comprehensive overviews of the functions and trends of NDBs globally. This literature is dominated by a perspective that emphasizes the role of state-backed financial institutions in ameliorating market imperfections that under-supply socially beneficial investments (Bruck, 1998; de Olloqui, 2013; Yeyati et al., 2004). Griffith-Jones and Ocampo 2018 distill this into five principle activities: (1) counteracting procyclicality: (2) promoting innovation and structural transformation: (3) enhancing financial inclusion: (4) supporting infrastructure investment: and (5) providing public goods. In this vein, this literature has examined the role of NDBs in promoting climate finance (Serra et al., 2013), financial services (Culpeper, 2012), and even entire markets (Mazzucato and Penna, 2016). In this endeavor, however, the literature largely neglects the political economy that surrounds these institutions, which is only examined for the case of large emerging countries, such as BNDES in Brazil (Hochstetler and Montero, 2013; Musacchio and Lazzarini, 2014; Studart and Ramos, 2018) and the China Development Bank (Sanderson and Forsythe, 2013; Xu, 2018).

European NDBs, however, have only recently gained some scholarly attention within the context of the Juncker Plan, despite the fact that their setting offers itself for a comparative analysis, as all of them exist in economically developed countries and largely within the same supranational context of the EU.[5] Here, Frigerio and Vandone (2018) find that European NDBs perform better financially than their state-owned commercial bank counterparts, and NDBs have been just as profitable in post-crisis Europe. Like Boitan (2016), this work is mainly concerned with the economic efficiency and productivity of the NDBs rather than

[5] See Wruuck (2015) for a good overview and the following chapters for single case studies.

understanding their political economy and engagement with the EU. In the latter vein, Mertens and Thiemann (2019, 2018) have emphasized that European NDB's horizontal (relationship with other development banks) and vertical relations (with supranational institutional structures) intensified over the past decade, signaling a dynamic conception of development banking for a broader understanding of the political economy of European integration. Taking up the thread from there, this requires first examining the diverse organizational and political manifestations of NDBs in the EU.

### 1.2.1 Defining NDBs

On the surface, the definition of an NDB is intuitive—it is a government-owned financial institution that engages in domestic economic activities to promote national economic goals. In practice, however, a definition becomes difficult to precisely determine as there are substantial variations in scope, mandate, size, financing vehicles, political governance, and risk tolerance (c.f. de Luna-Martínez et al., 2018). For the purposes of this book, we define an NDB as a financial institution with four characteristics, based upon the definition from de Luna-Martínez and Vicente (2012):

1. At least 50 percent of the equity is owned by the national government;
2. a long-term investment horizon;
3. a "promotional" mandate for a broad scope of scope of sectors and instruments;
4. a national, rather than regional or subnational, scope.

These criteria emphasize institutional design and stated objectives rather than the particularities of operation. It also helps ensure analytical comparability by holding key characteristics of ownership, mandate, and scope constant. As such, we have eliminated institutions that operate only within a subnational region, that have been privatized, that serve as municipal or community banks, or that function as state-holding companies with no promotional mandate.

With the emergence of the Investment Plan for Europe, European policy makers indeed settled for the terminology of "national *promotional* banks and institutions" (NPBIs), which have a mandate to carry out—somewhat interchangeably—"development or promotional activities" (EU 2015/1017, p. 10). Such definitional explorations are more than mere semantics, as the official European language of "promotional" clearly followed the German regulatory practice of a more market-supporting *Förderbank* (see Mertens, this volume). As this introduction will show, these definitional efforts are already part of the field dynamics this book seeks to capture, leading us to emphasize the more common term of development banking and its changing properties over time.[6] According to our definition above, this enables us to identify 27 NDBs within the EU, along with the European Investment Bank (EIB) (see Table 1.1).

Together, these NDBs have a combined balance sheet of EUR 1.53 trillion in 2017 or about 4.6 percent of the total European banking system[7], with Germany's *Kreditanstalt für Wiederaufbau*, KfW (EUR 472 billion), Italy's *Cassa Depositi e Prestiti*, CDP (417 billion) and France's *Caisse des Dépôts et Consignations*, CDC (358 billion)[8], comprising the three largest banks and accounting for nearly two-thirds of the total. In many cases, total assets have grown considerably between 2007 and 2017, most notably with the Bulgarian Development Bank or the Lithuanian Invega coming from very low base levels. Central and Eastern European NDBs, as well as the Spanish ICO, on the other hand, have seen a high degree of volatility in their growth (or decline) rates, more clearly resembling a counter-cyclical tool instead of investing in structural transformation. The only banks to see substantial negative growth of their total assets in this period are two smaller banks in Eastern Europe, Altum and ČMZRB, which signals more a reorientation of their activities than an overall shrinkage. Such variegation within a common trend of state-banking presence in the EU begs elaboration.

One area of significant variation among these institutions is the services provided (cf Rubio, 2018). In general, NDBs provide six types of support. First, NDBs can provide loans, usually targeted to a specific underprovided sector (e.g. SMEs or housing) and/or at a promotional rate. These can be administered directly to the firm or through a partnering commercial bank. Second, NDBs can provide guarantees to cover a predetermined amount of financial losses, either directly or indirectly through counter-guarantees. Third, NDBs can provide equity investments, which are most commonly distributed to start-ups or innovative companies, though some NDBs still/again take stakes in large firms. Fourth, NDBs can provide quasi-equity investments, a type of investing that is between equity and debt. This includes mixed financing instruments, mezzanine investments, subordinated loans, and preferred stocks. Fifth, NDBs can provide risk-sharing financial instruments. Finally, NDBs can provide a range of non-financial services that aid in their mission. This can include technical assistance, managerial advice, strategic planning, human capital development, and networking and mentorship services. As will be detailed in the rest of this volume, each NDB—as a result of historical legacy and political objectives—has opted for a different mix of

[6] In fact, the chapters in this book might use development banking, development finance, and promotional banks and institutions broadly interchangeably.

[7] See https://www.ecb.europa.eu/press/pr/date/2018/html/ecb.pr180619.en.html, last accessed October 22, 2019.

[8] Based on the consolidated accounts and including the 182bn Euro of the *Fond d'Epargne*, which is managed by the *Caisse des Dépôts et Consignations*.

**Table 1.1** National Development Banks in Europe

| NDB | Country | Year of creation | Total assets in million EUR (2017) | Total assets in % of GDP (2017) | Δ% 2007–2017 | Primary Activities |
|---|---|---|---|---|---|---|
| CDC (*Caisse des Dépôts et Consignations*) | France | 1816 | 358,543 | 15,64 | 62% | SMEs, public investment |
| CDP (*Cassa Depositi e Prestiti*) | Italy | 1850 | 419,533 | 24,41 | 104% | SMEs, innovation |
| BNG (*Bank Nederlandse Gemeenten*) | Netherlands | 1914 | 140,025 | 18,98 | 51% | Public investment |
| BGK (*Bank Gospodarstwa Krajowego*) | Poland | 1924 [1989] | 17,240 | 3,74 | 169% | SMEs, public investment |
| KfW (*Kreditanstalt für Wiederaufbau*) | Germany | 1948 | 472,347 | 14,39 | 28% | SMEs, exports, innovation, green tech |
| AWS (*Austria Wirtschaftsservice*) | Austria | 1954 [2002] | 358 | 0,6 | 279% | SMEs, innovation |
| SFPI (*Société Fédérale de Participations et d'Investissement*) | Belgium | 1962 [2006] | 2,296 | 0,5 | 46% | Innovation |
| SNCI (*Société Nationale de Crédit et d'Investissement*) | Luxembourg | 1977 | 1,442 | 2,61 | 39% | SMEs, exports |
| ICO (*Instituto de Crédito Oficial*) | Spain | 1971 [1999] | 42,200 | 3,62 | 5,8% | SMEs, innovation |
| SZRB (*Slovak Guarantee and Development Bank*) | Slovakia | 1991 | 572,9 | 0,67 | 8% | SMEs, public investment (via SIH) |
| Vaekstfonden | Denmark | 1991 | 1,611 | 0,55 | 301% | Innovation, SME |
| ČMZRB (*Českomoravská záruční a rozvojová banka*) | Czech Republic | 1992 | 831,98 | 0,46 | –59% | SMEs |
| SID (*Slovenska izvozna in rzvojna banka*) | Slovenia | 1992 | 2,497 | 5,81 | 74% | SMEs, exports |
| HBOR (*Hrvatska banka za obnovu i razvitak*) | Croatia | 1992 | 3,790 | 7,68 | 61% | SMEs, exports |
| MFB (*Magyar Fejlesztési Bank*) | Hungary | 1993 | 4,20 | 3,40 | 20,3% | SMEs, innovation, public investment |

*(Continued)*

**Table 1.1** *Continued*

| NDB | Country | Year of creation | Total assets in million EUR (2017) | Total assets in % of GDP (2017) | Δ% 2007–2017 | Primary Activities |
|---|---|---|---|---|---|---|
| Altum *(Latvijas Attistibas Finansu Institucija Altum)* | Latvia | 1993 [2013] | 451 | 0,05 | –65,9% | SMEs, innovation |
| ALMI | Sweden | 1994 | 864,4 | 0,19 | 70% | Start-ups |
| BDB (*Bulgarian Development Bank*) | Bulgaria | 1999 | 1,253 | 2,43 | 1055% | SMEs |
| Finnvera | Finland | 1999 | 10,337 | 4,62 | 414,6 | SMEs, exports, innovation |
| KredEx | Estonia | 2001 | 194,6 | 0,82 | | SMEs |
| Invega | Lithuania | 2002 | 256.3 | 0,61 | 2784% | Innovation |
| Bpifrance | France | 2012 | 52,414 | 2,29 | 308% | SMEs, exports, innovation |
| BBB (*British Business Bank*) | UK | 2012 | 1,1614 | 0,05 | n/a | SMEs |
| VIPA | Lithuania | 2013 | 33 | 0,08 | n/a | Public (infrastructure) investment |
| IFD (*Instituicão Financeira do Desenvolvimento*) | Portugal | 2014 | 100,78 | 0,05 | n/a | SMEs |
| SBCI (*Strategic Banking Corporation of Ireland*) | Ireland | 2014 | 762 | 0,26 | n/a | SMEs |
| Malta Development Bank | Malta | 2017 | 30 | n/a | n/a | SMEs, PPPs |
| EIB (*European Investment Bank*) | *EU-28* | 1957 | 602,657 | 4,36 | 95,88 | |

*Source*: Institutions' annual or financial reports; GDP from Eurostat national accounts; exchange rates, where used, from European Central Bank; authors' calculations.
*Note*: Data are from 2007 and 2017, except UK institutions (assets as of 31 March 2015) and SNCI (2008 and 2014); EIB measures refer to EU-28 GDP

services, leading to substantial diversity in operations, while also reflecting a reorientation towards greater market-supporting instead of market-steering instruments.

Another area of variation is the age of the institution. A few—such as France's CDC, Germany's KfW, Spain's *Instituto de Crédito Oficial*, ICO, and Italy's CDP—have existed for decades or centuries and, while they have undergone institutional changes, have remained important fixtures of their respective domestic economies. The age of these institutions strongly correlates with the variation in the total assets of the NDB, not only nominally, but also as a percentage of national GDP. Older NDBs in France, the Netherlands, Italy, and Germany all account for more than 15 percent; most banks, however, are only at a few percent. As Table 1.1 conveys, NDBs often emerge from political or economic crisis, like national unification or system transition. Since the 2008 financial crisis, some NDBs such as those in Latvia, and Slovakia, have been substantially restructured. Moreover, new NDBs have been established since 2012, in Ireland, Malta, Portugal, and the United Kingdom, and several other NDBs have been proposed across the EU. This not only includes Romania (Ban, 2019) and the Netherlands (see *Invest-NL*), but also Greece (Bastian, this volume) and the accession countries in the Balkans in order to create an infrastructure to channel European Union funds (see Rubio & Thiemann, this volume). In other words, newer NDBs have emerged in the face of European integration, underlining the point that size, age, and business models are interrelated features of a diverse development finance landscape in the EU.

An outcome of this variation in terms of size and age is the remarkable concentration in terms of asset size in only a few players in Western Europe[9]: the six largest Western European NDBs account for almost 97 percent of all NBD assets in the EU (see Figure 1.1). Adding the EIB to this picture shows that its asset growth over the past decade has made it the largest development finance actor within the EU (and also the largest multilateral development bank (MDB) globally), thereby crucially impacting the dynamic of what we below call the field of European development banking (see Griffith-Jones and Naqvi, this volume).

In this context, Figure 1.2 below charts the average asset size of NDBs, the average equity ratio of banks, and the role of EU funds in NDB's operational portfolio, for different European regions. We have differentiated the regions according to these criteria, which leads us to focus on a) large Western NDBs, b) NDBs in Central and Eastern Europe, c) smaller Western and Nordic NDBs (which

[9] Comparing NDBs on aggregated assets, however, can be a misleading endeavor. Some institutions such as KfW are structured as a corporate group that also includes several subsidiaries in development assistance or export finance, while in other cases these tasks are exercised by separate entities with separate balance sheets, as is true for France with CDC, Bpifrance, and the *Agence Française de Développement*. NDBs often also engage in substantial off-balance sheet activities, such as guarantees, depending on their funding targets, which might be even bigger than their on-balance sheet assets, but are not captured in such a comparison. Nevertheless, the fact of broad concentration in the Western countries in terms of the financial might of these institution remains.

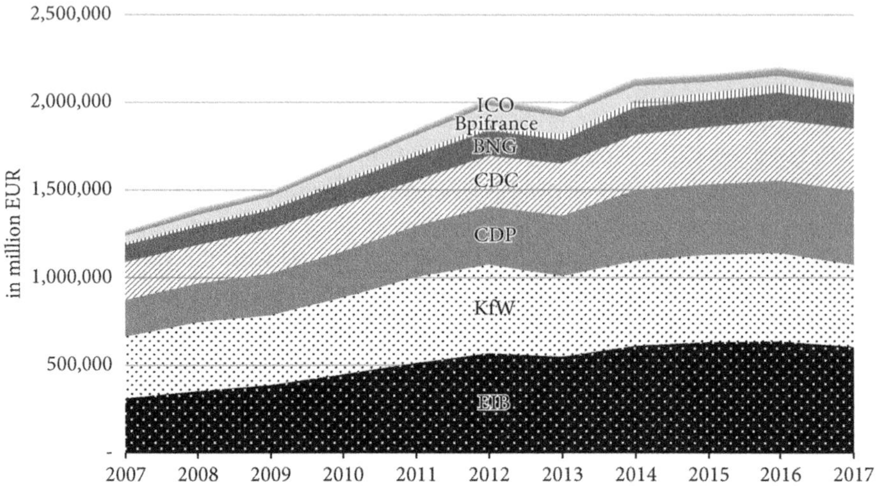


**Figure 1.1** Total assets for all NDBs in the EU and the EIB, 2007–2017
*Source*: Bloomberg, own calculations
*Note*: all banks from Table 1.1 are included

includes the Scandinavian countries, Austria, as well as Belgium and Luxembourg), and d) the Baltics. We further add a category e) for the NDBs founded post-crisis to account for the recent wave of new institutions as both conjunctural and transregional. The graph first highlights, again, the strong concentration of assets in the European core, and the relative smallness of both Baltic and post-crisis NDBs. What becomes further visible in the graph is that the smaller banks operate with a much higher equity ratio (hinting both at their lower credit rating and lesser ability to leverage but also at large off-balance sheet commitments such as credit guarantees). The third message the graph conveys reinforces the importance of a multi-level perspective on NDBs in the EU by zooming in on a European dimension of the business models, that is the mobilization and channeling of EU funds. These mainly include European Structural and Investment Funds (ESIF) and money from the European Fund for Strategic Investment (EFSI). Measuring mobilized EU funds as a share of NDB assets shows how some of the smaller (particular Baltic and post-crisis) NDBs build seemingly large parts of their business model on European money (Mikheeva and Juuse, this volume). Nominally, however, the larger Western NDBs obtain the lion's share of EFSI money (cf European Court of Auditors, 2019), while NDBs in CEE and the Baltics mobilize structural funds that do not play a (major) role in the core countries of the EU (Mérő and Piroska this volume; Rubio and Thiemann, this volume).

This initial stocktaking of European NDBs does suffice to summarize a few critical points that inform the following theoretical framework and the broader argument of this book. Clearly, our puzzle of national development banks in an

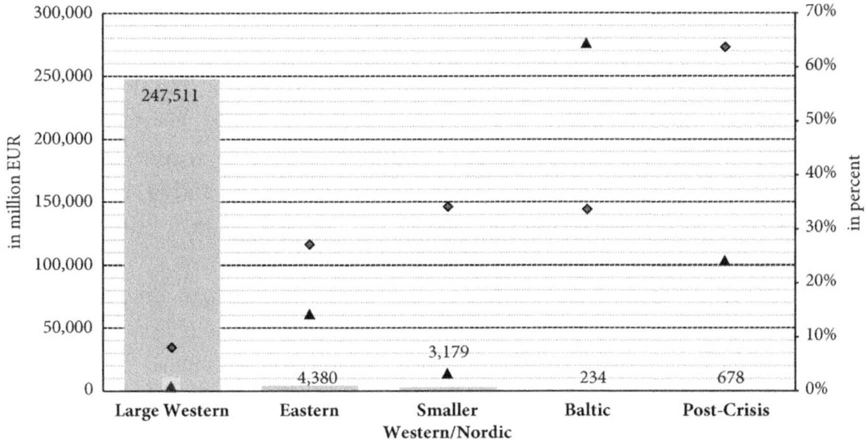


**Figure 1.2** NDB average total assets (bars, left), average equity ratio (diamonds, right), and EU money as share of total assets (triangles, right), by region in 2017

*Sources*: European Court of Auditors 2019; EU Commission 2017, EU Commission 2019; Bloomberg; various annual reports; own calculations

*Note*: EU money means resources from EFSI and ESIF channeled through NDBs between 2007 and 2017. Data for 'Post-Crisis' cover the British Business Bank, the Strategic Banking Corporation of Ireland, the Lithuanian VIPA and the Portuguese Instituicão Financeira do Desenvolvimento. The Malta Development Bank is excluded since it did not take up business before 2018. Bpifrance as a recombination of several existing institutions is categorized under 'Large Western'

integrated Europe is both a story of asset growth, which is more pertinent than mere counter-cyclical intervention, and a story of institutional transformation and diffusion. At the same time, our observations indicate strong variations and asymmetries in these trends, and among European NDBs, which suggest different capabilities, business models, and dependencies on specific resources to conduct strategic economic policy interventions. Despite the rapidly growing corpus of academic literature on NDBs, we find that there is currently no framework to adequately capture these observations. Thus, we propose a broader understanding of not just development banks, but also of the trends in European development *banking*.[10] That is, to take into view the institutional context of the promotional financing activities of NDBs in Europe, which have substantially evolved over the last 30 years as a consequence of shifting regulations, as well as incentives from European and national policymakers (Mertens and Thiemann, 2018). This analytical shift is necessary to us because NDBs do not operate in a vacuum: both political and economic pressures determine when and where NDBs can act.

[10] We understand development banking here as an institutional setting and not as a term to describe a specific set of tools available to public financial institutions for achieving, however defined, socio-economic progress.

### 1.2.2 Beyond NDBs: European Development Banking

In our view, five groups of actors shape the institutional setting and the evolution of the activities of NDBs in Europe: (1) national policy makers, (2) the European Union and its financial incentives, (3) the European Union regulatory bodies, (4) European development banking institutions (EIB and EIF), and (5) commercial actors such as other banks and investors. First, as national institutions, NDBs' primary task is to implement the priorities of their governments. NDBs' mandates reflect this fact, whereby the Member State government establishes the scope and financial instruments available to them. While the daily operations are often independent from political guidance, NDBs are influenced by political mandates and oversight, and sometimes projects require approval from the relevant ministries. Member States also provide financing to NDBs, or establish funds with specific purposes, giving them additional leverage to guide NDB operations.

Second, NDBs within the EU are also influenced by the political objectives of the European Commission (EC). As the 2015 communication demonstrated, the EC has its own political priorities in utilizing NDBs for its targeted investments in key sectors, suggesting that NDBs face pressures from supranational political institutions. However, unlike with Member State influence, the EC cannot directly give political guidance to NDBs; rather, it employs a variety of "carrots" to incentivize NDB participation. This has included budgetary means in terms of financial instruments for regional policies. It has also encompassed the Juncker Plan and InvestEU[11], both of which encourage NDBs to serve as financing partners for EU-led investment platforms that serve the broader interests of the EC. These financing platforms have become increasingly large in volume, providing a huge incentive for NDBs to participate.

Third, numerous regulatory actors work to constrain the agency of NDBs. Unique to European NDBs is the supranational regulatory authority of the EU. Of most importance is Eurostat, the agency that decides whether NDBs liabilities count as state debt, and DG Competition, which works to prevent anti-competitive behavior on the part of states. As such, DG Competition has taken a strict stance on NDBs through its State Aid regulations that prevent NDBs from intervening too directly in the economy. DG Competition has invoked this "stick" in numerous ways. For one, the courts have laid out important legal precedents to restrict NDB behavior. In addition, DG Competition has provided channels—such as block exemptions—that are free from regulatory oversight, provided the NDBs adhere to the guidelines. Additional regulatory guidance may come from DG ECFIN, DG FISMA, DG Regio, and others. However, regulations also provide

[11] InvestEU is planned to streamline the EU's existing investment-related financial instruments with access to the EU budget for both the EIB and NDBs, aiming to mobilize at least 650bn EUR of investment over the period of 2021–2027.

new opportunities for NDBs, thereby making regulatory actors an important force in shifting the contours of European development banking (see Volberding, in this volume).

Fourth, European-level development banking has also become both an important partner and competitor for NDBs. The European Investment Fund (EIF), established in 1994, provided the first Europe-wide agency that sought to promote and implement equity and debt instruments for SMEs. Since the EIF was administered jointly by the EC and the EIB, this provided an important connection between NDBs and European development banking. In the post-financial crisis period, this relationship has expanded to include the Juncker Plan and InvestEU. These programs have provided NDBs with an important channel for EU financial resources—both loans and guarantees—and have incentivized NDBs to support and co-invest with the EIB. The European Structural and Investment Funds (ESIF) have also been important channels for funds to newly admitted EU Member States in Central and Eastern Europe. However, these relationships have not always been collaborative. NDBs and the EIB have disagreed about who should take the leadership role in an expanding network of European development banking.

Finally, commercial actors are essential partners—all the while being competitors—for development banks. NDBs rely on private banks and private investors to act as co-investors or financial backers of projects. For the NDBs that issue bonds or utilize more complex financial vehicles, the private sector is an essential partner, also one that instills market discipline on the NDB. NDBs are therefore increasingly cognizant of the role that commercial banking plays in funding NDB projects, particularly as the financial instruments become more complex and more integrated with financial markets. This has been especially pronounced with the Juncker Plan and InvestEU. On the other hand, commercial actors can also compete with NDBs for investments. They are unafraid of lobbying domestic politicians if they sense that NDBs have encroached on their business.

Within these constraining and enabling factors, NDBs themselves have taken a proactive stance, seeking to actively shape these constraints. While they have grown in size, scope, and number in recent years, they have also grown more assertive in influencing the policy agenda. They have served as instigators of financial instruments, lobbied for reforms of State Aid, and built support within their home government. As part of this, a number of associations between NDBs have emerged. For instance, in 1999, the Network of European Financial Institutions for Small and Medium Sized Enterprises (NEFI) was established to support NDBs with SME financing programs and promote the expansion of these programs across the EU. In 2013, sixteen European NDBs and the EIB launched the European Long-Term Investors association (ELTI) in order to better coordinate changes to financing programs and represent the interests of the NDBs within the EU. Building on an EIB initiative in the early 2000s to coordinate among

"Institutions of the European Union Specialising in Long-Term Credit" (ISLTC), the Ecofin Council mandated the EIB in 2014 to set-up a task force with NDBs to support the Investment Plan for Europe. The latest InvestEU platform—which relies on the synergies between the EC, EIB, NDBs, and Member States—is the clearest evidence of this evolving development banking ecosystem.

Taken together, a complex web of relationships embeds NDBs within a larger context of development banking. New connections between actors have emerged, and a new awareness of their surroundings has been created. We contend that this book provides a novel lens for thinking about development banking in the European Union along these lines, and by doing so, requires a political economy account of the above observations. Not all NDBs are equal within this ecosystem, and some NDBs have had more success in pushing their interests at both the national and EU level. Moreover, European development banking exhibits changing properties over time and between countries, begging for a framework to understand how EU level regulation and investment vehicles have affected NDBs of various origins differently. To capture these evolving relationships within European development banking we now turn to our theoretical framework.

## 1.3 Theorizing European NDBs: The Field of Development Banking

In order to approach the dual challenge of dynamism and diversity in European development banking, we employ a field-theoretical lens, which analyzes the emergence and stabilization of a meso-level social order, a *field*, by focusing on power dynamics and strategic interaction between (individual or collective) actors (Fligstein and McAdam, 2012). We complement its focus on the interaction of incumbent and challenger banks within the field over how best to conduct development banking with insights from historical institutionalism and political economy accounts of the European integration process. We believe this lens is helpful for proposing a dynamic perspective on what NDBs in Europe are doing and how their activities are changing and why, particularly since fields develop over time within larger contexts and co-evolving adjacent fields.[12] In short, we argue that the answers to our initial questions reside in analyzing the evolution of a distinct European field of development banking, which begins to emerge in the early 1990s.

[12] Factors that link the core field to adjacent fields include, for instance, resource dependence, principal-agent relationships, power sharing and information flows. In the case of NDBs, commercial banking and state fields, but also foreign aid fields in which NDBs are involved fit this description (see Rubio and Thiemann, this volume).

A field establishes and operates according to changing "rules of the game," which are set both by bodies that are external to the field (such as national and supranational policy makers and bureaucrats) as well as by the *incumbents* within the field.[13] The latter, in our case the large national development banks and the EIB, are seeking to impose a conception of control, a normative vision of how development banking ought to be conducted that sustains their dominance in the field (Fligstein, 2001, 1996). A crucial feature that field theory allows us to see is that efforts to define "what is at stake" and the "rules of the game" involve both cooperative and competitive strategies. Key actors, mainly incumbents, do have the skills to manage resources, mobilize others, and form political coalitions to stabilize the field and secure their interest, but this may happen in the form of collaboration or domination. Faced with a continuous "jockeying" around field stakes and positions, formally constituted organizations—so-called *internal governance units* (IGU) such as the various associations involving European NDBs mentioned in section 1.2.2—take a central role.[14] In our case, cooperation and competition among development banks is structured by the size and power of the large NDBs, which in turn bring about different relationships with the European level such as the European Investment Bank.

Understanding the evolution of these relationships, historical institutionalist analyses can provide important insights. Historical institutionalism not only points to path dependencies, critical junctures, and incremental change, but it also enables the analysis to focus on the struggle over the rule-making and rule-interpretation that governs development banking and its activities, crystallizing in the idea of an ever-evolving institutional regime (Streeck and Thelen, 2005). Regularized interaction between European rule makers and NDBs as rule takers involves both common understandings and contentious interpretations of the rules of the field, shifting within its political and economic environment. What this linkage enables us and the chapters in this book to do is to think about the historical trajectories and, crucially, capacities and activities of NDBs within their national space and how these affect their involvement and position in a field that increasingly intertwines—and cuts through—"the national" and "the European."

[13] Incumbents wield disproportionate influence in the field and as Bourdieu (2005) points out, often nurture a strong relationship with state agents to shape these external rules in their favor, while "shared meanings tend to legitimate and support their privileged position within the strategic action field" (Fligstein and McAdam, 2012, p. 13). On the other hand, challengers (that we think are most of the smaller national development banks) "occupy less privileged niches within the field and ordinarily wield little influence over its operation" (ibid.) but are able to survive and sometimes gain from opportunity structures.

[14] These IGUs may appear as "neutral arbiters of field relations" but are usually engaged in reproducing and "naturalizing" the field in the interest of incumbents through lobbying or representative tasks, but also through regulation, enforcement, administration or the collective organization of field actors as such.

Zooming in on the historical trajectories of development banking in Europe supports the ability to identify common trends *and* their diverse manifestations. The European field, as this book shows, grows out of a multitude of national experiences that reflect Member State specificities regarding both their economic and political organization, as well as their integration in the wider European political economy. If field dynamics are to mirror patterns of different varieties of European capitalism and their interaction with waves of Europeanization, we need to pay attention to the potentially path-dependent national spaces of development banking. In other words, older NDBs emerge in the European field based on the compromises they made in their national field, but latecomers may emerge in the national field based on the compromises that were made in the European field. This intertwinement in turn has been crucially shaped by the dualist political economy of European integration.

The broader process of European integration has been characterized by the tensions between completing the common market project and national varieties of (democratic) capitalism (Hall, 2018; Streeck, 2014), accompanied by the tensions stemming from an uneven implementation and/or enforcement of liberalization policies producing a varied landscape of state interventionism (Bruszt and Vukov, 2017). Arguably, these tensions have increased due to the attempts of the EU to limit Member State public debt via the Maastricht treaty and its enforcement apparatus since 1992, as well as the multiple crises the European integration project has been undergoing since the 1990s, which have gradually shifted the power relations in favor of market-oriented "structural reforms" and fiscal austerity limiting net public investment (Streeck and Mertens 2013). These developments have accentuated the inequalities and frictions between a northwestern core and the southern, central, and eastern periphery, amplified by the sovereign debt crisis and subsequent Troika governance (Gambarotto and Solari, 2015; Magone et al., 2016).

Against the background of this literature, we expect the emergence and consolidation of a European development-banking field to be characterized by similar tensions. Development banks have always been discretionary instruments to relieve state budgets from cyclical or structural pressures, both within Member States and on the supranational level (see Mertens and Thiemann 2018, 2019). But as the specter of "secular stagnation" continued to haunt European policy makers in a post-crisis environment (Pichelmann 2015), the need to forge an integrated space of only quasi-fiscal investment vehicles may help to explain the timing of field-defining efforts. Still, like many other areas of European integration, this field is likely to be structured through a core-periphery dynamic, in which development banking does not evolve on a level playing field, but NDBs situated in powerful Member States benefit from exceptions those in weaker Member States do not (for the case of KfW, see Naqvi et al (2018)). In terms of constraints, stronger NDBs are likely to resist the pressures of the EU, while those that are smaller and newer rely more heavily on the EU (and incumbents) for technical assistance and regulatory guidance.

Such variegation has long been discussed by the literatures on Europeanization (e.g. Knill and Lehmkuhl, 2002) and European "varieties of capitalism" (Bohle and Greskovits 2012; Hay, 2004; Menz, 2005; Nölke and Vliegenthart, 2009; Schmidt, 2002), which serve as theoretical focal points in several of this book's chapters. In the context of describing the field and the developmental landscape across the EU, it is striking that Member States typically classified as "liberal" such as the UK and Ireland are indeed latecomers to the ecosystem of NDBs, while some "coordinated" and statist types of capitalism—Germany, Belgium, the Netherlands, and France, Italy, Spain—have long histories of development banking; and while development-finance institutions in the neoliberal Baltics are especially small according to our measures above, they play a much bigger role in the "embedded liberalism" of the Visegrád countries. Other cases, such as the Nordics or Portugal, are harder to squeeze into such a typology, but a field-theoretical lens on the evolving European political economy is broadly set to take such varieties into account.

## 1.4 Argument: The Making and Properties of the Field

To fully understand the dynamic structuration of the field over time, it is important to revisit the components that structure it as outlined in section 1.2.2. In our case, there are political actors (the EU and Member State governments), EU financing programs (such as the Juncker Plan, and InvestEU), regulators and their enforcement of regulation (DG Competition and State Aid), European development banks (EIB), commercial actors, and, of course, the NDBs themselves. As noted earlier, the field only exists when there is mutual recognition among actors, which is when the existence of the field is present in the strategizing of actors themselves. Over time, the relative strengths of the multitude of actors have shifted, leading to both restrictions and opportunities for new activities. In this way, we view the field as both holistic and interactive. It is holistic in the sense that it encompasses all actors within development banking, suggesting a much broader view than just NDBs themselves. These actors mutually recognize each other and take their actions into account when operating. Second, it is interactive because, within the field, influence is multidirectional and contested, based on more or less fluid coalitions and on competitive as well as cooperative relations (see Figure 1.3).

A particular feature of the field of development banking within the EU is the non-hierarchical power relationship between the EU level and most development-banking institutions within the field. EU institutions do not control NDBs, which are subject to national control, but rather can only guide and constrain them over

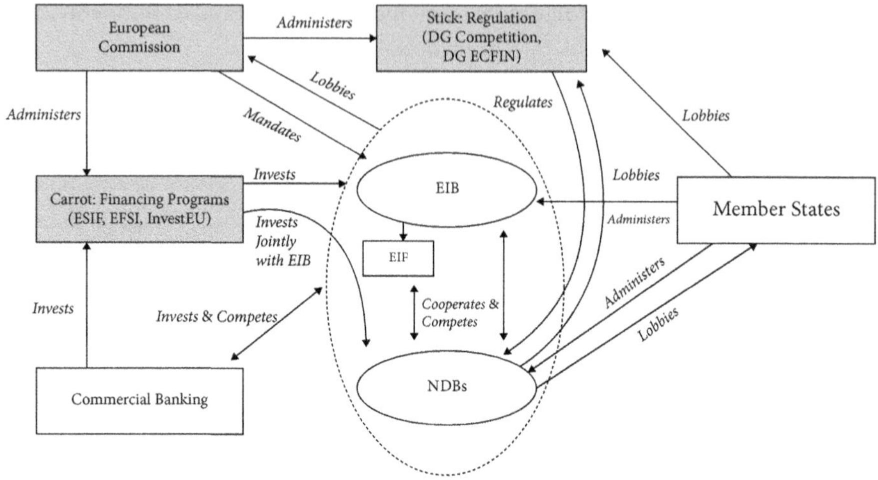


**Figure 1.3** The field of European Development Banking
*Source*: authors' own

time, using a "carrot and stick" approach. This non-hierarchical relationship of mutual dependence means that EU actors need to entice, rather than command, a relationship that is nicely illustrated by the way in which NDBs came to support the Juncker Plan in 2015. NDBs, for their part, have sought to advocate for their own views on how development banking should operate within the EU, seeking to shape both the carrot and the stick, and have used conjunctural opportunities, such as in the moment when the Juncker Plan needed support to flex their muscles. While this perspective of mutual dependency has been present in other areas of study within the European context, such as the financial sector following the crisis (Monnet et al., 2014), this is the first scholarship to do so within the context of development banking. For the moment, this representation suffices to convey the key relationships, but for better capturing the relations between the NDBs, the role of IGUs, and the national spaces of development banking, a few additions are in order.

In the current manifestation of the field, there is no single place for a supervisory authority. As some chapters will detail, Member States have in part lobbied for regulatory exemptions such as are visible in Art. 2.5 of the Capital Requirement Directive IV, splitting up the supervisory space into supranational and national authorities, including ministries and parliaments, on a case-by-case basis. In addition, as some NDBs become reliant on capital market financing, credit rating agencies become a constraining or enabling factor for state banks fulfilling their mandate, often depending on their sovereign's rating. In some instances, multilateral development banks (MDBs) beyond the EIB have also taken relevant positions for NDBs. They have acted either as partners in implementing multilevel financing programs (for the case of KfW see Mertens, this volume), or as funders and competitors in national contexts, contributing to a crowded space of development finance in some countries (see for instance the role of the EBRD and others in Bastian, this volume). Finally, internal governance units are more difficult to locate in a two-dimensional figure since they assume functions that govern relations between NDBs but also with the EIB and the Commission, such as ELTI and the task force within the EIB. As the importance of these additional elements changes over time, a dynamic perspective on the development banking field is required.

### 1.4.1 The Evolution of the Field of European Development Banking

To be sure, NDBs have existed in Europe since the early 19th century, and a handful of European NDBs have engaged in traditional industrial policy programs in the post-war period. However, the single market project entailed that the EU became suspicious of NDBs because of the risks they posed for economic integration and, as a consequence, increasingly regulated both NDBs as institutions and the tools they used to finance projects. In the first few decades of the EEC, NDBs were relatively minor actors, in part because a growing State Aid regime circumscribed their operations. For their part, NDBs possessed neither the opportunity nor the financial resources to link together. With little political recognition and limited interactions, a European development banking field could hardly have been said to exist.

This changed at a critical juncture in 1991/2, in the context of the recession brought about by the Bundesbank interest rate hike and the negotiations over the convergence criteria of the Maastricht treaty. The EC spearheaded the founding of the European Investment Fund (EIF) in order to mobilize investment in SMEs across the EU, which began its work in 1994. While the fund itself was modest in terms of volume, the EIF demonstrated a profound shift in how development banks were utilized by the EC as it engaged in (counter-cyclical) economic policy making. The EIF was officially led by the EIB, granting it both increased political legitimacy as an important economic institution as well as supplying it with financial resources to engage in investments. Its most important aspect for the field dynamics was that it created a potential for NDBs and EIB to work together, despite their traditional rivalry, based on the first modest usage of EU budgetary resources for so-called financial instruments (Mertens and Thiemann, 2019).

Through the 1990s, the projects of the EIF were expanded and replicated for other projects, and the encouragement of the EC for NDBs to apply counter-cyclical spending at the summit of Amsterdam in 1997 signaled a further "rapprochement" between these actors and, ushering in a "carrot" of EU policy, an opportunity for development banks. Through the announcement and these policy initiatives, the EC recognized that Member States' economies had systematic underinvestment in key sectors. However, the EC lacked the budgetary resources to provide all the investments and therefore relied heavily on the EIB group. Concurrently, Member States lacked the ability to intervene directly in the economy as a consequence of strengthening single market regulations and an increasingly aggressive DG Competition. In this conjuncture, NDBs began to emerge as potential actors within this space as the validation of the EIB emboldened their own efforts. In other words, just as field theory would predict (DiMaggio and Powell, 1983; Fligstein, 2001, 1996), national development banks increasingly started to take each other and the EIF into account. Moreover, this already involved an emerging understanding of these institutions as legitimate tools for policy makers to tackle structural and cyclical economic problems in the single market as a liberalization project.

Many NDBs were already in operation by the 1990s and were engaging in economic activities that broadly corresponded with the priorities of the EU. For instance, KfW assisted the privatization of Lufthansa (1994), Deutsche Telekom (1997), and Deutsche Post (1999), with KfW's continued equity participation in the latter two, but—as with many other existing NDBs—was also important in regional development programs, most notably the unification of East and West Germany (Harries, 1998). While these various activities had not been linked with either the EIB or other NDBs, there were signs of early connections (see Mertens, this volume). In 1999, the Network of European Financial Institutions for Small and Medium Sized Enterprises (NEFI) was founded, providing one of the first NDB networks within the EU. For its part, the EC also began to seek ways that leveraged its political and regulatory influence to guide development banking towards its own public policy objectives. In 2005, for instance, the EC ordered a review of the State Aid procedures (State Aid Action Plan, SAAP), which endeavored to leverage NDBs as partners (c.f. Hölscher et al., 2017).

The evolution of development-banking activities progressed steadily for the next decade, including forays of NDBs into venture capital (CDC and KfW) and securitization (KfW) jointly with the EIF; but the full field formation was triggered by the 2008 financial crisis and the ensuing Eurozone crisis. The sudden drop in economic activity and the evident need for investment dramatically shifted the interests of the actors—the EC and Member States became interested in quick counter-cyclical impulses, relying heavily on NDBs and the EIB to deliver them. In its wake, new financial instruments like the Project Bond initiative and the Juncker Plan sought to make more funds available for investment, while regulations by DG Competition, in particular State Aid, was streamlined to encourage block exemptions and investment platforms, which NDBs had advocated for (see Volberding, this volume).

For the European level, the EC created an important carrot and stick approach to guiding the field of development banking. First, since the EC cannot give direct political guidance to NDBs, it has instead provided incentives for NDBs to invest in key sectors. The EU's Juncker Plan provided funds for investment, attracting Member States and their NDBs to cooperate with the EIB. Structural funds (ESIF), budgetary procedures, and the EIF have also served as incentives for NDBs. Second, the EC has simultaneously strengthened the stick of regulation to circumscribe other activities. DG Competition has established important legal precedents to restrict particular economic interventions, but also modernized its regulations to streamline exemptions if NDBs adhere to certain procedural and sectoral factors. In line with the Investment Plan, both the Commission and Eurostat published related guidelines on how to make use of flexibilities within the fiscally prudent rulebook of the Union (European Commission 2015a; 2015b). Together, this carrot and stick combination transformed NDBs into partners for the EC. They were granted flexibility in implementation within the confines of EU policy. Nevertheless, this greatly encouraged NDBs to participate with the EIB and link with other NDBs to advocate for common goals.

The outcome of this evolution is that from a sparsely linked space of NDBs in the EU we have moved to a full-fledged field of European development banking. European NDBs are now subject to field dynamics—all relevant actors recognize their mutual existence and take them and their actions into account when devising new policies. NDBs have become a go-to tool for the implementation of both EU and Member State initiatives, a substantial transformation from the decades before. This recognition also holds for EU actors, such as several Directorate-Generals (DGs), as well as for NDBs that increasingly organize in transnational associations (ELTI, LTIC, NEFI) to pursue their objectives on the European level. NDB ascendance has also brought commercial banks into the field, as they too have found both an important partner and competitor to their operations. In charting the emergence of this new field in the EU, we find that NDBs have moved from mere rule takers into an important part of the rule-making network, transforming both the field and its constitutive interactions (Liebe and Howarth, 2019; Mertens and Thiemann, 2018; Moslener et al., 2018). In terms of our field-theoretical lens, this evolution produced a sort of "settlement" that enabled new lines of interaction with altered understandings of threats and opportunities (Fligstein and McAdam, 2012, p. 91), initiating further interactions to stabilize the field for the immediate rewards of incumbents.

The development-banking field continues to grow with recent EU initiatives, such as InvestEU, supplying further financial resources for the field. While the Juncker Plan initially attempted to mobilize EUR 315 bn of investment, its extension aimed at EUR 500 bn. The InvestEU program is targeting an investment volume of at least EUR 650 bn between 2021 and 2027. While all this summarizes the key events of the field's evolution and with it the growing visibility and legitimacy of development banking, it only hints at the politics of this financial integration process. The question over who gets to shape the rules of the game, both in terms of the reinterpretation of existing rules that limit development-banking activities, but also in terms of the use of EU budgetary means for such activities, has led to intense contestation not only between NDBs and external actors, but also between development banks themselves. For instance, NDBs—particularly the large ones—and the EIB both have an interest in growing the field of development banking to legitimize and expand their operations, yet both have a different vision over who should lead these activities in the field and under what conditions. Consequently, NDBs and the EIB have proposed various solutions to political actors (the EU and Member States), lobbied for changes to State Aid regulations, and promoted new financial instruments as solutions, as the chapters in this volume reveal in more detail. Crucially, this process has also carried implications for the very substance of development banking in the European Union.

### 1.4.2 The Properties of the Field of European Development Banking

The point of convergence in the field dynamics has been the joint push for financial instruments and the use of the EIF as the host, which allows both NDBs and the EIB to partner in projects based on financial engineering rather than to compete in traditional loan business. The implications of this convergence of these otherwise diverging interests have been two-fold. First, the field of development banking has provided a potential governmental infrastructure for industrial policy, although it has now been defined within the confines of new practices of development banking inspired by risk-sharing mechanisms, engaging the instruments of venture funds, guarantees and securitization, but also more old-fashioned subsidized and risk-sharing credits.[15] Second, as each NDB is endowed with different characteristics, the field has created disparities concerning the capacity of NDBs to tap into EU budgetary means and engage in such financial engineering, while funding in general has certainly transcended the national context.

We understand the first of these implications as key to providing an answer to the initial puzzle, since what we observe in the evolution in the field are signs of a settlement that suggests *the reinvention of development banking in the EU.* Such reinvention rests on development banks' capacities to mobilize private finance for investment in infrastructure, innovation, and especially SMEs; it is based on

[15] An example is the conditional loan to entrepreneurs by Bpifrance, which needs to be paid back fully only in case of success (see Thiemann and Volberding, this volume).

risk-sharing arrangements—including public-private partnerships—and financial instruments instead of old-style vertical industrial policy and thus more often "promotional" and market-supporting than "developmental" and market-steering; instead of "picking winners" and funding state-owned enterprises, it rather conforms with the discursive and regulatory constraint of "market failures" as a precondition for targeted financing. True, such distinctions are often difficult to draw as research on horizontal and "networked" industrial policies have suggested (Ó Riain, 2004; Mazzucato and Penna, 2016), but for those dynamics that emerge from the European level they clearly mirror a shifting consensus on what is legitimate action within the field (see e.g. section 2.2 in European Commission, 2015a) The European formula for this shift has become "from grants to loans" and "from subsidies to financial instruments" that allow the public sector to "do more with less." In this sense, it describes a shift from the post-war age of industrial policy to the financialized age under austerity rule.

In this sense, both the Juncker Plan and InvestEU reflect an understanding of the current historical situation as one with abundant private capital, which needs to reach the "real economy" and close post-crisis investment gaps. Instead of taxing financial wealth away for the purpose of public spending, governments employ development banks to reign in market failures to allocate capital for productive projects that may increase the global competitiveness of the EU. This reflects changing conceptions of what is at stake in the field of development banking as well as incremental institutional change, with potentially large implications for the distribution of risks among public and private actors as the former seek to steer the latter's investment decisions (see Griffith-Jones and Naqvi, this volume).

However, as our theoretical framework has suggested, this does not mean that all NDBs are equally empowered. The second implication of the field dynamics is that substantial variations exist in how these NDBs engage with the development banking field in both political and economic terms, meaning that some Member States stand to benefit more from these initiatives than others. For one, we find enormous discrepancy in the abilities of Member States to respond to—and shape—regulatory and financial pressures from the EU. While this largely accords with the findings of the academic literature on EU integration (Knill and Lehmkuhl, 2002; Hanf and Soetendorp, 2014), in the context of development banking, this may produce new inequalities in the distribution of funds and the viability of more urgently promoted European industrial policy (European Court of Auditors, 2019).

We thus contend that the diversity of NDBs and of the strategic goals of national policy makers produce partially idiosyncratic outcomes to similar pressures in an increasingly Europeanized field that cannot mute pressures from the domestic political economies. There, development banks need to engage in a delicate balancing act with the government, from which they derive their main legitimacy and also resources, and with private finance, which is essential for them to achieve their policy goals. As they steer their course of action and seek to maintain their "embedded autonomy" (Evans, 1995), there is the danger of being too close to either of these, threatening their technical independence as well as their potential to enroll private actors for the purposes of public policy. And yet, we do see an alignment of NDBs with the goals and techniques of financial instruments pushed by the European Commission, which envisions risk sharing agreements between NDBs and private actors to mobilize capital which fiscally constrained states no longer can.

In other words, the field has evolved in a way to promote a new version of light-touch European industrial policy that may or may not be in line with national industrial models (Fioretos 2001). Policy makers in favor of the common market project mostly agree that (visible) industrial policies are counterproductive in the age of liberalization (Stiglitz and Kaldor, 2013). Yet, Clift and Woll (2012) have highlighted the incentives of governments to enact policies that promote economic patriotism. That is, politicians engage in policy making that "shape[s] market outcomes to privilege the position of certain actors," which in practice results in the support of national industries (308; also see Thatcher, 2014). Accordingly, and within this new field, there are some indications that Member States have used NDBs to pursue their own national interests and protect key sectors and companies—sometimes acting as *de facto* sovereign wealth funds (Clift, 2013; Naqvi et al., 2018). Several chapters show how national development banks can be employed to follow "protectionist" industrial strategies that were supposedly sidelined in the process of European liberalization, though Member States' abilities have varied tremendously. And, in tandem with power discrepancies, this variation also has implications for the transformative power of this field with regard to pursuing progressive goals of industrial policy such as "inclusive and sustainable growth" or even with regard to a "truly European" endeavor—to which we will return in the conclusion of this book.

## 1.5 Structure of the Book

In order to substantiate these claims, this edited volume is divided in two thematic sections. The first three chapters (2–4) are dedicated to understanding the macro-level dynamics of the European development banking field, whereas the next seven chapters (5-11) contain case studies on European NDBs to investigate the variations in how individual NDBs interact with their governments, EU institutions, and each other. As such, the chapters examine two banks from wealthier and politically powerful EU members (Germany and France), two from semi-peripheral states that have slowly adapted but lacked EU-level political influence (Spain and Italy), several cases from recent enlargements to the EU that lacked any influence in establishing the rules and operations (the Baltics and Poland/Hungary), and one "negative" case where a development bank has failed to materialize yet (Greece). Taken together, the broad variation in case selection helps illuminate the political economic and power dynamics that have emerged in the European development banking field.

Chapter 2 by Eulalia Rubio and Matthias Thiemann focuses on the implementation of the EU budget through NDBs to examine the gradual evolution of the development banking field by the means of European resources as incentives for collaboration, or as a "carrot." Breaking down EU funding by NDB, the authors show how stepwise institutional innovation proceeds through the dialectical interplay of collaboration and conflict between the EIB, the NDBs, and the European Commission, with the Commission seeking to solve its own predicament of limited budgetary resources by first leaning on the EIB, and then, increasingly, on NDBs directly. The Juncker Plan and InvestEU have been the latest manifestations of this process, with the European Commission drawing on the EIB to leverage its limited resources but also seeking to diversify its potential partner base to do so.

In contrast, Chapter 3 analyzes DG Competition and State Aid, the "stick" of the EU. In the chapter, Peter Volberding argues that State Aid has served as an important regulatory tool to guide when, where, and how NDBs are permitted to intervene in the domestic economy. Through a detailed analysis of the evolution of the relationship between State Aid and NDBs from the 1950s to the present, he demonstrates that in the first few decades State Aid greatly limited NDBs, driving them to near extinction in the 1980s. However, beginning in the late 1990s, and accelerating after the 2008 financial crisis era, the EC has loosened State Aid to increase investment in sectors like SME, R&D, and green technology. For their part, NDBs began to assert their positions, not only carving out a role in implementing industrial policy, but also serving as financing partners for the EU.

Chapter 4 by Stephany Griffith-Jones and Natalya Naqvi then zooms in on the European Investment Bank and the Juncker Plan in terms of its properties for industrial policy and state-market relations. Showing the growth of both the EIB and the EIF over the past two decades, the authors highlight the increasing importance of engaging private investors in their financial operations. The authors propose an analytical distinction between "economic" and "financial" risk, arguing that operating on risk-sharing arrangements has led the EIB—and the Juncker Plan—to effectively accumulate the latter at the expense of the former, which has resulted not only in a trade-off between actual policy steer as envisaged by the Commission and increased leverage as a developmental strategy, but also in political tensions within the field.

In the second thematic section on NDB case studies, Daniel Mertens begins by analyzing the evolution of Germany's KfW within the EU in Chapter 5. Presenting

KfW as a key pillar of the German economic model that depends on export-led growth, he traces the imprint that Europe's largest NDB has left on the European field. Beginning in the 1990s, when the bank counseled and funded development banks in 14 transition countries in CEE, KfW became the first incumbent of the emerging field. Adapting itself to the incentives and constraints stemming from European integration during the 2000s, it continues to shape the field today with both the assertiveness of its financial firepower and business model, and the rationale of the reluctant but embedded hegemon that Germany is in the European Union.

The Italian *Cassa Depositi e Prestiti* is the focus of Chapter 6. Fabio Bulfone and Donato di Carlo locate the CDP and its transformations, which in part meant privatization, in the broader evolution of Italian capitalism within the European Monetary Union. Domestically, the glaring gap between the financial means of the deposit-administering bank and those of the sovereign makes CDP a crucial case for a development bank's stabilization role vis-à-vis the public budget. At the same time, the chapter illustrates the key tenets of the "reinvention of development banking," tracing the expansion of new financial activities and their partial transnationalization that were paradoxically linked to the partial privatization of CDP in 2003.

Chapter 7 analyzes Bpifrance, the other NDB originating from a powerful and wealthy EU member. In the chapter, Matthias Thiemann and Peter Volberding contend that the growth and expansion of Bpifrance, which is based on the inclusion of France's sovereign wealth fund, stands for a reinvigoration of French *dirigisme*. Bpifrance has consolidated the government's financial and technical support for key economic sectors to direct economic developments, but, unlike previous attempts, has heavily relied on financial markets actors and techniques to do so. Engaging enterprises like a venture capital firm and expanding the scope of intervention to new sectors, such as start-ups based upon research and innovation, Bpifrance represents the new form of promotional banking in the EU. Ultimately, the authors conclude that Bpifrance's holistic interaction with SMEs and start-ups, based on a broad array of financial and non-financial instruments distinguishes it from other NDBs, as does its ability to shape domestic markets and withstand pressure from the EU.

While these three cases exemplify the trend of development banking expansion and field emergence, Judith Clifton, Daniel Díaz Fuentes, Clara García and Ana Lara Gomez make a slightly different case for Spain's ICO in Chapter 8. While there is evidence for its insertion into a European field, particularly through growing EIB involvement since the accession years in the 1980s, ICO has mainly functioned as a counter-cyclical instrument after the crisis. And despite instances of "marketization" on both its liability and asset side of the balance sheet, its "reinvention" to serve a "hidden investment state" remains modest at best, partially reflecting entrenched political legacies.

Chapter 9 offers the first comparative case study of two Member States outside the euro area: Hungary and Poland. Dóra Piroska and Katalin Mérő similarly argue that these countries have only cautiously employed their development banks as their historical trajectories are riven by tensions that stem from post-social transition in the 1990s, the intricacies of the accession process of the 2000s, and the rise of illiberalism post-crisis. The authors contend that while development finance is valued as a political tool as such, both regimes promote tools that are under firm political control, potentially giving rise to mismatches with a truly European endeavor in state-led investment.

This is no less true for the Baltics as examined by Olga Mikheeva and Egert Juuse in Chapter 10, albeit for different reasons. Estonia, Latvia and Lithuania emerged rapidly from state-led industrial financing and instead adopted, more or less, profoundly (neo-)liberal economic models. While differences between them persist, existing development finance institutions in these countries have broadly followed a path of channeling European funds into their domestic economies in a "decontextualized" manner. Instead of expanding their strategic capacities, they are thus delegated to merely perform a managerial role within the peripheral context they are embedded in.

In the last of the case studies, Jens Bastian in Chapter 11 studies Greece as one of the three European countries, besides Cyprus and Romania, not to have established a fully-fledged development bank at the time of writing. While a Hellenic Development Bank is in the making, development finance has had a contested trajectory over the past thirty years. Beginning with the conglomeration and then privatization of the late industrial development bank ETBA, the Greek economy is familiar with a fragmented and crowded field domestically, populated by Greek, foreign, and multilateral development actors. Within the context of severe crisis and stark political tensions over the past decades, it is unclear what success a new national development institution will have.

Finally, with a multitude of insights from these chapters, the conclusion allows us then to reflect on the commonalities and variegations in European development banking. It asserts that the theorization of European development banking as a field helps elucidate recent trends in EU policy making. First and foremost, this encompasses the push to expand discretionary industrial policy in order to shape industrial capabilities at the EU level. Moreover, the chapter outlines the possible ways forward for the role of development banking in the single market and draws attention to the pitfalls. After all, the reinvention of development banking in the EU involves not only the potential to financially tackle the great challenges of our times but may also become part and parcel of a regime that either reifies "the market" or adheres to some sort of "regressive developmentalism." In this sense, we see in this book a specific lens to understand a broader conjuncture of democratic capitalism in Europe and, perhaps, beyond.

## References

Armendáriz de Aghion, B., 1999. Development Banking. Journal of Development Economics 58, 83–100.

Ban, C., 2019. Dependent Development at a Crossroads? Romanian Capitalism and its Contradictions. West European Politics 42, 1041–68.

Boitan, I.A., 2016. Examining the Role of National Promotional Banks in the European Economy: Emerging Research and Opportunities: Emerging Research and Opportunities. Hershey: IGI Global.

Bohle, D., Greskovits, B., 2012. Capitalist Diversity on Europe's Periphery. Ithaca: Cornell University Press.

Bourdieu, P., 2005. The Social Structures of the Economy. Cambridge: Polity.

Bruck, N., 1998. Role of Development Banks in the Twenty-First Century. Journal of Emerging Markets 3, 61–90.

Bruszt, L., Vukov, V., 2017. Making States for the Single Market: European Integration and the Reshaping of Economic States in the Southern and Eastern Peripheries of Europe. West European Politics 40, 663–87.

Cameron, R.E., 1953. The Crédit Mobilier and the Economic Development of Europe. Journal of Political Economy 61, 461–88.

Chandrasekhar, C., 2016. National Development Banks in a Comparative Perspective, in Rethinking Development Strategies after the Financial Crisis, Volume II: Country Studies and International Comparisons. New York: UNCTAD, 21–30.

Clift, B., 2013. Economic Patriotism, the Clash of Capitalisms, and State Aid in the European Union. Journal of Industry, Competition and Trade 13, 101–17.

Clift, B., Woll, C., 2012. Economic Patriotism: Reinventing Control over Open Markets. Journal of European Public Policy 19, 307–23.

Culpeper, R., 2012. Financial Sector Policy and Development in the Wake of the Global Crisis: The Role of National Development Banks. Third World Quarterly 33, 383–403.

de Luna-Martínez, J., Vicente, C., 2012. Global Survey of Development Banks. Policy Research Working Paper No. 5969. Washington DC: World Bank.

de Luna-Martínez, J., Vicente, C., bin Arshad, A., Tatucu, R., Song, J., 2018. 2017 Survey of National Development Banks. Washington DC: World Bank.

de Olloqui, F., 2013. Public Development Banks: Toward a New Paradigm? Washington DC Inter-American Development Bank.

DiMaggio, P.J., Powell, W.W., 1983. The Iron Cage Revisited: Institutional Isomorphism and Collective Rationality in Organizational Fields. American Sociological Review 48, 147–60.

Epstein, R.A., 2017. Banking on Markets: The Transformation of Bank-State Ties in Europe and Beyond. Oxford: Oxford University Press.

European Commission, 2015a. Working together for jobs and growth: The role of National Promotional Banks (NPBs) in supporting the Investment Plan for Europe (COM(2015) 361 final). Brussels: European Commission.

European Commission, 2015b. Making the best use of the flexibility within the existing rules of the stability and growth pact (COM(2015) 12 final/2. Brussels: European Commission.

European Commission, 2017. Summary of data on the progress made in financing and implementing financial engineering instruments reported by the managing authorities in accordance with Article 67(2)(j) of Council Regulation (EC) No 1083/2006. Available at https://ec.europa.eu/regional_policy/sources/thefunds/fin_inst/pdf/closure_data_fei_2017.pdf, last accessed 9 September 2019.

European Commission, 2018. Financial instruments under the European Structural and Investment Funds: Summaries of the data on the progress made in financing and implementing the financial instruments for the programming period 2014–2020 in accordance with Article 46 of Regulation (EU) No 1303/2013 of the European Parliament and of the Council. Available at: https://ec.europa.eu/regional_policy/sources/thefunds/fin_inst/pdf/summary_data_fi_1420_2017.pdf, last accessed 9 September 2019.

European Court of Auditors, 2019: European Fund for Strategic Investments: Action Needed to Make EFSI a Full Success. Special Report 03. European Union, Luxembourg.

Evans, P., 1995. Embedded Autonomy: States and Industrial Transformation. Princeton: Princeton University Press.

Fligstein, N., 2001. The Architecture of Markets: An Economic Sociology of Twenty-First-Century Capitalist Societies. Princeton: Princeton University Press.

Fligstein, N., 1996. Markets as Politics: A Political-Cultural Approach to Market Institutions. American Sociological Review 61, 656–73.

Fligstein, N., McAdam, D., 2012. A Theory of Fields. Oxford: Oxford University Press.

Fioretos, K.-O., 2001. The Domestic Sources of Multilateral Preferences: Varieties of Capitalism in the European Community, in Hall, P.A., Soskice, D. (eds), Varieties of Capitalism: The Institutional Foundations of Comparative Advantage. Oxford: Oxford University Press, 213–44.

Frigerio, M., Vandone, D., 2018. Bank Ownership and Firm-Level Performance: An Empirical Assessment of State-Owned Development Banks, in García-Olalla, M., Clifton, J. (eds), Contemporary Issues in Banking: Regulation, Governance and Performance, Palgrave Macmillan Studies in Banking and Financial Institutions. Cheltenham: Springer International Publishing, 197–219.

Gambarotto, F., Solari, S., 2015. The Peripheralization of Southern European Capitalism Within the EMU. Review of International Political Economy 22, 788–812.

Griffith-Jones, S., Ocampo, J.A. (eds), 2018. The Future of National Development Banks. Oxford: Oxford University Press.

Hall, P.A., 2018. Varieties of Capitalism in Light of the Euro Crisis. Journal of European Public Policy 25, 7–30.

Hanf, K., Soetendorp, B., 2014. Adapting to European Integration: Small States and the European Union. London/New York: Routledge.

Harries, H., 1998. Wiederaufbau, Welt und Wende: Die KfW—Eine Bank mit öffentlichem Auftrag. Frankfurt/Main: Knapp.

Hay, C., 2004. Common Trajectories, Variable Paces, Divergent Outcomes? Models of European Capitalism Under Conditions of Complex Economic Interdependence. Review of International Political Economy 11, 231–62.

Hochstetler, K., Montero, A., 2013. The Renewed Developmental State: The National Development Bank and the Brazil Model. The Journal of Development Studies 49, 1484–99.

Hölscher, J., Nulsch, N., Stephan, J., 2017. State Aid in the New EU Member States. JCMS: Journal of Common Market Studies 55, 779–97.

IMF, 2019. The Return of the Policy That Shall Not Be Named: Principles of Industrial Policy. IMF Working Paper No. 19/74. Washington D.C.: International Monetary Fund.

Knill, C., Lehmkuhl, D., 2002. The National Impact of European Union Regulatory Policy: Three Europeanization Mechanisms. European Journal of Political Research 41, 255–80.

Liebe, M., Howarth, D., 2019. The European Investment Bank as Policy Entrepreneur and the Promotion of Public-Private Partnerships. New Political Economy 0, 1–18.

Magone, J.M., Laffan, B., Schweiger, C., 2016. Core-Periphery Relations in the European Union: Power and Conflict in a Dualist Political Economy. London/New York: Routledge.

Mazzucato, M., Penna, C.C.R., 2016. Beyond Market Failures: The Market Creating and Shaping Roles of State Investment Banks. Journal of Economic Policy Reform 19, 305–26.

Menz, G., 2005. Varieties of Capitalism and Europeanization: National Response Strategies to the Single European Market. Oxford: Oxford University Press.

Mertens, D., Thiemann, M., 2018. Market-Based but State-Led: The Role of Public Development Banks in Shaping Market-Based Finance in the European Union. Competition & Change 22, 184–204.

Mertens, D., Thiemann, M., 2019. Building a Hidden Investment State? The European Investment Bank, National Development Banks and European Economic Governance. Journal of European Public Policy 26, 23–43.

Monnet, E., Pagliari, S., Vallée, S., 2014. Europe between Financial Repression and Regulatory Capture. Bruegel Working Paper No. 8. Brussels: Bruegel.

Moslener, U., Thiemann, M., Volberding, P., 2018. National Development Banks as Active Financiers: The Case of KfW, in Griffith-Jones, S., Ocampo, J.A. (eds), The Future of National Development Banks. Oxford: Oxford University Press, 63–85.

Musacchio, A., Lazzarini, S., 2014. Reinventing State Capitalism: Leviathan in Business, Brazil, and Beyond. Cambridge: Harvard University Press.

Naqvi, N., Henow, A., Chang, H.-J., 2018. Kicking Away the Financial Ladder? German Development Banking Under Economic Globalisation. Review of International Political Economy 25, 672–98.

Nölke, A., Vliegenthart, A., 2009. Enlarging the Varieties of Capitalism: The Emergence of Dependent Market Economies in East Central Europe. World Politics 61, 670–702.

Ó Riain, S., 2004. The Politics of High Tech Growth: Developmental Network States in the Global Economy. Cambridge: Cambridge University Press.

Pichelmann, K., 2015. When "Secular Stagnation" Meets Piketty's Capitalism in the 21st Century: Growth and Inequality Trends in Europe Reconsidered. Economic Papers 551. Brussels: European Commission.

Pierson, P., 1996. The Path to European Integration: A Historical Institutionalist Analysis. Comparative Political Studies 29, 123–63.

Rubio, E., 2018. Making Better Use of Public Funding: The Role of National Promotional Banks and Institutions in the Next EU Budget. Paris: Jacques Delors Institute.

Sanderson, H., Forsythe, M., 2013. China's Superbank: Debt, Oil and Influence—How China Development Bank is Rewriting the Rules of Finance. New York: Bloomberg Press.

Schmidt, V.A., 2002. The Futures of European Capitalism. Oxford: Oxford University Press.

Seikel, D., 2014. How the European Commission Deepened Financial Market Integration. The Battle Over the Liberalization of Public Banks in Germany. Journal of European Public Policy 21, 169–87.

Serra, L., Lorenzo, J.J.G., Smallridge, D., Trabacchi, C., Netto, M., Buchner, B., 2013. The Role of National Development Banks in Catalyzing International Climate Finance. Washington DC: Inter-American Development Bank.

Stiglitz, J.E., Kaldor, M. (eds), 2013. The Quest for Security: Protection Without Protectionism and the Challenge of Global Governance. New York: Columbia University Press.

Streeck, W., 2014. Buying Time: The Delayed Crisis of Democratic Capitalism. London/New York: Verso.

Streeck, W., Thelen, K.A. (eds), 2005. Beyond Continuity: Institutional Change in Advanced Political Economies. Oxford: Oxford University Press.

Streeck, W., Mertens, D., 2013. Public Finance and the Decline of State Capacity in Democratic Capitalism, in Schäfer, A., Streeck, W. (eds), Politics in the Age of Austerity. Cambridge: Polity Press, 26–58.

Studart, R., Ramos, L., 2018. The Future of Development Banks: The Case of Brazil's BNDES, in Griffith-Jones, S., Ocampo, J.A. (eds), The Future of National Development Banks. Oxford: Oxford University Press, 86–111.

Thatcher, M., 2014. From Old to New Industrial Policy Via Economic Regulation. Rivista della regolazione dei mercati 2, 6–22.

Thurbon, E., 2016. Developmental Mindset. The Revival of Financial Activism in South Korea. Ithaca: Cornell University Press.

Verdier, D., 2000. The Rise and Fall of State Banking in OECD Countries. Comparative Political Studies 33, 283–318.

Wade, R.H., 2012. Return of Industrial Policy? International Review of Applied Economics 26, 223–39.

Wruuck, P., 2015. Promoting Investment and Growth: the Role of Development Banks in Europe. EU Monitor: Global Financial Markets. Frankfurt/Main: Deutsche Bank.

Xu, Q., 2018. China Development Bank: Born Bankrupt, Born Shaper, in Griffith-Jones, S., Ocampo, J.A. (eds), The Future of National Development Banks. Oxford: Oxford University Press, 39–62.

Yeyati, E., Micco, A., Panizza, U., 2004. Should the Government be in the Banking Business? The Role of State-Owned and Development Banks. Washington DC: Inter-American Development Bank.

# SECTION I

# DEVELOPMENT BANKING AND EUROPEAN GOVERNANCE

# 2

# United in Diversity? Interests, Preferences, and Patterns of Engagement of Public Development Banks in the Implementation of the EU Budget

*Eulalia Rubio and Matthias Thiemann*

## 2.1 Introduction

The use of the EU budget for promotional purposes by National Development Banks (NDBs) and the European Investment Bank has become a major characteristic of the field of European development banking. Indeed, it has been a catalyst for the field's' evolution (Mertens and Thiemann 2018, Mertens, Thiemann and Volberding, this volume), with the founding of development banks post-crisis in Ireland (2014), Portugal (2014), Malta (2017), and the Netherlands (2017) directly motivated by the desire of national authorities to tap into European resources. This chapter traces how this fusion of public budgetary funds at the European level with the activities of development banks has come about over the course of the last four decades. While describing the changing relationship between the EIB, the Commission and NDBs since the 1970s, the chapter focuses in particular on the last two decades, when the interactions between the EIB and national development banks have intensified following a) the increasing share of EU budget support being provided through market-like financial instruments such as loans or equity (one of the core business of promotional banks) instead of traditional grants and b) the resurgence of promotional banking in the aftermath of the crisis.

When one looks at the use of EU budgetary funds by promotional institutions over time, the EIB stands out as the bank that has institutionalized and shaped this practice right from its beginnings in the 1980s. In order to understand its evolution, which involved an increasing pluralization of promotional actors taking part in their use, one needs to take into account the interests of two groups of actors intricately linked to the field of development banking in Europe: the EU

Eulalia Rubio and Matthias Thiemann, *United in Diversity? Interests, Preferences, and Patterns of Engagement of Public Development Banks in the Implementation of the EU Budget* In: *The Reinvention of Development Banking in the European Union: Industrial Policy in the Single Market and the Emergence of a Field.* Edited by: Daniel Mertens, Matthias Thiemann, and Peter Volberding, Oxford University Press (2021). © Oxford University Press.
DOI: 10.1093/oso/9780198859703.003.0002

Member States (which jointly are the principals of the EIB in their role as shareholders and are the direct superiors of NDBs and are members of the Council) as well as the European Commission itself which had an important input into the use of these funds.

The Commission, on the one hand, sought to retain command over the use of its funds, seeking to use them for what it perceived to be strategic goals of the Union. It initially saw the EIB as the most efficient and "natural partner" for the use of these funds, given its status in the treaties. Over time, however, it became wary of the intransigencies of the EIB with respect to how the funds should be allotted and the high fees the EIB charged for these services. It therefore began to call for more competition and a more open approach to NDBs. Member States, on the other hand, particularly since the 1990s under the increasing budgetary constraints of EMU, sought budgetary relief in terms of off-balance sheet stimulus programs financed by the EIB or their NDBs. As such, they have pushed for the expansion of these programs and tasked their domestic NDBs to access these funds, seeking support from EIB and NDBs in their attempt to generate economic stimulus. Consequently, the relationship which emerged between the EIB and NDBs over time then is characterized by both cooperation and tensions regarding access to EU budgetary resources, two aspects increasingly institutionalized in associations and coordinating bodies such as the EIB-NDB taskforce and mutual exchanges between the Commission and these actors.

To document this evolution, the chapter bases itself on eight expert interviews with ten members of the EIB, ELTI and the European Commission as well as extensive document analysis. It proceeds as follows: the next section reviews the history of closer cooperation between the EIB and the EU Commission from the 1970s until the late 1990s, which was fundamental for the development of the first generation of financial instruments using EU budget resources. Section 2.3 describes the major expansion of EU market-driven instruments during the 2000s, which created new opportunities for development banks to participate in the EU budgetary arena. Section 2.4 explains the resurgence of promotional banking following the 2008 crisis and how the latter led to more collaboration between the EIB group and big NDBs. Section 2.5 focuses on the Juncker Fund, which constitutes an important milestone in the building of more structured relationships between the EIB, the Commission, and NDBs. Section 2.6 describes today's variegated reliance of the EIB and national development banks on European funds. Section 2.7 analyzes the interests and strategies of different actors—EIB, the Commission, the Council, and NDBs—in the negotiations of the next generation of EU financial instruments covering the 2021–2027 period. Section 2.8 concludes, with some general reflections on the patterns of competition and collaboration between the EIB and NDBs and its likely evolution in the future.

## 2.2 The Early Years: The Build-Up of a Close Collaborative Relationship Between the EIB and the Commission in the Implementation of EU Funds

The history of the rapprochement between the EIB and the Commission dates back to the mid-1970s. Before this moment, the EIB—created in the Treaty of Rome (1957) as an independent legal persona—mainly behaved as Member States' bank and had little relationship with the Commission, in charge of a very small EU budget. This situation changed with the creation in 1975 of the first important EU structural fund, the European Regional Development Fund (ERDF). Following the Council's advice, the Commission gave to the EIB an important advisory role with respect to the implementation of this fund, which was reciprocated with the placement of a representative of DG Regional Policy on the EIB board of directors.

The growing collaboration between the Commission and the EIB in pursuing EU's cohesion goals intensified during the 1980s and 1990s, when the deepening of the single market following the approval of the 1986 Single Market Act and the Maastricht Treaty (1992) led to the establishment of a more ambitious and strategic-oriented EU cohesion policy (the 1988 reform of structural funds) and the doubling of the EU resources for cohesion policy (the first and second "Delors packages"). In this new context, Members States—in their double capacity as EIB stakeholders and members of the European Council—again requested the Commission and the EIB to better coordinate their actions (van der Zwet et al, 2016). In June 1989, operational guidelines were set on how to combine EIB loans with structural funds for infrastructure investments (Bussiere et al., 2008, p. 213–14) and references to the coordination of the structural funds with the operations of the EIB were also introduced for the first time in the EU structural funds' regulations. There were also calls to the EIB to further concentrate its lending in cohesion countries (European Council, 1992, p. 85). One of the consequences was that projects combining EIB loans with EU cohesion grants became more frequent: whereas in 1989 20 percent of EIB loans were combined with a EU budget grant, the figure rose to 31 percent in 1994 and to 39 percent in 1995 (Bussiere et al., 2008, p. 249).

The 1990s also saw another type of the EIB-Commission collaboration emerge. In a context of strong budgetary constraints imposed by the Maastricht convergence criteria, Member States would increasingly rely on the EIB off-balance capacity to boost employment and growth, in parallel to the Commission's budgetary actions. The first of such initiatives was the 1992 temporary "Edinburgh facility," an EIB-funded instrument of 5 billion ECU created "in full consultation with the Commission" (Bussière et al., 2008 p. 38) to accelerate the financing of capital infrastructure projects notably connected with Trans-European Networks

(TENs). This facility was extended in "June 1993 and endowed with an additional 3 billion" (ibid., p. 211). Similar EIB-Commission growth initiatives were launched by the European Council in 1997 (in the context of the "Amsterdam Special Action Programme–ASAP") and in 2003 (with the "European Action for Growth").

Curiously, these initiatives happened at the same time that the EIB faced intense scrutiny by Member States regarding its value added and its *raison d'être* in a liberalizing European banking system and with increasing calls by some Member States to receive a dividend from the EIB, which would have threatened the self-funded growth model of the institution.[1] Against this backdrop, the EIB adopted a more proactive approach, actively encouraging these sorts of joint initiative as a way of gaining legitimacy vis-à-vis the Member States. Thus, for instance, the EIB was behind the proposal of the Amsterdam Special Action Programme (ASAP), an initiative conceived to enable the Bank to inject additional loan finance of ECU 10bn into labour-intensive or job-creating innovative SMEs, health and education, urban renewal, the environment and trans-European networks (Bussiere et al., 2008, p. 208, 212). This strategy of moving closer to the European institutions by making the support of European policies the *raison d'être* of the EIB would be later on clearly enshrined by Philippe Maystadt, the EIB president between 2000 and 2012, which in 2001 would rebrand the bank as the "policy driven public bank" (Robinson 2009, 653) as a way of guaranteeing both resources and legitimacy (Robinson 2009, Kavvadia 2018).

During these years, the most accomplished and institutionalized form of EIB-Commission collaboration was the European Investment Fund (EIF), a spin-off from the EIB established in 1994. The EIF emerged from a joint working group of the EIB and the European Commission established in the late 1980s, which identified a market need for the provision of guarantees to SME lending due to the imminent introduction of Basel I in Europe (interview EIB official July 25, 2019). With a 1.5bn Euro of subscribed capital, the major shareholders of the EIF were to become the EIB (40 percent) and the Commission with 30 percent, the rest being offered to commercial and promotional banks. This subsidiary then installed a direct shareholder link between the Commission and the EIF, allowing it a much larger say on the actions of the latter when compared to the EIB itself (interview EIB Official, July 25, 2019). Furthermore, the EIF, right from the beginning, counted among its shareholders the KfW, CDC, and ICO, which held 60 million of subscribed shares, establishing in addition a direct link between the EIB and these NDBs.

During the second half of the 1990s and early 2000s, the EIF would become the Commission's natural partner for the implementation of the first EU financial instruments funded by the EU budget. This started in 1995 with the "Growth and

[1] Member States actually did withdraw 1 billion Ecu as dividends for the financial year 1998 (Bussiere et al 2008, 208), setting a dangerous precedent for future institutional growth.

**Table 2.1** First EIB-Commission collaboration initiatives, 1989–2003

| Date | Name | Description |
|---|---|---|
| Late 80s/ early 90s | Better coordination EU cohesion policy/EIB lending policy | Operational guidelines in EU cohesion policy rules to facilitate combination of EIB loans with Structural Funds for infrastructure investments, Council's calls to further concentrate EIB loans in cohesion countries |
| 1992 | Edinburgh Facility | EIB instrument of ECU 5bn aimed at accelerating the financing of big infrastructures connected with Trans-European Networks (TENs), set up "in consultation with the Commission" |
| 1994 | European Investment Fund | New EU financial body to support SMEs financing, owned by the EIB (40%), the Commission (30%) and commercial and promotional banks (30%) |
| 1997 | Amsterdam Special Action Program (ASAP) | EIB programme of ECU 10bn aimed at financing labor-intensive or job-creating innovative SMEs, health and education, urban renewal, the environment and trans-European networks, in coordination with Commission's actions |
| 1995–1998 | Growth and Environment guarantee scheme for SMEs (1995), Joint European Venture Initiative (1997), European Technology Facility Start-up a risk capital facility (1998) | Three first EU market-based instruments, financed by resources from the EU budget and managed by the EIF |
| 2003 | European Action for Growth | EIB program aimed at enhancing investment in trans-European network infrastructures (TENs) and innovation and R&D, including environmental technology, in coordination with Commission's budgetary actions |

Environment Guarantee Scheme for SMEs," a EIF guarantee scheme financed by ECU 9 million from the EU budget[2], and was followed in 1997 by three new instruments also backed by the EU budget: the European Technology Facility (EFT), a start-up risk capital facility; the Joint European Venture (JEV) Initiative; and the SME Guarantee Facility[3]. These various initiatives, which were maintained and strengthened under the EU budget for 2000–2006 (see Table 2.1

[2] "Commission approves pilot scheme to support environmental investments by SMEs ," CORDIS news, 1995, https://cordis.europa.eu/article/rcn/4472/es

[3] European Commission press release, "Commission proposes financial support for job creation by SMEs," Brussels, 21 January 1998, IP/98/61.

below), would herald a move away by the EIF from guaranteeing infrastructure projects, a task which was found to be much more capital intensive than the EIF could shoulder, towards SME funding and investment in venture capital. This would increase the EIF's reliance on EU budget funds and, over time, it would also imply an increasing interaction with NDBs, first and foremost the KfW and other large NDBs (interview former EIB official, July 30, 2019).

## 2.3 The Shift from Grants to Loans: The Expansion of EU Financial Instruments During the 2000s

These first EIF experiences in the management of the EU's budget instruments were overall satisfactory but they represented a very small part of the overall EU spending during 2000–2006 period. From 2007 onwards, however, the share of EU budget support spent in form of market-like financial instruments (i.e. loans, guarantees, equity or quasi-equity investments) instead of traditional grants would experience a significant increase. EU resources allocated to financial instruments would shift from €1.3bn in the 2000–2006 period to 12.5bn in the 2007–2013 and 64bn in the 2014–2020 period. The reasons for this "shift from grants to loans," as it is commonly known, were multiple. Before the start of the 2007–13 period, six Member States (Germany, France, the Netherlands, Sweden, the United Kingdom and Austria) had signed the so-called "1%-letter" declaring that EU expenditures should not exceed 1 percent of the Union's GNI in the forthcoming multi-annual budget (European Commission, 2014, p. 75–76). This strong, politically imposed budgetary limit would force the Commission to find new ways to maximize the leverage of EU funds in order to support the Lisbon growth strategy and accompany the accession of 10 new and poorer Member States (Schild, 2008). The need to do "more with less" would become again a necessity for the 2014–2020 budget, negotiated in the context of an economic recession and austerity policies.

The EIB engaged in "particularly intensive" co-operation with the Commission to develop new EU budget financial instruments (European Investment Bank Group, 2006, p. 55). The first was the Risk-Sharing Finance Facility (RSFF), a new innovative facility set up in 2007 and designed to support research-intensive companies and projects (Robinson and Bain, 2011, p. 85). In 2007 a new generation of SME guarantee and equity financial instruments was also established, as part of the new EU budget "Competitiveness and Innovation Programme" (CIP). Implemented by the EIF, the CIP was a more ambitious program than its predecessor (the 2000–2006 MAP), as it covered a wider geographical area, extended the targets of its support and had a larger budget (European Investment Fund, 2008, p. 26). Early in 2008 the Commission and the EIB signed another co-operation agreement establishing a Loan Guarantee Instrument for Trans-European Transport

Network projects (LGTT). This represented the first EIB infrastructure lending program backed by a guarantee from the EU budget (Núñez Ferrer and Infelise, 2015, p. 11). In late 2008 another financial instrument was set up, the ELENA facility, to provide financial and technical support to EU cities and regions implementing projects in the areas of energy efficiency, renewable energy and sustainable urban transport. In 2010, confronted with a drop in bank investment in infrastructures, the Commission and the EIB created a new type of financial instruments on a pilot basis, the "Project Bonds Initiative." Through this initiative, the EU budget would provide support to EIB guarantees offered to infrastructure bonds issued by private project companies.

In the area of cohesion policy, there was also a major increase in the amounts allocated to financial instruments. Encouraged by the Commission, Member States' cohesion policy authorities allocated more resources to financial instruments, from only 1.2bn in the period 2000–2006 to 16.4bn in 2007–13 and 18.8bn in the current programing period (2014–2020)[4]. This rapid expansion was not devoid of problems. The first evaluations from the 2000s evidenced the lack of expertise of cohesion managing authorities in setting up and managing such instruments, which translated into delays in launching and delivering the funds to final recipients and difficulties in finding the most appropriate set ups. To avoid these problems, two EIB-Commission policy initiatives were created to help national and regional managing authorities: JESSICA, managed by the EIB, provided support in setting up financial instruments in the field of urban development whereas JEREMIE, managed by the EIF, helped EU cohesion policy managing authorities to set up instruments in support of SMEs. Both initiatives worked the same way: the EIB or the EIF provided technical expertise to national managing authorities on how to set up a holding fund to manage these instruments. Additionally, they offered themselves to national authorities as possible managers of these holding funds.

In the EU's external field there was also a "shift from grants to loans." The pure-grant based approach which had inspired EU development aid until then was replaced by an approach which put the accent on combining grants and loans ("blending") to better coordinate the actions of the various national and EU aid actors by pooling the resources from the EU budget, Member States, public development agencies, financial institutions and other multilateral development financial institutions working in the field. Different EU blending platforms were created, covering all regions of EU external cooperation (Nuñez Ferrer and Behrens 2011).

[4] European Commission (2017b), Summary of data on the progress made in financing and implementing financial engineering instruments 2007–2013, Brussels October 2017; European Commission (2018), Summaries of the data on the progress made in financing and implementing the financial instruments for the programing period 2014-2020, situation at December 2017, Brussels November 2018.

The creation of all these new instruments covering EU's internal and external action translated into a significant increase in the amounts of the EU budget allocated to loans, equity, or other types of market-based instruments. As most of these new EU financial instruments were co-designed and implemented by the EIB group, the main beneficiary of this increase was the bank's group, and particularly the EIF. The strategic restructuring of the EIB group in June 2000—which moved all venture capital and SME loan guarantees to the EIF while placing infrastructure guarantees back into the EIB—and the greater volume of the EU financial instruments in support of SMEs reinforced the role of the EIF as the main financial partner for the Commission in the implementation of EU budgetary policies. From then on, the SME-related activities financed by the European Union's budget or by the EIB soon outstripped those financed by own funds (Bussiere et al., 2008, p. 245), meaning that the fee business earned by the EIF for these mandate activities would become of outstanding importance for the business model of the EIF (interview EIB official, July 26, 2019)[5]. In the context of this strategic shift, commercial banks increasingly withdrew from the EIF board whereas the engagement of NDBs increased, due to their predominant focus on SMEs. They became deeply involved, both as intermediaries in the implementation of EIF schemes in support to SMEs and as shareholders of the Fund[6].

The significant increase in volumes of EU financial instruments, however, also offered new opportunities for action to national development banks. In most of the cases, the Commission gave an exclusive mandate to the EIB for the implementation of these new EU budget instruments, but for some of them implementation was open to participation of other international or national financial institutions. However, in practice only one national development bank would be engaged, alongside with EIB, in implementing centrally managed FIs. This was the German KfW, which was one of the three entities (together with the EIB and the Council of Europe Development Bank) implementing the European Local Energy Assistance (ELENA) facility. The overall experience of the KfW, however, was disappointing, due to the high bureaucratic burden interaction with the EU budget entails (interview ELTI member, July, 2019), which is why the KfW closed its participation in these programs in 2016, while the EIB continued its mandate. KfW was also the only NDB participating in the newly created EU "blending platforms" for development cooperation, which can be explained by the fact that the KfW is among the rare public development banks having an explicit external mandate (see Mertens, this volume).

[5] This dependence on fees led the same official to speculate that the Commission has more power in the EIF than the EIB itself.

[6] Whereas in 2000, only 3 NPBIs were shareholders in the EIF, this number increased to 6 in 2007, 9 NPBIs in 2013 and 12 NPBIs in 2017 (EIF annual reports 2007, 2013, 2017).

As for the rest of national development banks, many of them became financial intermediaries of the EIF CIP guarantee facility, using it to extend their offer of "soft" SME loans. Big banks such as KfW and CDC also participated in the EIB-run "project bonds" pilot initiative, as bond issuer (CDC in two projects) or bond subscriber (KfW in one project) (EY, 2015). Finally, many national and regional development banks benefitted from the significant increase in the amounts of cohesion funding allocated to financial instruments. In many countries, national and regional cohesion management authorities relied on NDBs and regional DBs to design financial instruments and manage investment funds, despite the fact that EU rules incentivized the appointment of the EIB group and despite the existence of EIB-Commission initiatives favoring the involvement of EIB and the EIF in this field (JEREMIE and JESSICA).[7] The existence of experienced national or regional banks already implementing similar support schemes for SMEs weighted in the choice made by managing authorities (Schneidewind et al., 2013, p. 33). Overall, 13 NDBs were appointed as fund managers in the period from 2007 to 2013, mostly from Eastern Europe.[8]

The expansion of financial instruments to be administered not only by the EIB but also NDBs (see Table 2.2 below) now began to set a material incentive for Member States to establish such a bank. This incentive, in conjunction with the rediscovered role of development banks since 2008 in weathering a crisis, explains the new wave of founding NDBs in Europe.

## 2.4 The Rise of Promotional Banking in the Aftermath of the Crisis and the Development of NPBs' Group Consciousness

As the financial crisis hit the European Union in the last quarter of 2008 and in 2009, the field of European development banking vastly accelerated its activities, fulfilling its counter-cyclical role. At the European level, the EIB expanded its lending activities by 30 percent in 2009 and 2010, based on a capital injection of 67bn Euros in subscribed capital in 2009. Other large promotional banks, such as the KfW, also strongly increased their lending, to counteract the drop in private loans.

[7] In fact, whereas JEREMIE was expected to give a potentially strong role for the EIF in the management of financial instruments, in practice by October 2010 among the 30 holding funds established under the JEREMIE program only 11 were managed by the EIF (Van der Zwet et al 2016, p. 90).

[8] These NDBs were the Czech CZMRB, the three NDBs from the Baltics (Kredex, Altum and Invega), the Polish BGK and the Hungarian MFB, the Slovenian SID as well as the Slovak SZRB, the Swedish Almi and the Finnish Finnvera, the Spanish ICO as well as the French CDC and OSEO, the forerunner of BPIfrance (see European Commission, 2013). Most notable for their absence as fund managers in this multi-annual framework were both the KfW as well as the CDP in Italy, tasks taken over by regional development banks and local public guarantee bodies.

**Table 2.2** EU-level financial instruments, 2000s

| Year of creation | Name | Description | Implementing partner |
|---|---|---|---|
| 2007 | Risk-sharing finance facility | Risk-sharing instrument to support EIB investment in research-intensive companies and projects | EIB |
| 2007 | CIP SME guarantee and equity instruments | Guarantee and equity schemes in support to SMEs | EIF in charge of managing but many NDBs involved as financial intermediaries |
| 2007 | JEREMIE | Support to national and regional cohesion authorities to set up financial schemes in the area of SME financing | EIF |
| 2007 | JESSICA | Support to national and regional cohesion authorities to set-up financial instruments in the field of urban development | EIB |
| 2007–2012 | EU-Africa Infrastructure Trust Fund (ITF), Neighbourhood Investment Facility (NIF), Western Balkan Investment Framework (WBIF) | Various EU platforms for blending grants and loans in support to development of third countries | EIB, KFW, CEB, EBRD and national development aid agencies (e.g. French AFD, Italian SIMEST) |
| 2008 | Loan Guarantee Instrument for Trans-European Transport Network projects (LGTT) | Guarantee scheme to support EIB infrastructure lending | EIB |
| 2008 | ELENA facility | Provision of financial and technical support to EU cities and regions implementing projects in the areas of energy efficiency, renewable energy and sustainable urban transport | EIB, CEB bank and KfW |
| 2010 | Project Bonds Initiative | EU budget support to EIB guarantees offered to infrastructure bonds issued by private project companies | EIB implementing it, some NDBs participating as bond issuer (CDC) or bond subscriber (KfW) |

The crisis also prompted calls from the Council and the Commission to further coordinate the EIB and NDBs' actions. The first mentions of the need to further coordinate can be found in September 2008 when, in the context of an informal Ecofin council in Nice, the Italian Minister of Economy and Finance proposed to create a large network of public investment banks to better support the economic recovery in Europe (Bassanini and Reviglio, 2014, p. 2). This idea was not implemented at that moment but paved the way for the creation of the "Marguerite Fund" as part of the 2008 Commission's European stimulus plan. The Marguerite Fund is a pan-EU fund focused on energy, climate, and infrastructures. Co-financed by the EU Commission, the EIB, the four largest national development banks in Europe (KfW, CDC, CDP, ICO) and PKO.[9] It is situated in Paris, with the CDC jointly with the CDP playing a major role in setting it up and managing it (interview former EIB official, July 30, 2019). In addition, the collaboration of NDBs with the EIF and the EIB in the implementation of EU financial instruments was increasing, fueled by a re-dedication of EU funds. By the end of 2014, around €16bn of EU cohesion policy funding had been allocated to financial instruments. This represented a significant increase compared to around €1.3bn in the 2000-2006 period and €0.6bn euro in the 1994–1999 period (European Court of Auditors, 2016, p 20).

In the meantime, against the backdrop of a looming recession driven by the eurozone crisis and with most Member States applying budgetary austerity, the Council again resorted to the EIB to stimulate growth. In the European Summit of June 2012, a new extension of the EIB's capital by €10 billion was agreed, as part of a "European Growth Pact" promoted by the newly elected French president Hollande. However, this capital extension was largely used up to satisfy concerns of rating agencies about the rising leverage of the EIB due to its crisis engagement. This led to a sobering assessment by EU Council officials, who bemoaned the obsession of the bank's president with the banks triple A rating and were frustrated by its reluctance to lend. At the European Council of June 2013, the heads of state and governments urged the EIB to "implement its plan to increase its lending activity in the EU by 40% over 2013–2015." The Council 'conclusion also included an explicit reference to the need for "strengthening of the cooperation between national development banks and the EIB to increase opportunities for co-lending and exchanges of best practices" (European Council, 2013, p 6–7). As an EU council official put it, "We feel they haven't used the money boost enough, so we're looking at new ways to increase risk sharing" (EU Observer, 2013).

[9] PKO is the largest Polish bank, which is majority government owned. Its role was taken over by BGK, the actual Polish development bank in 2017 when the Fund was renewed.

In parallel to the Council's incipient interest in NDBs' financial capacities, and while the European debate on the investment gap intensified, the major NDBs developed more institutional forms for exchange and representation, thereby further institutionalizing the field. In 2009, the three major national development banks (CDC, CDP and KfW) joined forces with the EIB to create the Long-Term Investment Club (LTIC), with Augustin de Romanet, then CEO of CDC taking up the helm of this new institution. However, the Club was a rather informal platform for exchanges and discussion and had an international scope, trying to gather together very different long-term investment entities (promotional institutions, banks, private investors) from all over the world. Soon it appeared necessary to develop a more formal entity to represent only the interests of development banks in Europe. Thus, in 2013, the same four big public banks that promoted the creation of LTIC (CDC, CDP, KfW, and EIB) founded the European Long-Term Investment Association (ELTI), an association involving the 16 public long-term investors operating in the EU. 11 of these 16 members were national promotional institutions right from the beginning, due to the fact that ELTI was de facto transforming a previous informal annual meeting of NPBIs and the EIB into a formal one (interview former EIB official, June 25, 2019).

The infrastructure in terms of meeting space and office space for this new lobbying organization was provided by the "big 5" European NDBs (KfW, CDC, CDP, ICO and BGK) which jointly occupied a floor in Brussels. At the same time, the EIB also loomed large, the president of the new association being the president of the EIB, Werner Hoyer, and the new general secretary being a former EIB official, who prior to that post was responsible for LTIC. In organizational terms, ELTI at that point was basically one well connected individual, Secretary General de Crayencour, who used his long-standing contacts as an EIB representative in Brussels to represent the interests of the large long-term investors, mainly NPBIs and EIB in Europe. In addition, it stated as one of its goals to "strengthen cooperation, including at an operational level, between European financial institutions" (EIB Press release 2013). This at least was the rhetoric that Hoyer embraced when taking up the presidency of ELTI:

> "The ELTI association is a genuine European project. Following the EIB capital increase, it is yet another way to multiply our mutual leverage effect in federating the financial strength of our institutions for growth and employment through long term investment." He added: "I am honored and happy to be able to make the link between the work of the EU Bank and all the national Members of ELTI who are pursuing the same objective of supporting EU policy" (ibid).

And yet, behind the scenes, the EIB was opposed to intensifying these relationships if it meant granting NDBs access to the European budget, a resource that the EIB deemed central for its growth (interview former EIB official, July, 2019).

They had only agreed to the initiative because of stakeholder requests and had come to the conclusion that it would make the EIB look bad to officially oppose such an increase in collaboration and it would be best to place themselves at the center of this effort and block any initiatives that involved sharing these budgetary resources (ibid). As a result, several of the position papers by ELTI with proposals for how to ease access to the EU budget for NDBs were blocked by the EIB, causing frustration within ELTI (interview with a member of ELTI, July 2019). This stance however did not prevent NDBs from participating in the discussions leading to the negotiations of the EU budget 2014–2020, that took place between 2011–2013. To that purpose, they used different channels, notably their access to other EU-level interest associations such as the Network for European Financial Institutions for SMEs (NEFI), the European Association of Public Banks (EAPB) and the European Association of Mutual Guarantee Societies (AECM), insisting on subsidiarity and complementarity as main arguments.

In 2012, in the middle of the negotiations of the EU budget 2014–2020, the three associations named above published a joint statement on the next generation of EU financial instruments in support of SMEs. In this statement, they argued that "the EU principle of subsidiarity means that wherever possible, implementation should be carried out at the national or regional level" and that "the immediate actions taken by national promotional institutions since the start of the financial and economic crisis have illustrated the importance of promotional institutions and funds with a public mission" (AECM, EAPB and NEFI. 2012).[10] In 2014, in its annual meeting in Madrid, the NEFI members endorsed a joint statement on the "Key role of National Promotional Institutions in access to finance for SMEs" (NEFI 2014a), where they argued that National Promotional Institutions (NPIs) were key to ensuring complementarity between EU and national schemes and to provide targeted solutions for SME adapted to the specificities of national markets. They therefore argued that "NPIs should be first choice partners for the European Commission, EIB and EIF to contribute to the development and implementation of European policies for SMEs in the member countries."

The 2014 NEFI statement also made specific references to the Commission's efforts to update and simplify State Aid rules and raised one point which would become a persistent demand from European NDBs in subsequent years: the need to harmonize State Aid treatment between the different financial entities implementing EU funds ("equal State Aid rules should apply to all players involved in the implementation of structural funds and the EU budget, regardless of their

[10] The most active lobbying was exerted by NEFI, which during this period submitted various statements on Commission's specific proposals related with EU financial instruments (NEFI 2011a, b, 2013a), and on reforms in State Aid regulations, recommending some changes seen as desirable to facilitate NBD participation (de minimis as well as the General Block Exemption Regulation, NEFI 2013b, c, NEFI 2014b).

assignment (NPIs, commercial banks, EIB Group, etc.") (NEFI, 2014a, p. 2). The criticism here referred to the fact that, under EU State Aid rules, investment undertaken by the EIB Group is never considered as State Aid (as long as the EIB Group invests from its own resources), while State Aid rules apply in case of an investment with identical features undertaken by a national promotional bank. This put NBDs into a disadvantaged position as any participation in the implementation of EU funds had to be cleared by State Aid rules (except if covered by a block exemption or not exceeding the "de minimis" threshold) (see Volberding, this volume). Removing these regulatory constraints would reach a new level of urgency for NDBs with the expansion of EU level resources in the Juncker plan that began in 2015.

## 2.5 The Juncker Plan: The First Formal Recognition of NDBs as "Strategic Partners" in the Implementation of EU Funds

In July 2014, Jean Claude Juncker was elected as the new president of the Commission by the European Parliament under the promise to launch an ambitious "investment plan for Europe" to close the post-crisis investment gap. Rather than asking for new money, which in the context of budgetary austerity was deemed politically difficult, Juncker decided to rely on some sort of EIB-led financial engineering tool. At the end of November 2014, the Commission came up with a proposal to create a new EU-level instrument, the European Fund for Strategic Investments (EFSI)[11]. In fact, however, the main features of EFSI had been defined over the summer of 2014, based on the close collaboration of Juncker with the EIB (Hoyer 2015)[12]—leading the Commission staff to be furious over the fact that everything was already agreed before Juncker officially took office on 1st November 2014 (interview former EIB official, June 25, 2019).

With the EIB playing a crucial role both in terms of conceiving the plan and shaping its set-up (interview former EIB official June 25, 2019; Hoyer 2015), the overall terms of who should bear the risks were very favorable to the EIB: by taking the first-loss position, the EFSI would allow the EIB to increase its volumes of lending to activities with a higher risk profile without losing its triple-A rating. Besides, contrary to previous EIB-Commission instruments, EFSI's mandate would be very broad and flexible, leaving to the bank a wide degree of discretion to select projects and single-out investment priorities. Indeed, the EIB was given almost full operational control of the new instrument, with the EFSI steering

[11] Commission's Communication "An investment plan for Europe," Brussels, 26.11.2014 COM(2014) 903 final

[12] In a speech in Luxembourg in September 2015, Mr Hoyer, the president of the EIB went as far as stating that the idea of the EFSI was born in a conversation Juncker and Hoyer had had in the summer of 2014, before Juncker became Commission president (Hoyer, 2015, 12ff).

board located within the Bank and the EIB staff playing an important role as 'gate-keeper' of projects. In this vein, EIB president Hoyer characterized it as "nothing else than a managed account inside EIB backed by a 16 billion guarantee of the EU budget and 5 billion from EIB in order to increase the risk-taking-capacity of EIB" (Hoyer 2015, 15).[13]

The presentation of the Plan elicited mixed reactions, with many people criticizing the lack of major new public resources and the ambitious leverage target of the new instrument (just 8 billion euros from the EU budget, together with 5bn from EIB own resources were expected to mobilized up to 315bn of additional investments, see Griffith-Jones and Naqvi, this volume). To strengthen the proposal, the Commission would exert major pressure on Member States to increase the impact of the Fund with direct national contributions to EFSI's capital. However, despite the promise to exclude these contributions from the Structural and Growth Pact' deficit calculus and some initial interest expressed by the French and Italian governments[14], in the end no national governments would contribute to a Fund which would not guarantee a return in the form of investments in their territory.

Against this backdrop, the idea of making contributions indirectly, in form of co-investments from their "own" NDBs to EFSI projects taking place in their own territory, would gain ground (Marty, 2015a). Central in raising this idea were the French and Italian governments, backed by their banks—French CDC and the Italian CDP—which pushed for such access arguing that their local knowledge and capacities would make them well-prepared to play this role. KfW on the contrary was initially reluctant, with the then CEO of KfW, Schroeder, characterizing the use of EU budgetary resources as a "bureaucratic nightmare" (interview EIB official, July 25, 2019). To discuss, in more concrete terms, the possible contribution of NDBs to EFSI, an informal ECOFIN meeting in September 2014 in Milan demanded that the EIB develop a more institutionalized coordination with its national counterparts. Based on this paragraph, which was inserted on the suggestion of CDP (interview EIB official 25th of July 2019), a "National Promotional Bank Task Force" (NPB Task Force) was created, involving representatives of the EIB, the various NDBs and the Commission[15].

This group, which would form a central internal governance unit in the field of European development banking would then initially meet twice a year, with additional meetings with the big five and the EIB in Brussels (interview EIB official,

[13] For a detailed description and assessment of the EFSI proposal see Rubio, Rinaldi and Pellerin Carlin, 2014 and Griffith-Jones and Naqvi, this volume.

[14] Euractiv, "Member states seek guarantees for Juncker plan´s contributions."

[15] Given the absence of an official EU list of "National Promotional Banks," each Member State is invited to design the financial institution represented in the task force, which results in a heterogeneous list of 26 entities of different sizes and profile The list excludes some small NDBs (such as Latvian's ALTUM or Lithuanian's INVEGA) and includes some entities operating at regional level (Belgium's Société Régionale d'Investissement de Bruxelles and Participation Company Flanders).

July 25, 2019). In parallel to this, large and well-established NDBs started to mobilize to set out their position regarding EFSI. In a joint letter sent to the Commission in April 2015, the representatives of the five largest national development banks present in Brussels (KfW, CDC, CDP, ICO and GKG) announced that they "are prepared to contribute to the EU Investment Plan" and "ready to expand our activities with the complementary support of the increased EIB Group risk capacity." However, they made these statements conditional on four points: NDBs' contributions to EFSI should be exempted from State Aid rules, EFSI governance should avoid duplications, the EFSI guarantee fee granted shall be coherent with the Plan's objectives and NDBs shall benefit from access to EFSI.[16] Concerning the latter point, NDBs asked for *pari passu* access to the EFSI guarantee, i.e. they wanted to take advantage, in the event of an EFSI project co-financed with the EIB, of the same "first-loss" risk coverage as the EIB group (Marty, 2015b, p. 4).

To respond to these concerns, the Commission published in July 2015 a Communication clarifying several key principles for the collaboration of NDBs with the EIB and the Commission in the context of the Investment Plan[17]. While the Communication recognized the role of NDBs as key partners in the implementation of the Juncker Plan and clarified some points for the treatment of NPB's contributions to EFSI under EU fiscal and State Aid rules, it did not grant NDBs direct access to the EFSI guarantee. The document concluded by pointing out the possibility that "over time, this deepened cooperation could evolve into an integrated system of public investment banks, which would be able to apply proven products and best practices across Member States" (European Commission, 2015, p. 13). However, this expectation that EFSI would reinforce cooperation was only partially confirmed by reality. During the first years of implementation, EFSI proved to be both an engine to reinforce cooperation but also to intensify competition between EIB and NDBs. Two different dynamics emerged in the two different windows in which EFSI was structured, the SME Window (SMEW), implemented by the European Investment Fund (EIF) and providing support to SMEs and Mid-caps and the Infrastructures and Innovation Window (IIW), implemented by the European Investment Bank (EIB) and focused on big projects.

Under the SMEW, EFSI was basically used to extend the EU guarantee schemes in support of SMEs already managed by the EIF (in particular COSME LGF and InnovFin SME). Since NDBs were already involved in the implementations these instruments, its extension through the SME window was very effective and

[16] https://www.caissedesdepots.fr/sites/default/files/medias/cp_et_dp/CP_Lettre_commune_JCJuncker_21042015.pdf, last accessed 14th of October 2019.

[17] Commission's Communication " Working together for jobs and growth: The role of National Promotional Banks (NPBs) in supporting the Investment Plan for Europe, Brussels, 22.07.2015 COM(2015) 361 final.

satisfactory and reinforced the established cooperation between national banks and the EIF (interview member of ELTI, July 9, 2019; Rubio et al., 2018a). In contrast, under the IIW, EFSI was expected to push the EIB to develop riskier products and expand the volume of so-called EIB "special operations" (operations having a risk profile higher than conventional EIB loans). Yet, in a context marked by the scarcity of big infrastructure projects and with a strong political pressure to reach the 315bn target of additional investment mobiliszed, the EIB made use of the EFSI "first loss" tranche to provide more favorable financial conditions to mature infrastructure projects rather than searching for new, additional, riskier projects. The perception from NDBs was hence that EFSI was used by the EIB to enter the business of national promotional banks, creating competition among them (ELTI, July 9, 2019; EY, 2016, p. 29; Rubio et al., 2018).

The difficulties in cooperation were reflected in the first EFSI results (European Investment Bank 2017). By December 2017, one and a half years after the launch of EFSI, there were 140 EFSI operations co-financed with NDBs, representing only 23 percent of all signed operations. Not surprisingly, the share was much lower in the infrastructure window (14 percent) than in the SME window (31 percent). These overall results were further strongly differentiated geographically, revealing important differences between Western and Eastern NDBs in the level of engagement, stemming from different internal capabilities and external resource dependencies. A survey by Rubio et al., (2018a) shows that only very big entities from Western Europe (more than 100bn in total assets) are strongly involved in the implementation of EFSI whereas most very small banks (less than 1bn in total assets) have no experience at all with EFSI (Rubio etal., 2018a, p. 50). The same survey shows the difference in the pattern of participation between central and eastern European NDBs, more reliant on EU cohesion funds, and Western European NBDs, more engaged in the implementation of EFSI funds.

## 2.6 The Variegated Capabilities of National Development Banks to Use European Funds

The creation of EFSI in 2015 and its extension in 2017, the strengthening of EU budget instruments managed by the EIB on behalf of the Commission[18] and the significant increase of funds allocated to financial instruments under EU cohesion policy[19] have resulted in a growing, but differentiated implication of NDBs in the implementation of the EU budget. The relative importance of these different forms of engagement varies according to NDBs' size and geographical

[18] From €5.7bn allocated to these instruments in 2007–13 to €9bn in 2014–2020 (European Commission 2017c, p 6).

[19] From €12.5bn in 2007–13 to €21bn in 2014–2020 (European Court of Auditors 2017).

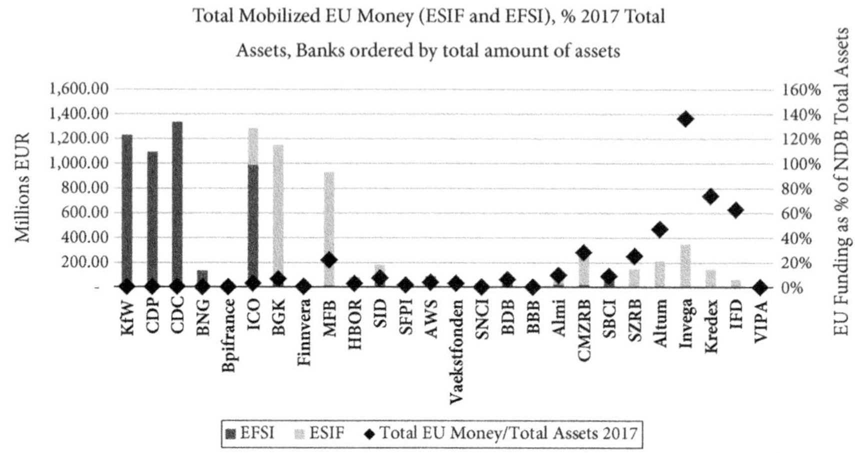


**Figure 2.1** Importance of EFSI and ESIF funds for national development banks in Europe

*Source*: own elaboration based on annual reports of NDBs and EU Commission reports on use of both funds, EC 2017; EC 2018

location. As shown in Figure 2.1, smaller banks tend to be more reliant on EU funds. EU funding represents more than 40 percent of the total assets of NDBs from the three Baltic countries (ALTUM, Invega and Kredex) and Portugal (IFD), and more than 20 percent of the banks from Czech Republic (CMZRB), Slovakia (SZRB). This strong correlation between NDB's size and EU funding is however partly explained by the fact that NDBs in central and northern European states are bigger on average than those in the East and South. Thus, very small NDBs tend to be located in countries receiving important amounts of EU cohesion funding—indeed, in all the six countries mentioned above (Baltic countries, Portugal, Czech Republic and Slovakia) cohesion policy funding represents more than 40 percent of total public investment (European Commission, 2017a, Figure 2.1, p. Xxiv). There are also differences as regards to the type of EU funding mobilized.

EU cohesion and structural funds (ESIF in EU jargon, grey in the bars above) are of great importance for eastern NDBs whereas they play a much lesser role, both in absolute and percentage terms, for Western European banks. Figure 2.1 above also shows that only big banks have mobilized significant amounts from the Juncker Fund (EFSI), even if in relative terms these amounts represent a tiny percentage of their total assets. This is in line with recent findings from a 2018 survey, which shows that small and medium Eastern NDBs are particularly worried about complex regulations and time-consuming procedures for setting up financial instruments under cohesion policy and ask for this bureaucratic burden to be eased in the future. They also complain about the lack of a "level playing field" with commercial banks for participating as financial intermediates in EIF debt guarantee schemes, hence calling on the Commission and the EIF to recognize them as "first choice partners" for the implementation of EU SME instruments. Big western banks share some of these concerns, but are also particularly critical of the EIB role under the IIW. They question the additionality of some EIB investments under EFSI and have an interest in directly managing financial instruments on behalf of the Commission and hence compete with EIB directly (Rubio etal., 2018a, pp. 56–57). These differences in size, geographical location, and experience with EFSI have translated into different interests and preferences as regards the EU budget and, ultimately, different positions in the negotiation of the next generation of EU financial instruments for 2021–2027.

## 2.7 Negotiating the InvestEU Fund

As the Juncker plan developed after 2015 and with the growing perception from big NDBs that the EIB was using EFSI to enter their business, the relationship between the EIB and NDBs at the institutional level worsened. ELTI members got more frustrated by the blockade of its lobbying activities through the EIB, which was an associate member. For that reason and upon the wish of the large Western NDBs, EIB's membership status was changed in 2016 from associate member to observer in order to allow the opinion of NPBIs to be clearly expressed (interview former EIB Official, June 25, 2019). Before, the EIB had blocked these initiatives, arguing that it made use of different channels to exchange and exert influence on EU institutions and that lobbying activities would irritate its EU partners. At the same time, the EIB was exerting influence, especially over the smaller NPBIs, by advising them not to oppose EIB interests too strongly or they might face problems in their collaboration with EIB with respect to both the global loans that the EIB advances as well as with respect to centralized FIs the EIB manages (interview EU Commission official, June 20, 2019, interview former EIB official, June 25, 2019).

From that moment onwards, ELTI actively participated in discussions about the extension of EFSI in 2016 (ELTI, 2016) and the beginning of the negotiations over the next Multi-Annual Financial Framework (see e.g. ELTI, 2017a, 2017b). In these papers, ELTI is presented as the association representing all NDBs[20] even if in practice it is dominated by big banks. The papers recognize the success of EFSI in promoting cooperation between the EIB and NDBs, particularly in the SME window but also implicitly show NDBs' dissatisfaction with the EIB's role in the IIW. In a 2017 paper on the next MFF, ELTI argues that "NPBIs should be able to either implement EU financial instruments directly and/or via the

[20] "Representing NPBIs, ELTI is ready to be an integral part in the forthcoming discussions about the design of EU financial instruments and is happy to work alongside EU Institutions to shape the EU budget for the benefit of European citizens and the European economy" (ELTI, 2017a).

intermediation of a third institution mandated by the EU Commission for this purpose" but that, in the latter case, "a clear institutional separation between the management of the financial instrument by the intermediary and its effective roll-out (doing the actual financing) by the NPBIs would be essential to (i) prevent conflicts of interest and (ii) to ensure an efficient and consensus based structuring framework and execution process" (ELTI, 2017b, p. 1).

In the meantime, whereas the Commission's official discourse on EFSI remained very positive (with EFSI recurrently presented as a "success"), internally there was some dissatisfaction among Commission officials with the way EIB manages the instrument. In particular, the perception was that the EIB did not sufficiently engage in taking riskier positions and that it had difficulties in reaching smaller projects. There was also the feeling that the Commission had lost control over the instrument, and that it had become too dependent on EIB's technical expertise (interview with an EC official, July 2, 2019). Against this backdrop, the idea gained ground of relying on the EIB as an implementing partner in the future while at the same time opening future instruments up to other partners also, as a way to push the EIB to look for better projects and for the Commission to regain the political guidance over the instrument.

In May 2018, the Commission came up with its proposal of the InvestEU Fund, a single instrument replacing both EFSI and all other 14 centrally managed financial instruments[21]. The new instrument was expected to have the EIB as "privileged partner"—a commitment taken in the preamble of the regulation to reserve 75 percent of the EU guarantee to the EIB—but implementation was opened to other eligible partners (NDBs and some multilateral development banks active in Europe such as the World Bank or the EBRD). A condition however was put to them. To implement the InvestEU Fund, they had to successfully go through a "pillar-assessment" procedure. In addition to that, there were important changes in the governance of the instrument. The EIB no longer had a seat on the steering board (as was the case in EFSI) and it was only present in an advisory board gathering representatives of all implementing partners. Thus, it was the Commission alone which would set the strategic orientation and carry out the risk management of the instrument.

The presentation of the InvestEU proposal left the EIB very shocked and upset (interview with EIB officials, July 26, 2018; interview first EC official, July 2, 2019; interview with ELTI member, July 9, 2019). Immediately after the publication, the bank expressed its astonishment that it had not been involved at all in the drafting of the proposal (unlike with EFSI and EFSI 2.0) and raised objections. It requested a clearer recognition of its role as a "privileged partner" and cast doubt upon the capacity of the Commission to manage the instrument alone, given the lack of

[21] See Rubio et al (2018b) for a detailed explanation of the proposal.

banking and especially risk management expertise (interview with second EC official July 2, 2019, interview EIB officials, July 9, 2019). At the same time ELTI members also expressed their views in different position papers and their demand for a "neutral and inclusive governance," which sees EIB and NDBs equally represented in the governance of InvestEU, generating a level playing field in terms of access to the instruments (ELTI, 2018b). During the fall of 2018 both ELTI and the EIB lobbied the two EU co-legislators—the European Parliament and the Council. The EIB, however, would be much more successful, particularly in convincing national finance ministers—who were both sitting in the Council of Economic Affairs (Ecofin Council) and on the EIB board. Here smaller, Eastern European member states were arguably conflicted, but due to the sway of the EIB regarding the funding of operations in these countries sided with the EIB. As a European Commission official put it:

> some of them (member states) were unhappy with EFSI because they believe they haven't benefitted enough of EFSI—It has mostly benefitted big western countries—but at the same time some are ... more prompt to the EIB influence ... I mean, let me use the term, blackmailing a bit, specially some of the small ones that rely on EIB funding , even if they have an NPBI, for access to the market they rely on the EIB for funding[22] ... and the EIB told them, "if you do not defend us anymore there will be consequences" ... I mean, they put pressure, and for some of them this was the explanation ... despite the fact that they were unhappy with the geographical imbalance and so on (interview with first EC official; July 2, 2019).

At the demand of the EIB, the Ecofin council called upon the Commission to negotiate bilaterally with the bank a "strategic partnership agreement" to reflect the central role of the EIB and to ensure that full use is made of its expertise. The Commission officials responded grudgingly to this demand, even if tensions were eased with the clear positioning of Jean-Claude Juncker who, in July 2018, stated at a press conference at the EIB that "the commission is the commission and the bank is the bank," thereby signaling that the Commission defers to the EIB in terms of expertise (interview with EIB officials, July 9, 2019). After five months of negotiations between the Commission and the EIB a compromise was reached in early 2019: the EIB got the 75 percent reserve of the EU budgetary guarantee included in the articles of the regulation (and not only in the preamble). In addition, the EIB was endowed with some extra-functions: 1) it will carry out the overall risk management of the instrument on behalf of the Commission; 2) it will assist, upon request, other implementing partners to pass the pillar

[22] Member States, especially those with lower credit ratings use global loans from the EIB to fund domestic projects, as the EIB has a triple A rating.

assessment; and 3) the EIB will give a non-binding opinion on the guarantee agreements the Commission prepares with other implementing partners. In the words of an EC official, the EIB accepted the plurality of implementing partners but "wants to frame the level-playing field" (interview EC official, July 2, 2019).

During January and February 2019, the Ecofin Council endorsed the changes agreed in the "strategic partnership agreement" and discussed other aspects of the InvestEU Fund proposal. On governance, the ministers of finance proposed to include the implementing partners on the steering board but to give greater representation to the EIB to reflect "the role of the EIB as the key implementing partner" (Council of the EU: 2019, p. 4). The Council also accepted the Commission's proposal to open up implementation to NDBs. However, during the Council meetings, some Member States—Croatia, Poland, Czech Republic, Slovenia, Sweden—expressed concerns about the possible concentration of the remaining 25 percent of the EU guarantee on those countries having strong and powerful NDBs[23]. To prevent this from happening, a specific reference was included into the text regarding the need to support smaller or less sophisticated NDBs in getting access to the EU guarantee. In early March 2019 negotiations started between the Council and the Parliament based on the Council's partial position. However, one issue which remained unresolved in the Council until the very last moment particularly well illustrates the tensions between the EIB, the Commission and NDBs over access to the funds: where to locate the secretariat of the InvestEU Fund.

The place of the secretariat is not a minor issue, as the secretariat is acting as a first gatekeeper by checking if all incoming proposals are compliant with EU rules, then sending them to the independent investment committee that evaluates them thoroughly. For the EIB, it was unimaginable to have their proposals first checked by Commission officials before being evaluated by the independent experts' committee. For the Commission, on the contrary, keeping the secretariat in Brussels was a way of subjecting all implementing partners to the same rules, as well as making sure that the EIB operations were fully aligned with EU laws and policies (interview with EC officials, July 2, 2019). NDBs also lobbied their own finance ministers to have the secretariat in Brussels, as one of the greatest fears for national banks was to have the EIB act as de-facto gatekeeper, threatening their access to the InvestEU Fund. Despite NDBs' lobbying efforts, on 15 March, the Ecofin Council agreed on placing the secretariat in Luxembourg[24], a decision which was reversed during the negotiations with the Parliament. A final

[23] "Soutien des États membres au partenariat Commission/BEI pour la gouvernance du programme InvestEUpost-2020", Agence Europe, Bruxelles, 22nd January 2019.

[24] Interview with European Commission official, July 2, 2019 and Agence Europe, « La Présidence roumaine du Conseil dispose enfin d'un mandat complet de négociation avec le PE sur le programme InvestEU », March 15, 2019.

compromise was reached in April, by which the secretariat will be hosted at the Commission but the EIB will have the right to send its proposals directly to the independent investment committee without passing through the secretariat.

Overall, what InvestEU means then is that the quasi-monopoly of EIB on financial instruments is broken, which is seen as a major rupture by observers (former EIB official, June 25, 2019; EIB officials, July 9, 2019). And yet the EIB maintains control over most of the resources from the European Commission. In this way the Commission proposal partly satisfies the political demands of NDBs, granting them a greater role, even if this role has been weakened over the course of the negotiations. An open question remains however: whether and to what extent will NDBs seize this new opportunity offered by the InvestEU Fund? According to one ELTI official, not all NDBs are convinced of the benefit of going through the "pillar assessment" and applying to gain direct access to InvestEU. They see a lot of additional bureaucratic requirements and the benefits are not as evident, especially for smaller NDBs, who have fewer opportunities for direct co-investment in big infrastructures and are more attuned to the intermediation of SME loans or the use of cohesion policy funding. At the same time, many of them may receive political pressures from the ministry of finance to do it, in order to ensure that the country receives an acceptable share of the 25 percent of the EU guarantee (interview with ELTI member, July 9, 2019).

It is also important to note the role of the Commission in encouraging and supporting NDBs to undertake the "pillar assessment" procedure in order to become vetted partners for future direct interactions between NDBs and the Commission. As noted by the ELTI official, the impression is that the Commission "needs to deliver (because) if the proposal is not accepted by other implementing partners [beyond the EIB], they have a problem, so it is very understandable that they are pushing now" (ibid, July 9, 2019).

## 2.8 Conclusion: Competition and Collaboration between EIB and NDB's over EU Budget Resources and Its Likely Evolution

This chapter has traced the evolution of the use of budgetary resources for financial instruments and hence for the purpose of development banking. We traced how from the 1970s onwards, this process has brought about and has been fueled by an ever-closer movement of the EIB towards the European Commission. This rapprochement also found an organizational expression in the creation of the European Investment Fund in 1994, where the EC held a direct share. Through its reorganization in 1999 and the creation of the risk capital facility in the EIB group, the EIF increasingly functioned as a node that brought together the EIB and Commission and NDBs (a trend much accelerated by the growth of centralized financial instruments). Based on these developing institutional linkages, the EIB, the European Commission and the NDBs increasingly formed a triadic relationship.

During the 2000s the EU Commission, constrained in its budgetary resources by the Member States, shifted to financial instruments to remedy its lack of financial prowess, making the EIB and the EIF its primary address. At the same time, financial instruments and the EIF induced positive experiences of direct collaboration between NDBs and the Commission. In addition, since the late 1990s. the Commission and the Member States needed the EIB, drawing upon her again and again to engineer an off-balance sheet stimulus for a faltering EU economy. The EIB, on the other hand, were very consciously moving ever-closer to the EU Commission rhetorically, depicting itself as the investment bank of the EU. This triadic form of collaboration was characterized by collaboration, induced by mutual need, and arguably the biggest winner in it was the EIB, strongly expanding its balance sheet (almost doubling it from 2007 to 2017) and its headcount.

Over time, however, this triadic relationship became increasingly characterized by conflicts and tensions. With the expansion of financial instruments and particularly after the creation of the EFSI in 2015, the Commission and NDBs became more and more dissatisfied with their collaboration with the EIB. For the Commission, over-dependence on the EIB to implement financial instruments is seen as problematic, and there is dissatisfaction over the EIB as opaque, as charging too high fees, and overly insisting on its independence in business matters, while acting as an agent of the Commission. The larger Western European NDBs are critical of the unique control of EU resources by the EIB, a concern they have brought to the InvestEU negotiations. For all NDBs, the recent expansion in the wake of the Juncker plan has brought about fears of overreach by the EIB, which is why they ask for the EIB to restrain its activities to those showing a clear value added. Insisting on subsidiarity and complementarity, NDBs exploit the fact that the EIB, based on its business model of large loans financed in wholesale markets, has too many problems servicing small-sized SME loans to position itself as the ideal local partner of the Commission.

Overall, the EU budget and its use for financial instruments has done a lot to create the field of development banking in Europe, where the relationship between NDBs and the EIB is structured by competition and cooperation regarding the EU budget. As a response, NDBs are now actively organizing in Brussels (ELTI) to structure future financial instruments and meet with the EIB semi-annually in the EIB-NDB taskforce. This intensified exchange between EU Commission, NDBs and EIB on how to design financial instruments to make them work means that coordination in the field has become much easier. However, this field is also characterized by very strong power asymmetries: small NDBs, particularly in Eastern Europe and those newly founded in peripheral countries, are highly dependent on EU resources, but have only limited capacities to implement them. At the same time large Western NDBs have only a limited need for EU resources, but a great capacity to implement them. And the larger NDBs not only have greater domestic resources at their behest, they also have a greater capacity to exert influence in Brussels to seek to engineer new ways of accessing funds, which would limit the hold of the EIB on these resources. The EIB, on the other hand, seeks to maneuver strategically between the Commission and the NDBs to satisfy their demands sufficiently, without losing their control over the financial instruments the EU initiates. How this struggle between these actors unfolds in the future will have a direct impact on how and where EU funds are channeled in the future as well as on the fate of these institutions themselves.

## References

AECM, EAPB, and NEFI, 2012. Financial Instruments—The Best Way to Reach EU Policy Goals? The Case of Access to Finance for SMEs. Available at http://www.nefi.eu/publications/.

Bassanini, F., Reviglio, E., 2014. Long-term investment in Europe. The origin of the subject and future. Paper presented at the Italian Embassy in France, 16th of March, 2014. Available at https://www.bassanini.it/wp-content/uploads/2014/06/Ambasciata-italiana-a-Parigi.pdf

Bussiere, É., Dumoulin, M., and Willaert, É. (eds), 2008. The Bank of the European Union: The EIB, 1958–2008. Luxembourg: European Investment Bank Press.

Council of the European Union, 2019. Proposal for a Regulation of the European Parliament and of the Council establishing the InvestEU Programme—Presidency Issues Note, 15 January 2019.

ELTI 2016. Investment Plan for Europe: Experience of National Promotional Banks and Institutions and possible improvements. ELTI position paper Brussels, 23 November 2016 available at http://www.eltia.eu/images/2016_11_23_ELTI_position_clean.pdf.

ELTI, 2017a. Future role of National Promotional Banks and Institutions in the Implementation of EU Funds. ELTI Position paper Brussels, July 2017. Available at http://www.eltia.eu/images/2017_07_17_Future_Role_EU_Funds_consolidated_-_clean.pdf.

ELTI, 2017b. Multiannual Financial Framework post 2020. ELTI Position Paper Brussels, 06 November 2017, available at http://www.eltia.eu/images/2017_11_03_Multiannual_Financial_Framework_for_the_European_Union.pdf.

ELTI, 2018a. Financial Instruments in the Next MFF—The Way Forward Regarding the Single Fund, Direct Access for NPBIs and the Single Rule Book. ELTI Position Paper: Brussels, 26 March 2018. Available at http://www.eltia.eu/images/eltiMFF3deff.pdf.

ELTI, 2018b. InvestEU: How to Concretely Deliver? Brussels, September 24, 2018. Available at http://www.eltia.eu/images/2018.10.02_-_InvestEU_-_How_to_concretely_deliver.pdf.

European Commission, 2013. Summary of Data on the Progress Made in Financing and Implementing Financial Engineering Instruments Co-Financed by Structural Funds. Situation as at 31 December 2012.

European Commission, 2014. European Public Finances, 5th edition.

European Commission, 2015. "Working Together for Jobs and Growth: The Role of National Promotional Banks (NPBs) in Supporting the Investment Plan for Europe", Brussels 22.07.2015, COM/2015/0361 final.

European Commission, 2017a. Seventh report on economic, social and territorial cohesion, Directorate-General for Regional and Urban Policy, September 2017.

European Commission, 2017b. Summary of data on the progress made in financing and implementing financial engineering instruments reported by the managing authorities in accordance with Article 67(2)(j) of Council Regulation (EC) No 1083/2006.

European Commission, 2017c. Report on financial instruments supported by the general budget according to Art.140.8 of the Financial Regulation as at 31 December 2016, Brussels, 25.9.2017, COM(2017) 535 final

European Council, 1992. Presidency conclusions of the Edinburgh European council, 11–12 December 1992.

European Council, 2005. Presidency conclusions of the Brussels European Council, 22–3 March 2005.

European Council. 2013 Presidency conclusions of the Brussels European Council, 27–8 June 2013.

European Court of Auditors, 2016. Implementing the EU budget through financial instruments—lessons to be learnt from the 2007–2013 programme period, special report. Luxembourg: European Court of Auditors.

European Court of Auditors, 2017. EFSI: an early proposal to extend and expand Opinion No 2/2016. Luxembourg: European Court of Auditors.

European Investment Bank (EIB), 2017. Report to the European Parliament and the Council on 2017 EIB Group Financing and Investment Operations under EFSI. Luxemburg: EIB

European Investment Bank Group, 2006. Annual Report 2005, Volume I: Activity Report. Luxembourg: EIB.

European Investment Fund (EIF), 2008. Annual Report 2007. Luxembourg: EIF

European Investment Fund (EIF), 2014. Annual Report 2013. Luxembourg: EIF

European Investment Fund (EIF), 2018. Annual Report 2017. Luxembourg: EIF

EU Observer, 2013. "EIB in spotlight as leaders eye increased business lending." 28. June 2013 https://euobserver.com/economic/120672).

EY. 2015, Ad-hoc Audit of the pilot phase of the Europe 2020 Project Bond Initiative. Final Report, December 2015.

EY, 2016, Ad-hoc audit of the application of the Regulation 2015/1017 (the EFSI Regulation). Final Report, 14 November 2016.

Hoyer, W., 2015. "The Investment Plan for Europe." Bridge Forum Dialogue, 27 October 2015. Available at https://forum-dialogue.lu/wp-content/uploads/discours-du-president-hoyer.pdf

Kavvadia, Helen. 2018. The European Investment Bank in a turbulent environment: Seen through its ever developing business model. Conference Paper

Marty, O., 2015a. Progress on the "Juncker Plan" Continues—But Are Member States Behind It? EPC Commentary, 18 March 2015.

Marty, O., 2015b. The Juncker Plan a Tangible Opportunity for Europe, Fondation Robert Schuman, European Issues, n 362, 23 June 2015.

NEFI, 2011a. Statement of NEFI on the Public consultation on a possible successor to the Competitiveness and Innovation Framework Programme (CIP). Available at http://www.nefi.eu/publications/.

NEFI, 2011b. Consultation of the European Commission's "Green Paper" for EU Research and Innovation funding Statement of NEFI. Available at http://www.nefi.eu/publications/.

NEFI, 2013a. Contribution of the Network of European Financial Institutions for SMEs to the European Commission's Green paper on long-term financing of the European economy. Available at http://www.nefi.eu/publications/.

NEFI, 2013b. NEFI comments on the DRAFT COMMISSION REGULATION (EU) No.../.. of 17.7.2013 on the application of Articles 107 and 108 of the Treaty on the Functioning of the European Union to de minimis aid. Available at http://www.nefi.eu/publications/.

NEFI, 2013c. NEFI comments to the draft guidelines on State aid for rescuing and restructuring nonfinancial undertakings in difficulty. Available at http://www.nefi.eu/publications/.

NEFI, 2014a. Key role of National Promotional Institutions in access to finance for SMEs. Joint Statement of the NEFI High Level Meeting, Madrid, 30th October 2014. Available at http://www.nefi.eu/publications/.

NEFI, 2014b. NEFI comments to the new Commission Regulation declaring certain categories of aid compatible with the internal market in application of Articles 107 and 108 of the Treaty ("General Block Exemption Regulation/GBER")—the 3rd round of public consultation. Available at http://www.nefi.eu/publications/.

Nuñez Ferrer, J., Infelise, F., 2015. Financial Instruments in Support of Territorial Development, Brussels: Committee of the Regions. Available at https://cor.europa.eu/en/engage/studies/Documents/financial-instruments-territorial-development.pdf

Nuñez Ferrer J., Behrens, A., 2011. Innovative Approaches to EU Blending Mechanisms For Development Finance, CEPS Special Report. Available at https://www.ceps.eu/wp-content/uploads/2011/05/EU%20Blending%20Mechanisms.pdf

Robinson, N., 2009. The European Investment Bank: The EU's Neglected Institution. Journal of Common Market Studies 47 (3), 651–73.

Robinson, N. and Bain, R., 2011. The implications of EIB and EBRD co-financing for the EU budget. Directorate-General for Internal Policies, Policy Department D: Budgetary Affairs. Brussels: European Parliament. Available at https://www.europarl.europa.eu/RegData/etudes/etudes/join/2013/490670/IPOL-JOIN_ET(2013)490670_EN.pdf

Rubio, E. Virel, F, and Pavesi, B., 2018a. Making Better Use of Public Funding: The Role of National Promotional Banks and Institutions in the Next EU Budget. Paris: Notre Europe-Institut Jacques Delors. Available at https://institutdelors.eu/wp-content/uploads/2018/07/TheRoleofNPBIsintheEUBudget-Rubio-July2018-1.pdf

Rubio, E.,Virel, F. 2018b. InvestEU Fund: A Rebranded "Juncker Fund"?. Policy Brief. Paris: Notre Europe-Institut Jacques Delors. Available at https://institutdelors.eu/wp-content/uploads/2018/09/InvestEUFund-Rubio-Sept18.pdf

Schneidewind, P., Radzyner, A, Hahn, M., Gaspari. E., Michie, R and Wishlade, F., 2013. Financial Engineering Instruments in Cohesion Policy, Directorate-General for Internal Policies, Policy Department B: Structural and Cohesion Policies. Brussels: European Parliament. Available at https://www.europarl.europa.eu/RegData/etudes/etudes/join/2013/495870/IPOL-REGI_ET(2013)495870_EN.pdf

Schild, J., 2008. "How to Shift the EU's Spending Priorities? The Multiannual Financial Framework 2007–2013 in Perspective," Journal of European Public Policy, 15 (4), June.

Van der Zwet, A., Bachtler, J., Miller, S.,Vernon, P., Dozhdeva, 2016. Review of the Role of the EIB Group in European Cohesion Policy, Study for the European Parliament's Committee on Regional Development. Brussels: European Parliament

APPENDIX 2.1

# List of interviews

Interview EIB official, July 26, 2018 (Telephone)
Interview EC official, June 20, 2019 (Brussels)
Interview former EIB official, June 25, 2019 (Telephone)
Interview with first EC official, July 2, 2019 (Brussels)
Interview ith second EC official July 2, 2019 (Brussels)
Interview EIB officials, July 9, 2019 (Brussels)
Interview EIB official July 25, 2019 (Telephone)
Interview former EIB official, July 30, 2019 (Telephone)
Interview member of ELTI, July 9, 2019 (Brussels)
Interview EIB official, July 26, 2019 (Telephone)

# 3
# State Aid and National Development Banks in the EU

*Peter Volberding*

## 3.1 Introduction

While EU-wide investment programs serve as a financial "carrot" for Member States, equally important is the EU's "stick"—DG Competition and State Aid regulation. From the 1950s, the EU acknowledged that political integration necessitated a level economic playing field that avoided beggar-thy-neighbor policies. To this end, Article 107 of the Treaty on the Functioning of the European Union (TFEU) required that Member States refrain from using public resources to support domestic firms or industries in ways that distorted cross-border economic activity (European Commission, 2008a). Since then, DG Competition has become a powerful force in limiting Member States' abilities to intervene in their domestic economies.

Within this context, State Aid provides a window into the dynamics between EU regulation and NDBs. With their intimate political connections and financing tools, NDBs have often been in the crosshairs of State Aid. In the 1960s, DG Competition began to aggressively target anti-competitive economic policies and, by the 1990s, had circumscribed many of the traditional operations of NDBs. In response, NDBs contested the tightening regulations and retooled to adapt to the changing guidelines, creating an iterative back-and-forth between regulators and NDBs. Since the financial crisis, a more balanced relationship between NDBs and DG Competition has emerged. NDBs have transitioned from antagonists of competition to a powerful institutional partner to, first, implement EU counter-cyclical financing, and later broader policy objectives. Both EFSI and InvestEU provided Member States with a respite from State Aid, so long as the investments hewed to EU policy objectives. The 2014 State Aid Modernization (SAM) similarly provided a streamlined process for NDBs to use block exemptions for their financing activities, within strict limits of total volume and sector.

Consequently, while NDBs have reemerged in European public policy, State Aid has profoundly impacted when, where, and how NDBs invest. State Aid has

Peter Volberding, *State Aid and National Development Banks in the EU* In: *The Reinvention of Development Banking in the European Union: Industrial Policy in the Single Market and the Emergence of a Field.* Edited by: Daniel Mertens, Matthias Thiemann, and Peter Volberding, Oxford University Press (2021). © Oxford University Press.
DOI: 10.1093/oso/9780198859703.003.0003

pushed NDBs towards EU investment priorities—including regional development programs, green investments, and SME promotion—but rather than solely relying on punitive measures, the EU has also provided thresholds and exemptions from State Aid to guide behavior. NDBs are therefore permitted latitude in investment decisions, but, in exchange, the EC and DG Competition set the regulatory parameters. Pushbacks from NDBs have also occurred, but these have been subtle, often indirect, and unevenly distributed. Stronger and older NDBs have been the most successful at navigating State Aid, as they possess both greater political access and stronger institutional capacity to maximize benefits from changing regulations. Post-crisis NDBs and NDBs from accession states are more dependent on EU funding and have been subjected to stricter State Aid rules, which have consequently created greater hurdles for these NDBs to chart independent paths and use the rules for maximum advantage.

Scholarship on State Aid has arisen from legal scholars (Nicolaides et al., 2008; Quigley, 2009) and economists (Crocioni, 2006; Neven and Verouden, 2008). There is also a literature on the impact of financial regulation on NDBs (Bassanini and Reviglio, 2011; Denzer-Speck and Lob, 2013). However, a much smaller literature has emerged around the political economy of State Aid (Blauberger, 2011; Cini, 2001; Kassim and Lyons, 2013; Lavdas and Mendrinou, 1999; Mause and Gröteke, 2017; Zahariadis, 2010), and even less on the interaction between State Aid and public banks (Grossman, 2006). No scholarship exists on the relationship of NDBs and State Aid, at either the national or EU level. This chapter seeks to investigate the political economy of State Aid by examining how a changing State Aid regime has engendered—and guided—both the reduction and resurgence of NDBs within the EU.

The chapter proceeds as follows. In sections 3.2 and 3.3, I provide a historical overview of State Aid and its relation to NDBs from the 1950s until the 2000s. Then, I analyze how a strengthening State Aid regime first circumscribed, and then enabled, the operations of NDBs to implement policies that accorded with EU policy priorities. Finally, I examine how the financial crisis served as a turning point for the relationship between State Aid and NDBs. State Aid now serves as a guiding force to nudge Member States and NDBs into the EU's favored sectors and financial instruments, though its impact on NDBs has been uneven.

## 3.2 Integration, State Aid, and NDBs

DG Competition is the primary EU regulatory body tasked with enforcing compliance in matters relating to antitrust, mergers, liberalization, and State Aid (European Commission, 2014a). Of central importance to this chapter are Articles 107, 108, and 109 in the TFEU. Article 107(1)[1] lays out the central pillar

[1] Formerly known as Article 87 of the TEC.

of State Aid, which says that "any aid granted by a Member State or through state resources in any form whatsoever which distorts or threatens to distort competition by favoring certain undertakings or the production of certain goods" is to be prohibited (European Commission, 2008a, p. 91). Article 107 (3) elucidates the exemptions, which include aid to promote regional economic development, support an important project of common European interest, support economic activities that do not adversely affect trade, aid cultural and heritage conservation, and promote any other categories specified by decision of the Council.[2]

DG Competition has been empowered with both regulatory objectives and legal authority to ensure Member State compliance. However, determining the specific interpretation of what constitutes aid is challenging. Generally, aid is declared legal if it relates to market exemptions (does not conventionally abide by market principles), market externalities (such as public goods), and market exceptions (which are moments of emergency) (Davies, 2013). Critical to the determination of aid is who has control over the funding. Article 107(1) of the TFEU posits that any aid granted "by a Member State or through State resources" is prohibited; this includes financing from EU sources that are administered by Member States or are under shared management. This also means that programs such as ESIF and ERDF normally fall under State Aid (Policy Department for Budgetary Affairs, 2018). However, if no Member State has authority over the funds, then the programs are generally outside the scope of State Aid, as an EU notice has clarified: "If [EU] resources are awarded directly by the Union, by the European Investment Bank or by the European Investment Fund, with no discretion on the part of the national authorities, they do not constitute State resources" (European Commission, 2016, p. 14). This includes ESIF, EIF, and EIB funds that are managed at the EU level, unless Member States provide guarantees or co-funding. In addition, the regulations of EU-led programs like COSME and Horizon 2020 state that investments should abide by State Aid principles, but these apply to the programs, not the implementing institutions like the EIB. If the EIB uses its own resources and controls the investment, State Aid rules do not apply.[3]

A number of additional EC guidances and legal precedents have set rules as to what constitutes aid, but the changing economic and political landscape, as well as more complex financial instruments, has meant that interpretations have evolved, an area that legal scholars term soft law (López, 2015; Rubini, 2009). This flexibility in interpretation—particularly when backed by political support from the EC—has enabled DG Competition to expand the set of precedents necessary

[2] Article 107 (2) also lists three exemptions—aid having a social character that is granted to individual consumers; aid for damage caused by natural disasters, and aid to the former East German states, though these are rarely invoked.

[3] http://ec.europa.eu/competition/state_aid/modernisation/joint_statement_en.pdf

to implement State Aid (Cini, 2001). Yet there is also difficulty in the political economy of the discretionary ability of DG Competition to interpret the law. Doleys (2013) describes a "dilemma of discretion" that has characterized State Aid—balancing the desire to centralize authority at the supranational level, yet avoiding the backlash of Member States to the policy.

State Aid can therefore be viewed through the lens of regulatory politics, with the relationship between State Aid and NDBs as a contested space over how the regulations are enforced (Buch-Hansen and Wigger, 2011; McGowan and Wilks, 1995; Warlouzet, 2016). On the one hand, State Aid provides a powerful tool for the EC to pursue its policy objectives, and is aware of the strategic implications of its regulatory tools (Botta, 2016; Cini, 2001). On the other, Member States and NDBs can resist—lobbying the EC, circumventing rules by exploiting loopholes, or stretching the legal precedents (López, 2015; Smith, 1998). This cat-and-mouse dynamic has characterized the evolution of State Aid, though the particular composition of national interests, EU policy objectives, and NDB strength has shifted. At times, as in the 1980s and 1990s, the EC cracked down on Member States' activities in industrial policy and pushed NDBs to near extinction; at others, such as the period following the 2008 financial crisis, the EC succumbed to economic urgencies and lobbying from Member States to open new avenues of state investment.

While the presence of State Aid has been substantial, its distributional impact has been uneven. DG Competition has contributed to the purported reduction in national (Pierson, 1996) and subnational (Streb, 2013) autonomy over domestic economic policy making. Sectors such as the automotive industry, finance, SMEs, green technology, and regional development policies have gained exemptions (Davies, 2013; Lyons and Zhu, 2013), yet others have not. Furthermore, there is substantial variation among Member States. Newly admitted EU states have been treated legally the same as older EU members (Hölscher et al., 2017), but overall lacked the political capacity to affect changes at the regulatory level (Zahariadis, 2013). In fact, these challenges began even before accession, a hurdle that older NDBs did not have to contend with (Cremona, 2003). Conversely, larger and wealthier countries have been able to both navigate the regulatory changes and impact the political side of regulation, even if they also receive more negative State Aid decisions (Buts et al., 2011; Clift, 2013). Nevertheless, State Aid has served as a powerful tool to shape the field of European development banking.

## 3.3 NDBs and European Competition Policy: 1951–2000

Beginning in the 1950s, NDBs were relatively minor players in Member State economies, in large part because direct state intervention was widespread. Through the 1970s and 1980s, however, shifting political coalitions and economic integration pressures prompted the ascent of DG Competition, which, through the 1990s, curtailed the limited reach of NDBs.

### 3.3.1 The Early Years of NDBs and European Integration

Early European integration enthusiasts were cognizant of the dangers posed by state support. In 1950, the French Minister for Foreign Affairs, Robert Schuman, promoted the creation of a common market for coal and steel along with the establishment of a public authority to regulate these markets (Leucht, 2008). However, these nascent attempts at regulating interstate markets were heavily influenced by political lobbying, and the fledgling institutions did not officially legislate as a regulatory body (Warlouzet, 2010, p. 7). In 1957, the founding of the European Economic Community (EEC) emphasized free market dynamism with limited public interventions (Gerber, 1998). While the newly established EC appeared to have less formal authority than the previous High Authority, the scope was far wider, even though Articles 85 and 86 on regulation were determined later. The negotiations in 1961 resulted in the adoption of Regulation 17/62, which established a notification system and, if the EC suspected anticompetitive practices, it could launch an inquiry and rule on the validity of the support. This marked the beginning of a centralized institution for EU competition policy (Allen, 1983).

It quickly became clear to the Competition Commissioner, von der Groeben, that the institution would be unable to handle the increasing number of notifications. His solution was to implement block exemptions, "whereby the Commission would be able to exempt certain types of agreements, *en bloc*, from the prohibition against restrictive agreements" (Warlouzet, 2010, p. 12). However, disagreements amongst states prolonged the implementation until 1965, and block exemptions were only permitted in 1967. Following the changes, DG IV (now DG Competition) was flooded with notifications. Instead of adjudicating each case separately, DG Competition has instead preferred deciding precedent-setting cases, such as *Grundig-Consten*. Nevertheless, the leniency of the DG Competition in its regulatory role was obvious: large industrial restructurings and capital infusions from the British, French, and German governments were all but ignored in the 1960s and 1970s (Buch-Hansen and Wigger, 2010, p. 27).

During this initial period, the focus of State Aid was to limit the overt financial subsidies to national industries and export promotion. Germany's KfW implemented investments targeting SME financing, industrial promotion, and the securing of raw materials abroad (Grünbacher, 2005). Spain's ICO was established in 1971 to coordinate NDBs and other state-owned banks, indirectly to support industrialization. Nevertheless, NDBs remained relatively small economic players because, in the absence of a strong regulatory regime, they provided no advantage over direct state intervention.

### 3.3.2 The 1980s and 1990s: The Ascent of DG Competition and the Pressure to Reform

The promotion of a strong competition policy gained traction following the Single Market Act (SMA). Central to this strategy was the increasing usage of precedent-setting court cases.[4] As a result, from 1985 under the leadership of the newly-appointed Competition Commissioner Sutherland, challenges to State Aid were aggressively brought before European courts (Buch-Hansen and Wigger, 2010; Cini and McGowan, 1998). Equally important, DG Competition gained the responsibility of regulating mergers (McGowan and Wilks, 1995).

The rising strength of DG Competition can be attributed to a number of factors. First, European industrialists grew increasingly frustrated with Europe's stagnating economic situation. In 1983, they formed the European Roundtable of Industrialists (ERT) to lobby for greater integration, a quality they admired about the US (Buch-Hansen and Wigger, 2010). Second, a changing ideological and political environment that reflected neoliberalism took hold in Continental Europe, mirroring that of the Anglo-American countries (Buch-Hansen and Wigger, 2011). Third, the presidency of Jacques Delors spurred a revival of EU institutions, gaining the support of affiliated institutions like the ECJ. Block exemptions were expanded and new issue areas were incorporated into DG Competition's policy mandate. The EC seized on this opportunity to promote the completion of a single market couched in language that competition between private enterprises was good for economic growth (Warlouzet, 2010, p. 17). To further reinforce the market orientation, the EC began using the Market Economy Investor Principle (MEIP) to determine if financial assistance constituted aid by comparing the assistance to what the free market would have provided in its absence (López, 2015).

In the 1990s, DG Competition looked to expand upon its newly-established authority in merger control to liberalize previously state-owned sectors (McGowan and Wilks, 1995, p. 153). First, the Single European Market (SEM) entered into force; second, a new more aggressive Competition Commissioner was appointed; third, there were discussions on revising the old merger threshold and strengthening the legal recourses for DG Competition; and finally, a revived interest in free trade agreements (ibid). Yet the rapid expansion of power came at a cost. DG Competition was once again inundated with cases, and a serious backlog

[4] For a detailed legal examination of important precedents, see Stuart and Roginska-Green (2016).

developed. While proposals were floated to decentralize implementation to national courts, it was decided to keep authority within DG Competition in order to maintain harmonization across the EU.

More pertinent to the operations of NDBs was the strengthening of State Aid in the 1980s and 1990s. Smith (1998) argues that three factors explain why DG Competition was able to gain influence. First, the increasing reliance on the language of Community rules and impartiality attempted to depoliticize the functions of DG Competition. Second, rules of the ECJ on State Aid cases reinforced the ability of DG Competition to suspend aid, demand information, and obtain compensation. In particular, four precedent-setting court cases clarified the ability of DG Competition, with the 1984 *Intermills* decision providing a landmark case for State Aid rules as it demonstrated that state financial support could be broadly interpreted to include not only direct subsidies, but also subsidized loans, guarantees, and tax breaks (Smith, 1998, p. 67).[5] What resulted was a much more hostile environment for state-owned entities. Together, these legal precedents greatly increased the regulatory power of State Aid.

The larger NDBs were greatly influenced by the changes in State Aid regulation, and some like KfW were forced to reorganize and reorient their operations (see Mertens this volume). Outside of the existing Western NDBs, however, State Aid also began exerting influence on NDBs in accession countries. In 1997, the EU-10 began enshrining State Aid regulations in national law in preparation for the EU and, in comparison to other measures, compliance with State Aid in the new states was remarkably high (Blauberger, 2009a). However, the greater impact would be felt later, as unfamiliarity with State Aid procedures limited the ability of NDBs in new Member States to fully leverage State Aid rules to their advantage.

## 3.4 A New Era: European Regulation and NDBs since 2000

By 2000, DG Competition's growing regulatory power translated into more aggressive enforcement of regulations with regards to types of aid and notification procedures. However, the financial crisis reversed the long-standing EC apprehension about NDBs, and NDBs were tagged first to supply counter-cyclical financing, and later to pursue a more ambitious industrial policy. NDBs also became more powerful advocates themselves in shaping the regulations. Therefore, following the

[5] In particular, *Intermills* found that capital injections used for operating aid for troubled companies can constitute State Aid. Other precedent-setting cases included *Meura* (1986), which allowed the EC to reach a negative decision if full information is not provided; *Boussac* (1990), which allowed the EC to demand information within one month or be able to declare a violation of State Aid; and *Alutechnik* (1990), which reinforced the power of the EC to recover aid and prohibit Member States from relying on "legitimate expectations" when disbursing aid.

financial crisis, NDB expansion was tolerated—and even encouraged—so long as NDBs adhered to the rules and policy objectives of State Aid.

### 3.4.1 The Early 2000s: Continued Strengthening of State Aid

The legal precedents from the 1980s and 1990s—particular that of *Intermills*—finally caught up with the institutions of NDBs by 2000. Member States had often provided public banks with statutory guarantees, and in Germany, the law provided these through a guarantor liability (*Gewährträgerhaftung*) for its state-owned financial institutions, which included NDBs (KfW). While Commissioner van Miert first voiced his concerns in 1996, in 1999, the European Banking Federation filed a complaint regarding government guarantees of public banks. The EC and German government entered into consultations in 2001, and ultimately adopted a declaration on public credit institutions (the Amsterdam Declaration) that concluded that not all agencies regulated by public law are bound by State Aid. Exemptions to this rule could be granted, but only if the operations are in the "general economic interest" of the European economies (Moser and Pesaresi, 2002). A four-year grace period was implemented, and any investment with that guarantee in 2001 was grandfathered in until 2015 (Moser and Pesaresi, 2002, p. 10). Germany was forced to relinquish its state guarantee of public banks, an outcome known as *Verständigung I.*

In 2002, Germany and the EC entered into consultations to limit the guarantees of NDBs. Two new issues surfaced: "Firstly, a subsidiary obligation (*Nachschusspflicht*) in some Länder for owners of savings banks to provide institutional security funds (*Institutssicherungsfonds*) with financial means, and, secondly, state guarantees to so-called free savings banks" (Moser and Pesaresi, 2002, p. 10). On March 1, 2002, the Commissioner announced conditions for Germany. First, the investments could not discriminate under EC law. Second, investments could be made in areas predetermined to be in line with competition regulations, and these investments must be directly related to their public promotional task (VÖB, 2014, p. 30). Other exemptions included co-investments with the EIB, the granting of loans and other financing to government and special purpose associations of public legal form, and export financing outside the EU. In short, the German government could maintain its guarantee so long as bank activity remained promotional and non-competitive. This agreement was later termed *Verständigung II* (VÖB, n.d.).

The agreements between the EC and German government had a substantial impact on European development banking. Within Germany, this required the restructuring of state-owned banking sector (Grossman, 2006). IPEX, KfW's export finance arm, was also forced to be legally separated and required to adhere to commercial principles. Second, the decision strengthened the role of DG Competition, setting an important precedent. Existing and candidate EU countries were required to adhere to these principles of state ownership in the banking sector. It also contributed to the harmonization of economic policymaking. With this ruling, the "Commission extended its attention to *less visible State interventions* in the form of state guarantees to banks which constitute *operating aid*" (Moser and Pesaresi, 2002, p. 4, emphasis original).

While DG Competition had successes in the early 2000s in asserting its regulatory authority, there was a simultaneously growing acknowledgement that State Aid could also help nudge Member States and NDBs to support EC public policy objectives (Interview with EU Official #2, 2016). One way to achieve this would be to use State Aid as a guiding stick. Central to this perspective was the idea that State Aid could be streamlined in ways that allowed Member States and NDBs to retain investment decisions, but that still adhered to the EU single market vision. Or perhaps more importantly, adhered to the economic policy priorities of the EU (Blauberger, 2009b).

An important first step in the rethinking of State Aid came in June 2005, when the EC announced the State Aid Action Plan (SAAP) in order to deliver less and better aid. As the Competition Commissioner, Neelie Kroes stated, the SAAP aimed to "ensure Member States have a clear, comprehensive and predictable framework, so that they can provide state aid which contributes to cohesion, competitiveness and high quality public services" (European Commission, 2005a). The EC set out three guiding principles for the reform. First, the EC would seek a partnership with Member States to reduce the administrative burden by expanding block exemptions. Second, State Aid would pursue an economic approach that tried to focus on improving the functioning of markets, often through investment means that also minimized market distortions. Finally, the EC set policy priorities on what would be permitted under block exemptions; these were noted to be R&D, innovation, risk capital, public services, transportation, energy and environmental sustainability, and social and regional cohesion (European Commission, 2005b). These reflected the broader change at the EC to move European investment to these strategic sectors, particularly from the Lisbon Strategy.

Very quickly, the EC adopted guidelines and frameworks based upon the SAAP. For instance, key guidelines were adopted on innovation (2005), regional aid (2006), risk capital (2006), and environmental protection (2008), as well block exemptions on regional aid (2006) and de minimis rules (2006). DG Competition noted that these changes brought about significant clarification on how Member States could abide by State Aid rules while simultaneously increasing funding (Schwarz and Foeckling, 2008). Therefore, by the mid-2000s, the EC began to use State Aid to support their policy objectives of channeling the activities of state support into particular areas of the economy, rather than just as a regulatory tool.

### 3.4.2 Post-2008: The Financial Crisis, State Aid Reform, and the Partnership with NDBs

The 2008 financial crisis proved to be another turning point for State Aid and the evolving European development banking field. State rescues of commercial banks highlighted the need for government involvement in the economy, but also revealed new areas of contestation over how the soft law aspects of State Aid should be implemented (Doleys, 2012; Lyons and Zhu, 2013; Reynolds et al., 2009). NDBs were some of the first institutions to be able to provide counter-cyclical financing and emergency rescues of commercial banks. Simultaneously, EU policy objectives shifted towards areas of investment in innovation, R&D, and SME financing to pursue growth (Ulnicane, 2016). For the EC, the need to increase investment required a different perspective on State Aid. The SAAP had already laid the groundwork for the new, more collaborative relationship with NDBs. NDBs seized the opportunity to better respond to State Aid, and, in particular, adapted their operations to take advantage of new opportunities (Interview with EU Official #2, 2016). This evolution also allowed NDBs to test the limits of State Aid regulation.

The crisis unfolded just as the more ambitious SAAP reforms to simplifying State Aid were being implemented. One of the first major transformations took place in June 2008, when the EC clarified the application of Articles 87 and 88 to guarantees. According to the notice, DG Competition clarified that funding by public authorities for companies could be compatible with regulations if they are made under conditions that a private market investor would have accepted (the Market Economy Investor Principle), and established the minimum margin on interest rates based on investment risk.[6] The notice also established policies for guaranteeing SMEs and raised the threshold of aid notification of financing up to EUR 2.5 million per company, which could also be pooled (European Commission, 2008b).

Additionally, DG Competition in July 2008 revised the General Block Exemption Regulation (GBER). The GBER granted automatic approval for 26 categories of State Aid in the core policy areas defined in the SAAP, so long as public authorities adhered to certain limits of funding. SME financing particularly benefitted from the expansion of GBER (European Commission, 2008c). In addition, Commissioner Neelie Kroes detailed new additions to the simplification package. This included streamlined methods for investigations, new procedures to swiftly

[6] According to the communication, a state guarantee would be considered not aid if the minimum annual premium (also known as the "safe-harbor premium") were charged upon the amount that is effectively guaranteed by the state. This ranges from 0.0% to 0.4%, based on credit rating agencies' ratings on credit quality. See the *Official Journal of the European Union* (OJ C 14, 19.1.2008) for details.

approve cases where notification is complete, and the ability to use national courts to enforce State Aid (Kroes, 2008).

Critically, these notices clarified the parameters of State Aid regulation and provided Member States and NDBs predictable latitude to take advantage of these updates without the threat of punitive action. The EC signaled two changes. First, market-preserving state interventions in key sectors like SME finance would not only be tolerated, but ultimately supported by the EU. State Aid viewed subsidized financing as less distorting than grants, a view that the Commission wanted to spread to NDBs (Interview with EU Official #3, 2016). Second, NDBs would be treated as partners. This gained added emphasis as NDBs became important partners to distribute counter-cyclical financing, from KfW in Germany to Finnvera in Finland. Ultimately, this provided NDBs with an opportunity—intended or not—to engage with and shape the future direction of State Aid.

#### 3.4.2.1 New Partnerships, and New Opportunities: EFSI and NDBs

As the crisis unfolded, the EC recognized that NDBs might need to be more than just tolerated—they could serve as partners in implementing EU public policy objectives. The EIB-managed European Fund for Strategic Investment (EFSI), which in its initial configuration aimed to achieve EUR 315 billion in mobilized investment, recognized that NDBs could serve as financing partners within Member States. NDBs welcomed the change as a way to reestablish themselves within European public policy. However, by October 2015, institutions from France, Germany, Italy, Luxembourg, and Spain had only committed EUR 33 billion. Moreover, most was earmarked for co-financing projects within their respective countries. In order to encourage contributions, the EC provided incentives:

> We did want to encourage [the establishment of NDBs], but we wanted to encourage a business model that was focused on market failures that was also at arm's length from the government, so you don't have political decision on specific loans. And we were dangling the carrot that once you did meet these criteria, any lending that these banks do will not count towards the Stability and Growth Pact's debt limits.
>
> (Interview with EU Official #4, 2016)

Even though the quantity of financing from NDBs disappointed, it was critical in solidifying a paradigmatic shift away from grants and towards financial instruments, as well as promoting NDBs as channels for structured funds (Interview with EU Official #3, 2016). The financial crisis solidified NDBs as not only conduits for countercyclical financing, but also as partners for EU funds.

Second, the EC encouraged Member States without an NDB to establish one and laid out regulations for their adherence to State Aid (European

Commission, 2015a). Existing Member States with NDBs, particularly France and Germany, were concerned that the communication was designed to circumscribe the authority of NDBs, but these concerns were later ameliorated when the document endorsed the creation of new NDBs (Interview with EU Official #3, 2016). These new banks in the UK, Portugal, and Latvia were all assessed by DG Competition to ensure adherence to State Aid regulation (European Commission, 2015b, c.f. 2014b), and a consultative process strongly guided their structure and activities (Interview with EU Official #3, 2016). In fact, the EC saw the establishment of new NDBs as a boon to propagating their influence over state financing:

> Part of the imperative is to focus and encourage member states to make investments in infrastructure, but also to consider private financing and PPP models for infrastructure rather than to strain budget finances . . . You also force member states to generate projects that are viable and not just funded through grants.
> (Interview with EU Official #4, 2016)

The EC sought not only to expand the ability of states to use NDBs as a way of spurring investment, but also to guide how these investments were implemented. The sudden growth of new NDBs also concerned the EIB, which feared that NDBs would become powerful competitors to their own business (Interview with EU Official #4, 2016).

The shift in the EC's perspective on State Aid had another effect—NDBs obtained the ability to collaborate—and contest—the governance of State Aid. For example, Bpifrance had developed a method for calculating the recoupable advance under State Aid. This innovation proved to be so successful that the EC asked for the tool to be transferred to other institutions (Thiemann and Volberding, this volume). NDBs also began to lobby, either directly or through their Member States' governments, for increased responsibilities and broader exemptions from State Aid (Interview with EU Official #2, 2016; Interview with EU Official #4, 2016). Additionally, EU public policy was beholden to NDBs, giving them more ability to assert their interests. The Juncker Plan relied on the contributions of NDBs and, as Franco Bassanini, the head of Italy's CDP, stated, "were these [NDB] guarantees considered as illegal state aid, we can forget about the Juncker plan."[7] This would foreshadow the changes made with the InvestEU platform.

### 3.4.2.2 State Aid Modernization and GBER 2012–2014

The SAAP and financial crisis elevated NDBs into important economic partners to the EU. Yet, to many NDBs, the State Aid rules were complex enough to hinder the implementation of more ambitious investment projects. NDBs particularly

[7] "EU governments want state aid leeway on EU investment plan," *Reuters*. 13 April 2015.

sought further clarifications and simplifications to State Aid in order to gain regulatory certainty. Therefore, in 2012, the State Aid Modernization (SAM) was designed to update the activities of DG Competition. According to Joaquin Almunia, the former head of DG Competition, there were three reasons for the reforms: to ensure that State Aid rules supported Europe 2020 objectives; to prioritize enforcement in the internal market; and to streamline decision-making processes (Almunia, 2012). The driving principle remained the same; State Aid rules are "designed to ensure that the interventions of [NDBs] are well-targeted to remedy market failures and thereby contribute to economic and financial development, while at the same time not distorting markets, crowding out private operators or keeping companies alive that would otherwise have exited the market" (European Commission, 2015a, pp. 5–6). SAM focused on facilitating the disbursement of state support that is well-designed and targeted at common market failures, obviating the need for a possibly lengthy review process. The streamlined regulations no longer required *ex ante* approval in three categories: investments that are in line with *de minimis* regulations, included in a block exemption regulation, or approved under specific State Aid guidelines.

Central to SAM was a revised GBER that simplified procedures by granting authorization without prior notification. The EC hoped that two-thirds of all investments would ultimately qualify for GBER within five years, and up to 90% after that. GBER streamlined exemptions in three important ways. First, more categories were eligible for exemption. Second, new forms of exemption within existing categories were added. Third, exemption thresholds were raised. For instance, the threshold for notification within investments in R&D and innovation doubled from EUR 7.5m to EUR 15m per enterprise. For SMEs, it has increased from EUR 1.5m to EUR 15m per SME that covers the full development cycle of a business of seven years (DG Competition, 2014a). Similar increases were implemented for promotional schemes as well. To ensure compliance, the EC implemented new rules for transparency.

Outside of GBER, the thresholds for policy review have been raised. For instance, DG Competition announced new compatibility conditions above the 15m GBER threshold as long as "the aid measure is granted in cases where market failures have been convincingly demonstrated" (DG Competition, 2014b, p. 2). In particular, funding for R&D and innovation are largely exempted from the new rules. According to the Commission, this "will enable, among others, R&D-intensive companies and companies in industries with high upfront investments costs to access the necessary amount of finance right from their creation, through a sequence of investment rounds, without being constrained by the current restrictions on maximum annual tranches" (DG Competition, 2014b, p. 2). More aid will be allowed for innovation clusters and pilot projects, and if the project is implemented within the framework of EU Joint Undertakings (a public-private scheme), then the threshold rises to EUR 20m (DG Competition, 2014c). For

SMEs, the new rules allowed for annual investment tranches of up to EUR 2.5m, instead of the previous limit of EUR 1.5m. The regional aid regime was also modernized to strengthen its effectiveness, mainly by prioritizing SMEs and other locally based enterprises (DG Competition, 2014d). In the area of risk finance, the new guidelines also lift the old restriction of a 70 percent equity stake to allow a wider range of financial instruments, such as quasi-equity, loans, guarantees, or hybrid financial instruments (DG Competition, 2014b).

The new rules allowed for more flexibility, including public-private partnerships, as long as the actions did not interfere in the market. These regulations effectively incentivized states to support their SMEs, perhaps even to the extent of establishing one of their NDBs to coordinate the funding schemes. As Barbara Cattrysse explained, "[t]he objective of the risk finance State aid rules is to encourage Member States and private investors to provide on a risk sharing basis repayable financing at preferential conditions to SMEs, so as to help them become more competitive at a global level" (Cattrysse, 2014, p. 697). In addition, these State Aid rules may be more flexible, as they can relieve the pressure on governments during times of budgetary constraints. The inclusion of private finance was also meant to add vitality to the process (Cattrysse, 2014, p. 697). Efficiency of investments has been widely cited as the single most important reason for expanding these exemptions, enabling Member States to quickly and efficiently implement new programs (Interview with EU Official #2, 2016).

The SAM program highlights three important facets of EU policy. First, EU development policy is heavily reliant upon market-based financing, and these efforts have strengthened in recent years (Mertens and Thiemann, 2018). The revisions relaxed the policies on financial instruments, allowing for funding to be channeled through loans and risk guarantees, but also through public-private partnerships. The focus on exemptions of innovation, R&D, and the environment also highlight the disproportionate weight that the new sectors have. These trends can be clearly seen in GBER. In 2000, only EUR 124m was invested, and was roughly evenly split between SME financing and other programs. In 2017, more than EUR 41bn was channeled through block exemptions, with significant amounts going to environmental investments and regional development promotion (see Figure 3.1). For example, Germany, Sweden, Denmark, and Finland have a relatively high proportion dedicated to environmental projects. Italy and the UK give more to research and development, while Poland, France, the Czech Republic, Hungary, and Greece have emphasized regional development programs. These numbers suggest that the EC has been successful in redirecting funds towards its target investment areas, much as the creators intended (Interview with EU Official #4, 2016).

Second, NDBs continue to serve as an important mechanism for delivering State Aid. Since 2015, more than 96 percent of new measures that have been reported for the first time fell under GBER, an increase of 28 percent compared to

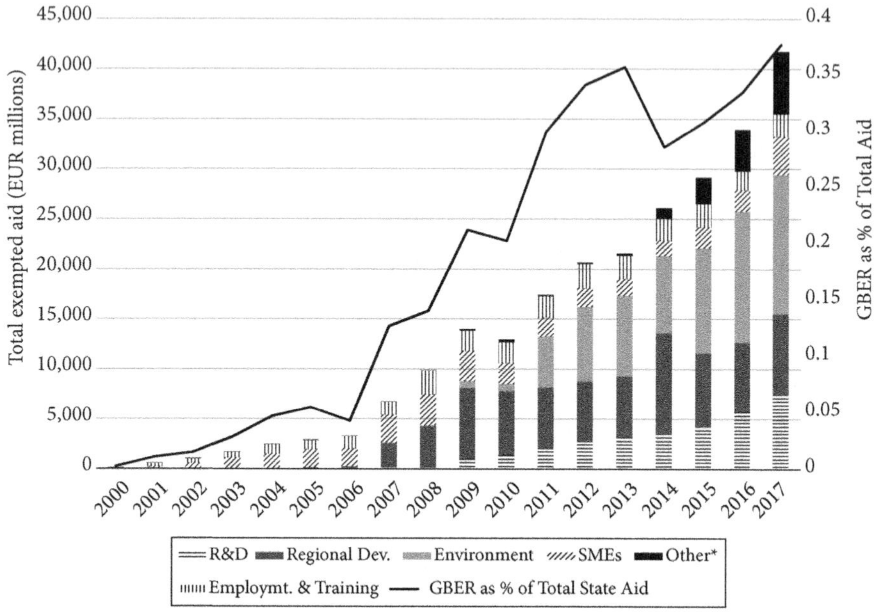


**Figure 3.1** Total Block Exempted Aid and GBER as % of State Aid in the EU-28, 2000–2017
*Source*: Eurostat.

2013. GBER now accounts for 48 percent of total State Aid spending, up from just 25 percent in 2010 (European Commission, 2019). While not all of GBER is administered through NDBs, it is acknowledged that GBER is best implemented through institutions that have close links with policy makers (Interview with EU Official #3, 2016). This was a consequence of the financial crisis, which fundamentally changed the perspective of the EU towards NDBs. Instead of serving as a pariah of state interventionism, NDBs have gained institutional advantages from the EC to serve as the official conduits (Interview with EU Official #1, 2016). For their part, 16 European NDBs established the European Long-Term Investors (ELTI) in an attempt not only to coordinate financial resources, but also to "represent, promote and defend [their] shared interests" and "inform the EU and its institutions on the role and potential" as sources of long-term funding (ELTI, 2013, p. 2). Therefore, while DG Competition still strictly regulates NDB intervention, the Commission has acknowledged that a robust promotion of the single market cannot entirely preclude national investment mechanisms or ignore their interests.

Finally, there is significant variation in how each country leverages the increasing availability of block exemptions, suggesting that while legally equal, NDBs have been impacted by State Aid in different ways. For example, of the EUR 41.7bn channeled through block exemptions, Germany, France, Poland, and Italy account for more than half the amount, or EUR 22bn; the bottom 20 countries combined account for just over EUR 9bn. Incidentally, the largest beneficiaries of block exemptions are also those with large NDBs. The reasons for these disparities in leveraging State Aid are numerous, but one is certainly that the regulatory regime has impacted Member States in unequal ways.

For instance, even though Germany's KfW was forced to undergo restructuring, the settlement was lenient, as there is no indication that "Germany was required to provide specific evidence of market failure to support these activities and there is no time limit on the mandate of these banks" (Taylor, 2017, p. 141). This stands in sharp contrast to new NDBs from the UK to Malta, which were required to obtain DG Comp approval of the institution prior to establishment, were more limited in their institutional flexibility and breadth, and were only approved for a few years before reassessment. The Latvian Single Development Institution (now Altum) similarly needed approval from the EC to begin channeling capital, even though the operations carried out interventions that were legacies of the three preceding NDBs (Taylor, 2017, p. 145). Nevertheless, DG Competition has noted that the gap between Member States is closing; between 2010 and 2017, the correlation between State Aid spending per capita and GDP per capita more than halved, indicating that newer Member States have been catching up. In fact, total State Aid expenditure as a percentage of GDP is highest in Hungary (2.67 percent), Latvia (1.77 percent), and Poland (1.59 percent), while Ireland (0.23 percent) is the lowest (European Commission, 2019).

Contestation simultaneously occurred through legal cases as well. Since 1998, there have been 14 State Aid cases involving NDBs. Of those, two were found not to constitute aid, and the other 12 had no objections raised. It is interesting to note that only one case (Estonia's Kredex in 2005) involved an NDB not from Germany, France, or Scandinavia. Yet drawing conclusions from State Aid cases is difficult since it is unclear who raised objections to the NDB, or whether additional cases affected NDBs indirectly. In addition to cases, NDBs can also issue notifications that defend a particular funding scheme as compatible with State Aid. Of the 33 notifications since 1998, KfW has by far the most notifications (20), with Poland's BGK and Austria's AWS at a distant second with 4 each (see Appendix). While direct conclusions are difficult to draw, these numbers do similarly suggest differences in the institutional capacity of NDBs. In this way, cases and notifications may be interpreted as the ability of NDBs to push back on the limits of State Aid, a capability that is concentrated in larger, Western NDBs.

### 3.4.3 Post-EFSI: A Direct Partnership Emerges with InvestEU

While EFSI and SAM demonstrated a new-found willingness of the EC to cooperate with NDBs, the protracted economic stress showed the EC that an even deeper partnership with NDBs would be beneficial. In 2018, the InvestEU platform was announced as the successor to EFSI. Unlike EFSI, InvestEU would seek to not only harmonize the numerous credit lines and guarantees of the EU, but it would also seek to empower NDBs to become direct implementing partners of investment funds. This remarkable transformation has elevated NDBs to important European economic actors and has assisted in expanding a new industrial policy.

InvestEU allows Member States to allocate up to 5 percent of their Cohesion Fund to one of the four policy envelopes in the fund, which will then be used to finance projects within the member's territory. In exchange for the buy-in, InvestEU lessens the regulatory threat of State Aid rules, as cohesion funds that have been allocated through InvestEU will be automatically declared compatible with State Aid rules as long as certain clear conditions are fulfilled (European Commission, 2018). This is a consequence of the EC's direct management of the fund, the prioritization of projects with additionality, and independent nature of the administering. In contrast to the Juncker Plan, however, the Member State will have more say in the selection of projects and implementing partner, allowing governments to appoint their own NDB to design and implement the final project (Rubio and Virel, 2018). InvestEU also allows NDBs to cooperate to obtain funding via InvestEU without the EIB serving as an intermediary institution. NDBs can even receive funding from InvestEU, so long as it encompasses investments in at least three Member States (see Rubio and Thiemann, this volume).

NDBs have welcomed the evolution, though they have also recommended additional changes to fully maximize the participation of NDBs. Specifically, ELTI has recommended that NDBs undergo a pillar assessment that grants them access to EU funds without needing to go through ex ante assessments, as this would expedite the process of fund disbursement. A harmonized regulatory approach would also decrease uncertainty over the deployment of financial instruments and enable NDBs to respond to market conditions faster. Moreover, ELTI has also advocated a revision of State Aid procedures so that NDBs are treated equally to commercial banks, particularly when mixed funds and guarantees are used (ELTI, 2018).

Ultimately, the dual nature of the InvestEU platform highlights the EC's carrot and stick approach in guiding NDBs. While EU funds are made available as an incentive, they are encouraged to be administered via EU-monitored financial channels. In return for participation, projects that meet the EU's guidelines for both sector and financing method are freed from the threat of regulation, allowing Member States greater flexibility and predictability in their investments. Consequently, it now may be easier to establish a new NDB that engages in delivering "aid" rather than commercial products because the EC has elucidated ways that accord with State Aid, such as GBER, that do not require ex ante notification. Commercial operations, on the other hand, can take time to go through the cumbersome State Aid notification process. Therefore, while NDBs have certainly undergone a resurgence in policy relevance, they have done so within the constraints of State Aid.

## 3.5 Conclusion

While it initially helped circumscribe NDBs until the early 2000s, State Aid has now helped steer NDBs to participate in the broader objectives of European public policy. As such, NDBs may have growing funds, but State Aid rules have constrained when, where, and how NDBs have been able to operate. Crucially, however, these newfound operations have reflected the public policy objectives of the EC and have consequently nudged NDBs to move into sectors (SMEs, green investment, and innovation) and financing methods (market-based financing) that have featured prominently in EU policy statements. Yet rather than simply wielding a punitive stick, the EC now also offers a respite from State Aid to guide NDB action. The SAM, GBER, and recent programs like the Juncker Plan and InvestEU have used State Aid minimum thresholds and exemptions to maintain NDB compliance.

To be certain, NDBs have also pushed back against the stick of State Aid. State Aid cases and notifications, indirect lobbying through national finance ministries, and investment consultations have all served as ways of NDBs seeking to contest State Aid. However, as has become evident, NDBs possess varying abilities to push back. Larger and older Western NDBs not only have been the most active in lobbying efforts and State Aid cases and notifications, but they have also, on average, been more active in utilizing GBER. These findings suggest that they possess the institutional capacity to understand and respond to the changing State Aid regime, which is a subtler contestation response to maximize flexibility under regulation. Conversely, those NDBs from accession states have largely been "rule takers" of State Aid. Post-crisis NDBs are also subjected to more intense vetting than older ones and are required to undergo periodic reviews—another aspect that older NDBs are exempted from. Whether this "rule taking" tendency is a consequence of weaker institutional capacity, dependency on European funding, or even from self-imposed restrictions requires further investigation.

What the future holds for the relationship between EU regulation and NDBs remains uncertain. The EC's willingness to allow NDBs to occupy the policy making space at the national level has opened opportunities, but also a number of unresolved—and fiercely contested—topics. First, the increasing complexity of financial instruments has created difficulties in calculating State Aid as most are implemented through commercial banks or private contractors (Interview with EU Official #2, 2016). Second, new issue areas present challenges to existing interpretations of rules. Third, there are persisting questions about the relationship of NDBs with the EIB, and perhaps whether the EIB will eclipse NDBs

(Interview with EU Official #4, 2016). These dynamics might be mitigated, however, by the fact that NDBs can now use InvestEU funds without the EIB as an intermediary. Fourth, even though State Aid regulations theoretically apply equally to all NDBs, in practice disparities in influence and capacity persist. Nevertheless, what is certain is that State Aid regulation will remain an important stick of the EU, guiding and constraining NDBs for years to come.

## Bibliography


Allen, D., 1983. "Managing the Common Market: The Community's Competition Policy." In H. Wallace, W. Wallace, C. Webb (eds), Policy-Making in the European Communities, Sage Publications, London.

Almunia, J. 2012., Presenting the State Aid Modernisation Initiative. European Commission, Brussels.

Bassanini, F. Reviglio, E., 2011. "Financial Stability, Fiscal Consolidation and Long-Term Investment after the Crisis." OECD Journal: Financial Market Trends vol. 2011 (1), 1.

Blauberger, M., 2011. "State aid control from a political science perspective." In E. Szyszczak (ed.), Research Handbook on European State Aid Law. Cheltenham UK: Edward Elgar.

Blauberger, M., 2009a. "Compliance with rules of negative integration: European state aid control in the new member states." Journal of European Public Policy vol. 16, 1030–46.

Blauberger, M., 2009b. "Of 'Good' and 'Bad" Subsidies: European State Aid Control through Soft and Hard Law'. West European Politics vol. 32, 719–37.

Botta, M., 2016. "Competition Policy: Safeguarding the Commission's Competences in State Aid Control." Journal of European Integration vol. 38, 265–78.

Buch-Hansen, H. and Wigger, A., 2011. The Politics of European Competition Regulation: A Critical Political Economy Perspective. London: Routledge.

Buch-Hansen, H. and Wigger, A., 2010. "Revisiting 50 Years of Market-Making: The Neoliberal Transformation of European Competition Policy." Review of International Political Economy vol. 17, 20–44.

Buts, C., Jegers, M., and Joris, T., 2011. "Determinants of the European Commission's State Aid Decisions." Journal of Industry, Competition and Trade vol. 11, 399–426.

Cattrysse, B. 2014. "The Newly Adopted Risk Finance State Aid Rules." European State Aid Law Quarterly vol. 1, 689–97.

Cini, M. 2001. "The Soft Law Approach: Commission Rule-Making in the EU's State Aid Regime." Journal of European Public Policy vol. 8, 192–207.

Cini, M. and McGowan, L., 1998. "Competition Policy in the European Union." New York: St. Martin's Press.

Clift, B., 2013. "Economic Patriotism, the Clash of Capitalisms, and State Aid in the European Union." Journal of Industry, Competition and Trade vol. 13, 101–17.

Cremona, M., 2003. "State Aid Control: Substance and Procedure in the Europe Agreements and the Stabilisation and Association Agreements." European Law Journal vol. 9, 265–87.

Crocioni, P., 2006. "Can State Aid Policy Become More Economic Friendly?" World Competition vol. 29, 89–108.

Davies, W., 2013. "When Is a Market Not a Market?: 'Exemption', 'Externality" and "Exception" in the Case of European State Aid Rules'. Theory, Culture & Society vol. 30, 32–59.

Denzer-Speck, D. and Lob H. 2013. "Promoting Long-Term Investments under Changing Regulatory Framework Conditions: The Case of Germany's KfW Bankengruppe." Long-Term Investors Club.

DG Competition, 2014a. State Aid Modernisation—A Major Revamp of EU State Aid Control (No. 11), Competition Policy Brief. Brussels: DG Competition.

DG Competition, 2014b. A New Rule Book for Risk Finance State Aid (No. 1), Competition Policy Brief. Brussels: DG Competition.

DG Competition, 2014c. Supporting R&D and Innovation in Europe: New State Aid Rules (No. 5), Competition Policy Brief. Brussels: DG Competition.

DG Competition, 2014d. Guidelines on Regional State Aid for 2014–2020 (No. 14), Competition Policy Brief. Brussels: DG Competition.

Doleys, T., 2012. "Managing State Aid in a Time of Crisis: Commission Crisis Communications and the Financial Sector Bailout." Journal of European Integration vol. 34, 549–65.

Doleys, T.J., 2013. "Managing the Dilemma of Discretion: The European Commission and the Development of EU State Aid Policy." Journal of Industry, Competition and Trade vol. 13, 23–38.

ELTI, 2013. The European Long Term Investors Association (ELTI) Launches Its 2014 Action Plan. European Long Term Investors Association. Brussels: ELTI.

ELTI, 2018. Financial Instruments in the Next MFF: The Way Forward Regarding the Single Fund, Direct Access for NPBs and the Single Rule Book. European Long Term Investors Association. Brussels: ELTI.

European Commission, 2019. State Aid Scoreboard 2018: Results, Trends and Observations Regarding EU28 State Aid Expenditure Reports for 2017. Brussels: DG Competition.

European Commission, 2018. The InvestEU Programme: Questions and Answers (No. MEMO/18/4010).

European Commission, 2016. Commission Notice on the Notion of State Aid as Referred to in Article 107(1) of the Treaty on the Functioning of the European Union. Official Journal of the European Union 2016/C 262/01.

European Commission, 2015a. Working Together for Jobs And Growth: The Role of National Promotional Banks (NPBs) in Supporting the Investment Plan for Europe (COM(2015) 361 final). Brussels: European Commission.

European Commission, 2015b. State aid SA.36904 (2014/N)—MLB development segment and creation of the Latvian Single Development Institution. Brussels: European Commission.

European Commission, 2014a. Competition: Making Markets Work Better. Brussels: European Commission.

European Commission. 2014b. State Aid SA.37824 (2014/N)—Portuguese Development Financial Institution. Brussels: European Commission.

European Commission, 2008a. Consolidated Versions of the Treaty on European Union and the Treaty on the Functioning of the European Union. Official Journal of the European Union 115.

European Commission, 2008b. Commission Notice on the Application of Articles 87 and 88 of the EC Treaty to State Aid in the Form of Quarantees. Official Journal of the European Union 115.

European Commission, 2008c. Special Edition. Competition Policy Newsletter. Brussels: European Commission.

European Commission, 2005a. State Aid: Commission Outlines Comprehensive Five Year Reform of State Aid Policy to Promote Growth, Jobs and Cohesion (No. IP/05/680). Brussels: European Commission.

European Commission, 2005b. State Aid Action Plan: Less and Better Targeted State Aid: A Roadmap for State Aid Reform 2005–2009. Brussels: European Commission.

Gerber, D.J., 1998. Law and Competition in Twentieth-Century Europe: Protecting Prometheus. Oxford UK: Clarendon Press.

Grossman, E., 2006. "Europeanization as an Interactive Process: German Public Banks Meet EU State Aid Policy." Journal of Common Market Studies vol. 44, 325–48.

Grünbacher, A. 2005. Reconstruction and Cold War in Germany: The Kreditanstalt für Wiederaufbau (1948–1961). Aldershot UK: Ashgate Publishing.

Hölscher, J., Nulsch, N., and Stephan, J., 2017. "State Aid in the New EU Member States." Journal of Common Market Studies vol. 55, 779–97.

Kassim, H. and Lyons, B., 2013. The New Political Economy of EU State Aid Policy. Journal of Industry, Competition and Trade vol. 13, 1–21.

Kroes, N. 2008. The State Aid Action Plan: A Roadmap for Reform and Recovery.

Lavdas, K. and M. Mendrinou., 1999. Politics, Subsidies and Competition: The New Politics of State Intervention in the European Union. Brussels: European Commission.

Leucht, B. 2008. "Transatlantic Policy Networks in the Creation of the First European Anti-Trust Law: Mediating Between American Anti-Trust and German Ordo-Liberalism," in W. Kaiser, B. Leucht, and M. Rasmussen (eds), The History of the European Union: Origins of a Trans- and Supranational Polity 1950–72. New York: Routledge.

López, J.J.P., 2015. The Concept of State Aid Under EU Law: From Internal Market to Competition and Beyond. Oxford UK: Oxford University Press.

Lyons, B. and Zhu, M., 2013. "Compensating Competitors or Restoring Competition? EU Regulation of State Aid for Banks During the Financial Crisis." Journal of Industry, Competition and Trade vol.13, 39–66.

Mause, K. and Gröteke, F., 2017. "The Economic Approach to European State Aid Control: A Politico-Economic Analysis." Journal of Industry, Competition and Trade vol. 17, 185–201.

McGowan, L. and Wilks, S., 1995. "The First Supranational Policy in the European Union: Competition Policy." European Journal of Political Research vol. 28, 141–69.

Mertens, D. and Thiemann, M., 2018. "Market-Based but State-Led: The Role of Public Development Banks in Shaping Market-Based Finance in the European Union." Competition and Change vol. 22, 184–204.

Moser, S., Pesaresi, N., 2002. "State Guarantees to German Public Banks: A New Step in the Enforcement of State Aid Discipline to Financial Services in the Community." Competition Policy Newsletter vol. 2, 1–11.

Neven, D. and Verouden, V., 2008. "Towards a More Refined Economic Approach in State Aid Control," In N. Mederer, N. Pesaresi, and M. Van Hoof (eds), EU Competition Law—Volume IV: State Aid. Deventer, NL: Claeys Casteels.

Nicolaides, P., Kekelekis, M., and Kleis, M., 2008. State Aid Policy in the European Community: Principles and Practice. The Hague, NL: Kluwer Law International.

Pierson, P. 1996. "The Path to European Integration—A Historical Institutionalist Analysis." Comparative Political Studies vol. 29, 123–63.

Policy Department for Budgetary Affairs, 2018. "State Aid and EU Funding: Are They Compatible?" Brussels: Directorate General for Internal Policies of the Union.

Quigley, C., 2009. European State Aid Law and Policy.; Oxford UK: Hart Publishers.

Reynolds, M., Macrory, S., and Chowdhury, M., 2009. "EU Competition Policy in the Financial Crisis: Extraordinary Measures." Fordham International Law Journal vol. 33, 1670.

Rubini, L., 2009. "The Definition of Subsidy and State Aid: WTO and EC Law in Comparative Perspective." Oxford UK: Oxford University Press.

Rubio, E. and F. Virel, 2018. "InvestEU Fund: A Rebranded Junker Fund?" Jacques Delors Institute.

Schwarz, B. and Foeckling, J., 2008. "The New Approach to State Aids," European Commission (eds), in the New Approach To State Aids—Recent Reforms Under the State Aid Action Plan and Next Steps.

Smith, M.P., 1998. "Autonomy by the Rules: The European Commission and the Development of State Aid Policy." Journal of Common Market Studies vol. 36, 55–78.

Streb, H., 2013. "State Aid Policy, Territoriality and Federalism: EU Scrutiny and Control of Regional Aid and the Supranationalisation of Subnational Autonomy in

Federal Member States." Journal of Industry, Competition and Trade vol. 13, 129–41.

Stuart, E. and Roginska-Green, I., 2016. Sixty Years of EU State Aid Law and Policy: Analysis and Assessment. The Hague, NL Kluwer Law International.

Taylor, I., 2017., "Application of the State Aid Rules to the Creation of Development Banks: Is There Scope for Simplification?" Journal of Antitrust Enforcement vol. 5, 130–49.

Ulnicane, I., 2016. "Research and Innovation as Sources of Renewed Growth? EU Policy Responses to The Crisis." Journal of European Integration vol. 38, 327–41.

VÖB. 2014. "Promotional Banks in Germany: Acting in the Public Interest." Berlin: VÖB.

VÖB. n.d. Bundesverband Öffentlicher Banken Deutschlands: Förderbanken https://www.voeb.de/de/themen/foerderpolitik/foerderbanken-neu.

Warlouzet, L., 2016. "The Centralization of EU Competition Policy: Historical Institutionalist Dynamics from Cartel Monitoring to Merger Control (1956–91)." Journal of Common Market Studies vol. 54, 725–41.

Warlouzet, L., 2010. "The Rise of European Competition Policy, 1950-1991: A Cross-Disciplinary Survey of a Contested Policy Sphere." EUI Working Paper. EUI Robert Schuman Centre for Advanced Studies; Florence, Italy

Zahariadis, N., 2013. "Winners and Losers in EU State Aid Policy." Journal of Industry, Competition and Trade vol. 13, 143–58.

Zahariadis, N., 2010. "State Aid and Partisan Government in the European Union." Social Science Quarterly vol. 91, 436–54.

APPENDIX 3.1

# List of Interviews

#1, Interview EU Official, 25 February 2016, Brussels.
#2, Interview EU Official, 25 February 2016, Brussels.
#3, Interview EU Official, 26 February 2016, Brussels.

## APPENDIX 3.2

# State Aid cases involving European national development banks and total number of notices, 1998 to 2018

| Bank | Country | Year | Case | Outcome | Notices |
|---|---|---|---|---|---|
| **KfW** | Germany | 2010 | Entrepreneurs-fonds de la KfW pour le fonds de roulement et des investissements | Decision does not constitute aid | 20 |
| | | 2008 | KfW run loan component of German Konjunkturprogramm | Decision not to raise objections | |
| **CDP** | Italy | | None | | 0 |
| **CDC** | France | 2014 | Aide d'État accordée par la CDC au projet de R&D « TOURS 2015 » de STMicroelectronics dans le cadre du programme d'investissement d'avenir | Decision not to raise objections | 0 |
| | | 2001 | Garantie accordée par CDC à sa filiale CDC Ixis | Decision not to raise objections | |
| **Bpifrance** | France | | None | | 0 |
| **ICO** | Spain | | None | | 0 |
| **BGK** | Poland | | None | | 4 |
| **BNG** | Netherlands | | None | | 0 |
| **Finnvera** | Finland | 2002 | Finnvera loan program for the processing and marketing | Decision not to raise objections | 0 |
| | | 2004 | Amendment of Finnvera loan program for the processing and marketing of agricultural products | Decision not to raise objections | |
| | | 2005 | Finnvera plc's loan and guarantee scheme to fisheries | Decision not to raise objections | |
| | | 2007 | Tax exemption to Finnvera Oyj | Decision does not constitute aid | |
| | | 2009 | Temporary Framework guarantee measure | Decision not to raise objections | |
| | | 2014 | SME Rescue and Restructuring Aid Scheme of State-owned specialised financing company, Finnvera plc | Decision not to raise objections | |

| Bank | Country | Year | Case | Outcome | Notices |
|---|---|---|---|---|---|
| **HDB** | Hungary | | None | | 0 |
| **VIPA** | Lithuania | | None | | 0 |
| **Invega** | Lithuania | | None | | 0 |
| **Vaekstfonden** | Denmark | 1998 | Vaekstfonden | Decision not to raise objections | 0 |
| | | 2011 | The calculation methodology for the Large Growth Guarantee Scheme | Decision not to raise objections | |
| **SID** | Slovenia | | None | | 1 |
| **SZRB** | Slovakia | | None | | 0 |
| **SFPI** | Belgium | | None | | 0 |
| **Kredex** | Estonia | 2005 | Short-term export-credit guarantees provided by kredex | Decision not to raise objections | 1 |
| **Almi** | Sweden | 1999 | Almi | Decision not to raise objections | 0 |
| **BBB** | UK | | None | | 0 |
| **CMZRB** | Czech Republic | | None | | 0 |
| **SBCI** | Ireland | | None | | 1 |
| **HBOR** | Croatia | | None | | 2 |
| **Altum** | Latvia | | None | | 0 |
| **IFD** | Portugal | | None | | 0 |
| **SNCI** | Luxembourg | | None | | 0 |
| **BDB** | Bulgaria | | None | | 0 |
| **AWS** | Austria | | None | | 4 |

*Source*: DG Competition, author's calculations

*Note*: cases have, however, been approved for the creation of the BBB, MDB, Altum, UK Green Investment Bank, and IFD. Other categories include cultural projects, natural disasters, social support, and heritage promotion.

# 4

# Leveraging Policy Steer? Industrial Policy, Risk-Sharing, and the European Investment Bank

*Stephany Griffith-Jones and Natalya Naqvi*

## 4.1 Introduction

In the wake of the financial crisis of 2007–9, and the Eurozone debt crisis of 2009/10, there has been renewed support for public regional and national development banks, as the limitations and problems of a purely private financial sector have become more evident to different strands of economic thinking (see for example, Griffith-Jones and Ocampo, 2018). In this context, the European Investment Bank (EIB) became the key implementing partner of the Juncker plan, in particular the European Fund for Strategic Investment (EFSI) (2015–2020), and later InvestEU (2021–27), which promised increasing investment in Europe against the backdrop of severe budget constraints on Member States. However, rather than committing additional EU budgetary funds, these programs aim to increase private investment through leveraging largely existing funds reallocated from the EU budget as well as use a small contribution from existing EIB capital. Being able to leverage its own capital and operate on co-funding with private investors, the EIB has not only managed to double its balance sheet and workforce since the 2007 financial crisis, having tripled them over the course of the last 20 years (Table 4.1), but has also been largely responsible for introducing new and innovative financial products into the field of development banking.

While a substantial portion of the EIB support remains concentrated in traditional instruments, an increasing proportion of support, especially under EFSI, relies on highly leveraged lending, with somewhat heavier reliance on risk sharing with the private financial sector, and the use of increasingly complex financial instruments and products, rather than direct lending or simple on-lending using traditional instruments like loans.

What enabled this rise both of the EIB and the use of complex financial instruments in public development banking? This chapter examines the reasons for the

Stephany Griffith-Jones and Natalya Naqvi, *Leveraging Policy Steer? Industrial Policy, Risk-sharing, and the European Investment Bank* In: *The Reinvention of Development Banking in the European Union: Industrial Policy in the Single Market and the Emergence of a Field.* Edited by: Daniel Mertens, Matthias Thiemann, and Peter Volberding, Oxford University Press (2021). © Oxford University Press. DOI: 10.1093/oso/9780198859703.003.0004

**Table 4.1** EIB Group balance sheet size and workforce, 1999–2017

| EIB Group | 1999 | 2007 | 2010 | 2017 |
|---|---|---|---|---|
| Total Assets in billion EUR | 201,104 | 310,808 | 446,521 | 602,657 |
| Number of Employees | 1,011 | 1,569 | 1,882 | 3,204 |

*Source*: EIB Annual Reports

EIB's post-crisis expansion, as well as the form this expansion has taken, and outlines potential consequences of the use of leverage and financial innovation to increase investment: this expansion is a sort of Keynesianism *sans dire*, as opposed to traditional more fiscal-based Keynesian measures.

We argue there are three factors that enabled the rise of the EIB and innovative financial instruments: first, the real and perceived budget constraints of Member States created incentives for EU policy makers to rely on instruments and financial products that could create maximum leverage in order to "do more with less" public resources. Second, risk-sharing instruments and innovative financial products are highly beneficial for private financial actors, as they tend to increase their profitability through the provision of explicit or implicit subsidies, while socializing their risk of losses. Third, this could be facilitated because national development banks could, to an extent, join in regarding these financial instruments, allowing for more cooperation. This alignment of interests and incentives among EU policy makers, private investors, national policy makers and NDBs provided the rationale, support, and legitimacy for the significant expansion of the EIB and the various mechanisms used to attract private investors.

In order to evaluate the potential consequences of these initiatives, we distinguish between "economic" risks arising from natural uncertainty relating to investments in certain types of projects or sectors and "financial" risks that are related to financial products or intermediaries themselves, and create the danger of subsidizing the profits of private investors, while socializing their risk of losses. While policy makers want the EIB to take mainly the former, the mode of EIB engagement with private investors inevitably makes more likely the latter; and might even be encouraged by the incentives set for the EIB. This results in a trade-off between increased leverage and policy steer as well as between control over projects due to the number of intermediaries involved and the need to make projects attractive to private investors.

We argue that the post-crisis expansion of the EIB, enabled by EFSI, has been effective in increasing loan volume to meet targets, and has led to some very significant achievements. These include enabling the EIB and the European Investment Fund (EIF) to provide long-term funding to help maintain, or prevent larger reductions of, private investment in the post-crisis period, and to take more "economic" risk, leading to valuable real economy investments, that may increase productivity and competitiveness, as well as facilitate structural transformations that otherwise would have not taken place. However, Member States' budgetary constraints have created incentives for EFSI and thus the EIB to focus on increasing leverage, at the expense of policy steer. While this was less of a problem for EFSI, especially in its first phase, which focused on counter-cyclical long-term finance provision, the use of similar mechanisms in InvestEU, which has a greater focus on structural transformation, makes it potentially difficult to achieve public policy objectives. This is especially the case as it is unclear whether performance-related conditionalities are being enforced against financial intermediaries. More worryingly, the use of complex financial products and opaque pricing methods with terms that may be too generous for private investors has in some cases generated excessive "financial risk," possibly distracting from the need for greater "economic risk-taking." Therefore, in evaluating the types of instruments these initiatives use to finance investment, two related issues emerge. The first concerns the types of risks various instruments entail for the public sector. The second concerns the trade-off between increasing loan volume through leverage and policy steer.

## 4.2 Analytical Framework for Risk-Taking

There is a key distinction in the nature of risk that is essential to clarify, both from an analytical point of view and a policy perspective. This framework is important for evaluating initiatives like EFSI and InvestEU, but could be applied to others, like World Bank and IFC schemes.

There is first the "economic" type of risks: these are basically related to the natural uncertainty associated with projects or sectors. These are typical in infrastructure projects, where risks of construction difficulties and delays prevail, especially in engineering ambitious projects, like the Channel Tunnel (Griffith-Jones, 1993). Such "economic" risks are also very prevalent in the funding of innovative companies, such as start-ups, often based on potentially excellent ideas, but lacking assets for guarantees, and/or track record. Financing of SMEs is generally considered more risky in most countries, except in countries like Germany, with very decentralized banking systems (which allow for a greater knowledge of companies, thus reducing asymmetries of information (Stiglitz and Weiss, 1981)), and a long tradition of broadly successful lending to SMEs[1]. Very importantly, "economic" risks can also relate to sectorial or cross-sectorial innovation that may lead to major increases in productivity and/or significant structural transformation, for example to a greener economy (see Mazzucato, 2013).

[1] SME financing becomes riskier if financial crises happen, when the benefits of diversification are reduced.

Also assuming "economic" risk implies lending to or investing in countries that are (usually temporarily) seen as less creditworthy by financial and banking markets, especially, during and in the, often long, aftermath of financial crises, or other shocks with major macroeconomic effects. Examples of EIB activities that take on such risk in the post-crisis era include financing for renewable energies that utilize new technologies, such as innovations in offshore wind, as well as the expansion of financing for crisis-hit and austerity-affected Southern European countries.

More basic instruments created by the EIB, especially those that do not involve financial intermediaries, may hold "economic," but not "financial" risk. These "economic" types of risks are in sharp contrast with "financial" risks created by financial actors, often partly hidden by opaque and complex structures, and whose impact only often emerges *ex post* in crises situations. The alleged, and sometimes legitimate, aim may in some cases partly be to increase leverage of public resources, and for this reason may be backed also by policy makers, with the aim of "doing more with less" (Mertens and Thiemann, 2018). "Financial" risks stem from a contractual reallocation of risk, which makes certain investments for financial actors more attractive by increasing profitability or minimizing their risk of losses. However, it is difficult to know *ex ante* how much risk the actor is willing to accept, and this creates a risk of offering too many rewards to private actors, while requiring too little "economic" risk taking. This may increase risks for the public sector, which are not paid for, or not sufficiently paid for, by the private sector, and generate contingent public liabilities that could become quite large and potentially costly.

The distinction between "economic" and "financial" risk was less important in the immediate aftermath of the 2008/9 and the Eurozone debt crisis, as there was a great need to counter-cyclically increase lending volume to maintain investment as the private financial sector became risk averse. However, now that the private financial sector has become more willing to lend (see interview material)[2], and even does so at very low margins, there is not much benefit to most countries and sectors, in de-risking the private sector even further. Indeed, they may even need to be held back from causing a bubble in certain sectors (see interview material). However, there remains a need to take "economic" risk, especially for sectors important for industrial policy/structural transformation, or developmental objectives, such as green energy, innovative companies, or riskier less developed EU countries. Financial risk on the other hand needs to be limited in total scale, very carefully evaluated *ex ante*, to avoid large contingent liabilities, and thus possible future significant losses. Indeed, the EIB has repeatedly emphasized its growing risk-management expertise, having hired many risk managers since

[2] See list of interviewees at the end of this chapter.

the 1990s and recent reform proposals seek to further strengthen it (*Financial Times*, 7 August 2018). The open question is whether this risk-management expertise is able to deal with financial engineering risks and what this would imply for the EU's industrial policy goals.

## 4.3 EFSI, InvestEU, and Industrial Policy: Leverage vs Policy Steer

Industrial policy is defined as "any policy that attempts to affect the evolution of specific industries through state intervention in order to effect national efficiency and growth" (Chang, 1994). It includes the allocation of subsidies to private actors, in exchange for these actors performing economically valuable functions they otherwise would not. In order for this to work, it is vital the public sector is able to strictly monitor and enforce performance-related conditionality on the recipients of subsidies and withdraw support if the conditionalities are not being met (Amsden, 1992).

Importantly, there is some trade-off between the EC's objectives of achieving policy steer for public policy purposes, most recently with major emphasis on the European Green Deal and achieving the highest possible loan volume through leverage. On the one hand, increasing the loan volume through leverage is positive, as it should facilitate higher levels of investment. However, there is a risk that the greater the loan volume achieved through involving private intermediaries, the more indirect the operations become, and the less strategic direction the European institutions can exert over projects. Involving too many intermediaries makes monitoring and enforcing conditionalities more difficult. When it comes to involving private intermediaries in particular, the range of projects can be limited, because some projects cannot be made attractive to private lenders even though a subsidy is given. These projects may however be very socially or economically valuable. While high leverage at the expense of policy steer may have been more appropriate for EFSI as it focused on counter-cyclical funding, InvestEU is more focused on industrial policy, and therefore should rethink the balance between leverage and policy steer.

### 4.3.1 Consequences of the Leverage Mechanism: Leverage vs Policy Steer

While the leverage mechanisms of EFSI are very attractive for policy makers due to EU budget limitations, these mechanisms also make it more difficult to provide policy steer, for example as part of an industrial policy, because the instruments that provide leverage also make the activity much more indirect. EFSI is a much more indirect instrument than grants given out by various EC DGs (or increased public investment by national governments), or more traditional loans given by EIB for three reasons.

First, the EC guarantee must be pooled at the Commission level, rather than be comprised of a set of very specific instruments. Second, if leverage is to be achieved through a public intermediary like the EIB, which can use the guarantee to increase loan volume funded on international capital markets, the activities become subject to the constraints of a bank. If the EIB is to keep its AAA rating, which enables it to borrow cheaply on international capital markets, one factor is that it cannot take excessive risk. Finally, if private sector funds are to be catalyzed at the project level, the activity must be made attractive for private investors/lenders. This means that conditions that make the project too risky or un-bankable for them cannot be implemented.

In sum, there is a trade-off between achieving specific policy objectives, especially ones that involve a lot of risk, and leverage, because in order to achieve leverage, the project must be bankable (see interview material). According to one interviewee from the EIB:

> EC wants to square the magic circle. They want high leverage with low risk for EU budget where the remuneration is market based...they want high volume and they want to focus on un-bankable policy priorities...you cannot have the same policy steer you have with these instruments; that's the price you pay for the leverage (interview, EIB Official).

## 4.4 History and Evolution of the EIB's Focus on Financial Engineering and Instruments

Established in 1958 with the Treaty of Rome, the EIB initially provided infrastructure financing, usually through long-term fixed interest rate loans, backed by the guarantees of its shareholders, the EU Member States[3]. The EIB has since broadened its activities, most importantly with the founding of the European Investment Fund in 1994 and its increasing use of European budgetary means for financial instruments in the 2000s (see Rubio and Thiemann, this volume; Kavvadia, 2018; Mertens and Thiemann, 2019). It currently focuses on four sectors: innovation; SMEs; infrastructure; and environment. As of 2017, the stock of EIB loans was concentrated mainly in transport (28.7 percent), global loans (23.6 percent), energy (14.8 percent), health and education (7.4 percent), water and sewage (6.4 percent) and industry (6.3 percent) (EIB, 2017a, 8).

[3] Loans were given both directly, as well as through local financial intermediaries (global loans), in the case of lending to SMEs.

The EIB essentially took little risk on its activities due to the Member State guarantees, and has always had an AAA credit rating, which it could use to cheaply finance its activities on international financial markets, and then on-lend very cheaply through direct loans to its customers (Kavvadia, 2018; Clifton et al., 2018; Honohan, 1995). Although the EIB was constrained by mandate not to provide interest subsidies itself through cross-subsidization or out of its own capital resources, it acted as a conduit for interest rate subsidies from EU budgetary subventions for special programs (Honohan, 1995, p. 328).

From the late 1970s onwards, the EIB began changing its business model to take on more risk. The instruments evolved. The EIB began giving loan guarantees[4] rather than doing on-lending from the late 1970s onwards (Kavvadia, 2018). Guarantees have two important advantages: first, they provide leverage, that generates economic gain resulting from the additional economic risk taken, and second, they are like a revolving fund and resources can be used again if there are no major losses[5]. On the other hand, if major losses occur (for example during a financial crisis, when uncorrelated risks become correlated), and the provisions are not sufficient, for example because the risk of losses was underestimated, and the guarantees have not been fully priced, then governments (taxpayers) have to pay, and thus contribute additional resources.

The EIB also began relaxing requirements for Member State guarantees and using equity instruments (Honohan, 1995). In 1994 the EIB founded the European Investment Fund (EIF) to provide financial institutions with guarantee instruments for SME finance[6]. In the 1990s, the EIB also started funding public-private partnerships due to their perceived value for money, as they could be accounted for outside Member States' balance sheets. By the 2000s, the EIB had become the single largest lender for PPP projects in Europe (Liebe and Howarth, 2019). Reportedly, the financing of PPPs has significantly fallen in recent years; in part since this instrument does not sufficiently deliver on public policy goals but entailed precisely financial engineering risks that disproportionately benefited private investors (European Court of Auditors 2018). At that time, the EIB started to grow considerably. Subscribed capital and borrowing increased between 1996 and 2006 from EUR 62bn to 164bn and from EUR 18.6bn to 48bn respectively. Loan volume and the balance sheet total increased from EUR 23bn to 46bn and from 135bn to 304bn respectively over the same period (Kavvadia, 2018).

The EIB's approach to innovation also changed over this period. Until 2007, innovation was only funded through grants. In 2007, the EC and the EIB set up

[4] In exchange for a guarantee fee paid to the EIB, the EIB agrees to reimburse a fixed percentage of losses on the financial institution's loan or loan portfolio. The aim is to encourage the FI to increase its lending in a particular area.

[5] It is argued by some EIB officials that guarantees are less risky than grants because with grants there is certainty that the funds will not be paid back (Interview material).

[6] https://www.eif.org/who_we_are/history, last accessed on 7 October 2019.

the Risk Sharing Finance Facility (RSFF) with the stated aim of improving access to finance for activities in the field of R&D and innovation. It was built on the principle of *pari passu* (equal) credit risk-sharing between the EC and the EIB, which was designed to give the EIB capital relief, and therefore allow it to take more risk by providing loans or guarantees with a sub-investment grade risk profile[7]. This could be said to be the first time the EU institutions used financial engineering to make risk-sharing agreements, and was to become the blueprint for EFSI (see interview material). After the first mid-term review, the risk-sharing agreements between EC and EIB changed from *pari passu* to portfolio. This meant the EC would take the first loss, and the EIB the residual, allowing the EIB to take even more leverage (see interview material).

## 4.5 Risk-Sharing in the Post-2008 Context

Following the 2007/8 North Atlantic financial crisis and the 2009/10 Eurozone debt crisis, and the devastating austerity implemented in Europe in its wake, investment levels and growth plummeted. The problem was particularly acute in the European Union as growth and investment levels recovered far more slowly than, for example in the United States, or Asia. It was widely argued at the time that this necessitated a strong counter-cyclical investment response by member states (for a synthesis of these arguments, see Stiglitz, 2019, especially Chapter 3; see for previous discussions, for example Bofinger, 2016; Griffith-Jones and Cozzi, 2017).

However, in the context of the debt crisis, the creditor governments (especially Germany, but also the Netherlands and Finland) blocked a traditional Keynesian response at both the national and EU levels[8]. EU countries were prevented from increasing their national deficits to fund investment by an extremely rigid interpretation of the Stability and Growth Pact. An alternative option would have been to increase EU level investment through increasing the EU budget or through further increasing directly the capitalization of the EIB to enable it to increase loan volume. Although it was difficult to formally expand EU level investment (e.g. via Structural Funds), because the budget had already been approved till 2020, supplementary funds could have been made available had Member States been willing to increase their contributions to the EU budget. This approach was again blocked by the creditor countries.

[7] See https://www.eib.org/en/infocentre/press/news/all/risk-sharing-finance-facility-rsff.htm, last accessed on 7 October 2019.

[8] In 2012 the EIB's paid-in capital was doubled with contributions from all Member States—leading to significant increases in lending, guarantee, and equity operations by the EIB Group (for the original proposal, see for example Griffith-Jones and Kollatz-Ahnen, 2012). However, this was far from sufficient, leading to calls for a further recapitalization.

Therefore, although a more traditional Keynesian response would arguably have been more efficient in 2010, as it would have allowed for maximum policy steer while minimizing financial risks, and possibly been cheaper in the long run, this was politically not feasible at the time. Increased investment, therefore, was a key demand for Juncker from the S&D (Social Democrats in the European Parliament and institutions), to achieve their support for him to be elected as President of the European Commission. The result was the EFSI, and its incorporation into Juncker's program for the election thus was a key offer for S&D to support him for this position (see interview material). The EFSI was formulated under real and perceived severe fiscal constraints, as a Keynesian mechanism *sans dire*, with no additional public money. The EIB/EIF became the natural institution to implement EFSI, given its long-established record in lending to/investing in infrastructure and SMEs.

The European Fund for Strategic Investment (EFSI), which is the core of the post-crisis Investment Plan for Europe (the "Juncker Plan"), aims to provide much needed investment for Europe, as well as to facilitate structural change to a greener, more dynamic, and more equal economy. Emphasis was placed on financing more risky investment, both in this structural transformation, and to help finance the crisis hit countries more, as well as the newer member countries of Central and Eastern Europe.

In 2014 EFSI was launched as a EUR 16bn guarantee from the EU budget, which comes mainly from existing research and innovation and transport budget lines, complemented by a EUR 5bn allocation of the EIB's own capital, given EU budget limitations[9], with the aim of mobilizing total investment of EUR 315bn. In 2016, EFSI was extended, and EFSI 2.0 increased the EU budget guarantee to EUR 26bn and the EIB's capital allocation to EUR 7.5bn. The total amount of EUR 33.5bn aims to leverage additional investment of at least EUR 500bn between 2015–2020. Essentially a small fraction of the EU budget is used as a guarantee for EIB projects that have a higher risk profile than the usual ones.

The aim is to push the EIB to increase "additionality" by increasing the percentage of its lending that supports higher risk projects and involves new clients, to adopt a junior position with respect to co-financiers, and, in order to reduce the risks taken by private investors, to increase the chances of attracting their investment (Claeys and Leandro, 2016; interview material). The implicit aim is therefore to increase the EIB's "economic risk" by supporting valuable projects and clients that could not secure funding on their own.

EFSI has two components: the innovation and infrastructure window (IIW) managed by the EIB, focusing on bigger projects; and the SME window implemented by the EIF, which basically extended the financial instruments already in

[9] http://www.europarl.europa.eu/legislative-train/theme-new-boost-for-jobs-growth-and-investment/file-extension-of-efsi, last accessed on 7 October 2019.

use before the plan, such as COSME and InnovFin[10]. Since the EIF and NDBs were already involved in the implementation of these instruments, its extension through the SME window was very effective and satisfactory and reinforced the established cooperation between national banks and the EIF (Rubio, 2018). Therefore, about a fourth of the transactions of the EFSI are estimated to have been channeled through national development banks, thus increasing the role these banks play in the EU (on the political tensions this collaboration implies, see Rubio and Thiemann, this volume).

In contrast, under the IIW, the EFSI was expected to push the EIB to develop riskier products and expand the volume of so-called EIB "special operations" (operations having a risk profile higher than conventional EIB loans). Yet, in a context marked by some scarcity of big infrastructure projects and with a strong political pressure to reach the 500bn target of additional investment mobilized, the EIB would in many cases make use of the EFSI "first loss" tranche to provide more favorable financial conditions to mature infrastructure projects rather than searching for new, additional, riskier projects.

The political decision to create an investment plan based on leverage rather than additional public money created incentives to use the EIB as the key implementing partner for EFSI, due to its ability to add leverage through raising funds on the private capital markets (the internal multiplier). Had more public money been channeled from national budgets to the European level, the Commission would instead have played a greater role.[11] Furthermore, in order to achieve the necessary loan volumes, policy makers were incentivized to rely on the involvement of financial intermediaries to as great an extent as possible, as these added further leverage (the external multiplier). These included public NDBs, but also private financial lenders and investors, such as commercial banks and institutional investors (discussed in greater detail below).

For the next EU budget (2021–27), the Commission is developing the continuation of EFSI, with some modifications as the InvestEU Fund. The InvestEU Fund will consolidate various EU financing programs and instruments into one, which should lead to economic efficiency gains, and politically may be more desirable, due to greater decentralization, though may be more bureaucratic. InvestEU will follow the Juncker Plan model of mobilizing additional private funds for additional investment. This is expected to allow the EU budget to provide a €30bn guarantee, which is then expected to crowd in an additional total of EUR 650bn of public and private investments over the 7-year period. This will result in investment far greater than is possible via for example public investment, in the context

[10] See https://www.eif.org/what_we_do/efsi/index.htm, last accessed on 7 October 2019.

[11] However, the European Commission is not a shareholder of the EIB and hence has limited capacity to directly steer the EIB's action via the official governance structure. This has been the cause of conflict between the two (see Rubio and Thiemann, this volume).

of Member States' budget constraints, or via conventional EIB activities, as took place before EFSI. NDBs will play an even larger role in InvestEU; indeed, the EU guarantee can be granted directly to NDBs, up to a certain proportion.

## 4.6 EFSI, Financial Products and the Role of Private Investors

EFSI has a high overall multiplier target of 15x[12]. The first step is the internal multiplier of 3x, where the EFSI guarantee of 33.5bn Euros from the European budget is expected to generate 100bn of EIB financing on international financial markets. The second step is the external multiplier of 5x, where the internal funds of 100bn are expected to catalyze additional private and public financing to reach a total mobilized investment volume of 500bn (Claeys and Leandro, 2016). In practice, the external multiplier varies across financial products, so the 5x target applies to the entire portfolio of operations. The overall multiplier target of 15x is the relation between expected total investment mobilized (500bn) and the initial EFSI guarantee (33.5bn) (EIB 2019a). The final mobilized investment is measured as the Eligible Project Investment Cost (EPIC) defined according to EIB Methodology.

Under the infrastructure window, in terms of product type, traditional senior loans have the lowest (expected) external multiplier of 3x, followed by junior debt (5x), with equity type products having the highest multiplier of 15x, (EIB, 2019a, 4). Direct operations include inter alia investment loans, framework loans, direct guarantees and credit enhancement provided to investment projects, hybrid-debt instruments, equity-type financing for corporates and project finance, and quasi-equity financing for SMEs and Mid-Caps, and have multipliers ranging from 3x to 8.9x. Intermediated operations tend to have a higher external multiplier due to the so-called "catalytic effect" which is the co-financing provided by the public or private financial intermediary (which may be an NDB, private bank, leasing company, or investment fund). The external multiplier of intermediated operations is calculated by multiplying the catalytic effect by the project level external multiplier (EIB 2019a, 6).

EFSI has taken a number of steps including the creation and use of new financial instruments (financial innovation), especially in EIB operations, whilst EIF operations for SMEs relied mainly on existing instruments and encouraging the greater involvement of public and private actors, in particular NDBs and institutional investors. For instance, in 2016 the EIF build together with KfW a European initiative to foster SME securitization, based on the EIF's line of

[12] The EIB's EFSI Multiplier calculation methodology for the infrastructure window and the EIF's EFSI Multiplier calculation methodology for the SME window follows the same principles, although laid out in different documents (EIB 2019a; EIB 2019b).

business since the late 1990s (Kraemer-Eis et al., 2015)[13]. The mobilization of private capital may achieve higher levels of investment, by "doing more with less fiscal resources," but also generates potential risks, via contingent liabilities that need to be properly accounted for and provisioned for.

### 4.6.1 Financial Instruments and Products Used in EFSI

Aiming at the mobilization of private capital, the expansion of the EIB after 2008 has indeed come with significant financial innovation. EFSI has widened its range of financial products to include not only EIB/EIF traditional loans and guarantees, but also credit enhancement products, using the RSFF blueprint, and equity type products. The EFSI operational strategy further specifies the different products that the EIB Group can use to deploy EFSI. These include senior and junior loans, risk-sharing instruments, capital market instruments (e.g. corporate hybrid bonds), equity or quasi-equity participations (European Court of Auditors, 2019, p. 18). Under the Infrastructure window, in addition to relying on traditional long-term senior loans (about 60 percent of the total) the EIB expanded the use of existing higher-risk products and developed new ones. These include corporate hybrid bonds which focus on low-risk utilities, infrastructure aggregation platforms, asset-backed securities mezzanine that supports lower rated beneficiaries, layered funds mezzanine, captive funds and investment platforms that target NDBs, venture debt and other "quasi-equity" products (ICF, 2018, pp. 54–55). The EIB has conducted securitized transactions under the infrastructure window in partnership with the EIF. As of March 2019, EUR 5bn of guarantees under securitization have been signed as part of 24 transactions (see interview material).

In 2014, the RSFF had also turned into InnovFin, and both the size of the funds, as well as the range of financial products was increased[14]. COSME, the EU program for Competitiveness of Enterprises and SMEs, operated by EIF, was also set up in 2014 to 2020, with a budget of €2.3bn, in order to provide financing support for SMEs[15]. COSME has a Loan Guarantee Facility that aims to enable financial institutions to increase loan and lease finance to SMEs, as well as an Equity Facility for Growth that provides risk capital to equity funds that invest in SMEs.

Under the SME window of EFSI, the EIF continues to rely on existing products already used under COSME, InnovFin, the Cultural and Creative Sectors Europe Guarantee Facility (CCS), the Employment and Social Innovation Programme (EaSI) and the EIB-EIF Risk Capital Resources mandates. It was reportedly an

[13] This business segment grew rapidly until the 2008 crisis, but then significantly slowed down. EIF's securitized transactions total 8.2bn EUR between 2004 and 2015 (EIB, 2017b).

[14] See https://www.eib.org/en/products/blending/innovfin/index.htm, last accessed on 7 October 2019.

[15] See https://ec.europa.eu/docsroom/documents/9783, last accessed on 7 October 2019.

advantage that for the SME window, EFSI, especially initially, used existing, well-tested product lines. It may have contributed to the more rapid deployment of EFSI finance for SMEs, which especially initially were seen as more successful. Since 2016, three new products were added to the SME window, including uncapped guarantees for riskier (subordinated) loans to innovative SMEs and small mid-caps; capped guarantees for EaSI; and Investment Platforms. There is on-going discussion between the EIF and the European Commission about using securitization as part of the SME window, but as of early 2019 no securitized products have been rolled out (ICF, 2018, pp. 56–57) although the EIF has been conducting SME securitization since the 1990s outside of EFSI (EIB 2017b).

The EIF's volume of operations has been increased very significantly thanks to EFSI, growing from EUR 3.3bn in 2014 to almost EUR 10bn in 2018, that is more than tripling in four years (interview material; see Table 4.2). EIF's focus is to enhance access to finance for SMEs as part of its EU mandate, but it also provides ecosystem support like the development of the European venture capital market, as well as developing the market for private investors, via a fund to co-finance with private investors. It also helps develop fintech, crowd funding, etc. EIF is a for-profit organization for their shareholders while EIB is non-profit—this means they need to have a different pricing model.

In terms of products, EIF covers the whole financing chain, starting with funding for seed capital to later-stage growth to mid-cap market, but also is active in more mature markets with guaranteed products. EIF does not finance SMEs directly, but always goes through intermediaries—the guarantee is provided to banks or counter guarantees are provided to guarantee institutions (NDBs mainly like Bpifrance, KfW). The counterparty must do riskier business than they would do normally if they get EIF guarantees. For example, COSME is a first loss guarantee and the financial intermediary needs to take at least 20 percent of risk, to have "sufficient skin in the game."

COSME has a very high target leverage of 20–30; that is 1 euro should catalyze 20–30 euros. EIF achieves that because it is targeting very high-risk SMEs—the rules for the banks are such that they need to target high risk or un-served SMEs in order to receive the guarantee. The financial intermediary is the owner of their portfolio but within a certain framework and criteria that EIF specifies, they

**Table 4.2** EIF total assets and employees, 1999–2017

| EIF | 1999 | 2007 | 2010 | 2017 |
|---|---|---|---|---|
| Total assets in million EUR | 463,0 | 1024,0 | 1196,0 | 2489,3 |
| Number of employees | 42 | 135 | 215 | 479 |

*Sources*: EIF various Annual Reports (note that EIF deploys EU funds and engages predominantly in guarantees; allowing it to deploy 9.6bn Euros in 2017, even though assets itself are 2.5bn Euros (EIF Annual Report 2017)

report back to EIF. EIF is more focused on whether the loan is given or not, so price is secondary, but they do check that the benefit of resources is passed to the SME (see interview material).

Some guarantees are free; some are not. There are usually embedded costs to the intermediary in the product; as the intermediary has to serve higher risk clients, there is an implicit cost in the product even if the guarantee is free. Risk increase is defined by EIF for a commercial bank, for example if they lend more to the bottom quartile of the existing loan book (in terms of credit ratings) or lend to segments of SMEs not currently served. This is a matter that seems to require further study, especially if guarantees are given free, in times when SMEs already have access to credit from banks, and the sectors are not so innovative or risky; in such cases, it would seem that guarantees should be priced fully for the intermediary.

Because COSME is focused on smaller transactions, over 1 million SMEs have been supported. EFSI support has also not just increased the number of SMEs served, but also riskier SMEs, in more countries. However, some sectors and niches therein remain neglected, as are start-ups on the side of debt. Here, equity products have gained momentum, not only implying more risk than loans, but also having the advantage of being able to "capture the upside" if projects are more profitable than expected.

One such instrument being currently applied under EFSI is venture debt to support "innovative enterprises." If business does well, the EIB also gets part of that higher profit as compensation for taking a higher risk. This is done usually by an equity-linked instrument (warrants) or profit participation. Venture debt also has the virtue of financing the growth stages of companies, for example for scaling up from pilot to mass manufacturing, further development of R&D, and international expansion. 2000 cases have been reviewed annually, but only 75 operations signed till now. However, the amount is meaningful, implying a portfolio of EUR 1.6bn, which implies a portfolio mobilized of EUR 14.9bn (see interview material).

### 4.6.2 Relationship with Financial Intermediaries and the Role of Private Investors

#### 4.6.2.1 Private Intermediaries and Policy Steer

An important component of the leverage in EFSI comes from private financial sector lending or investment. EIB can either co-finance projects with private banks and investors, and/or use a private financial intermediary. The advantage of involving private intermediaries is that this increases leverage, and in theory enables better risk assessment and monitoring of projects due to local knowledge and relationships. On the other hand, this creates the danger of taking excessive "financial risk" and decreases policy steer. This is because only projects with the potential to be bankable in the short to medium term can attract private investors. For example, if the EC wants to finance energy efficiency projects that are not just applying current technologies, but investing in new technologies, such an activity might be too risky to be attractive to private investors, even with EIB support. In a similar manner, basic research cannot be financed in this manner, as there is no way to make it bankable.

The SME window in particular relies mainly on intermediaries, while the infrastructure window co-finances a large portion of its portfolio directly, as the scale of transactions is much bigger.

Private banks can be involved through traditional on-lending[16], or through "de-risking" the private bank's loan portfolio, with the expectation that they will then increase lending to beneficial areas. For an example of the latter, the EIF can make a bilateral loss-sharing agreement with a financial institution under which the EIF reimburses the financial institution for up to a certain percentage of the principal losses incurred on a portfolio loans, in exchange for a guarantee fee. This arrangement is used especially for SME lending. The EIF hopes that sharing a portion of the risk will encourage the financial institution to expand their SME lending, especially to more risky SMEs. This should also help the financial institution to increase business volume without exceeding their risk limits (country, industry exposure, single obligor) and would reduce the amount of capital the FI needs to allocate towards the SME portfolio[17].

According to the EIF, private banks prefer to receive transactions that involve de-risking and securitization over traditional on-lending because it is more flexible for the banks' portfolio management strategies. Additionally, because securitization makes SME risk tradable, it is seen by some to have the added benefit of capital market development, in line with EU objectives on the Capital Market Union (see interview material). It should, however, be pointed out, that other commentators (see for example Finance Watch, 2016) have been critical of the emphasis on securitizing loans to SMEs, pointing to the potential large risks of such transactions, as was shown in the case of US securitization of mortgages that contributed to the US sub-prime crisis and subsequently to the North Atlantic financial crisis.

#### 4.6.2.2 Private Investors and Risk Assessment

One of the main aims of the Juncker plan and EFSI is to provide finance to valuable projects that would not get financed on private markets, or through normal EIB channels due to their high risk. Although these risky projects might not be bankable in the sense of resulting in short term profits, they are vital for long-run

[16] Where a low interest loan is given to the intermediary, which then on-lends the funds at a slightly higher interest rate, profiting from the spread.

[17] https://www.eib.org/infocentre/publications/all/acp-fs-risk-sharing-guarantees.htm, last accessed 31 March 19.

growth and structural transformation. The Juncker plan envisions doing this by getting the EIB to take on more risk than it normally would. While EFSI (in its Phase 1) initially had a counter-cyclical focus in the post crisis environment, EFSI 2.0 and InvestEU have more of a structural transformation objective.

The EU institution's matrix for assessing whether this developmental role is being played is to take into account the risk profile of the EIB's financial products, rather than that of the final beneficiaries. This can be problematic in some cases, as "economic" and "financial risks" can at times diverge, and projects that the EIB classified as "high risk" according to the EFSI objectives may in fact only be risky in the financial sense. In some cases, the same project was classified as a riskier EFSI project rather than a normal EIB project, purely because the financial products changed to riskier ones (interview material).

For example, the EIB's Board of Directors had approved financing for the investment program of a listed energy company through a traditional senior loan outside of EFSI. This approved loan was never signed as the EIB then offered the company a Corporate Hybrid Debt product, which it was developing at the time. Due to the use of this new product, the rating of this operation was downgraded, qualifying it as a "Special Activity" under EFSI. This was because the new financial product offered weaker contractual protection, and a longer grace period for interest repayments, as compared to the senior loan. In this case, while "financial" risk to the EIB increased, the "economic" risk of the project clearly remained the same (interview material; European Court of Auditors, 2019, 26). This is complicated by the fact that the EIB makes complex contractual arrangements with private agents.

#### 4.6.2.3 Collaboration with National Development Banks

The EIB's cooperation with Member States' national development banks (NDBs) has been strongly enhanced as part of EFSI, including its leverage strategy. As discussed above, participation of an NDB as a financial intermediary increases EFSI's leverage due to the catalytic effect. NDB participation also helps with overcoming fiscal constraints. Although NDBs' activities do count as contingent liabilities, they do not count towards the Maastricht criteria (EC 2015). Cooperation between the EIB and NDBs can take four forms: 1. Co-investment, taking place at the project level; 2. Intermediated financing where the EIB provides loans or guarantees to NDBs for on-lending; 3. Risk-sharing instruments where the EIB makes an agreement to cover up to a certain percentage of credit risk associated with a portfolio of loans[18]; 4. Collaborative investment platforms that involve joint cooperation among the EIB Group, several NDBs and potentially other IFIs, the latter especially in the context of InvestEU (EIB, 2016). An

[18] This reduces the exposure of the NDB to certain sectors or client segments and frees up capital and other resources to grant new loans.

example is the EIF-NPI Securitization Initiative (ENSI) that aims to provide more SME finance through boosting the SME securitization market (ICF, 2018, pp. 58–59; see Mertens and Thiemann, 2018). As of December 2017, EUR 7.4bn of funds have been signed with NDBs, 2.7 under the SME window, and 4.7 under the infrastructure window[19].

Cooperation with NDBs rather than private financial actors has the potential to increase "economic" risk-taking while reducing "financial" risk taking. Since NDBs are public actors not bound purely by short-term profit motives, and benefit from public guarantees, they may be more likely to take on "economic" risks than private financial actors. Furthermore, excessive subsidies or de-risking by the EIB would go back to the public sector rather than benefit private actors. Furthermore, NDBs, being closer to the firms are more likely to engage in taking on economic risks; also due to their capacities to overcome asymmetric information better.

#### 4.6.2.4 Assessing the Consequences of Risk Sharing Arrangements

While funding projects with "economic risk" is good, taking excessive "financial risk" through complex financial products or through too high risk sharing with the private sector creates the danger that the public entities (and ultimately the taxpayers) will bear the risks, while the private sector reaps all the rewards. It could also have negative long-term budgetary implications via contingent liabilities.

This leads to the issue of the distribution of risks of losses and profits, between the public actors (in this case EIB and European Commission funds, for example granting guarantees), and the private financial actors (lenders and investors). If in the aim to attract additional private lending or investing, financial products are created that generate too much additional financial risk, and transfer too high a proportion of that risk to the public sector, (especially without transferring any of the potential upside of profits to the public sector), then this is highly undesirable from a welfare and public policy perspective. This is particularly the case if these instruments lead to high losses, which can only be known *ex post* in the future; such losses could be costly to the public sector, if the instruments are not properly priced, and can generate future problems if there are no adequate provisions against such potential future losses.

Because many of the projects have long maturities, it is hard to know for certain what the longer-term possible losses, and thus budgetary implications of the risk-sharing agreements, are before loans become due [see interview material]. However, there are a number of clues:

[19] See https://www.eib.org/attachments/strategies/efsi_2017_report_ep_council_en.pdf, last accessed 7 October 2019.

1. Nature of financial instruments

The use of opaque new financial instruments can increase unnecessary "financial risks", of the type that resulted in the 2007 subprime mortgage crisis, without increasing necessary and valuable "economic risks". Excessive securitization and financial innovation should be avoided, and traditional instruments used wherever possible, even if this sacrifices some leverage. EFSI should use instruments that also capture the upside for the public sector, as pioneered for example by venture debt, and impose strictly monitored conditionalities on intermediaries in return for EFSI support. It is worth noting, however, that the bulk of infrastructure lending under EFSI continues to be conducted through traditional instruments, including direct loans, for larger projects.

2. Pricing of guarantees

If loan guarantees are underpriced, or have no charge, then this is an implicit subsidy for the recipient. The implicit subsidy is not a problem per se but does become problematic if it is excessive beyond what is required to attract the private investors' participation, or if it does not come with performance-related conditionalities. If future losses were to become very high, for example in another financial crisis, they could imply large liabilities for EU member governments, precisely at a time when fiscal budgets are tight. This is why it is important that: a) guarantees covering risks are properly costed, and an appropriate fee is charged for them, b) that adequate provisions are made, and that, c) there is adequate sharing of risks between the private and the public sector.

There is evidence that, though the EIB and EIF pay fully the price of the European Commission guarantee, it is likely that an important part of EFSI guarantees granted to commercial banks do not price fully their cost (ser interview material). Above all, the pricing of guarantees seems to be opaque. This is reportedly in contrast with loans, where products are more fully standardized and more transparent. It is difficult to ensure the level of implicit subsidy in guarantees given, but further research is required on this important topic, research that would be welcomed by the EIB itself (see interview material).

3. Level of provisions

EFSI has lowered provisions from the 20 percent required in the RSSF to 9 percent. This increases the risk of potential losses for EU institutions in the case of increased default, were there to be another economic downturn, or worse another financial crisis. Lower provisioning regulations free up capital, which fit with EFSI's aims to do more with less but is illogical. If EFSI is supposed to increase risk taking, they would be expected to also increase provisioning. In fact, as pointed out above the opposite seems to have happened, further increasing potential risks for the public sector.

If EFSI wants to take more risk, it is key it identifies higher risk projects/sectors/countries, as opposed to identifying higher risk financial products as it currently does in its risk evaluations. A problem is that some countries' governments like the Dutch and the Danish reportedly do not favor a more sectorial approach, which would give priority to EFSI lending/investing in particular sectors. InvestEU does however seem to move towards greater sectorial priorities through the establishment of policy windows controlled by policy DGs, which seems positive from an industrial policy perspective (see below).

4. Performance related conditionalities
Attaching performance related conditionalities—for example increased lending to economically more risky SMEs, in new/underserved sectors/countries, etc.—to any subsidies/cheap funding/guarantees given to financial intermediaries are necessary in order to make EFSI operations effective in terms of catalyzing additional private investment and achieving policy steer. In risk-sharing operations, the EIB assumes the risk on underlying transactions in order to support the origination of an EFSI eligible new portfolio of loans. In partial delegation models, EIB retains the right to approve/reject any addition to the portfolio. In full delegation models, the EIB delegates the selection of the loans based on pre-defined criteria to the financial intermediary (ICF, 2018, p. 57). It is key that the EIB and EIF set and strictly monitor whether financial intermediaries are taking increased economic risk on worthwhile projects.

What does this foreshadow for InvestEU? The form of InvestEU was debated between the EC, EIB, and NDBs. Complaints arose from NDBs that EIB was not passing enough of the benefits of the EC guarantee as part of EFSI to them. The NDBs were therefore in favor of getting direct access to the EC guarantee as part of InvestEU, and this was reflected in the EC's original InvestEU proposal. This happened because various EC DGs felt that giving the EIB such a prominent role in EFSI had resulted in a loss of their strategic control over the projects. Previously, the DGs had funded projects directly through grants to achieve specific policy objectives, or via EIB loans, whereas the EFSI mechanism required projects to be bankable, and risks to be pooled, and so resulted in very different types of projects being financed (see interview material).

The EIB strongly objected to giving NDBs direct guarantees on three grounds (see also Rubio and Thiemann, this volume). First, it would decrease the visibility of the EIB, and the EIB would have to compete with other funding partners for the guarantee. Second, the EIB objected to the EC directly negotiating guarantees with national actors and aggregating the risk due to its lack of experience with banking. They believed that without the EIB playing the role of intermediary or at least advisor, Member States' taxpayer money could be put at risk, as guarantees are a contingent liability and Member States are guarantors of the EU budget. Finally, they believed the proposed governance mechanisms in InvestEU were suboptimal because they allowed for purely internal governance involving only

EC DGs and excluding the EIB's expert opinion. Under EFSI, key documents have to be approved by the EIB board, which is essentially comprised of the Member States, giving the Member States a "double voice."

Although details are not yet final at the time of writing, the EIB and Member States concerned about contingent liabilities that would be assumed by the European Commission via NDBs were successful in negotiations. The outcome was that EIB got 75 percent of the guarantee, there would be a banking partnership between EC and EIB when negotiating guarantees with other bodies, like NDBs (through an advisory role for EIB), and governance arrangements would remain similar to those under EFSI. This seems broadly positive, as the EIB has more experience than many NDBs, especially newer ones in avoiding contingent liabilities. The compromise within the EC gave the DGs greater control over the projects, thus potentially enhancing policy steer. Implementing partners would fund via four policy windows: SMEs, social, R&D and digitalization, and sustainable infrastructure, each under control of the relevant DG (see interview material).

## 4.7 Conclusions: Achievements, Risks, and Lessons for InvestEU

EFSI has resulted in important achievements, including the significant leverage it is providing on scarce EU budget resources to help provide lending and guarantees to new riskier businesses, important innovative projects, and additional resources to countries that have suffered from the Eurozone crisis, or who are new EU members, as well as supporting increased investment in the EU more broadly. It has also allowed the EIB and the EIF to significantly increase their operations, in its important role of catalyzing financing, especially for SMEs. However, this chapter has shown how the EIB's mode of engagement with private investors creates a trade-off between policy steer—implied in European moves towards a industrial policy—and the higher leverage ratios, implied in a strategy to mobilize private resources.

This trade-off is also linked to the crucial distinction between "economic risk" and "financial risk." While funding projects with "economic risk" is valuable, taking excessive "financial risk" through complex financial products or through excessive risk sharing with the private sector is not. Socializing the risks, while privatizing the rewards leads to excessively subsidizing private financial intermediaries without necessarily increasing the funding of "economic risk." This is highly undesirable from a welfare and public policy perspective. If the EIB wants to take more risk, it is key that it identifies higher economic risk projects/sectors/countries, and focuses more on final beneficiaries, as opposed to identifying higher risk financial products, and focusing on financial intermediaries, as it currently does in its risk evaluations. The unwillingness of the European Commission and Member States behind it to put in additional budgetary resources may create obstacles to increasing "economic risk," while creating incentives for greater "financial risk-taking."

Similarly, while the mobilization of private capital brings benefits, achieving higher levels of investment, by "doing more with less fiscal resources," it also generates potential risks, via contingent liabilities, that need to be properly accounted for, and provisioned for. There is also a risk that the greater the loan volume achieved through involving private intermediaries, the more indirect the operations become, the harder it becomes to impose conditionalities, and the less strategic direction the European institutions can exert over projects.

For this reason, InvestEU should focus more on "economic risk" and less on "financial risk." This is especially important as it is more oriented towards structural transformation rather than counter-cyclicality, and so control over the instruments becomes more important, and loan volume somewhat less important. This becomes easier to implement if greater resources are granted by the European Commission and/or Member States to the EIB. When private intermediaries are used, performance related conditionalities should be imposed and monitored, where feasible. In the end, the financial sector must serve the real economy, and financial objectives, for example, the development of capital markets, must never be an end in itself.

## References

Amsden, A. H.,1992. Asia's Next Giant: South Korea and Late Industrialization. Oxford: Oxford University Press.

Chang, H.-J., 1994. The Political Economy of Industrial Policy. New York, NY: St. Martin's Press.

Claeys, G., Leandro, A., 2016. Assessing the Juncker Plan After One Year. Bruegel. http://bruegel.org/2016/05/assessing-the-juncker-plan-after-one-year/(accessed 31.03.19).

Clifton, J., Díaz-Fuentes, D., Gómez, A.L., 2018. The European Investment Bank: Development, Integration, Investment? JCMS: Journal of Common Market Studies 56, 733–50.

European Commission, 2015. "Working Together for Jobs and Growth: The Role Of National Promotional Banks (NPBs) In Supporting the Investment Plan for Europe." Communication from the Commission to the European Parliament and the Council. Available at: http://europeanmemoranda.cabinetoffice.gov.uk/files/2015/07/11283-15.pdf (accessed 20.09.19)

EIB, 2016. Rules Applicable to Operations with Investment Platforms and National Promotional Banks or Institutions. Available at https://www.eib.org/attachments/strategies/efsi_steering_board_rules_applicable_to_operations_with_investment_platforms_and_npbs_or_institutions_en.pdf (accessed 20.09.19)

EIB, 2017a. EIB Financial Report. Available at: https://www.eib.org/attachments/general/reports/fr2017en.pdf (accessed 20.09.19)

EIB, 2017b. Evaluation of the EIF's SME Securitisation Activities, 2004–2015. Available at: https://www.eif.org/eib.org/attachments/ev/ev_report_eif_sme_securitisation_activities_en.pdf (accessed 20.09.19)

EIB, 2019a. EIB EFSI Multiplier Methodology Calculation. Available at https://www.eib.org/attachments/strategies/efsi_steering_board_efsi_multiplier_methodology_calculation_en.pdf (accessed 20.09.19)

EIB, 2019b. EIF-EFSI Multiplier Calculation Methodology. Available at https://www.eib.org/attachments/strategies/efsi_steering_board_eif_efsi_multiplier_methodology_calculation_en.pdf (accessed 20.09.19)

European Court of Auditors, 2019. European Fund for Strategic Investments: Action Needed to Make EFSI a Full Success. Special report no 03/2019. Available at https://www.eca.europa.eu/en/Pages/DocItem.aspx?did=49051 (accessed 20.09.19)

Finance Watch, 2016. Statement at the Committee on Economic and Monetary Affairs (ECON) of the European Parliament ORGAnised the Public Hearing on Securitisation on Monday 13 June 2016, Brussels.

Griffith-Jones, S., 1993. Loan Guarantees for Large Infrastructure Projects: The Issues and Possible Lessons for a European Facility. Report prepared for the Commission of the European Communities. Luxembourg: European Communities.

Griffith-Jones, S., Cozzi, G, 2017. The Roles of Development Banks: How They Can Promote Investment, in Europe and Globally, in Noman, A. and Stiglitz, J. (eds). Efficiency, Finance, and Varieties of Industrial Policy: Guiding Resources, Learning, and Technology for Sustained Growth. New York: Columbia University Press. 131–55.

Griffith-Jones, S., Kollatz-Ahnen, M., June 18, 2012. Stimulating Europe. *Financial Times*.http://www.stephanygj.net/press/sgj-e-forum.pdf (accessed 20.09.19).

Griffith-Jones, S., Ocampo J.A. (eds), 2018. The Future of National Development Banks. Oxford: Oxford University Press.

Honohan, P., 1995. The Public Policy Role of the European Investment Bank within the EU. JCMS: Journal of Common Market Studies 33, 315–30.

ICF, 2018. Independent Evaluation of the EFSI Regulation. Brussels: European Commission.

Kavvadia, H., 2018. Small Words, Big Changes: Understanding the EU Bank Through Its Business Model. Paper for the XVIII World Economic History Conference. Boston: MIT.

Kraemer-Eis, H., Passaris, G., Tappi, A., Inglisa, G., 2015. SME Securitisation—at a crossroads? EIF Working Paper 2015/31. Luxembourg: European Investment Fund.

Liebe, M., Howarth, D., 2020. The European Investment Bank as Policy Entrepreneur and the Promotion of Public-Private Partnerships. New Political Economy, 25 (2), 195–212.

Mazzucato, M., 2013. The Entrepreneurial State: Debunking Public vs. Private Sector myths. London: Anthem Press.

Mertens, D., Thiemann, M., 2018. Market-Based but State-Led: The Role of Public Development Banks in Shaping Market-Based Finance In the European Union. Competition & Change 22, 184–204.

Mertens, D., Thiemann, M. (2019). Building a hidden investment state? The European Investment Bank, national development banks and European economic governance. Journal of European Public Policy, 26(1), 23-43.

Rubio, E., 2018. Making Better Use of Public Funding: The Role of National Promotional Banks and Institutions in the Next EU Budget. Paris: Jacques Delors Institute.

Stiglitz, J.E., 2019. Re-Writing the Rules of the European Economy. FEPS. Brussels. https://www.feps-europe.eu/attachments/publications/book_stiglitz-web-pp.pdf

Stiglitz, J. E., Weiss, A., 1981. Credit Rationing in Markets with Imperfect Information. The American Economic Review, 71(3), 393–410.

APPENDIX 4.1

# List of Interviews

#1 Ambroise Fayolle, European Investment Bank, Vice-President
#2 Julie Chevaillier, European Investment Bank, Advisor to Vice-President Ambroise Fayolle
#3 Alessandro Izzo, European Investment Bank, Head of Project Finance Division, Western Europe, Operations Directorate
#4 Caroline Gaye, European Investment Bank, Head of Unit Mandator Management, Institutional Mandates Division, Operations Directorate
#5 Markus Berndt, European Investment Bank, Director of Institutional Strategy
#6 Matthieu Bertrand, European Investment Bank, EFSI and CEF Mandate Officer
#7 Shiva Dustdar, European Investment Bank, Head of Innovation Finance Advisory
#8 Jaroslav Toth, European Investment Bank, Innovation Finance Advisory
#9 Edward Calthrop, European Investment Bank, Senior Economist, Environment, Climate and Social Office
#10 Helmut Kramer-Eis, European Investment Fund, Head of Research and Market Analysis
#11 David Gonzales Martin, European Investment Fund, Head of Growth and Investment Programs,
#12 Martin Puc, European Court of Auditors, Senior Auditor
#13 James Mcquade, European Court of Auditors, Senior Administrator
#14 Matthias Kollatz, Finance Senator for Berlin, formerly European Investment Bank
#15 David Rinaldi, Director of Research, Foundation for Progressive European Studies
#16 Estelle Goeger, European Commission, Team Leader, DG Ecfin
#17 Lukas Vesely, European Commission

# SECTION II

# THE MANY FACES OF DEVELOPMENT BANKING IN THE EU

# 5

# A German Model? KfW, Field Dynamics, and the Europeanization of "Promotional" Banking

*Daniel Mertens*

## 5.1 Introduction

Of all the European national development banks, the largest one, Germany's *Kreditanstalt für Wiederaufbau* (KfW), has probably received the most scholarly attention. Equipped with public funds and guarantees, a broad mandate, and privileged policy access, it is long-acknowledged to have served the purpose of fostering the German export-led growth regime and its underlying competitive structure of small- and medium-sized industrial firms (Shonfield, 1965). Recent scholarship has examined KfW's historical origins (Grünbacher, 2004), its continuing role in supporting German industrial policy and mission-oriented finance (Mazzucato and Penna, 2015; Naqvi, Henow, and Chang, 2018), its support for Germany's sustainable infrastructure (Griffith-Jones, 2016), and its proactive engagement as a policy entrepreneur (Moslener, Thiemann, and Volberding, 2018).

Much less is known, however, about how the bank has conceived and performed its role in the wider European economy and polity, and particularly the Single Market. As cross-border and multi-level interactions among development finance institutions to kick-start investment have become more salient since the multiple crises of the European integration project, the KfW is perceived as having taken a prominent role in these endeavors (Mertens and Thiemann, 2019). Given Germany's powerful and outward-oriented position in Europe (Story and Walter, 1997; Bulmer and Paterson 2013), this observation begs further examination. How precisely did Germany's major state-owned bank engage in such interactions and for what political purpose? What is the history of this leadership and how has the KfW impacted the evolution of a European field of development banking?

Daniel Mertens, *A German Model? KfW, Field Dynamics, and the Europeanization of "Promotional" Banking*
In: *The Reinvention of Development Banking in the European Union: Industrial Policy in the Single Market and the Emergence of a Field.* Edited by: Daniel Mertens, Matthias Thiemann, and Peter Volberding, Oxford University Press (2021). © Oxford University Press. DOI: 10.1093/oso/9780198859703.003.0005

This chapter applies the field-theoretical lens of this volume in combination with insights from research on Europeanization and policy diffusion to answer these questions and bring attention to the "conceptions of control" that KfW as an incumbent has been able to imprint on the emerging development banking field—foremost its emphasis on SME finance and on the practices of "promotional" banking. However, this has not been the result of a pure power exercise but has rather been contingent on the historical conjunctures of European integration, which altered the form of KfW's incumbency and its status of being *primus inter pares*. Drawing on KfW archival sources, information from expert interviews, official documents from both European and German public entities, press material from KfW and EU institutions, as well as public news coverage, the chapter reconstructs this process by examining two key areas of KfW's transnational engagement in Europe since 1990: (1) bilateral activities such as loans for and counseling of existing and newly founded development institutions; and (2) the involvement in supranational and multilateral governance processes that shapes KfW's relationships with both EU institutions, notably the European Investment Bank, and fellow development institutions.

Seeking to illustrate the mechanisms through which KfW has left its imprint on the European field, I begin by discussing the conceptual framework of field dynamics as involving diffusion processes (section 5.2). I proceed by laying out the role of the bank in the German political economy and the related principles of promotional banking (section 5.3). Subsequently, in the empirical part, I reconstruct the Europeanization processes around German promotional banking in three steps, from the KfW's mandate in the transition economies of Central and Eastern Europe (CEE) in the 1990s (section 5.4.1) via its enmeshment in both the consolidation of the Single Market project and the financial crisis (section 5.4.2) to the post-crisis engagements in the European Union (section 5.4.3). I will conclude with a discussion about the KfW's role for both field dynamics and economic integration in Europe more broadly (section 5.5).

## 5.2 Field Dynamics and the Europeanization of "Promotional" Banking

As the European integration process has fueled new multinational policy fields (Fligstein and McAdam, 2012), not only in development banking, I begin by linking field theory to the literature that has focused specifically on the political processes and mechanisms forging such meso-level social orders on the continent: Europeanization and diffusion scholarship. Europeanization designates the process by which the political and economic dynamics of the EU "become part of the organizational logic of national politics and policymaking" (Ladrech, 1994, p. 69) as well as the institutional formation of a common European space that relies on specific norms, procedures and interactions between a given set of actors, without necessarily supranationalizing policy making processes or institutional structures. For instance, EU regulatory action and the provision of European structural funds (or an equivalent funding scheme such as EFSI or InvestEU) have altered national opportunity structures and triggered institutional change as well as new political and organizational strategies (Knill and Lehmkuhl, 2002; see Rubio and Thiemann as well as Volberding in this volume).

Scholars have usually examined such processes of Europeanization by tracing the spread of policies and institutions across time and space, what is called "diffusion" (Börzel and Risse, 2012). This literature provides a range of conceptual tools to tackle such phenomena, but for the sake of simplicity I follow Gilardi and Wasserfallen (2019, 1) in distinguishing four mechanisms by which policies or institutions may Europeanize: Here, policy makers are said to be influenced

(1) "by the success or failure of policies elsewhere", i.e. *learning*;
(2) "by policies of other units with which they compete for resources", i.e. *competition*;
(3) "by the pressure from international organisations or powerful countries", i.e. *coercion*; and
(4) "by the perceived appropriateness of policies", i.e. *emulation*.

A noteworthy strand of this literature highlights the need to inquire into the agency (and politics) of political and technical elites in the process of economic policy diffusion (Dyson, 2007, Börzel and Risse, 2012), and the need to distinguish between vertical and horizontal diffusion in Europeanization. While the latter "treats the decision to adopt regulatory reform as an 'interdependent' decision that is taken within a group of actors who closely observe each other", the former focuses on the interaction between inter-/supranational and the domestic level (Levi-Faur, 2005). Thus, in the case of development banking, horizontal processes of Europeanization mainly rely on the interactions between national development banks (NDBs), whereas vertical processes depend on interactions between the supranational level in shape of the European Commission or the European Investment Bank, for instance, and either a particular NDB or the community of NDBs as a whole.

For considering the role of an incumbent as the KfW, it is worth remembering that the "diffusion of public policies is never just the conduct of rational agents looking for the best solutions that 'work', but is always highly embedded in political and institutional interests and specific historical contexts" (Smith, 2013, 3). Ideology, power and expectations about political (e.g. electoral or distributional) consequences guide relevant actors not only when policies or institutions are adapted, but already when agenda-setting takes place (Gilardi and Wasserfallen, 2019). This thinking overlaps considerably with field theory's emphasis of "conceptions of control" in the structuring of emergent fields. Where "incumbent" organizations seek to use their power to reinforce their position, they are also able to prescribe—or at least greatly influence—how competition and collaboration work in a given setting, and provide "cognitive frames to interpret the actions of other organizations"—whereas "challengers", i.e. usually smaller, less resourceful organizations "must find a place in the existing set of social relationships" in order to survive (Fligstein, 2001, 18).

Applying these conceptual notions to the role of the KfW in Europe seems useful for two reasons. First, KfW's activities can be understood as critical to the development banking field, simply because it is the largest development bank in Europe. It seems difficult to conceive of a Europeanized space for investment-oriented public financial institutions without the *Kreditanstalt* (or Germany, for that matter) being on board. Second, the KfW as a government-owned body has traditionally been instrumental to the furthering of German economic and political interests; relating the emergent field to those interests helps to carve out both its character and implications.

For the remainder of this chapter, I will therefore focus on the Europeanization of German development banking as represented by KfW, which has followed a very specific business model in the German political economy, described domestically as "promotional" banking—a term that has found its way into the self-definition of the European field. Therefore, before I delve into the question of how KfW has actively shaped processes of Europeanization and in turn has been subject to such processes, the next section addresses the political and economic foundations of Europe's largest NDB.

## 5.3 The KfW: A "German Institution"

KfW was founded in 1948 as the government-owned bank through which Marshall Aid funds were channeled into the reconstruction of the German economy. This original task of providing long-term loans for the rebuilding of basic industries, housing and infrastructure also gave it the English name, "Reconstruction Loan Corporation". Over the decades, however, its priorities shifted with the economic and political environment, anchoring development aid, export finance and the financing of small-and-medium-sized enterprises—the *Mittelstand*—firmly in its identity as a public bank and, in fact, financial conglomerate. When comparing NDBs across Europe, it is key to reflect that KfW is a *group* that has under its one roof all sorts of financial activities for which other countries may use several entities. This being mainly a result of the post-Reunification expansion of its activities and integration of other state-owned institutions, the KfW stepped up its activities further after the financial crisis. Today it has more than 6,300 employees—which is more than double the workforce of the EIB—and total assets of EUR 486 billion—which makes it the third largest bank in Germany (KfW, 2018; see Figure 5.1).

As a first approximation to its current tasks, the KfW Group's new business amounted to 76.5 billion EUR in 2017 with lending to municipalities, households, and credit institutions accounting for almost 40 percent of new expenditure, while SME finance alone accounted for 29 percent; both combined constitute (broadly) the domestic lending activity of the bank. Export and project finance (18 percent) and development finance (13 percent) account for the bank's main international business. And most recently, the group has founded KfW Capital to invest in venture capital funds. Within these categories, the KfW in recent years has set priorities regarding renewable energy and promoting energy efficiency, particularly in its domestic business pillars, i.e. SME, infrastructure (i.e. municipality) and retail finance (KfW, 2018).

If one takes these activities as a proxy for government priorities in structural policies, one can swiftly acknowledge the reflection of key traits of the German political economy at large: the strong prevalence of SMEs; the proximity to other public entities, yet as well the private sector (corporatist-consensual); plus a strong outward orientation (cf. Katzenstein, 1989). Grünbacher (2001, 68) has argued accordingly that the "Kreditanstalt's activities, its task and structure made it into a 'German institution' in the sense that it was a very important part of… the 'corporate market economy', not a mere distributing institution for Marshall Plan counterpart funds." In this process, the KfW became one of the prime

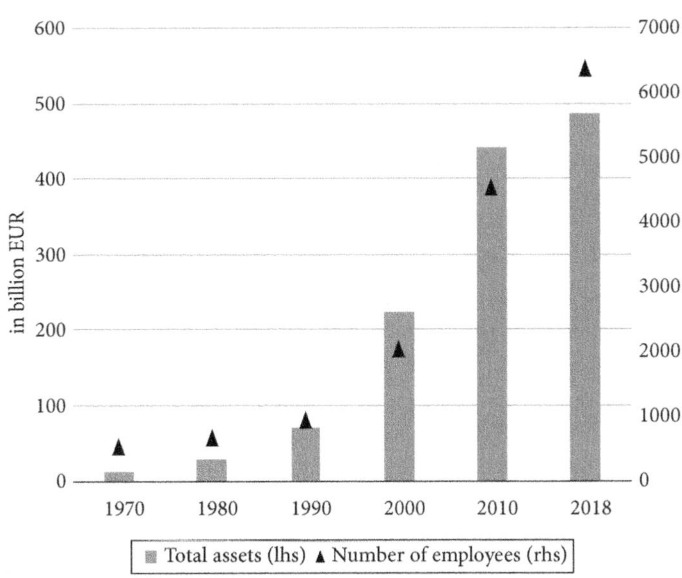


**Figure 5.1** Total assets and number of employees at KfW Group, 1970–2018
*Source*: KfW annual reports

instruments for the government to "intervene directly in the market whenever the government felt it necessary." This notion of a "German institution" is also reflected in the governance of the KfW, where ministers of both federal and state governments, bureaucrats, parliamentarians, trade unionists, and bank and industry managers sit side-by-side in the governing organs of the bank, while the ownership composition of *Bund* (80 percent) and *Länder* (20 percent) reflects German federalism.

Most importantly, as Shonfield (1965, 277) has noted, the KfW is a "characteristic German arrangement" in the sense that although the state bank is in charge of the distribution of funds for investment, "in practice the choice was often determined by the commanders actually in the fields – the individual commercial banks." And indeed, from its inception, the KfW was confronted with concerns over its relationship with the commercial banking sector. With the help of its "denazified" leading figure Hermann Josef Abs, who also was to become KfW's first chairman, the financial industry made sure that direct lending would remain the exception rather than the rule (Grünbacher, 2004, 40) and in its daily operations the *Kreditanstalt* would follow something that is often termed *Hausbankenprinzip* (relationship lending) or *Durchleitungsprinzip* (pass-through loans or on-lending). These principles reflect that the KfW had and has no branches, and it would usually be the commercial banks who deal with the final customer and assume the credit risk, while they can make use of quasi-public funds and mix them with their own products. In other words, the KfW is a second-tier development bank, reflecting a broader public-private settlement over the channeling of funds for economic policy making.

The core of German "promotional" banking thus lies within the process of KfW employing its triple-A-rated status to obtain cheap capital market funding and pass it through the commercial banking sector, who receives a margin for doing the risk assessment, to the target customer or purpose—crucially SMEs. Any profits made by KfW, which are not its primary objective, are retained and reinvested. In this sense, on-lending is said to be a source of autonomy for development banks by reducing the options for political lending, while somewhat appeasing—on competition grounds—the potentially hostile commercial banking sector and adhering to the liberal notion of "competitive neutrality". Therefore, the KfW relies on a dense network of private, public, and cooperative banks and co-exists with a second-tier network of 17 subnational, state-owned promotional banks. Although this banking practice reflects a peculiar public-private division of labor that is characteristic of many areas of the German political economy—from the housing market to labor market institutions—it has also become a reference point in the emergence of the European field of development banking, as the main section of this chapter will show.[1]

[1] It is worth noting, however, that this promotional set-up was only consolidated in the early 1970s, when the reconstruction purposes of the KfW were largely fulfilled (Winkler, 1999).

Nonetheless, throughout its history, the KfW served the specificities of the German political economy in several other respects. First, it was instrumental in fostering the postwar export-led growth regime, which "lacked a large enough domestic market to sustain economic growth and which therefore depended on selling abroad and [to] regain markets lost during and after the war" (Grünbacher, 2004, 207). This was mainly realized through its export and development aid business, securing foreign markets, mitigating the risks companies have when expanding or selling abroad, and promoting capital exports to reduce the appreciation pressure on the currency—without, however, this having to be a matter of parliamentary discussion (KfW Archive HA-VW21; Grünbacher, 2004; Naqvi et al., 2018).

Second, the KfW time and again took the role of the shareholder in the state's name under various historical circumstances. In the mid-to-late 1990s, following its own boost after German Reunification, it served as an off-balance-sheet vehicle for the state when it took over the shares of the former public companies Telekom, Deutsche Post, and Lufthansa from the federal government in order to alleviate the latter's budget problems (FAZ, January 30, 2003, 45). In 2018, the latest instance, the bank was called upon to act strategically-protectionist when it had to buy a 20 percent stake in the network operator 50Hertz to block a stake purchase from a Chinese state company (*Financial Times*, July 27, 2018). While these cases are instructive regarding KfW's array of political functions, the main section will center more on its institutional set-up and somewhat "ordinary" operations for understanding the processes of Europeanization.

## 5.4 "Doing Europe" in and through the KfW: The Vertical and Horizontal Europeanization of "Promotional" Banking

*"Germany and the KfW, we are too big as that we could hide"*
*(Interview KfW officials, 24 April 2018)*

For and through KfW, Europeanization has come in many different forms and had, to some extent, material consequences earlier than elsewhere in the EU. When evaluating these forms, I will mainly distinguish between two sorts of activities that have facilitated the emergence of a European field of development banking. First, bilateral activities such as loans, counseling and joint projects with existing and newly founded European development institutions; and second, participation in multilateral and supranational governance schemes, including associational activities. Besides these, I will review the regulatory impact of the integration process on KfW with its feedback effects on field dynamics. One should note, however, that some of the activities reconstructed below have been novel only within their intra-European context and are thus distinguished from collaborations and practices that have taken place earlier in the context of development aid.[2]

For historical context, much of the international activity of the KfW during the Cold War era was driven by a combination of foreign policy considerations in the "battle of the systems" and requirements stemming from the political constitution of the export-led growth regime, in between which the KfW regularly pointed to its statutory sovereignty when it felt that the political wish to employ it was ignoring sound banking criteria. In turn, "whenever it became active the bank did so either with the consent or on the more or less explicit wishes of the federal government" (Grünbacher, 2004, 255). This is the background for the process tracing that follows, beginning in the 1990s leading up to the most recent post-crisis developments.

### 5.4.1 Transition in the East, Single Market in the West: The 1990s from a KfW Field Perspective

Just as the founding of the EIF in the early 1990s represents a supranational landmark for the European field of development banking to come (see the introduction to this volume), the political transformations impacting the role of the KfW at that time were nothing short of game-changing. After the collapse of the Soviet bloc led into what is called post-socialist transition, KfW became a key financier of the social and economic restructuring in East Germany, initiating a fundamental expansion of its balance sheet, equity base and headcount (Harries 1998; see Figure 5.1). Beyond its borders, Germany took advantage of its proximity to, knowledge of, and mutual interest with CEE economies in an "attempt to achieve influence" through cross-border cooperation (Wedel 2001, 102).[3] Between 1994 and 2004 the German government ran the so-called TRANSFORM-Program, worth EUR 843 million, that institutionalized German aid for Central, Eastern and Southeastern European as well as the NIS economies with the objective to "enable them to take their place within the community of democratic, market-based states" (German *Bundestag* Drucksache 15/5815, 136). Herein, the Ministry of Finance, the Ministry of Economic Affairs and the Foreign Office mandated the KfW to lead the coordination of their economic advisory services in these

[2] This holds true, for example, for the pioneering collaboration between the development arm of KfW and the British Commonwealth Development Corporation, which goes back to the early 1980s to "help aid co-ordination in the EEC" (FT, 11 Dec 1981), or similarly for the employment of "blended finance" in the EU which has come to fruition in the context of financial assistance to developing countries (see Volberding 2018). Furthermore, loans to development finance institutions in developing economies have also been long established parts of the KfW international toolbox (KfW Archive HA-VW7). Such instances are illustrative of the importance of "adjacent fields".

[3] It is important to recall that these countries had been the former trading partners for the German Democratic Republic (GDR) but also the old export markets for the bygone German empire (Gross, 2016), stirring concerns about a renewed "*Drang nach Osten*" (see Webber, 2001).

**Table 5.1** KfW Credit Lines to CEE development banks, 1995–2001

| Country | Financing purpose | Agreed credit volume (in million EUR) |
|---|---|---|
| **Bosnia and Herzegovina** | SMEs | 7.7 |
| **Croatia** | SMEs | 30.7 |
| | Infrastructure/Tourism | 100.6 |
| **Estonia** | SMEs | 15.3 |
| | Energy | 5.1 |
| **Hungary** | SMEs | 40.9 |
| | Infrastructure/Energy | 46.0 |
| **Latvia** | SMEs | 23.0 |
| **Lithuania** | SMEs | 10.1 |
| **Macedonia** | SMEs | 15.0 |
| **Poland** | SMEs | 60.0 |
| | Infrastructure | 10.0 |
| **Romania** | SMEs | 25.6 |
| **Slovak Republic** | SMEs | 32.6 |
| | Housing | 33.0 |
| **Slovenia** | SMEs | 20.0 |
| **Ukraine** | SMEs | 15.3 |
| ***Total*** | *SMEs* | *296.2* |
| | *Other* | *194.7* |

*Source*: KfW 2001, from Clement and Reppegarther 2002, Table 7

countries for the buildup of "democracy and social market economy" and, more specifically, provide advisory services in the area of banking, insurance and stock exchanges to develop financial markets for both the imminent wave of privatization and the capital accumulation process at large, but also to build capacities for SMEs. This prominently included the counseling, and due to capital shortage, also financing, of revived or newly founded development banks. Table 5.1 shows that between 1995 and 2001, loans of almost EUR 400 million had been agreed upon, of which roughly a third was supposed to go to the Croatian HBOR and a fifth to the Hungarian MFB.

The KfW understood counseling these development banks to mean the export of its own model, as its chairman Vogt put it (FAZ, May 18, 1993, 17). This included a corporate governance framework that would secure a fair degree of autonomy in daily operations, a funding mix that entails capital market financing, not-solely-for-profit orientation, and the principles of subsidiarity and on-lending (Clement and Reppegarther, 2002). Mainly the Croatian, the Macedonian, the Slovakian, and to some extent, the Hungarian institutions followed that model, while the Polish and Lithuanian governments decided against it, and again others did struggle with survival in the face of political instability (ibid.).

These variegated outcomes did not just flow out of efficiency considerations over newly established markets but were also about political control, domestically and geopolitically. For instance, CEE was the field in which competition in "institutional transplantation" to the transition economies took place among donors of the liberal-capitalist west (Zavisca, 2012). The dynamics in development banking counseling, however, seem aptly captured by the development anthropologist Janine Wedel (2001, 8) who noted of Western aid to Eastern Europe that

> aid appears more like a series of chemical reactions that begin with the donor's policies, but are transformed by the agendas, interests, and interactions of the donor and recipient representatives at each stage of implementation and interface. Each side influences the other, and the result if often qualitatively different from the plan envisioned.

This notion may be worthwhile keeping in mind when assessing more recent endeavors of NDB counseling, and so is remembering the context in which the KfW went East.

KfW's advisory and financing services to development banks in CEE were embedded in a political strategy that was as much geopolitical as it was economic. As the Ministry of Economic Affairs (1995, 8) stated, "[e]conomic and political stabilization, including processes such as the development of new sales markets and possibilities of cooperation, are the goals of a policy of concrete support as conducted by the German government", a strategy that it later deemed successful in terms of foreign trade promotion (German *Bundestag Drucksache* 13/3944).[4] At the same time the KfW was convinced internally that promoting SMEs and development banks in CEE would be both efficient in terms of the larger political mission and in terms of its own model's legitimacy (Winkler, 1999). As Table 5.1 illustrates, the vast majority of credit lines were earmarked for SME finance.

Besides the economic dependencies that these strategies held in store for CEE economies (Nölke and Vliegenthart, 2009), what lasted was that many of the development banks founded then have become part of the current landscape of active institutions and thereby involved in the recent European investment

[4] While in this process there was no direct aid tying, the construction of loan syndicates and provision of technical expertise (German engineering) still allowed for the support of German industry. The Financial Times at the time provided an instructive illustration of this. When Germany financed the modernization of Albania's only international airport in Tirana in 1996 with 33.7 million USD, this was based on a lending consortium of Berliner Bank, KfW and export credit agency Hermes, which allowed for a credit maturity of 40 years on 0.75 per cent interest: "The airport contract was awarded over two years ago to a consortium led by Siemens, the German electrical engineering group. Civil engineering work will be carried out by Walter Bau, the second largest German construction group" (*Financial Times*, March 21, 1996).

schemes. Their models have retained their early KfW marks that they received from a mix of "coercion" and "emulation", as the policy diffusion literature suggests. From the perspective of KfW, its engagement in the transition economies gave it not much growth in personnel and funds when compared to the programs it ran domestically in the face of Reunification. But it levelled up the bank's experience, on which it should be able to capitalize in the European integration process, and broadened both its business opportunities and capacities to act, not least because it was then given the possibility of having external representative offices (former KfW board member Wolfgang Kroh, in Bohnet, 2015, 178). In other words, this outward orientation to Central and Eastern Europe made KfW the first among its peers and thereby the earliest incumbent of a field in its early stages. This interpretation is also reflected in the fact that amid its activities in CEE, KfW also decided to open an office in Brussels in 1996, representing the kernel of what would later become a shared representative office for the large Western NDBs and ELTI. This being an early move in the field, KfW also began to extend global loans to Western European public and commercial banks, which became part of its business from then onwards.

### 5.4.2 Going West and the Reordering of KfW: The Rollercoaster Decade of the 2000s

Against the background of the 1990s and the transition boom of founding new development banks in Central and Eastern Europe, the 2000s seem to be calm seas at first glance. Only the freshly merged Belgian SFPI made for a new dot on the European map in 2006. For KfW, however, the decade began and ended with a bang.

On 1st of March 2002, the German government and the European Commission found a compromise on how to structure its public banking sector prospectively, in order to conform with EU state aid regulations (see Volberding in this volume for more details). This Monti-II-Agreement, or *Verständigung II*, did not only have consequences for German *Landesbanken* and savings banks, but also for the KfW. The agreement resulted in the Promotional Bank Restructuring Act (*Förderbankenneustrukturierungsgesetz;* German *Bundestag Drucksache* 15/1127), which involved the precise definition of the promotional business the KfW could conduct and meant the disincorporation of export financing, leading to the founding of the KfW IPEX bank in 2008. A remarkable amendment in the context of Europeanization, however, was the specification that the KfW now had the function of

> [g]ranting other financings in the interest of the German *and European* economy. The tasks of KfW in this area include a) projects in the interest of the

> European Community that are cofinanced by the European Investment Bank or similar European financing institutions, b) export financings outside the member states of the European Union, the other contracting states of the Agreement on the European Economic Area, and states with official status as candidates for accession to the European Union aa) on a syndicated basis or bb) in countries lacking sufficient financing offers.
>
> (Law concerning KfW, Art. 2 IV; own italics)

This amendment thus codified an increasing European orientation of the bank's business[5], explicitly mentioned the cooperation with European financing institutions in serving projects in the interest of the EU and allowed for export financing in line with that interest. As will be detailed below, the amendment indeed foreshadowed a greater multi-level engagement of the KfW, with both the EIB group—especially the EIF—and several supranational grant programs and financial instruments. In other words, "Europe" became a statutory-granted playing field for the KfW, an area of strategic action.

Yet, the reordering of the KfW had another dimension for the European field of development banking, which linked back to a core feature of "promotional" banking, the on-lending. In a parliamentary hearing following the Monti-II-Agreement, KfW chairman Reich responded to concerns of the German commercial banking sector and policymakers over the principle of subsidiarity:

> The separation of competitive business from promotional business and the clear definition of what promotional business is, and with the proviso that promotional business should go through the 'Hausbanken', mean that the term subsidiarity is sufficiently and clearly defined, at any rate much clearer than subsidiarity as such in the KfW Act to date. *This is what the EU wants. One has to be aware of the fact that this law or this agreement, which was made last year with the EU, will have a blueprint character for all funding institutions in Europe, i.e. in Europe all other funding institutions will be structured in a similar or comparable way*
>
> (German *Bundestag Drucksache* 15/743, 7 May 2003; own translation and italics).

If one takes the communication on "The role of National Promotional [sic!] Banks (NPBs) in supporting the Investment Plan for Europe", which the Commission released in 2015, as a benchmark, Reich had a point. The 2015

[5] In fact, the bank's annual reports of 2000 and 2001 had temporarily revealed the expense category for "investment finance in Europe", which had grown from 1 per cent of new promotional business in 1999 to almost 5 per cent in 2001. The KfW itself announced: "Europe is becoming a domestic market and KfW is part of the process. For small and medium-sized firms national frontiers in Europe are becoming less and less important. KfW is also increasingly Europeanizing its promotion and financing small and medium-sized enterprises in western Europe" (KfW annual report 2001, p. 48), which should be seen in the context of the 1999 founding of NEFI (see Rubio and Thiemann in this volume).

document was written to provide "guidance to Member States intending to set up a new NPB, building on best practices" and directed the guiding principles towards the alleviation of market failures. It stressed that "[w]hen operating in markets already served by commercial banks", which is likely to be the case everywhere in the EU with regard to SME and infrastructure finance, NPBs are advised to distribute their "products indirectly through the commercial banking sector" in order to maintain "a level playing field in the financial markets", i.e. serving "competitive neutrality" (European Commission 2015, 3–4).

However, insiders contend that there is no uniform official position of the Commission on on-lending, even though it is considered good practice in order to increase the leverage of an operation, even in small countries (interview European Commission officials, March 27 2019). Given that the potential risks the communication highlights[6] are understood in the German context to be sufficiently well mitigated by the KfW's governance framework, the Monti-II-agreement and the following Act codified this for the first time, suggesting that from then on it served as a foil on which further action in the European field built.

Beyond these governance considerations, the *Verständigung II* to some extent also simply institutionalized KfW's already existing European-focused activities. After the experience of financing both commercial and development banking in CEE, the KfW began to hand out global loans to public and private banks in Western Europe from the late 1990s onwards. The KfW proclaimed that with these loans it would account for the "increasing economic interrelations within Europe" that required the "further Europeanization of KfW SME financing" (KfW press release, June 13, 2002). However, funds were also available for infrastructure finance and housing projects, more generally signaling the political will to further the common market project, both in trade and finance. Between 2000 and 2004, EUR 5.5 billion had been transferred to West European banks (KfW press release, November 25, 2004), a sum that is more than ten times the volume Table 5.1 revealed for CEE credit lines between 1995 and 2001. In 2007 alone, the volume of global loans was EUR 1.7 billion, which was 2.6 percent of KfW's financing operations, mainly going to financial institutions in France, Austria, Spain, and Portugal.[7] These global loans, as we now know, were emblematic of a wider trend of German capital exports that were instrumental in the German growth regime but facilitated increasing imbalances between Euro area countries

[6] These risks entail: "Losses to the guarantor governments stemming from substandard underwriting; Misallocation of investments due to political interference; Maintaining inefficient market structures, sectors with overcapacity or supporting undertakings in difficulty; Crowding out of private sector financiers, thus holding back financial sector development" (European Commission 2015, 4).

[7] Yet, when the financial crisis had reached Germany in 2008, the KfW came under pressure (see below) and was quick to announce that global loans to European counterparts would only be handed out to the extent that there would "not be any impairment of domestic SME financing as a result" (KfW press release, 6 November 2008).

(Mertens, 2017; Fuller, 2018). But for the KfW, this turn to Western Europe entailed both new business opportunities and a new source of legitimacy within the European (Monetary) Union.

This notwithstanding, some of these global loans had been agreed upon under the umbrella of the Commission's PHARE[8] program, some of which was jointly managed by the Council of Europe Bank and the KfW since 2000 and involved both bank and EU budgetary resources. Indeed, it was a sign of the times as the 2000s saw an increasing entanglement of the KfW with European financing institutions, which had found their way into the bank's legal framework after *Verständigung II*. Its role varied by program, ranging from a co-funding to a managing institution, and in many cases it was the expression of closer operational cooperation with the EIB group that happened in parallel to CDC involvement and mainly entailed risk-sharing frameworks and loan facilities. Two observations, however, are noteworthy. First, over the decade several multilevel/multilateral programs emerged, such as the Galaxy Fund (2004)[9] with CDC, EIB, KfW, and the Italian Sanpaolo IMI, the European Post-2012 Carbon Fund (2008) with CDC, EIB, ICO, KfW and NIB, and the first Marguerite Fund (2010) set up by CDC, CDP, EIB, KfW, ICO, and the Polish state-dominated PKO (later succeeded by BGK). All of them heralded a growing interaction between NDBs and the EIB, even though only the large NDBs could get involved.

Second, KfW's involvement was exceptional to the extent that it was the only NDB that also joined genuinely supranational initiatives. In 2008, most notably, KfW became a partner in JASPERS, a technical assistance facility for those Member States that joined the EU in 2004 and 2007, which was jointly established by the Commission, the EIB, and the European Bank for Reconstruction and Development (EBRD). This partnership, which lasted until 2013, was again inspired by KfW's engagement in CEE in the 1990s. As the EIB proclaimed,

> [t]his cooperation will enable JASPERS to make use of KfW's experience and professional expertise in the financing of projects and its long record of successful cooperation and project co-financing with the EIB and EBRD in a large number of different countries. KfW staff assigned to JASPERS will join the existing expert staff in the regional offices of JASPERS in Warsaw, Vienna and Bucharest.
>
> (EIB Press Release BEI/08/67)

[8] PHARE initially stood for "Poland and Hungary: Aid for Restructuring of the Economies" but more broadly prepared the accession process of CEE economies.

[9] The Galaxy Fund marked the first occasion the Commission invested in a fund and, according to the KfW, was supposed to lay the basis for further institutional cooperation between CDC and KfW. Then chairman Reich stressed that it resulted from the view that further liberalization and privatization of public infrastructure was needed, generating potential for mobilizing private equity (KfW press release, March 22, 2004).

Similar supranational fund structures throughout the 2000s, in which the KfW participated as the sole NDB were provided by the European Fund for Southeast Europe and the Green for Growth Fund. Finally, the ELENA facility under shared management from CEB, EBRD and KfW was set up in 2009 to focus on energy efficiency. In other words, when it came to targeting regions in CEE, the KfW was both in demand and able to reassert its key position in the consolidating European field.

While one could be led to assess these early field dynamics on efficiency and expertise grounds, they also involved strategic action of the participating institutions. Obviously, these programs provided new business and more often than not were conceived as win-win situations (in other words, they were "carrots"); at the same time, NDBs would also engage in order to have one's own specifics perceived positively in Brussels, to ensure fair treatment on other issues (the "stick") (interview NDB lobbyist, March 27, 2019). In other words, the mechanisms that drove the Europeanization of "promotional" banking during the 2000s entailed both learning and emulating processes, while competition and coercion were particularly relevant for KfW's organizational change in the face of European integration.

The decade of the 2000s, as mentioned above, however, ended with a second bang for the KfW, which was its involvement in the transatlantic financial turbulences. On the morning of September 15, 2008, just hours after Lehman Brothers filed for bankruptcy, the KfW transferred EUR 320 million to the insolvent bank for a swap deal. After this expensive mismanagement was revealed by the *Frankfurter Allgemeine Zeitung*[10] only days later, the biggest German tabloid was quick to name KfW the "dumbest bank in Germany". This added insult to injury, because the scandal fueled an already existing debate over KfW's risk-management and supervision that came from a second financial entanglement with the unfolding crisis: KfW's ownership of the SME-bank IKB *Deutsche Industriebank* (cf. Moslener et al., 2018). Since the summer of 2007 IKB had been in trouble due to its engagement with the US subprime market and sequences of financial misconduct, after which KfW stepped up both its stakes and employed its emergency funds to avoid insolvency (German *Bundestag Drucksache* 16/7977), before it finally sold off its stake to the private equity firm Lone Star.

The intense political debate triggered by these events ultimately led to a sea change in the KfW's supervision. Having been supervised by the Ministry of Finance in cooperation with the Ministry of Economic Affairs ever since, the 2013 KfW regulation implied further supervisory competencies for the Federal Financial Supervisory Authority (BaFin) and added legal obligations to some of

[10] "320 Millionen für Lehman: Die berühmteste Überweisung," September 18, 2010; available at https://www.faz.net/aktuell/wirtschaft/unternehmen/320-millionen-fuer-lehman-die-beruehmteste-ueberweisung-11040466.html [last accessed on 30 April 2019].

the theretofore voluntary risk-management and reporting practices.[11] This change, however, did not alter the bank's legal status in German banking law. Policy makers made sure that the KfW would still count as a public sector entity and not as a credit or financial services institution, which, among other things, enabled its further exemption from key European financial regulations. Today, this is visible in the provisions of the Capital Requirement Directive (IV), which explicitly exempts KfW and the German promotional landscape from the scope of the regulation.

The immediate turbulence of the financial crisis affected the European position of the bank also in other, ambiguous ways. Global lending was put on hold for Western European entities as the interbanking market broke down, while CEE financial institutions continued to receive KfW loans, mainly for the purpose of SME support (KfW annual reports, 2008; 2009), partly reflecting the need to stabilize the production chain of German goods. KfW's firepower also turned strongly to counter-cyclical action instead, bolstering the government's stimulus packages. In terms of field dynamics, this turn, first, led the bank "in close consultation with the federal government" to further advocate for "blending" EU budgetary funds with federal funds in order to increase available resources (KfW annual report, 2012, p. 90). Second, in combination with the overall mild course of the crisis in the German economy, it washed away the IKB and Lehman episode among European financial publics: except the disaster of some *Landesbanken*, the German public banking sector, including the KfW, were increasingly seen as key to the mitigation of the credit crunch (Münnich, 2016). This lay at least one foundational brick for a prominent role of the KfW in the European development banking field post-crisis.

### 5.4.3 The New Normal? Post-Crisis Europeanization and the Role of KfW

When asked about the banks' European activities after the crisis, officials from the KfW (April 24, 2018; October 17, 2018) and the German Ministry for Economic Affairs (September 27, 2018) stressed the bank's own slogan "*Bank aus Verantwortung*" (a bank committed to responsibility). Here, officials contend that Germany's superior economic position implies "responsibility for Europe", something that former chairman Ulrich Schröder (2008-2017) had emphasized when signing a global loan agreement with Spain's ICO: "As the promotional bank of the Federal Republic of Germany, we actively exercise our responsibility for

[11] It is an interesting side note that the members of the supervisory board, who are usually not too familiar with the technicalities of the financial sector, now receive regular trainings in financial market regulation (informal exchange with supervisory board member, 29 January 2019).

strengthening international partnership between promotional banks and for actively designing (*Gestaltung*) European networks" (KfW press release, February 11, 2013; own translation). In other instances global loans have been presented as "another building block in our longstanding European engagement and cooperation with European promotional banks" (KfW press release on global loan to Italian CDP, November 26, 2014; own translation) or as a "manifestation of the good cooperation between the KfW and the BGK as important European promotional banks" (KfW press release, February 11, 2015; own translation).

As a matter of fact, global loan business with Western counterparts made a comeback to KfW business in the period following the peak of the banking and sovereign debt crisis and was almost showcased by the bank. The German newspaper *Frankfurter Allgemeine Zeitung* promptly titled "Germany is becoming too small for the KfW"[12], alluding to several reports that addressed the growing size of the bank, and argued that it would not do this out of altruism. Asked for the reasons, officials point to the European policies of the German federal government that have pushed for austerity in the European Union:

> The motivation comes from that the federal state says, "I want you to do this business for political reasons". The background is of course not only that you are not stuck in the austerity corner, but also that you say that "governments, where we have the feeling they make an effort with budget consolidation, we want to give other impulses". And then KfW is the implementing partner of German European policy, in the end of the day.
>
> (Interview KfW officials, 24 April 2018; own translation)

It is also against this background that the KfW was the first NDB in 2015 to pledge 8bn EUR to the Investment Plan for Europe, thereby compensating for the reluctance of the Ministry of Finance under Wolfgang Schäuble to contribute direct fiscal resources to any European-level investment program; and thereby making a first move which other NDBs then could follow.

These activities point again to KfW's explicit cross-border mandate and its elevated position for handing out loans to its European counterparts (interview European Commission official, October 10, 2018). Here, it is worth remembering that the KfW benefits from the German government's prime rating on international financial markets. Its triple-A rating for most of the post-crisis period meant that, by and large, the KfW did not have funding problems, which is crucial for two reasons. First, it did not need one of the primary products that the

[12] "Der KfW wird Deutschland zu klein," 21 February 2015, available at: https://www.faz.net/aktuell/wirtschaft/kreditvergabe-der-kfw-wird-deutschland-zu-klein-13438440.html [last accessed 6 February 2018].

EIB is offering to NDBs, which is funding through global loans.[13] Second, instead, it had the capacity to pass through its advantage on capital markets to other development banks through its own global loans. And if the KfW finds politically demanded loans not to be viable on banking terms, it may claim guarantees from the government to assure its sound refinancing position. A peculiar case of this is the first rescue package to Greece in 2010, where the German government had its share handled by the KfW, who then loaned EUR 15.2 billion to Greece—a deal that, up to 2018, delivered EUR 400 million in interest revenues (Financial Times, June 22, 2018).

This is, however, not the only practice that has found its way from the 1990s into the current context. In its communication on the "role of National Promotional Banks", the European Commission has highlighted its intention to facilitate the establishment of new institutions in Member States. Here, it contended that "[n]ew NPBs can benefit from the experience of established peers in a variety of ways to help them meet the above objectives. Several recently-created NPBs, such as the Portuguese Development Financial Institution and Ireland's SBCI relied on ad hoc bilateral cooperation with fellow NPBs" (European Commission, 2015). The KfW has taken on a prominent role in these "ad hoc" cooperations, sometimes in collaboration with the Commission and the EIB. In the case of Portugal, the KfW announced that the Portuguese "promotional bank shall promote SMEs after the *role model of the KfW by using pass-through loans*. In the founding stage KfW has supported the Portuguese government with its know-how. The capital base was provided by EU structural funds and public resources" (KfW press material online, own translation and italics)[14]. And as the case of the Irish SBCI further confirms, diffusion through counseling resembles in principle the ways practiced in the 1990s.

> In numerous workshops, KfW has shared with its Irish partners its expertise in all aspects of promoting medium-sized enterprises and thereby contributed to the efficient setup of this new institution. Furthermore, the federal government has mandated the KfW to negotiate a global loan agreement with SBCI. These negotiations have been completed this week, so that the KfW supports SBCI also financially, with a global loan of EUR 150 million, guaranteed by the federal government, to finance investment credit to small and medium-sized enterprises in Ireland (KfW press release, October 3, 2014, own translation)

[13] This is different for the *Länder*-based regional promotional banks who partly use EIB *and* KfW refinancing as well as other European funds in the implementation of cohesion policy.

[14] Available at: https://www.kfw.de/KfW-Konzern/Newsroom/Pressematerial/Themen-kompakt/Europa/Kooperation/ [last accessed on 6 Feb 2018].

Officials have depicted these bilateral activities as in part demand-driven, confirming the bank's leaflet statement that "KfW's expertise in promoting small and medium-sized enterprises is sought after not only in Germany, but across Europe."[15] One of the interviewees (interview KfW officials April 24, 2018) describes the counseling activities as reflective of the benchmark status of the KfW:

> When governments want to found new promotional banks or restructure them, KfW often is somewhat of that big role model . . . because we have that incredibly long experience. And our second strong focus is our on-lending model . . . because that's a great advantage, in principle, for every promotional bank – we don't have to make the risk-assessment of the loans.

The demand-driven aspect of the counseling, however, has become evident in the case of the UK. In 2012, Richard Barwell, then senior economist at the Royal Bank of Scotland, wrote in the *Financial Times*: "The Germans have found a way of channeling cheap funds to SMEs without breaching state aid rules. We should copy it" (Financial Times, May 24, 2012). As early as 1993, the UK government had looked to KfW to consider a long-term credit institution particularly for its SMEs (Financial Times, November 2, 1993), and now the 'stick' of the Commission seemed to have a diffusion impact that was both 'learning' and 'emulation', against the probable 'coercive' consequences of state aid approval (also see Volberding this volume).[16] Indeed, after the crisis, the KfW became involved by providing its expertise in the founding process of the British Business Bank, and later was invited to the House of Commons when it debated the possible founding of a national investment bank. Table 5.2 lists the official bilateral activities of the KfW between 2012 and 2015 that affected post-crisis field dynamics and shows that the timing of KfW support for Spain, Portugal, Ireland (though not Greece) was closely linked to the phasing out of the EU's financial assistance programs for these countries.

The push and pull factors in these domains also provide insights into the evolution of the European field as such, implying lessons from the 1990s experience in CEE. The diffusion of specific practices or policies in European development banking, KfW officials (April 24, 2018) argue,

[15] For the case of Greece and the failed Institution for Growth, see Bastian, this volume.

[16] As one interviewee noted: "The interesting thing is pressure for homogenization, is the Commission. Because the authority in front of which the institutions have to justify, is the Commission . . . if you see that several programs in Europe work better and you have a better chance to come through at the Commission—but that is less peer pressure, but rather that you say, okay, there were solutions in other countries, that works with European competition law. And you could say that we are less likely to catch a bloody nose there" (interview KfW officials, April 24, 2018).

**Table 5.2** KfW core bilateral activities, 2012–2015

| Year | Type | Receiving institutions |
|---|---|---|
| 2012 | Counseling/Memorandum of Understanding | Green Investment Bank (UK)<br>British Business Bank (UK) |
| 2013 | Global loan 800m EUR (SMEs on-lending)<br>Global loan 200m EUR (SMEs equity) | ICO (Spain) |
| 2013 | Counseling/Funding (SMEs) | IfD (Portugal) |
| 2014 | Counseling/Funding 100m EUR (SMEs on-lending) | IfG (Greece) |
| 2014 | Counseling/Global loan 150m EUR (SMEs on-lending) | SBCI (Ireland) |
| 2014 | Global loan 500m EUR (SMEs on-lending and energy efficiency) | CDP (Italy) |
| 2015 | Global loan 100m EUR (SME finance) | BGK (Poland) |

*Source*: KfW press releases; own compilation. Further activities involved the exchange of expertise and personnel; total global loan volume including CEE not available

has to be consensual. You will not have a small one agree on something which is against their interests…So this is rather classical soft power and…not limited to Germany and the KfW. It's all too decentralized, diverse and colorful for that.

This is critical to the extent that incumbents cannot merely impose their view on smaller institutions but need (to create) some sort of consensus. In addition, and in marked difference to the field emergence of the 1990s, the post-crisis period featured a supranational policy to promote the founding and involvement of NDBs, and a broader presence from both the EIB and other large NDBs in the European policy space, who would also provide expertise and funding. In other words, Bpifrance and CDC, partly CDP and others, were also ready to provide bilateral counseling support, with each having their own comparative advantages in financing SMEs and infrastructure. The founding report of the Portuguese IFD is a case in point for an increasingly crowded field, as it details: "Along the year, contacts were developed with similar entities (Bpifrance, ICO, BBB, KfW, BGK, HBOR), in an exercise of benchmarking but also to assess the possibilities of collaboration" (Instituição Financeira de Desenvolvimento, 2015, 9).

Furthermore, with the expansion of EFSI, and InvestEU looming large, Member States could now also resort to technical assistance bodies, who would offer support in leveling up NDBs, such as the structural reform support service (SRSS). The SRSS had emerged from the "Task Force for Greece" to engage with Member States in implementing structural reforms in a wide array of policy areas. Within the area of financial sector support, member states were recently enabled to request support for streamlining internal processes or even founding a "promotional bank", in line with the Commission's push. In these processes of technical support, KfW is not the only household name, but Bpifrance and external consultancies do have their own role and reputation (interview European Commission officials, March 27, 2019).

This is not to say that KfW lost its template function for the development banking field.[17] Especially in the context of EFSI, within which KfW matched more than 1.2 bn EUR of EU funds, and of InvestEU, for which KfW has been one of the two NDBs *ex ante* fulfilling the requirement of a "pillar assessment" preconditioning access to the EU budget, the German promotional bank's advantageous capacities came to the fore once more—and added "competition" to the diffusion dynamics of the field.

But beyond that, the post-crisis field dynamics have brought about a greater diversity in and embeddedness of NDB actor constellations that need coordination through internal governance units. The now more visible associations, networks, and fora around NDBs (see Rubio and Thiemann, this volume) shape the diffusion of promotional bank practices more than ever before, which has also made it harder to pin down a specific source of influence. Still, only few institutions within the associations have the capacity to deal with complex questions, which consequences would unfold in the long-term, and have the power resources to mobilize other institutions for "what is at stake" (interview NDB lobbyist, March 27, 2019). In this regard, KfW has not only initiated and led some of the NDB networks but has also been the partner institution of the EIF to set up a post-crisis initiative with NDBs for promoting securitization markets for SMEs (Mertens and Thiemann, 2018). On other occasions, however, it was the Italian CDP and the French CDC (Marguerite Fund) or Bpifrance (equity collaboration) who set the pace, not to speak of the EIB group.

As the strength of support for specific European investment policies and blending practices among NDBs is thus likely to remain fragmented along some traditional lines of economic thinking (cf. Brunnermeier, James and Landau, 2016), the question of incumbency power also resides with individual lobbying resources. As Table 5.3 shows, KfW as well as the main French development institutions and the Italian CDP have resources at their command that enable them to make their voices heard, even outside of the collective interest bodies they participate in. The post-crisis period, therefore, reflects some sort of "embedded incumbency" in the consolidation of the field that remains shaped by the struggle for power positions.

[17] As the Commission and Eurostat notes: "In context of the 2016 EDP [excessive deficit procedure, D.M.] dialogue visit, the largest German 'Förderbank' (promotional bank) 'Kreditanstalt für Wiederaufbau' ('KfW') was examined in detail, particularly given that the operations and the structural setup (including the governance) of the entity were used as a model template for other promotional banks that were established in other Member States" (European Commission and Eurostat 2019, p. 39). For adverse regulatory effects of such visits, however, see Piroska and Mero in this volume.

**Table 5.3** NDB interest representation on EU level

| Organisation name | Country head office | Lobbying costs** | Lobbyists (FTE) | # of meetings |
|---|---|---|---|---|
| KfW Bankengruppe | Germany | 900000 - 999999 | 5.5 | 52 |
| Cassa Depositi e Prestiti s.p.a. | Italy | 100000 - 199999 | 3.25 | 24 |
| Caisse Des Dépôts | France | 700000 - 799999 | 3.75 | 14 |
| Bpifrance | France | 100000 - 199999 | 1.25 | 5 |
| Agence Française de Développement | France | 200000 - 299999 | 4 | 4 |
| Bank Gospodarstwa Krajowego (BGK)* | Poland | 100000 - 199999 | 3 | 3 |
| Instituto de Crédito Oficial (ICO)* | Spain | 75000 | 0.75 | 0 |

*Source*: Lobby Facts Database, retrieved 17 April 2019

*Notes*: *currently not on lobby register;

**declared annual spending on lobbying, latest financial year available; FTE =full-time equivalent;

# of meetings "covers meetings held since November 2014 with commissioners, their cabinet members or directors-general at the European Commission; other lobby meetings with lower-level staff may have taken place, but the European Commission doesn't publish information about such meetings"

## 5.5 Conclusion: Soft power, Europeanization and the Emergence of a Field

Among the key requirements for a new field to emerge, Fligstein and McAdam (2012, 88) argue, actors must achieve a degree of consensus not only over "what is at stake" and legitimate action, but also that "there is a set of relatively fixed actors in the field whose roles and comparative status/power are consensually defined by others in the strategic action field." From the information and views gathered from documents and interviews, there is little doubt that the KfW is a fixed point of reference for strategic action in the European field of development banking. This is as much true for domestic actors throughout Europe who have sought orientation when (re-)structuring their own development institutions as it is true for supranational policy makers who have tried to mobilize both financial power and technical expertise.

From the position of the KfW this amounts to "soft power", a notion that has long been part of its internal narrative, reasserting its confidence without over-stretching legitimacy (KfW Archive HA-AS19). The KfW has been able to capitalize on regulatory, organizational and structural advantages, which it employs in the construction of the European field of development banking. At the heart of this has been a stark focus on the financing of SMEs and the practice of on-lending as a pillar of "promotional banking", which the KfW exported partly on mandate from the federal government and made a feature of the field. Here, the double rationale of expanding business for the bank and serving German policy consideration on the European continent has been evident from the political mandate to facilitate the transition to capitalism in Central and Eastern Europe after the collapse of the Soviet Union to the global loan and counseling missions in austerity Europe.

In this light, the chapter underlines the need to understand field dynamics in European development banking as based on unequal resources, fragmented policy access, and diverse historical-political legacies, which requires reflection regarding the properties we see emerging in EU investment policies, from industrial policy to the Green Deal. But the historical reconstruction of KfW's transnational engagement presented here is not enough to provide a full picture of its distributional implications, requiring further examination of the perspectives of recipient institutions across the EU. In addition, as Gilardi and Wasserfallen (2019, 9) have noted, "[w]hether one criticises or welcomes the diffusion of a certain policy is less a question of how the process of diffusion unfolds, but rather depends on whether one is an advocate or opponent of the policy itself". When there is a shared consensus over the need to bolster sustainable infrastructure and SME financing on the basis of on-lending practices, the KfW's experience and expertise can certainly be of great use.

However, different diffusion mechanisms and politics have implications for what works and how. For instance, research on the diffusion of stock exchanges indicates that "practices adopted through a process of mimesis [or 'pull'] were more likely to thrive, but those adopted owing to coercive processes [or 'push'] were less likely to do so" (Weber et al., 2009, 1320). This is a delicate question for European policy makers attempting to leverage NDBs for some sort of supranationally-devised investment policies through regulatory and quasi-fiscal guidance, but it also evokes a discussion about the dominance of German ideas and practices in the conduct of European economic policies, or—more precisely—about the "ordoliberalisation of the EU" (Nedergaard, 2019). Much of the European benchmarking of the KfW taking place in the emergence and consolidation of the development banking field points into this direction but will require a more systematic comparative analysis of current lending practices among NDBs. Certainly, as the early field presence and power position of the KfW has partially given way to a more engaged and embedded actor constellation, the conditions under which German promotional banking europeanizes will continue to evolve, and ultimately hinge on the inroads European integration at large will make.

## References

Bohnet, M. 2015. Geschichte der deutschen Entwicklungspolitik: Strategien, Innenansichten, Zeitzeugen, Herausforderungen. München: UVK/Lucius.

Börzel. T.A., and T. Risse. 2012. From Europeanisation to Diffusion: Introduction. West European Politics 35 (1), 1–19.

Bulmer, S., and Paterson, W.E. 2013. Germany as the EU's Reluctant Hegemon? Of Economic Strength and Political Constraints. Journal of European Public Policy 20 (10), 1387–405.

Brunnermeier, M., James, H., and Landau, J.-P. 2016. The Euro and the Battle of Ideas. Princeton: Princeton University Press.

Clement, H., and A., Reppegather. 2002. Effektivität der Förderbankkredite für KMU in Mittel- und Osteuropa. (Unter besonderer Berücksichtigung der Situation in Ungarn und Ukraine), Arbeiten aus dem Osteuropa-Institut München, No. 239.

Dyson, K., 2007. Economic Policy, in P. Graziano, P., Vink, P.M. (eds), Europeanization. New Research Agendas. Houndmills: Palgrave Macmillan, 281–294.

European Commission, 2015. Working together for jobs and growth: The role of National Promotional Banks (NPBs) in supporting the Investment Plan for Europe (COM(2015) 361 final). Brussels: European Commission.

European Commission and Eurostat. 2019. EDP Dialogue Visit to Germany. Ref. Ares(2019)4259829 - 04/07/2019. Luxembourg: European Commission.

Fligstein, N. 2001. The Architecture of Markets: An Economic Sociology of Twenty-First-Century Capitalist Societies. Princeton: Princeton University Press.

Fligstein, N., and D. McAdam. 2012. A Theory of Fields. Oxford: Oxford University Press.

Fuller, G.W. 2018. Exporting Assets: EMU and the Financial Drivers of European Macroeconomic Imbalances. New Political Economy 23 (2), 174–91.

Gilardi, F. and F. Wasserfallen. 2019. The Politics of Policy Diffusion. European Journal of Political Research 58 (4), 1245–56.

Griffith-Jones, S. 2016. National Development Banks and Sustainable Infrastructure: The Case of KfW. GEGI Working Paper 006.

Gross, S.G. 2016. Export Empire. German Soft Power in Southeastern Europe, 1890–1945. Cambridge: Cambridge University Press.

Grünbacher, A. 2001. The Early Years of a German Institution: The Kreditanstalt für Wiederaufbau in the 1950s. Business History 43 (4), 68–86.

Grünbacher, A. 2004. Reconstruction and Cold War in Germany: The Kreditanstalt Für Wiederaufbau (1948–1961). Aldershot: Ashgate Publishing.

Harries, H. 1998. Wiederaufbau, Welt und Wende: Die KfW—Eine Bank mit öffentlichem Auftrag. Frankfurt am Main: Knapp.

Instituição Financeira de Desenvolvimento (IFD) 2015. Annual Report (Relatório e Contas 2015). Porto: IFD.

Katzenstein, P.J. 1989. Industry and Politics in West Germany. Toward the Third Republic. Ithaca: Cornell University Press.

KfW, 2018. KfW at a Glance. Facts and Figures. Frankfurt: KfW Group.

KfW Archive HA-AS19. "Dr. Engel, Aufsätze und Vorträge (16–29), Band II, und Diverses (1969–1978)". Berlin: Historisches Konzernarchiv der KfW.

KfW Archive HA-VW21. "Dr. Hankel, Akte/1, 1953–1965". Berlin: Historisches Konzernarchiv der KfW.

KfW Archive HA-VW7. "Statistisches Material, 1972–1974". Berlin: Historisches Konzernarchiv der KfW.

Knill, C., and D. Lehmkuhl. 2002. The National Impact of European Union Regulatory Policy: Three Europeanization Mechanisms. European Journal of Political Research 41 (2), 255–80.

Ladrech, R. 1994. The Europeanization of Domestic Politics and Institutions: The Case of France. Journal of Common Market Studies 32 (1), 69–88.

Levi-Faur, D. 2005. The Global Diffusion of Regulatory Capitalism. The ANNALS of the American Academy of Political and Social Science 598 (1), 12–32.

Mazzucato, M., and Penna, C., 2015. The Rise of Mission-Oriented State Investment Banks: The Cases of Germany's KfW and Brazil's BNDES. SWPS 2015–26. Available at SSRN: https://ssrn.com/abstract=2744613.

Mertens, D. 2017. Putting "Merchants of Debt" in Their Place: The Political Economy of Retail Banking and Credit-Based Financialization in Germany. New Political Economy 22(1), 12–30.

Mertens, D., Thiemann, M., 2019. Building a Hidden Investment State? The European Investment Bank, National Development Banks and European Economic Governance. Journal of European Public Policy 26, 23–43.

Moslener, U., Thiemann, M., and Volberding, P. 2018. National Development Banks as Active Financiers: The Case of KfW, in S. Griffith-Jones and J.A. Ocampo (eds), The Future of National Development Banks, Oxford: Oxford University Press, 63–85.

Münnich, S. 2016. Readjusting Imagined Markets: Morality and Institutional Resilience in The German and British Bank Bailout of 2008. Socio-Economic Review 14 (2), 283–307.

Naqvi, N., Henow A., and Chang, H.-J. 2018. Kicking Away the Financial Ladder? German Development Banking under Economic Globalisation. Review of International Political Economy 25 (5), 672–98.

Nedergaard, P. 2019. The Ordoliberalisation of the European Union? Journal of European Integration 42 (2), 213–230.

Nölke, A., and Vliegenthart, A. 2009. Enlarging the Varieties of Capitalism: The Emergence of Dependent Market Economies in East Central Europe. World Politics 61 (4), 670–702.

Shonfield, A. 1965. Modern Capitalism. The Changing Balance of Public and Private Power. Oxford: Oxford University Press.

Smith, M.P. 2013. The Global Diffusion of Public Policy: Power Structures and Democratic Accountability. Territory, Politics, Governance 1 (2), 118–31.

Story, J., and Walter, I. 1997. Political Economy of Financial Integration in Europe: The Battle of the Systems. Manchester: Manchester University Press.

Volberding, P. 2018. Marketizing Development: KfW and the Rise of Financial Instruments for Development. Dissertation. Harvard Government Department.

Webber, D. 2001. New Europe, New Germany, Old Foreign Policy? German Foreign Policy Since Unification. London: Cass.

Weber, K., Davies, G.F., and Lounsbury, M. 2009. Policy as Myth and Ceremony? The Global Spread of Stock Exchanges, 1980–2005. Academy of Management Journal 52 (6), 1319–47.

Wedel, J.R. 2001. Collision and Collusion. The Strange Case of Western Aid to Eastern Europe. New York: St. Martin's Griffin.

Winkler, A. 1999. Promotional Banks as an Instrument for Improving the Financing Situation of Small and Medium-Sized Enterprises in the Transition Economies of Central and Eastern Europe: Some Observations Based on the Development of the German Financial System, Würzburg Economic Papers, No. 2e, University of Würzburg.

Zavisca, J.R. 2012. Housing the New Russia. Ithaca: Cornell University Press.

APPENDIX 5.1

# List of Interviews

#1 Interview KfW official, May 24, 2016, Frankfurt
#2 Interview KfW officials, April 24, 2018, Frankfurt
#3 Interview German Ministry for Economic Affairs, September 27, 2018, Berlin
#4 Interview KfW official, October 17, 2018, Frankfurt
#5 Interview EC official, October 10, 2018, Brussels
#6 Interview EC officials, March 27, 2019, Brussels
#7 Interview NDB lobbyist, March 27 2019, Brussels
#8 Interview EIB official, March 28, 2019, Luxembourg

# 6

# Privatization, Crisis, and the Transformation of Cassa Depositi e Prestiti

*Fabio Bulfone and Donato Di Carlo*

## 6.1 Introduction

State intervention has always been the defining feature of Italian capitalism (Molina and Rhodes, 2006; Schmidt, 2002; Shonfield, 1965). Historically, the Italian state had a ubiquitous presence in the economy, acting as a fully fledged entrepreneur through an extensive network of public utilities and state-owned enterprises (Martinelli,1981; Prodi, 1974). Direct state ownership spanned many sectors including banking, oil and gas, electricity, iron and steel, chemicals, motorways, and telecommunications (Cassese, 2014; De Cecco and Pedone, 1995). The centrality of state intervention makes Italy and its NDB *Cassa Depositi e Prestiti* (CDP) an ideal vantage point to explore the field of development banking—which, by its very nature, sits at the intersection between states and markets.

At the core of the Italian post-war model lays a complementarity between the banking sector, then predominantly publicly-owned (Ciocca, 2004), and the tight control over the banking and credit system exercised by the Bank of Italy (Lutz, 1962). Before the restructuring of the 1990s, the banking sector comprised five types of credit institution which engaged mostly in short-term lending (Ceriani, 1962). The provision of medium and long-term credit for real-estate investment, as well as industrial and infrastructural development, was instead the task of a plethora of "special institutes" which mushroomed throughout the 20th century, making the Italian field of development banking rather crowded[1]. For instance, the *Consorzio di Credito per le Opere Pubbliche* (Crediop) was created in 1919 with the participation of several Italian credit institutions (among which was the CDP) to fund public works while the *Istituto di Credito per le Imprese di Pubblica Utilita'* (ICIPU) was established in 1924 to finance strategic public infrastructure (e.g. electricity and telephone grids and hydroelectric plants). Both institutions raised capital in the bond markets, enjoying a state guarantee (Asso

[1] The brief review which follows is based on Ceriani (1962, 141–51) and Cassese (2014, 247–90).

Fabio Bulfone and Donato Di Carlo, *Privatization, Crisis, and the Transformation of Cassa Depositi e Prestiti* In: *The Reinvention of Development Banking in the European Union: Industrial Policy in the Single Market and the Emergence of a Field.* Edited by: Daniel Mertens, Matthias Thiemann, and Peter Volberding, Oxford University Press (2021).  DOI: 10.1093/oso/9780198859703.003.0006

and De Cecco, 1994). The *Istituto Mobiliare Italiano* (IMI) was launched in 1931 to sustain the recapitalization of Italian industry through medium/long-term lending and the acquisition of equity stakes in strategic corporations. *Mediocredito* was founded in 1952 to support small and medium enterprises (SMEs) in the industrial sector with shipping credit and export financing. The *Cassa per il Mezzogiorno* (CASMEZ) was instituted in 1950 to overcome the socio-economic backwardness of the Southern part of the country through strategic infrastructural investments and industrialization (Felice, 2007; Felice and Lepore, 2013). Along similar lines, after the war, the Italian government put pressure on its European peers for the establishment of a European Investment Fund meant to protect structurally weaker economies from the liberalizing pressures arising from the four freedoms enshrined in the European Economic Community. The fund was to be the forerunner of the European Investment Bank (EIB) established in 1958. From its establishment until the 1990s, the EIB would channel a large share of its development aid to the *Mezzogiorno*, operating in conjunction with CASMEZ (Bussière, Dumolin, and Willaert, 2008, Ch.2).

This brief historical excursus shows how, throughout its history, CDP was neither the sole nor the major institution active within the field of development banking in Italy. Yet, while the wave of privatizations and liberalization has since the 1990s wiped out the other domestic developmental institutions, CDP has instead broadened its scope and mandate, becoming the pivotal player in the Italian development banking field. This rise to prominence required a radical process of internal restructuring whose watershed moment can be traced to the 2003 transformation into a joint-stock company. The privatization of CDP paved the way for a broadening of its mandate, gradually transforming CDP into a full-fledged NDB. In fact, CDP has evolved from being a Directorate-General within the Treasury to becoming today, as the *CDP Group*[2], the country's third largest lender—with over €400bn in total assets (Figure 6.1). Besides growing in size, CDP broadened the scope of its activities and has become increasingly active domestically, but also at the European and international level. This foreign expansion took off in particular after the launch of the Juncker Plan. As a result of this process, CDP now fulfils three key roles within the Italian model of capitalism. First, it acts as a full-fledged NDB which, like its large European counterparts, provides credit to SMEs, finances infrastructural investment and social housing projects, and supports the internationalization of strategic firms. Second, it

[2] Hereinafter, the chapter deals only with CDP S.p.A., and not with the overall CDP Group. "The Group" was formed during 2012 as a result of a consolidation and reorganization of CDP Spa's subsidiaries. In addition to the parent company CDP Spa, the reorganization included within the scope of the group: CDP GAS S.r.l. ("CDP GAS"), CDP RETI S.r.l. ("CDP RETI"), CDP Investimenti Società di Gestione del Risparmio, S.p.A. ("CDPI SGR"), Fintecna S.p.A. ("Fintecna"), Fondo Strategico Italiano S.p.A. ("FSI"), SACE S.p.A. ("SACE"), Simest S.p.A. ("SIMEST") and Terna S.p.A. ("Terna") and their subsidiaries and associates. For more details see CDP (2012, 18–31).

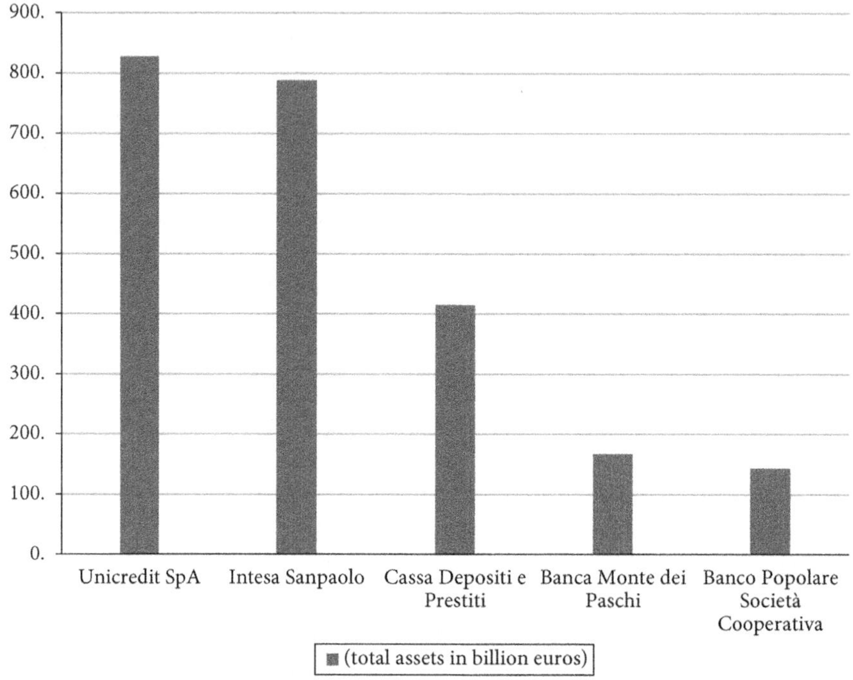


**Figure 6.1** CDP Group's balance sheet in relation to the largest Italian banks in the first half of 2017

*Source*: *Statista* 2019. N.B. Data for Cassa Depositi e Prestiti here refers to CDP Group

provides financial support to the Italian sovereign via two channels: the liquidity deposited in a bank account held at the Treasury and the purchasing of Italian sovereign bonds. Third, CDP acts as a state holding, having progressively acquired large minority stakes in domestic companies operating in strategic economic sectors (Ninni, 2013, pp. 153–4).

The present chapter analyses this transformation, focusing in particular on the post-privatization period when most of today's CDP defining traits were set out. We focus only on the parent company CDP S.p.A. (simply CDP hereinafter). Section 6.2 provides a bird-eye perspective on the historical origins of CDP, tracing the most significant regulatory and organizational changes which resulted from the privatization process onwards. The second part of the chapter illustrates in detail the progressive broadening of CDP's mandate since its partial privatization. Section 6.3 analyzes CDP's activities in the aftermath of the privatization and until the Eurozone crisis, when a series of regulatory changes paved the way for a further broadening of CDP's mandate. The post-crisis period is covered in detail in section 6.4. In section 6.5 we survey the European dimension of CDP's activities with a particular focus on its involvement in the Juncker Plan. Lastly, a concluding section takes stock of our findings, trying to delineate the main features of the Italian development banking field.

## 6.2 Between Path-Dependence and Innovation: An Overview of CDP's Regulatory and Organizational Transformations

Italy was among the first countries in Europe to equip itself with a NDB. CDP's establishment actually predates the foundation of the Italian unitary state. Its creation was an idea of the Piedmontese elite ruling over the Kingdom of Sardinia, the forerunner of the Kingdom of Italy. CDP's predecessor[3] was founded in Turin in 1840, borrowing the idea from the French *Caisse des dépôts et consignations* (CDC) (De Cecco and Toniolo, 2014, 7). CDP was established in 1850 and eventually institutionalized within the Italian legal system in 1863 (Battilossi, 1999, 98), after the country was unified in 1861.

In 1875 CDP became the "central bank" of the country's postal offices, which were allowed to offer retail customers savings accounts protected by the state's guarantee. Given the widespread diffusion of postal offices across the Italian peninsula, the reform aimed at mobilizing the savings of the rural population through CDP to use them for the implementation of works of public utility. The state guarantee was crucial to overcoming the time inconsistency problem arising between deposits which were risk-averse and eligible to be refunded at short-term and the long-term strategic mission of investment for the early infrastructural development of the country (De Cecco and Toniolo, 2001, XVIII).

Thus, throughout its history and until privatization in 2003, CDP retained an exclusive focus on public entities and, besides financing the provision of public goods, fulfilled the crucial social function of introducing rural segments of the Italian society into saving. Postal savings have in fact constituted the bulk of CDP's funding ever since 1875. Postal savings are collected via two financial instruments: the postal passbook savings accounts (*libretti postali*), and the postal savings bonds (*buoni postali fruttiferi*).

From its infancy, CDP was called to carry out two main functions which remain important today. CDP's first core function, and purpose for its establishment, was to provide funding at favorable rates to subnational governments for investment in public infrastructures and anticipate payments by the public administration. The second function was to finance the central government, i.e. the Treasury, through two main channels: the purchasing of sovereign bonds and the provision of the abundant liquidity originating from the postal savings. This liquidity is provided via a current account held by CDP within the Treasury (Bassanini, 2015b, 440). These two functions have made up for the backbone of CDP's lending activities with the balance between the two being determined by the Treasury. In other words, while the private savings of Italian citizens determine the size of CDP's funding base, the distribution of lending activities between the Treasury and subnational governments is determined by the Treasury's

[3] Founded under the name of *Bank for deposits and anticipation of funds for public works*. See Battilossi (1999, 64–73); De Cecco and Toniolo (2001, XVI–XVIII).

liquidity needs (De Cecco and Toniolo, 2014, 14). Della Torre (2001, 10–11) shows that the provision of capital to subnational governments for infrastructural spending has been CDP's prevalent activity before 1895 and during the period 1945 to the mid-1970s, while the provision of liquidity to the Treasury has been predominant during the period 1900–1945 and after the mid-1970s. By the early 2000s, CDP's exposure vis-à-vis the Treasury amounted to 60 percent of CDP's assets and CDP's liquidity within the Treasury constituted 15 percent of the Treasury's total debt (Battilossi, 2014, 61).

### 6.2.1 CDP's Privatization

At the end of 2003, the ruling center-right coalition led by Silvio Berlusconi opted for the formal privatization[4] of CDP. *De jure*, CDP was separated from the state and transformed into a private entity under the legal form of a joint-stock company (*Societa' per Azioni, S.p.a.*). A 30 percent equity share was acquired by 65 domestic banking foundations, yielding proceeds of 1.048bn euros (MEF, 2005, 17). The remaining 70 percent stayed[5] with the Ministry of the Economy and Finance (MEF). At the same time, part of CDP's liquidity deposited in the Treasury (a total of approx. 160.5bn in 2002) was employed by the MEF to transfer to CDP participations in key state-owned public utilities[6]. This operation contributed to a 11 billion euros reduction of Italy's public debt stock (Banca D'Italia, 2004, 67), all the while preventing the loss of *de facto* control[7] over strategic domestic firms.

CDP's legal mutation is best understood in relation to the structural constraints imposed by the process of monetary and economic integration in Europe (EMU) and by the EU competition policy framework. On the latter aspect, the creation of a single market implied a stricter pan-European regulation of state aid (see Volberding, this volume), subsidies and public procurements, meant to reduce the scope for state intervention in the economy (Thatcher, 2014). With regard to the former, by signing the Maastricht treaty, Italian policy makers purposefully committed to a *vincolo esterno* (Dyson and Featherstone, 1996), i.e. to a supranational

[4] Art. 5 D.L. n. 269, September 30, 2003; transformed into law through L. n. 326, November 24, 2003.

[5] A provision of the Law Decree 269/2003 mandated that the Treasury should always retain the absolute majority of the shares.

[6] The government sold a 10.35% equity interest in the electricity provider *ENEL* (for 3.15bn euros), 10% in the multinational oil and gas company *ENI* (for 5.31bn euros) and 35% in the postal services provider *Poste Italiane* (for 2.51bn euros).

[7] Through a decree from June 18, 2004 (n.59627), the MEF established the criteria for the management of the participations by CDP. In every action regarding the management of its portfolio of participations, CDP S.p.a. is subjected to *prior* and *binding* consultation with the MEF. CDP is obliged to reach an agreement with the MEF prior to any operation aimed at disinvesting or transferring CDP's equity stakes in the participations. See Corte Dei Conti (2008, 109).

regime which pre-empts the full-fledged use of domestic fiscal policy by a severely indebted sovereign. Thus, throughout the 1990s Italy underwent a process of fiscal adjustment (Chiorazzo and Spaventa, 1999; Spaventa and Chiorazzo, 2000) not compatible with the generous pattern of fiscal spending underpinning the state-led model of development of the post-war era (Barca, 1999; Cassese, 2014; De Cecco and Pedone, 1995; Shonfield, 1965).

Needing additional financial resources to shore-up public finances, the government launched the largest wave of privatizations in Western Europe (Barucci and Pierobon, 2007; 2010). Moreover, it sharply reduced expenditures for public investment (gross fixed investment), which declined from 3.6 percent of GDP in the mid-1980s to about 2 percent in the mid-1990s. As a result, by the early 2000s, it was widely acknowledged that Italy's infrastructural endowment lagged behind its European peers (especially with respect to the railway system, airports and electricity grids) (Battilossi, 2014, 72–77; De Cecco and Toniolo, 2014, 15). Willing to address these urgent issues through the implementation of a more activist industrial policy, but limited in its fiscal capacity by the constraints of the Stability and Growth Pact (SGP), the government engineered the privatization of CDP in order to exclude its balance sheet from public debt calculations, as was already the case for the French CDC and the German KfW (Interview 1) (De Cecco and Toniolo, 2014, 16–17). As long as CDP was part of the public administration, in fact, Eurostat considered postal savings as *liabilities* of the public administration vis-à-vis the private savers, therefore including them in public debt calculations. With the transformation of CDP into a market unit, postal savings would be excluded from these calculations, paving the way for the expansion of CDP off the government's books. As a necessary condition to carrying out this operation, Eurostat asked the government to open CDP's capital to private investors, which led the Minister of Finance, Giulio Tremonti, to turn to banking foundations.

Banking foundations are not-for-profit organizations engaged in charitable and philanthropic activities, which they fund thanks to the bank dividends they receive as shareholders (McCann, 2007). In Italy, their origins date back to the early 1990s when, through a series of legislative acts, the government decided to privatize the traditional *Casse di Risparmio* (savings banks) owned by public authorities (the state, local government or foundations). The government imposed the transformation of publicly-owned savings banks into joint-stock companies, and to shelter them from foreign takeovers it created 89 foundations that acted as trustees for the newly-privatized banks' capital (Giorgino and Tasca 1999). Although the foundations were required to gradually hand over control over the banks, only one fourth of them has fully disinvested from their original banks (Jassaud 2014).

Various features of the banking foundations made them suitable as CDP's shareholders in the eyes of the government (De Cecco and Toniolo, 2014, 17–20). First, foundations are well rooted in local communities across the peninsula. This made them an attractive partner for CDP in two ways. First, they would be a precious source of political and economic information regarding the territories in which the Rome-based CDP would have to operate its lending activities thereby minimizing information asymmetry. Second, the banking foundations constituted the perfect match with CDP's public interest mission (Interview 5) given their nature as patient institutional investors attentive to lending profitability, sustainable growth and the welfare of local communities[8] (Bassanini, 2011; Bassanini and Gorno Tempini, 2014). Third, in a country with a bank-based credit system, an underdeveloped stock exchange, few institutional investors, and with the main domestic banks busy with a process of state-led consolidation (Bulfone, 2017) foundations were the only financial investors that had the financial capacity to buy a large stake in CDP.

Tremonti saw the involvement of banking foundations also as a way to stabilize the banking sector during the delicate process of consolidation that was underway in Italy as well as in other European countries (Interview 1)[9]. In fact, the foundations were allowed to participate in the redistribution of the high dividend yields of the profitable companies which the Treasury had transferred to CDP. Since the foundations were the controlling shareholders of most Italian banks, Tremonti hoped that channeling the dividends towards the foundations would indirectly strengthen the ownership structure of the main domestic banks. Indeed, the investment in CDP has proved rather remunerative, with foundations earning more than 1.08bn between 2004 and 2011 (Battilossi, 2014, 91). As a result of their entry into CDP's ownership, the foundations enjoy voting rights and veto powers in the annual general meetings; appoint one third of CDP's Board members and appoint the majority of members in other governance institutions.

In sum, despite having been initially driven by budgetary constraints, the privatization had a profound impact on the field of development banking, opening CDP's ownership to a new actor: private banking foundations. Furthermore, the new statute adopted after privatization paved the way for the progressive broadening of CDP's mandate and its transformation into a full-fledged NDB, a process we describe in detail in the next three sections of the chapter.

[8] As Giuseppe Guzzetti, president of *ACRI* (the organization for the representation of the foundations), put it: "Our presence in the capital of CDP is the arrival point of a long-term trajectory. Today we are called to inaugurate a new path and to guarantee . . . the growth of the country, especially through our presence in local communities which is guaranteed by our extensive presence in the Italian territory" (authors' translation from Italian). See Righi (2007).

[9] Tremonti's offer was also a political move to normalize the relationship with the banking sector which was at the time rather tense (Interview 2). In fact, in 2001 Tremonti had tried to limit the private nature and the statutory autonomy of the foundations through a legislative act with which it increased the political control over their board. The foundations appealed to the Constitutional Court winning the case and defending their autonomy (Filtri, Guglielmi, and Carzana, 2014, 14).

### 6.2.2 Organizational Changes

CDP S.p.a. has been reconfigured with a hybrid system of corporate governance in which public and private logics coexist within the new privatized entity. As a sign of continuity, legislation re-established CDP's mission along its historical lines of activity: the financing of any public-law entity using repayable funds rose from postal savings and the financing of the construction or upgrading of public service infrastructures. All of these activities must be conducted ensuring adequate returns on investment for the shareholders and preserving long-term financial stability. As a novelty, the legislation now allowed CDP to "raise funds through the issue of securities, borrowing and other financial operations without state guarantees" (CDP, 2005, 19).

As a result, the new CDP became subject to a twofold organizational and accounting separation. Activities of general economic interest which employ postal funding under state guarantee are operated through the *separate account* in conformity with general guidelines established by the MEF[10]. All other activities are carried out through the *ordinary account,* under market-oriented logics, and with the employment of resources from institutional investors in financial markets or banks. This organizational change was necessary to comply with EU regulations on state aid and domestic competition. Given the state guarantee which postal funding enjoys in light of its social and economic importance, EU regulations required CDP to distinguish between functions of public interest with a state guarantee from other market operations to be conducted in competition with other market players (CDP, 2012, 21).

In terms of supervision, CDP has been subjected to the "informative supervision" by the Bank of Italy, but no regulation specific to CDP has been issued so far. Similar to other development institutions, CDP is classified as an "Other Monetary Financial Institution" by the ECB. It is subjected to the Eurosystem's reserve requirement, but neither to the Capital Requirements Directive (2013/36/EU; CRD IV) nor the Capital Requirements Regulation (575/2013; CRR). CDP is subjected to the monitoring of a bicameral Parliamentary Commission (Commissione di vigilanza sulla Cassa Depositi e Prestiti) and the scrutiny of the National Court of Auditors (Corte dei Conti).

Besides these accounting and regulatory innovations, CDP has undergone a profound transformation with respect to its workforce. The changes have been substantial both in *quantitative* and *qualitative* terms. Table 6.1 documents CDP's staff expansion over the period 2005–2018. Since the crisis, the number of total employees almost doubled, up to 787 from 434 in 2010. Of these, the biggest

[10] Through a decree from October 6th 2004, the MEF sets out the criteria for determining the terms and conditions of lending and funding under the separate account, although guaranteeing CDP with operational autonomy (CDP 2005, 21–4) It also established postal savings as a service of general economic interest.

**Table 6.1** CDP's personnel structure

| Year | 31/12/2005 | 31/12/2010 | 31/12/2018 |
|---|---|---|---|
| Total employees *(numbers)* | 426 | 434 | 797 |
| Senior Management *(dirigenti)* | 32 | 37 | 82 |
| Middle Management *(quadri)* | 126 | 150 | 373 |
| Office employees *(impiegati)* | 268 | 247 | 324 |
| Average age | 48.5 | 45 | 44 |
| Female employment *(as % of total staff)* | n.a. | 42 | n.a. |
| University graduates* *(as % of total staff)* | 33 | 52 | 73 |

*Source*: Authors' elaboration based on CDP's annual financial statements. *Bachelor' or master's degree, doctorate or other post-graduate qualification

expansion is registered among middle management positions. In 2006 a new "performance-oriented" system of human resource management was introduced to enable the management to assess employees' performance on the basis of tasks and target specified *ex ante* (CDP, 2006, 47). Furthermore, in 2005 a far-reaching plan for personnel restructuring was implemented with the aim of hiring figures with the professional skills required to upgrade the company's skills profile in light of the company's new operations (CDP, 2005, 35). This process has gradually led to a reduction of 4.5 years in the employees' average age (from 48.5 in 2005 to 44 in 2018) and a remarkable increase in their educational level.

The new hiring policy has been coupled with the expansion of in-house and external training. The expansion of investment on training has been especially steep in the aftermath of the crisis (Figure 6.2). As of 2014, CDP provided an average of 32 yearly training hours[11] per employee—a fivefold increase vis-à-vis the immediate post-privatization period. Also, employees exchange programs have been established between CDP and the other major European NDBs (CDC, KfW, ICO, EIB) (CDP, 2011, 95) to generate synergies aimed at ensuring the reciprocal transfer of knowledge and generating opportunities to work together (CDP, 2011, 111).

This gradual transformation in the profile of CDP's staff is evident also when looking at the first line of management with a growing number of executives coming from previous experiences in private investment banking. Since the privatization, CDP has seen a broadening of its mandate, in a dynamic that further accelerated as Italy got embroiled in the Eurozone crisis. As a result, in less than two decades, CDP went from fulfilling relatively simple tasks such as financing the public administration and managing postal savings, to acting as a full-fledged

[11] CDP provides employees with technical training in the areas of financial, administrative and regulatory matters together with IT skills and English language.

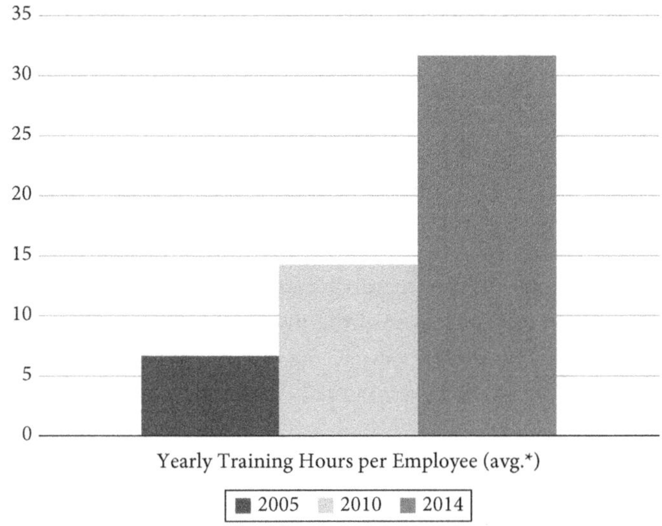


**Figure 6.2** Yearly training hours offered by CDP to its employees
*Source*: Authors' elaboration based on CDP's annual reports, various years
*Note*: calculated as "total employees"/"Yearly Training Hours". Data on training hours not available after 2014

"public investment bank." This transformation, which we analyze in more detail in the following sections, required the acquisition of expertise on issues including synthetic investment products, securitization, foreign currency transactions and equity that was available only in the private sector (interviews 3 and 4). The opening of CDP's ownership to private investors, its transformation into a joint-stock company and the growing weight of managers with previous experience in the private sector contributed to increasing CDP's room for maneuver vis-à-vis the executive. While on the one hand, as private investors, the foundations share a concern for the profitability of their investment, thereby opposing investments with uncertain prospects. On the other, the new managerial team brought procedures for the evaluation of new investment projects in line with those applied by private investment banks. In the words of CDP's CFO: "CDP is not an institution dealing with economic policy, CDP is a *national promotional institution*. Interventions in support of some sectors that go beyond the logic of the market cannot be financed with CDP's deposits and loans... Operations of vertical industrial policy should be done by someone else" (Interview 3).

## 6.3 The Short 2000s: CDP's Early Operations in the Aftermath of Privatization

Having described the internal legal and organizational transformation of CDP resulting from its transformation into a joint-stock company and privatization, we will now provide a detailed analysis of the process of gradual expansion and diversification of its mandate. Throughout the last two decades, along with its historical functions of lender to public entities for infrastructural investment and financier of the central government through its liquidity holdings within the Treasury and bonds' purchases, CDP has progressively taken up new roles in support of the Italian economy. It is possible to distinguish two phases in this transformation, with the crisis acting as a watershed moment (Figure 6.3). During the first phase, the main novelties in CDP's undertakings consisted in the start of lending for infrastructural investment through the ordinary account for project and corporate finance operations, and the undertaking of a new role as holding company of state-owned enterprises. It was after 2009 that further legislative changes paved the way for CDP's expansion in support of the enterprise sector (see section 6.4).

The first operations conducted through ordinary account lending were initiated in 2005. The ordinary account comprises lending activities funded through several sources: the emission of Euro Medium Term Notes (EMTN) and multi-currency commercial papers; repurchase agreements; credit lines with the European Investment Bank (EIB), the European Central Bank (ECB) and the Council of Europe Development Bank (CEB). CDP has granted an average of 1.1bn euros per year (calculations based on CDP's financial reports) of new loans for operations of project finance or corporate finance (e.g. providing loans to public utilities, i.e. firms operating in the energy, logistics and the construction sector, or universities).

After privatization CDP took up as well the role of holding of state-owned public utilities. In 2003 the Finance Ministry transferred to CDP the participations previously held by the government in Enel S.p.a., ENI S.P.A. and Poste Italiane S.p.a. Apart from its positive repercussions on public finances, the operation was deemed strategic for at least two reasons (Corte Dei Conti, 2008, 109). First, given that Poste Italiane collects postal savings on behalf of CDP through its offices, receiving a fee for this service, the acquisition of a stake in Poste by CDP strengthened the mutual relationship between the two firms. Secondly, remunerative participations in Enel and Eni help diversifying CDP's revenue stream besides proceeds from financial intermediation and liquidity holdings in the Treasury[12]. In December 2004, CDP acquired from Finmeccanica S.p.a. a 10 percent indirect equity interest in STMicroelectronics N.V.—a strategic Italian-French company, global leader in research and development of semiconductors and high-tech products. In September 2005, CDP acquired a 29.99 percent equity stake in Terna S.p.a., the high-voltage electricity provider and operator of the national electricity grid. The operation came under the spotlight of the Italian Energy

[12] In 2004 CDP earned 207.1m euros in dividends from Enel. In 2005, it earned 925.6m euros in dividends mostly generated by Eni and Enel. In 2006 it earned 1.037bn euros in dividends with the greatest part coming from Eni, Enel and Terna. See Corte Dei Conti (2008, 117).

| | | | | |
|---|---|---|---|---|
| **Public Entities exclusive focus** | 1850 | Loans to local authorities | | |
| **Privatisation and development of infrastructure segment** | 2003 -> 2009 | *Ordinary Account* | Revolving Fund for Enterprises | |
| | | *F2i Fund* | Terna Acquisition | |
| **Expansion of mission to companies** | 2009 -> 2010 | *Marguerite Fund* | SME support funds | |
| **Transformation and development in globalization and venture capital** | 2010 -> | Fondo Investimenti per l'Abitare (FIA) | Export Bank Agreement | *Inframed Infrastructure Fund* |
| | | Post-disaster reconstruction Fund | Increase equity investment in ENI | European Energy Efficiency Fund (EEEF) |
| | | Fondo Italiano di Investimento (FII) | Fondo Strategico Italiano | Kyoto Fund |
| | 2012 | Fintecna acquisition | SACE and SIMEST acquisition | Fincantieri Acquisition |
| | | SNAM acquisition | Fondo Investimenti per la Valorizzazione (FIV) | Advances on general government payables |
| | | IV Qatar/FSI for "made in Italy" | Streamlining of equity portfolio | IV KIA/FSI "FSI Investment" |
| | | HomeFund | Capital Goods Fund | Enterprises Platform Fund |
| | | FII -Private Debt FII -Venture Capital | European Investment Fund | |

Functions by categories: Public Entities and Territory / *Infrastructure* / Enterprises / Strategic Assets.

**Figure 6.3** Snapshot of the evolution of CDP's main activities (1850–2012)

*Source*: authors' elaboration based on CDP, 2012, p. 11.

watchdog (AEEG) for the possible emergence of a dominant position in the electricity market due to CDP's combined ownership of both the main electricity provider (Enel) and the grid operator (Terna). Eventually, the Antitrust authorized the operation conditionally on CDP selling its participation in Enel. In 2010 CDP and the MEF engineered a swap of participations to comply with the regulators' requirements. CDP transferred back to the MEF its stakes in Enel, Poste and STMicroelectronics in exchange for a 16.38 percent stake in Eni. With these ownership transfers the government aimed at curbing Italy's public debt, so to avoid breaching the SGP fiscal criteria, all the while preventing the loss of control over strategic state-owned enterprises.

In parallel, decidedly more international, CDP gradually entered the private equity segment starting in September 2006, when it acquired 40 percent of the shares in Galaxy S.àr.l. ("Galaxy")—a Luxembourg company investing in transportation infrastructure projects on the initiative of other NDBs—and established the F2i SGR investment fund in partnership with a number of leading Italian pension funds and banking foundations, Italy's two largest banking groups (Intesa Sanpaolo and UniCredit) and two global investment banks (Lehman Brothers and Merrill Lynch). In December 2009, CDP launched, together with the EIB and other leading European NDBs, the "2020 European Fund for Energy, Climate Change and Infrastructure SICAV-FIS Sa," aka the "Marguerite fund" to finance programs in the energy, environmental and transport sectors in across the EU.

## 6.4 The 2010s: The Eurozone Crisis and CDP's Transformation

Italy escaped a financial crisis and survived the first phase of the Eurozone crisis well owing to the retail focus of its banking sector. However, the anemic growth of the economy and the weakness of the then-ruling Centre-Right executive led market operators to question the sovereign's capacity to service its enormous public debt, leading since 2011 to a dramatic worsening of borrowing conditions on the bond market.

Italy's involvement in the Eurozone crisis had a profound impact on the economy. Between 2008 and 2015 the index of manufacturing production fell by 22 percent (Lucchese, Nascia, and Pianta, 2016). This contraction was in turn triggered by a dramatic decline in the level of private and public investment (Bassanini and Reviglio, 2014)—from an already low pre-crisis level. It is in this context of systemic crisis and severe budgetary constraints that CDP was asked to expand its mandate in support of the Italian economy through "off-balance sheet" interventions (Mertens and Thiemann, 2018). As with CDP's privatization, foreign models like KFW, CDC and BNDES were decisive sources of inspiration for this transformation (Bassanini, 2015a).

In agreement with the government, CDP reacted to the aggravation of the structural weaknesses of the Italian economy by broadening the scope of its activities. In the initial phase of the crisis, CDP focused on channeling funding towards SMEs via the banking sector in order to tackle the credit crunch. Since 2014, as credit conditions somewhat improved but growth remained elusive and investment levels low, the management switched the focus to the provision of patient equity investment, risk-sharing instruments and joint financial products (Interview 4).

The first step in CDP's post-crisis transformation took place in 2011 when its mandate was broadened allowing for the acquisition of participations in companies considered strategic by virtue of their sector of activity, level of employment, revenue, or their impact on the Italian production system. At the insistence of banking foundations, CDP was allowed to invest only in firms in a stable financial equilibrium and characterized by adequate prospects of profitability (Bassanini, 2015a; Chamber of Deputies, 2014).

This legal reform laid the foundation for the creation of the holding company Italian Strategic Fund (ISF). Initially endowed with a capital of EUR 4.4bn, the ISF was created to provide long-term equity investment through the acquisition of large stakes in strategic firms. To prevent CDP from investing in loss-making and non-strategic companies, a 2014 Law Decree established that the ISF should be allowed to invest only in specific strategic sectors. When operating outside these sectors, the ISF could invest only in firms with a net annual turnover of not less than EUR 300m and at least 250 employees. Finance minister Tremonti supported the creation of ISF in a failed attempt to prevent the takeover of the Italian diary multinational Parmalat by the French Lactalis (Interview 5) (Battilossi, 2014). The fund's ultimate goal is to favor the emergence of sizeable global players (La Repubblica, 2015), thereby tackling one of the historical weaknesses of Italian capitalism: the shortage of large global multinationals. Since 2012 the ISF has acquired participations in different sectors including telecommunications networks, pharmaceuticals, electricity engineering, tourism and oilfield services.

In 2016 CDP rebranded the ISF CDP Equity as part of a planned reorganization of its holdings. The rationale behind this change was to differentiate between a portfolio of long-term holdings and shorter-term investments in high-growth potential companies (CDP, 2018). During the crisis, the Treasury continued as well to transfer stakes of state-owned firms to CDP as a way to obtain short-term financial relief. Consequently, CDP now owns stakes in ENI, Fincantieri, Poste Italiane and the energy network operators Snam, Terna, and Italgas.

CDP's equity investments are part of a broader effort to provide financing to strategic and high-growth potential firms throughout their entire lifecycle, for which, according to the 2019–2021 business plan, CDP aspires to mobilize EUR 83bn through a leverage effect (CDP, 2018, 93). CDP aims at helping firms from their establishment, with the ambition of becoming the main player in Italy's venture capital market, to their eventual restructuring after an industrial crisis. To this end CDP participates as anchor investor in the "QuattroR SGR" fund specializing in the industrial turnaround of firms which, despite financial problems, have adequate growth prospects (CDP, 2015). The participation in the "QuattroR SGR" fund required a further broadening of CDP's mandate to allow investments in unprofitable companies on the basis of special conditions (Giachetti Fantini 2018). As with the French Bpifrance (see Thiemann and Volberding's chapter), in the aftermath of the crisis CDP stepped up its operations in support of the internationalization of Italian companies acting as an integrated "Export Bank" (CDP, 2015, 26). CDP's emergence as Italy's reference export-supporter involved, as well, the acquisition of the state-owned export agencies SACE and SIMEST in 2012. Like in the pre-privatization era, CDP maintained a focus on the development of the infrastructural networks and the financing of the public administration (for which, according to its investment plan, CDP envisages mobilizing up to EUR 25bn for the 2019–2021 period). In this regard, to tackle the huge drop in infrastructural investment in Italy, which reduced the number of investment projects that could be financed, CDP is taking a more pro-active role developing technical skills to stimulate the launch of new infrastructural projects (Interview 4). As part of the strengthening of the infrastructural network CDP is involved in the development of Italy's fiber-based internet network through its participation in Open Fiber, co-owned with the electricity company ENEL. Recently, CDP has progressively built up a 9.89 percent stake in the former telecommunications monopolist Telecom Italia which is also investing in the fiber network hoping to create synergies between the two firms (Interview 3).

As part of its effort in support of the public administration CDP provides consulting services to local administrations to improve the management of European structural funds. CDP invests as well in real estate, focusing in particular on two goals: the enhancement of state-owned real estate assets and the strengthening of social housing. CDP focused on this latter goal in response to an impetus coming from the banking foundations (Interview 5) which conceived of social housing as an integral part of their mandate to foster the welfare of local communities (Interview 2). Since 2014 CDP has also been given the task of managing and coordinating the financial resources devoted to the financing of international development cooperation initiatives. This led CDP to take one of KFW's key functions. It should nevertheless be highlighted that, contrary to its German counterpart (see Mertens' chapter in this volume), CDP took up this role only recently and the resources allocated for this purpose are still very limited. For instance, for the period 2019–2021 CDP aims at mobilizing up to EUR 3bn (CDP, 2018, 2).

Apart from these main lines of intervention, due to the profound impact of the crisis CDP was called on to expand the scope of its operations in support of the economy and of public finances (interview 5). For instance, with a total commitment of EUR 820m CDP was one of the main investors in the private equity funds

Atlas I and Atlas II[13] (CDP, 2018). Created in 2016 the funds were tasked with the recapitalization and the management of non-performing loans of a group of ailing Italian banks, and in particular the two medium-sized lenders Banca Popolare di Vicenza and Veneto Banca. While most large private banks, including the two systemic Unicredit and Intesa-Sanpaolo only invested in Atlas I, CDP was the only large credit institution contributing to both funds. Due to the eventually negative outcome of the recapitalization operation, by 2018 CDP's stake in Atlas had lost most of its value (Moschella and Quaglia, 2020). The losses have been entirely borne by CDP's income statements, leading the Court of Auditors to question the investment as it did not appear to fulfil the minimal requirements in terms of profitability (Corte Dei Conti, 2019, 20; Giachetti Fantini, 2018). While CDP's management was aware of the risks inherent in this operation, it nevertheless deemed it necessary to prevent the spreading of systemic risk throughout the banking sector. According to the management this is in line with CDP's developmental mandate as financial stability is a necessary pre-condition for economic growth (Interview 4 and 5).

The rise in interest rates on Italy's sovereign bonds, and the contemporary increase of CDP's firepower due to the countercyclical nature of postal savings, led CDP to strengthen its long-term commitment to the provision of liquidity to the Treasury. Aiming to increase CDP's leverage in supporting the economy, in early 2016 the management and the Ministry of Finance agreed to increase the interest rate on the Treasury bank account. The additional resources coming from the increase in the remuneration of the bank account are vital to maintaining CDP's profitability levels. CDP provided another financial lifeline to the Treasury by embarking on a campaign of purchasing sovereign bonds. This bond purchasing campaign was launched when, at the peak of the crisis, the Treasury asked the main domestic credit institutions to intervene in the bond market to stabilize the interest rates (Interview 5). As a result, between 2007 and 2012 the value of government bonds held by CDP skyrocketed. From around 200 million euros it increased up to 21.4 billion (De Cecco and Toniolo, 2014, 255), eventually reaching 35 billion euros by 2015 (Bassanini, 2015a, 2–3). As of end of 2018 CDP holds 57 billion euros of government bonds (CDP, 2018, 184–404).

CDP's growing activism does not come fully uncontested. Potential tensions may arise due to the different priorities of the main stakeholders. In fact, CDP's management is tasked with a developmental mission, the banking foundations pursue a profitability-oriented policy of investment, but the government may have an incentive to pursue investment policies to maximize consent in the short-term. In fact, as seen in the introduction, Italy's situation is unique in the mismatch between an extremely large and financially strong NDB and a cash-strapped sovereign. Given this dynamic, the executive could theoretically put pressure on

[13] Atlas II was rebranded Italian Recovery Fund in 2017.

CDP's management to invest in projects that are neither strategic nor financially sustainable in the pursuit of short-term electoral gains (Bassanini, 2015a, 1; Macchiati, 2013, 293; Ninni, 2013, 151). However, there are a number of legal, supervisory and statutory barriers which contribute to limiting the scope for political interference on CDP's investment decisions. First, Eurostat considers CDP a "financial intermediary" therefore keeping it outside the scope of the Public Administration, meaning that its liabilities are not included in debt calculations. Eurostat's definition of "financial intermediary" states that the intermediary bears the bulk of the business risk and manages its activities under market conditions, in particular when granting loans. If CDP did not fulfill these requirements, it might lose its status (Osservatorio Conti Pubblici, 2018). Second, the ownership of CDP is open to private shareholders, the Banking Foundations, which by their nature seek to obtain financial returns on their investment, therefore having strong incentives to prevent inefficient investment allocations (Interview 3). Finally, CDP is subject to the control and supervision of the Italian Court of Auditors, the market watchdog Consob and the Italian Parliament (Osservatorio Conti Pubblici, 2018). Apart from these regulatory limitations, in contrast to other industrial holdings of the past like the conglomerate *Istituto di Ricostruzione Industriale* (IRI), CDP is managed by executives that have previous experiences in the private sector, and has internal procedures for the evaluation of the financial sustainability of potential investments that are similar to those of private investment banks.

During the crisis these different legal, statutory and supervisory constraints helped CDP's managers to resist calls to acquire stakes or provide financial support to loss-making companies. For instance, CDP decided not to invest in the chronically loss-making flagship carrier Alitalia despite pressure from the government to do so (Bassanini, 2015a, 1; La Repubblica, 2018), with banking foundations being particularly vocal in opposing the deal (Cillis, 2018). Similarly, CDP's management objected to the operation, finding that, although the firm could be considered strategic, the investment would not meet the standards in terms of financial sustainability (Interview 4 and 5).

At the end of 2018 CDP presented its business plan for 2019–2021, according to which it aspires to mobilize EUR 203bn in support of the Italian economy, of which EUR 111bn would come from own resources and an additional EUR 92bn from private investors and governmental authorities (CDP, 2018, 92).

## 6.5 The European Dimension and CDP's Involvement in the Juncker Plan

This internal restructuring was accompanied by a change in CDP's statute when, with the 2016 Budget Law, CDP was qualified as a "National Promotional Institution."

This was a necessary premise for participation in the European Fund for Strategic Investment (EFSI). EFSI is the central pillar of the Investment Plan for Europe (or Juncker Plan), the flagship economic proposal of the Juncker Commission (see Rubio and Thiemann; Griffith-Jones and Naqvi, both this volume).

The Juncker Plan required CDP to step up its European dimension, strengthening its ties with both the EIB and the other NDBs, and acting as a catalyzer between private and public and between the European and the domestic levels (Interview 3). CDP, the other NDBs and the EIB were called to join forces in different initiatives ranging from the co-investment in common projects, to the establishment of investment platforms (IPs). IPs are special instruments through which EFSI investment is channeled to fulfill specific goals at Member States' level (Mertens and Thiemann, 2018, 194).

What makes EFSI's funding particularly attractive for NDBs is the guarantee from the EU budget that allows the EIB to co-finance projects that would have a higher risk profile than the usual ones, thereby increasing leverage (see Griffith-Jones and Naqvi, this volume). The EFSI guarantee can be used to finance projects in a wide array of sectors across all EU Member States, and the type of support provided can be very varied (loans, guarantees/counter-guarantees, mezzanine and subordinated finance, equity or quasi-equity participations) (Rubio, 2018, 34). The EU guarantee on part of the credit risk is particularly important for CDP to reduce its risk profile and increase its lending activity (Interview 4). In fact, due to its strong ties with the Ministry of Finance, CDP has the same long-term rating as the Italian government, which is considerably lower than the triple A rating of the EIB or of KFW[14]. The attractiveness of the EU guarantee, coupled with expertise in channeling lending to the real economy acquired throughout the previous decade (Interview 3), explains why CDP was among the most active and successful NDBs in attracting EFSI funding. CDP was responsible for the setting up of all the three investment platforms approved under SMEW in 2016 and 2017 (European Court of Auditors, 2019). As a result, Italy received by far the largest financial inflow in the framework of the SMEW pillar: 4.8 of the 10.9 billion euros mobilized (European Court of Auditors, 2019, 49). Overall, in 2017 Italy was the second largest recipient of EFSI funding with euro 6.1 billion, close to France in first place with 6.3 billion (EIB and EIF 2018).

In the 2021–2027 budgetary framework, the EFSI structure will be integrated into the InvestEU Fund. The rationale behind the InvestEU initiative is to bring together under the same roof all the different investment and financing instruments provided by the EU. The target is to trigger at least euro 650 billion in additional investment with an EU budget guarantee of euro 38 billion. Although the EIB remains the privileged implementing partner of the EU for the InvestEU

[14] At the time of writing, November 2019, CDP had the following long-term ratings: BBB (Standard and Poor's), Baa3 (Moody's) and BBB (Fitch).

program, implementing 75 percent of the guarantee, unlike with EFSI, NDBs will have direct access to the remaining 25 percent of the EU guarantee. The possibility of NDBs having direct access to the EU guarantee sparked a heated debate between the EIB, NDBs and the European Commission (see Rubio and Thiemann, this volume). Like the other large NDBs, CDP was among the main supporters of the proposal to have direct access to the EU budget guarantee claiming that, due to its deeper knowledge of the local market of Italy, it could help improve effective channeling and strengthen the complementarity of EU funding (Interview 4). The negotiations on the issue of the EU guarantee led to the re-emergence of an underlying tension between CDP and the EIB. In fact, while on the one hand the EIB is a privileged partner of CDP, and this synergy was strengthened within the EFSI framework, on the other hand the EIB has historically been CDP's main competitor in the financing of development projects in Italy (Interview 4).

## 6.6 Conclusions: CDP and the Reinvention of Development Banking in Italy

The development banking field in Italy is defined by the interaction between seven classes of actors: 1) CDP and its management; 2) the Italian sovereign and national policy makers; 3) the banking foundations; 4) European development banking institutions like the EIB and the EIF; 5) the Commission and relevant Directorate Generals like Eurostat; 6) domestic and European regulatory bodies; and 7) private and commercial banks. Given CDP's long history, some of these actors are tied together by long-standing mutual interactions. When comparing the current field of development banking with the situation of the post-war period, one notices that it underwent a process of rationalization. While in the immediate post-war decades a myriad of state-owned developmental institutions operated on the Italian market, often with very specialized mandates, these functions have now mostly been taken over by CDP and its subsidiaries.

As elsewhere in Europe, the crisis has led to a further reshaping of the development banking field, altering existing relationships and leading to the emergence of new synergies. Along with many of the field dynamics common to other EU Member States, we observe two features that are unique to the Italian case. First, the important mismatch between the financial means of a severely indebted sovereign and those of CDP. Second, the key role played by banking foundations in the governance of CDP.

By virtue of their developmental mandate and domestic focus, NDBs are closely tied to their respective sovereigns. This is true also in the case of Italy with the government owning a large stake in CDP and appointing its leading managerial figures and board members. However, the Italian dynamic is unique in that there is a clear mismatch between the financial strength of CDP, powered by high levels of citizens' postal savings Figure 6.4), and the financial struggles of a government burdened by very high levels of public debt, issued in a currency which the sovereign does not control (De Grauwe, 2013). Since its establishment, providing liquidity to the Treasury has been one of CDP's main functions (Figure 6.5). Still, today, CDP remains a *unicum* in that it is the only large European NDB that holds more than 40 percent of its financial resources in the form of liquidity deposited within the Treasury. Furthermore, as borrowing conditions worsened during the crisis, CDP stepped up its effort in purchasing Italian government bonds (Interview 5). As a result, between 2007 and 2018 the value of bonds held by CDP rose from 200 million to 57 billion euros.

If, on the one hand, this function of "shadow financier" has led the National Court of Auditors to raise an eyebrow (Corte Dei Conti, 2008), on the other it must be acknowledged that CDP's backup provides a countercyclical stabilization in the market for sovereign bonds, allowing the sovereign to have access to patient domestic capital in hard times. However, the mismatch between CDP's financial means and the sovereign's political ambitions may contribute to tensions with regard to CDP's autonomy in pursuing its developmental function. In fact, the cash-stripped government may be tempted to put pressure on CDP to invest in unprofitable firms or in projects of dubious developmental potential in the pursuit of short-term electoral gains. Here, European regulations on state aid and

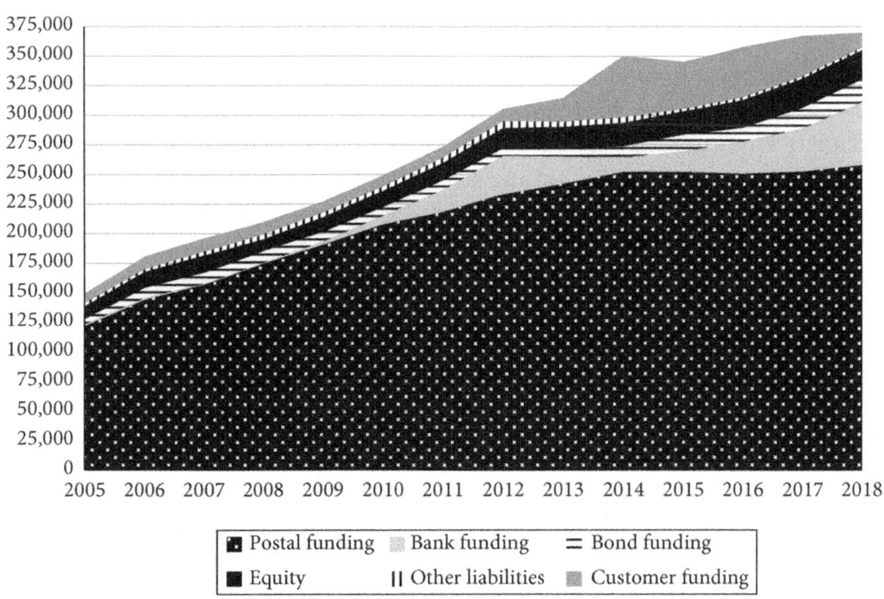


**Figure 6.4** CDP's liabilities and equity since its privatization
*Source*: authors' elaboration based on CDP's annual reports

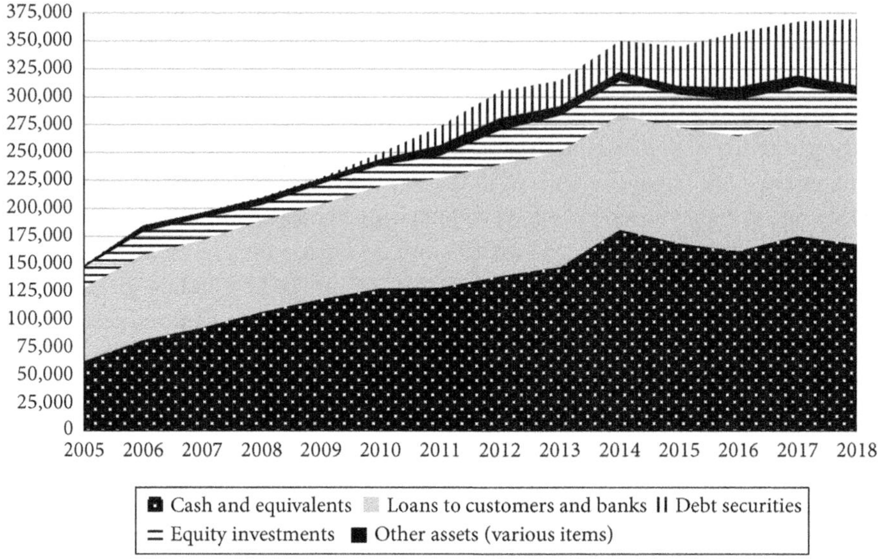


**Figure 6.5** The expansion of CDP's financial assets since its privatization
*Source*: Authors' elaboration based on CDP's annual reports, various years
*Notes*: *the bulk of "Cash and equivalents" is constituted by liquidity deposited in the Treasury*
*The bulk of "Debt securities" is constituted by Italian government bonds*
*The item "Equity investments" represents CDP's function of holding of state-owned enterprises*
*The item "Loans to customers and banks" provides a proxy for CDP's "pure" developmental function*

competition policy can play a decisive role in strengthening CDP's autonomy vis-à-vis the sovereign. In fact, to retain its status as Financial Intermediary and continue to be excluded from public debt calculations, CDP needs to avoid investing in loss-making projects. By owning a direct stake in CDP, banking foundations play a central role in minimizing the scope for these political manipulations. This is another unique feature of the Italian case. In fact, their role as profit-making private investors leads foundations to side with CDP's management against political pressures to invest in loss-making projects.

The double defense against political intrusion created by the EU regulations and the role of the foundations has become even more important in the post-crisis period. In fact, the concomitant worsening of the sovereign's borrowing conditions and the strengthening of CDP's investment firepower due to the countercyclical nature of postal savings led to an increase in the political pressure on CDP to take a more active role in support of the economy. When evaluating CDP's transformation from the point of view of its relationship with the sovereign, one could argue that, paradoxically, CDP's restructuring has simultaneously expanded and diminished the government's scope for the implementation of an activist developmental policy. On the funding dimension, the privatization has moved

CDP outside the public administration, and the related budgetary constraints, thereby paving the way for its balance sheet's expansion and functional diversification. However, the government's scope for discretionary control of the NDB is now significantly constrained by the presence of private shareholders attentive to the profitability of the banks' operations. Hence, while the government conceived of CDP's privatization as a way to circumvent the SGP's straitjacket by implementing industrial policy measures "off-balance sheet" (Mertens & Thiemann, 2018), as a result of it CDP has also gained room of maneuver for independent action vis-à-vis the sovereign by adopting practices typical of private banking. This "marketization" of developmental banking is common to CDP's counterparts across Europe, but also to state-owned companies active in strategic network industries. In fact, despite being often still state-owned, over the last three decades these firms went from semi-autonomous corporations that were part of the public administration to highly internationalized multinationals operating according to market rules (Bulfone, 2020; 2019).

The crisis also led to an opening of the Italian development banking field to the exterior, in a dynamic common to other EU Member States. This process was characterized by the increased activism of the EIB and the Commission in Italy as well as by a growing foreign activism of CDP. It is when looking at the mutual relationship between CDP and the EIB that this profound transformation appears all the more visible. In the pre-crisis period, the EIB was essentially perceived as a rival of CDP, as the European bank had often replaced CDP as the main investor in the infrastructural development of post-war Italy. The crisis, and in particular the launch of the Juncker Plan, led to the establishment of new forms of cooperation between CDP, the EIB and EIF, with CDP emerging as one of the most active NDBs in attracting funding in the framework of the Juncker Plan. However, these new forms of cooperation cannot fully eliminate dynamics of competition within the European NDB field. In fact, in the post-crisis period, the EIB stepped up its investment in Italy often outbidding CDP in the financing of important infrastructural projects by virtue of its better rating (Interview 3). Similarly, the relationship between CDP and its foreign counterparts is characterized by the co-existence of dynamics of rivalry and cooperation. On the one hand, CDP and the other European NDBs—in particular KFW and CDC—have engaged in common lobbying efforts to influence the content of important legislation like the Juncker Plan or InvestEU (Interview 4). Similarly, CDP was among the main advocates for the establishment of multilateral investment projects involving different NDBs and/or the EIB like the Marguerite Fund. On the other hand, however, by virtue of the national scope of their promotional mandate, NDBs often provide financing and equity support to large multinationals that are direct competitors on the global market (Interview 3). This, by extension, leads to the emergence of unavoidable competitive dynamics within the field which, to a certain extent, limit the scope for cooperation among the organizations populating it.

Finally, in the post-crisis period, CDP has stepped up its support to the commercial banking sector acting as a financer. In the initial phase of the crisis, CDP responded to the credit crunch affecting Italy by making additional financial funds available to SMEs and Mid-Caps through the banking sector. These allowed new credit lines to be opened for non-financial firms, while at the same time avoiding to create a direct competition between CDP and the commercial banking segment. However, the most important support CDP gave to the commercial banking sector came with the participation in the Atlas I and Atlas II funds, vital in preventing the crisis affecting small and middle-sized lenders from spreading to the entire banking sector. CDP also acts as partner of the commercial banking sector, co-financing large infrastructural projects with private banks.

To sum up, over the last two decades CDP underwent a process of radical transformation going from being a Directorate-General within the Treasury tasked with providing credit to the public administration, to an entity combining the roles of full-fledged NDB and public holding. CDP nowadays gives credit to SMEs, favors internationalization and provides patient equity investment to strategic firms, invests in social housing and aid for development, and stabilizes the economy by providing countercyclical financing to the Treasury through the liquidity held in the bank account and through the purchase of sovereign bonds. While infrastructural investment, one of CDP's main tasks since its establishment, witnessed a relative decline in terms of resource allocation, this has more to do with the lack of available investment opportunities meeting CDP's standards and to the growing competition from the EIB for the financing of large infrastructural investments (Interview 3). CDP's rise to prominence was contemporary to the progressive withdrawal of the Italian sovereign from the economy which took place since the 1990s due to the combined effect of privatizations, EU-driven market integration of formerly protected industries and exogenously imposed budgetary austerity. Given these constraints, the expansion of CDP's mandate can be seen, in a path-dependent logic, as a way for the state to maintain a certain presence in Italian capitalism despite the severe budgetary constraints. However, considering its autonomy and its limited mandate, CDP's presence in the economy is still significantly less pervasive than that of the post-war Italian state.

## References

Asso, Pier Francesco, and Marcello De Cecco. 1994. Storia del Crediop: tra credito speciale e finanza pubblica: 1920–1960. Laterza.

Banca D'Italia. 2004. Bollettino Economico. Numero 42. Rome: Bank of Italy, March 2004. https://www.bancaditalia.it/pubblicazioni/bollettino-economico/2004–0001/index.html

Barca, Fabrizio. 1999. "Compromesso senza riforme nel capitalismo italiano." In Storia Del Capitalismo Italiano, edited by Fabrizio Barca. Roma: Donzelli Editore.

Barucci, Emilio, and Federico Pierobon. 2007. Le privatizzazioni in Italia. Roma: Carocci editore.

Barucci, Emilio, and Federico Pierobon. 2010. Stato e mercato nella Seconda Repubblica. Il mulino.

Bassanini, Franco. 2011. Le Fondazioni di origine bancaria e la Cassa Depositi e Prestiti. Fondazioni, issue May-June 2011.

Bassanini, Franco. 2015a. "La 'mutazione' della Cassa Depositi e Prestiti: bilancio di un quinquiennio (2009–2015)." Rassegna Astrid.

Bassanini, Franco. 2015b. "La politica industriale dopo la crisi: il ruolo della Cassa Depositi e Prestiti." L'industria, 36(3): 435–54.

Bassanini, Franco, and Giovanni Gorno Tempini. 2014. "Presentazione," in Marcello De Cecco and Gianni Toniolo (eds) Storia della Cassa depositi e prestiti: Un nuovo corso: la società per azioni,. Bari: GLF editori Laterza.

Bassanini, Franco, and Edoardo Reviglio. 2014. "Long-term investment in Europe: The origin of the subject and future prospects." Rassegna Astrid (11), published online (2014): 13.

Battilossi, Stefano. 1999. Storia economica d'Italia. Annali, vol 2. Bari: Editori Laterza.

Battilossi, Stefano. 2014. "La nuova Cassa Depositi e Prestiti." Storia della Cassa Depositi e Prestiti. Un nuovo corso: la società per azioni, Roma-Bari: Laterza.

Bulfone, Fabio. 2017. "Insider job: corporate reforms and power resources in France, Italy and Spain." Socio-Economic Review 15 (2): 435–59.

Bulfone, Fabio. 2019. "The state strikes back: industrial policy, regulatory power and the divergent performance of telefonica and telecom Italia." Journal of European Public Policy, 26(5), 752–771.

Bulfone, Fabio. 2020. "New forms of industrial policy in the age of regulation: A comparison of electricity and telecommunications in Italy and Spain." Governance, *33*(1), 93–108.

Bussière, Éric, Michel Dumolin, and Émilie Willaert. 2008. The bank of the European Union: the EIB, 1958–2008. Luxembourg: European Investment Bank.

Cassese, Sabino. 2014. Governare gli italiani. Storia dello Stato. Il Mulino.

CDP. 2005. Report and Financial Statements at 31st December 2005. Rome: Cassa Depositi e Prestiti.

CDP. 2005. 2006. Report and Financial Statements at 31st December 2006. Rome: Cassa Depositi e Prestiti.

CDP. 2005. 2011. Report and Financial Statements at 31st December 2006. Rome: Cassa Depositi e Prestiti.

CDP. 2005. 2012. Report and Financial Statements at 31st December 2012. Rome: Cassa Depositi e Prestiti.

CDP. 2015. Report and Financial Statements at 31st December 2015. Rome: Cassa Depositi e Prestiti.

CDP. 2018. Report and Financial Statements at 31st December 2018. Rome: Cassa Depositi e Prestiti.

Ceriani, L. 1962. "'The commercial banks and financial institutions'." In Sayers, Richard Sydney (ed.), Banking in Western Europe. Clarendon Press, Oxford.

Chamber of Deputies. 2014. Cassa depositi e prestiti: principali linee di intervento. Rome: Italian Parliament.

Chiorazzo, Vincenzo, and Luigi Spaventa. 1999. "The prodigal son or a confidence trickster? How Italy got into EMU," in From EMS to EMU: 1979 to 1999 and Beyond, 129–55. Springer.

Cillis, Lucio. 2018. "Alitalia, Fs restano sole. Si sfilano Lufthansa, Eni e Leonardo." La Repubblica https://rep.repubblica.it/pwa/generale/2018/10/30/news/alitalia_fs_restano_sole_si_sfilano_lufthansa_eni_e_leonardo-210427384/.

Ciocca, Pierluigi. 2004. The Italian financial system remodelled. Springer.

Corte Dei Conti. 2008. Relazione sul risultato del controllo eseguito sulla gestione finanziaria della Cassa depositi e prestiti S.p.a. per gli esercizi 2004, 2005 e 2006. Rome: Corte Dei Conti.

Corte Dei Conti. 2019. Relazione sul risultato del controllo eseguito sulla gestione finanziaria della Cassa depositi e prestiti S.p.a. per l'esercizio 2017. Rome: Corte Dei Conti.

De Cecco, Marcello, and Pedone Antonio. 1995. "Le istituzioni dell'economia." Storia dello Stato italiano dall'Unità ad oggi, a cura di Raffaele Romanelli, Donzelli, Roma: Donzelli.

De Cecco, Marcello, and Toniolo, Gianni. 2001. Storia della Cassa depositi e prestiti. Bari: Laterza.

De Cecco, Marcello, and Toniolo, Gianni. 2014. Storia della Cassa depositi e prestiti: Un nuovo corso: la società per azioni. GLF editori Laterza.

De Grauwe, Paul. 2013. "Design Failures in the Eurozone: Can they be fixed?" London School of Economics, LEQS paper (57). London

Della Torre, Giuseppe. 2001. "Fatti stilizzati per una storia quantitativa della Cassa depositi e prestiti," in Marcello De Cecco and Toniolo Gianni (eds), Storia della Cassa Depositi e Prestiti, 3–37. Bari: Editori Laterza.

Dyson, Kenneth, and Kevin Featherstone. 1996. "Italy and EMU as a 'Vincolo Esterno': empowering the technocrats, transforming the state." South European Society and Politics 1 (2): 272–99.

EIB, and EIF. 2018. 2017 EFSI Report. Luxembourg, https://www.eib.org/attachments/strategies/efsi_2017_report_ep_council_en.pdf

European Court of Auditors. 2019. European Fund for Strategic Investments: Action needed to make EFSI a full success. 2019. Luxembourg.

Felice, Emanuele. 2007. Divari regionali e intervento pubblico: per una rilettura dello sviluppo in Italia. il Mulino.

Felice, Emanuele, and Amedeo Lepore. 2013. "Le politiche di sviluppo nel Sud dell'Italia rivisitate: storia d'impresa e conti regionali relativi all'intervento della «Cassa per il Mezzogiorno»." Rivista economica del Mezzogiorno 27 (3): 593–634.

Filtri, Andrea, Antonio Guglielmi, and Andrea Carzana. 2014. Italian Banking Foundations. Milan,

Giachetti Fantini, Michela. 2018. "La 'Straordinaria Mutazione' del Ruolo di Cassa Depositi e Prestiti nel Passaggio dallo Stato Azionista allo Stato Investitore." federalismi.it (6/2018), published online November 16, 2018.

Giorgino, Marco, and Roberto Tasca. 1999. "The Italian Experience." In Banking Privatisation in Europe, 179–235. Springer.

Jassaud, Nadège. 2014. Reforming the corporate governance of Italian banks. WP 14-181 1498310710. Washington: International Monetary Fund.

La Repubblica. 2015. "Fsi: 'L'Italia ha bisogno di venti Luxottica, investiamo per far crescere le imprese'." 2015/04/27/. Accessed 2019/08/26/17:07:34. https://www.repubblica.it/economia/affari-e-finanza/2015/04/27/news/fsi_litalia_ha_bisogno_di_venti_luxottica_investiamo_per_far_crescere_le_imprese-113024583/.

La Repubblica. 2018. "Fra Tim, Open Fiber, Ilva e Alitalia la Cdp si lancia nello slalom gigante." La Repubblica https://www.repubblica.it/economia/affari-e-finanza/2018/04/16/news/fra_tim_open_fiber_ilva_e_alitalia_la_cdp_si_lancia_nello_slalom_gigante-193999174/.

Lucchese, Matteo, Nascia Leopoldo, and Pianta Mario. 2016. "Industrial policy and technology in Italy." Economia e politica industriale 43 (3), published online 2016: 233–60. https://link.springer.com/article/10.1007/s40812-016-0047-4.

Lutz, Vera. 1962. "The central bank and the system of credit control," in R.S. Sayers (ed.), Banking Western Europe, edited by. Oxford: Oxford University Press.

Macchiati, Alfredo. 2013. "La Cassa Depositi e Prestiti dopo la trasformazione: ovvero «ai posteri l'ardua sentenza»." Mercato Concorrenza Regole 15 (2): 287–98.

Martinelli, Alberto, 1981. "The Italian experience: a historical perspective," in Vernon, Raymond and Yair Aharoni (eds) *State-Owned Enterprise in the Western Economies, Croom Helm: London.*

McCann, Dermot. 2007. "Globalization, European integration and regulatory reform in Italy: liberalism, protectionism or reconstruction?" Journal of Modern Italian Studies 12 (1), published online 2007/03/01: 101–17. doi:10.1080/13545710601132995.

MEF. 2005. La Relazione sulle Privatizzazioni. Relazione al Parlamento sulle Operazioni di Cessione delle Partecipazioni in Societa' Controllate Direttamente o Indirettamente dallo Stato. Rome: Ministero dell'Economia e delle Finanze, http://www.dt.tesoro.it/it/attivita_istituzionali/privatizzazioni/relazioni_parlamento.html

Mertens, Daniel, and Matthias Thiemann. 2018. "Market-based but state-led: The role of public development banks in shaping market-based finance in the European Union." Competition & Change 22 (2), published online 2018/04//: 184–204. doi:10.1177/1024529418758479.

Molina, O., and Rhodes, M. 2006. "Mixed Market Economies." European Politics and Society, Newsletter of the European Politics & Society Section of the American Political Science Association 5 (1).

Moschella, M., and Quaglia, L. 2020. European Banking Union to the Rescue? How Supranational Institutions Influenced Crisis Management in Italy, *South European Society and Politics*, 24: 4, 421–40. https://www.tandfonline.com/doi/abs/10.1080/13608746.2020.1728957.

Ninni, Augusto. 2013. "La cassa depositi e prestiti: il ritorno dello stato-guida (e oltre) in politica industriale." Economia e Politica Industriale, FrancoAngeli Editore, vol. 2013(3), pages 141–155.

Osservatorio Conti Pubblici, Italiani. 2018. CDP e i conti pubblici. https://osservatoriocpi.unicatt.it/cpi-archivio-studi-e-analisi-cdp-e-i-conti-pubblici.

Prodi, Romano. 1974. "Italy," in Vernon, Raymong. *Big business and the state: changing relations in Western Europe*. Harvard University Press.

Righi, Stefano. 2007. "La Doppia Anima della CDP Spa." Corriere Della Sera, 21/5/2007. Accessed 20/9/2018. http://archivio.corriere.it/Archivio/interface/view.shtml#!/MjovZXMvaXQvcmNzZGF0aW1ldGhvZGUxL0AyMjc0MjY%3D.

Rubio, Eulalia. 2018. Making better use of public funding: The role of national promotional banks and institutions in the next EU budget. 2018. Paris: Institut Delors. table 6.

Schmidt, Vivien A. 2002. The futures of European capitalism. OUP Oxford.

Shonfield, Andrew. 1965. "Modern capitalism." The changing balance of public and private power, London.

Spaventa, Luigi, and Vincenzo Chiorazzo. 2000. Astuzia o virtù? come accadde che l'Italia fu ammessa all'Unione monetaria. Donzelli Editore.

Thatcher, Mark. 2014. "From old to new industrial policy via economic regulation." Rivista della regolazione dei mercati 2: 6–22.

APPENDIX 6.1

# List of Interviews conducted

| Interview Number | Interviewee | Role/organization | Place of the Interview | Date of the Interview |
|---|---|---|---|---|
| Interview 1 | Giulio Tremonti | Former Italian Finance Minister | Milan | 11/06/2019 |
| Interview 2 | Official in the top echelon of ACRI | Associazione di Fondazioni e di Casse di Risparmio Spa (ACRI) | Rome | 31/05/2019 |
| Interview 3 | Chief financial Officer | CDP | Rome | 10/06/2019 |
| Interview 4 | Joint interview with multiple CDP's executives | CDP | Rome | 10/06/2019 |
| Interview 5 | Franco Bassanini | Former President of CDP | Rome | 30/05/2019 |

# 7

# The Rise of Bpifrance

## The Rebirth of a Dirigiste State?

*Matthias Thiemann and Peter Volberding*

### 7.1 Introduction

The field of development banking in Europe has changed substantially since the 2000s. Spearheaded by the European Investment Fund (EIF), development in Europe today increasingly involves venture capital, fund of fund investments, and investment in skill formation of entrepreneurs. The national development bank that manifests this trend the most in Europe is Bpifrance, which emerged in 2013 as a merger of dispersed developmental institutions. Bpifrance, which is smaller and more agile than the much larger and older Caisse des Dépôts et Consignations (CDC) not only complements the work of the CDC, but actually brings an entirely new interventionist dynamic to the field of development banking in France. At the same time, and despite all these new techniques for intervening in the economy, we argue that this rekindled form of intervention is a continuation of a tradition of *dirigisme* in France, albeit reinvented. With Bpifrance, the state is no longer directly picking winners, but rather seeking to stimulate entrepreneurial activities through the provision of loans, equity investment, and fund activities.

In this chapter, we contextualize this institution's expanding role as a public financial institution in France within a longer trajectory of state involvement in the economy. Specifically, we ask: To what extent is Bpifrance's precipitous growth a reinvention of *dirigisme*, and how do the financial activities of Bpifrance compare to previous French state interventions as well as to the operations of other European NDBs? We contend that Bpifrance is not merely a vestige of decades of French *dirigisme*, but rather a reinvention of it, seeking to adjust both to the new industrial policy goals of the French government in the 21st century, to conditions of EU State Aid (s. Clift, 2013), and to new practices in financial markets. In this respect, Bpifrance's status as a wholly owned French institution means that it can function as a state tool to direct investment and foster growth in strategic sectors. However, it does so not based on the direct allocation of credit, which would clash with EU state aid regulations, but rather based on co-financing and risk sharing arrangements with private banks and investment funds, enticing

Matthias Thiemann and Peter Volberding, *The Rise of Bpifrance: The Rebirth of a Dirigiste State?* In: *The Reinvention of Development Banking in the European Union: Industrial Policy in the Single Market and the Emergence of a Field.* Edited by: Daniel Mertens, Matthias Thiemann, and Peter Volberding, Oxford University Press (2021). 
DOI: 10.1093/oso/9780198859703.003.0007

them to engage in the financing of SMEs and start-ups using loan subsidies, credit guarantees, and risk capital. In this way, Bpifrance, which in 2013 united a disparate developmental landscape in France, has quickly become an important economic tool for the French government to intervene in the economy.

With a balance sheet of EUR 72 billion and an operational profit of more than EUR 2 billion in 2017—and more than EUR 10 billion over the last six years—Bpifrance provides a spectrum of financial and business services to French enterprises. In particular, it has increased the role of one of its predecessors, CDC Entreprises, as an active investor in both funds and funds of funds investment in start-up companies. It acts as an anchor investor in this market segment, while at the same time increasing its co-lending operations with commercial banks, with an emphasis on providing lending and equity financing for SMEs and innovative enterprises. Concurrently, Bpifrance has strengthened its position as an important blockholder of large, strategic French companies such as Peugeot or Orange. Finally, in 2017, Bpifrance adopted the mantel of France's export insurance, with an initial funding of EUR 19 billion (Bpifrance, 2018a) and, in 2019, it incorporated the branch of its larger brother, Caisse des Depots et Consignation (CDC International) that collaborates with sovereign wealth funds to invest in France.[1] In short, Bpifrance has provided a one-stop shop of publicly-backed financial instruments for French firms—a fact we argue constitutes a new form of *dirigisme*,[2] an expression of the will of the French government to directly intervene in the development of the economy to shape its future path.

A confluence of forces arising from domestic pressures, economic crisis, and European integration has hastened this integration into one institution and, critically, shaped how Bpifrance interacts with the French economy. In contrast to the previous form of *dirigisme*, Bpifrance instead relies extensively on financial markets to implement state policy, much like the EU itself (Braun et al., 2018). It has diversified its targeted sectors beyond large industrial conglomerates that it desired to become national champions to target the often-neglected SMEs and innovative start-ups. This more granular approach to investment and promotion has granted Bpifrance much more flexibility than its much larger, less flexible holding company, the CDC. Unlike the CDC, which is its 50 percent shareholder, Bpifrance is subject to considerable direct influence by the French state executive who holds the other 50 percent, and hence can be used as a tool for the state to direct investment and foster growth in strategic sectors to a much greater degree.[3]

[1] https://www.bpifrance.fr/Qui-sommes-nous/Nos-metiers/Fonds-propres/Fonds-directs-Bpifrance/Capital-Developpement-Transmission-International/Fonds-souverains-Bpifrance/Actualites2/(article)/, last accessed on October 7, 2019.

[2] To be clear, important differences from the old *dirigisme* remain, the most notable ones being the lack of an administrative unit developing five-year plans for the economy (cf Loriaux, 1991) as well as the central bank engaging in credit allocation (Monnet, 2018).

[3] The peculiar governance arrangement of the CDC, which limits the influence of the executive, stems from the time of the founding of the CDC in 1816. After the defeat of Napoleon and the ensuing

Furthermore, in contrast to other NDBs, Bpifrance also acts as an active investor much like a venture capital fund, providing services from seed capital to membership on the board of directors.

The chapter proceeds as follows. First, we examine the contours of the original French *dirigisme* in the post-WWII period with an emphasis on public finance institutions and their attendant instruments. By tracing the origins of French *dirigisme* up to the 1980s, we examine how the French state intervened and steered the economy in this period (Loriaux, 1991; Loriaux et al., 1997), providing a foil with which we can compare and assess Bpifrance's current operations and institutional structure. Second, we analyze the creation of Bpifrance as a consequence of the consolidation of state-backed financial instruments and initiatives, a dynamic which developed before the crisis and accelerated in its aftermath, and brought about a newfound capacity for the French state executive to intervene and steer the development of economic sectors deemed crucial for the future. We then evaluate Bpifrance's current activities within the French economy to tease out how far this new capability reaches, and which dynamics can be observed over the last six years. Third, we embed the growth of Bpifrance in its European context, investigating how far State Aid regulations, as well as EU promotional initiatives, have influenced the activities of Bpifrance. Finally, we conclude with thoughts on the future of *dirigisme* within France, as well as lessons for NDBs more broadly.

## 7.2 Dirigisme Old Style: 1946–1973

The French state during the post-war recovery played a strong role directing economic growth (Zysman, 1984). Back then, the Treasury of France and the Central Bank directed much of the savings into the industrial sectors deemed important to the economic growth and national security of France (Hall, 1986, Monnet, 2018). It did so by, inter alia, making use of a broad range of financial institutions under the direct influence of the state to invest in strategic sectors. These institutions included the CDC, a national development bank which, due to its particular history, was subjected to the French parliament, but not to the Treasury, the *Caisse d'Epargne*, the *Fond de Développement economiques*, and, during the 1950s, the *Fond de Modernisation de l'équipement*. These different institutions jointly formed the "Treasury Circuit," whereby a large part of French savings was directed into strategically important sectors (Loriaux, 1991). This circuit shielded large French companies from the vagaries of market finance, maintaining their competitiveness and allowing them to draw on state finances to pursue projects of

state bankruptcy, in order to again attract the savings of the French, the new CDC was not placed under the direct control of the State Executive, but under indirect control by the French parliament.

innovation deemed vital to the competitiveness of the French industry. These interventions were often directed at large state-owned conglomerates, such as for the French electricity provider to install nuclear power plants, as well as innovation projects, such as Concorde, but they also impacted smaller scale agricultural activities (Monnet, 2018). Using its industrial policy and planning capacities, the state actively designed the future structure of the French economy (Hall, 1986).

Since the late 1970s, this Treasury circuit has largely been dismantled by Treasury officials themselves, due to an internal analysis which emphasized the inflationary tendencies that this circuit provoked in the context of the new post-Bretton Woods regime (Loriaux, 1991; Monnet, 2018; Schmidt, 1996). In this view, the inability to devalue the Franc, in conjunction with the existing overdraft economy used by the large state-owned companies, generated an inflationary bias in the French economy that was detrimental.[4] Accelerated by the U-turn of the French socialists in 1982, state ownership was dramatically reduced, in particular giving way to the privatization of large banks and the liberation of French savings in the 1980s (Levy, 2006), seen by many as the end of the "old dirigisme" (Schmidt, 1997). The direction of credit and tax incentives to steer the development of the French economy had been dismantled and the state engaged massively in selling its stakes.

And yet, at the same time, the French Treasury did not simply withdraw from financial markets. Rather, Finance Minister Beregevoy sought to modernize and internationalize French financial markets in order to facilitate the privatization of large state-owned companies.[5] In the same market-shaping spirit, the French state in the early 1980s, deeply dissatisfied with the lack of venture capital in France, intervened to nurture an asset-management and a private equity industry (Granier and Bedu, 2019; O'Sullivan, 2007), an endeavor which would call forth further state interventions in the 1990s (see below). At the same time that the state sought to reshape financial markets, public financial actors, such as the French promotional banks for SMEs of the era, barely escaped their dissolution by the state (Gaston-Breton, 2015). As will be detailed, Bpifrance is the outcome of consolidating the remnants of these remaining tools for state intervention at the behest of the French state and joining them with those parts of the CDC that were central to the attempts of the French state to modernize financial markets and make them finance the "real economy." The final catalyst, however, that would bring these dispersed institutions together was the sovereign wealth fund FSI, created in 2008 by Sarkozy, which would signal the re-emergence of an interventionist state.

[4] On the difficulties of state owned companies in this new era, see Berger (1981).

[5] See O'Sullivan (2007). For a diverging perspective, see Culpepper (2010).

## 7.3 Forerunners of Bpifrance

The origins of the banking arm of the Bpifrance reside in the early 1920s, when a small public bank was set up to promote the hotel industry (1923), joined in 1936 by the *Caisse Nationale des Marchés de l'Etat*. Over the course of the rocky 1930s and 1940s, these institutions managed to remain solvent and became important in the reconstruction of the hotel industry and tourism in the French provinces from the 1940s onwards (Gaston-Breton, 2015). Regrouped in 1980 as the CEPME (*Crédit d'Equipement des Petites et Moyennes Entreprises*), the newly merged bank ran into serious financial difficulties in the early 1990s. Partially due to advancing deregulation and liberalization, which ate into its margins (Gaston-Breton, 2015, p. 91), the new bank produced losses of more than 1 billion Francs during the 1993–1995 period.[6] Despite the opinion of the Treasury and the private banks of the time, the Presidents' office decided to maintain these institutions for the purpose of industrial policy and instead to readjust them to focus exclusively on SMEs (Gaston-Breton, 2015, p. 108). It was to be fused with the public provider of guarantees for loans of banks to SMEs, Sofaris, in 1996, and was renamed the *Banque du Développement des Petites et Moyennes Entreprises* (BDPME). While retaining its branch network, an important institutional pillar for the future local reach of Bpifrance, it would from now on be directed to co-invest rather than compete with private French banks, accommodating the opposition by the Treasury and private banks.

Over the next decade, the BDPME would find a new profitable niche in the French financial system by expanding its cooperation with private banks, regional funds, and regional actors, based on its branch network (ibid, p. 134). In December 2002, the French state became the majority owner of the bank by buying up the shares of cooperative banks, the other main shareholder being the CDC. The state then used its newfound majority ownership to direct the bank in 2005, at the behest of the new Minister of Finance Sarkozy, to merge with the National Agency for the Valorization of National Research (ANVAR)[7], as well as the national agency for SMEs (ANPME). Together, these agencies formed OSEO, a new bank that co-located guarantees, credit provision, and venture capital for SMEs, as well as supported research and innovation. While a challenge in terms of organizational cultures, the merger of these different institutions proceeded rather well (interview Bpifrance bankers, March 26, 2019), a fact probably helped by the beneficial business environment of the years up until 2008.

[6] "La Banque du Développement des PME chapeautera le CEPME et la Sofaris," *Les Echos*. 15 July 1996.

[7] ANVAR is another state-led agency founded in 1967 to promote innovation among SMEs through research grants and financing (OECD, 2014, p. 247).

This re-organization and concentration of developmental capabilities to support SMEs was initiated and orchestrated by a network of former state officials—operating in the private sector—and their former colleagues—operating at the center of power in the presidential administration (Gaston-Breton, 2015, pp. 108; 158), a pattern which would repeat itself in the creation of Bpifrance seven years later. As an organizational blueprint for the future Bpifrance, OSEO had already established a regional network of offices and operated closely with the regions, and, rather than on-lending to other banks, always directly engaged with the SMEs it financed. OSEO's characteristics—namely, innovation finance for SMEs, regional offices, and direct contact with SMEs—would later provide the core of operations for Bpifrance. On this path towards an even larger merger, the 2008 financial crisis proved to be a turning point for OSEO, which together with the CDC became one of the main tools to implement the counter-cyclical policies of the state. OSEO did so by providing credit to SMEs, CDC by engaging in the provision of finance for the housing sector and its contribution to the FSI (interview Bpifrance official, April 23, 2018).

First, the important countercyclical plan of "relance des PMEs" was delegated to OSEO, where it operated on behalf of the state and, in compliance with State Aid regulation, guaranteed EUR 6.7 billion of loans. It administered EUR 2 billion of participatory loans and, based upon a EUR 450 million capital increase by the state, actively supported the state program of "Investing into the Future" with another 2 billion in loans. Independently of these state-financed efforts, OSEO expanded its balance sheet by 70 percent, from 7.4 billion to 12.68 billion, and doubled its extension of loans from 2 to 4 billion between 2008 and 2011. It also expanded its guarantee business, more than doubling it from 2007 to 2009 (OSEO, 2012, p. 9). By the end of 2012, OSEO operated 37 local agencies in France (a rather unique feature, given that most NDBs do not have any local agencies), employed 1641 employees, and entertained productive relationships with the French state, commercial banks with which they co-lent, as well as the 84,000 companies they financed. As such, it provided a fertile basis and the organizational kernel for the future Bpifrance.

The second pillar of activities for the future Bpifrance would stem from outside OSEO's remit and development banking proper, but instead from the involvement of the CDC in the fund managing industry. The French state engaged in this industry from the 1990s onwards to make financial markets contribute to the financing of technological and entrepreneurial innovations. In these attempts, CDC PME (later renamed CDC Entreprises) was a forerunner as one of the initial fund of fund managers in the French fund industry beginning in the late 1990s (Bouchara, 2003; interview with Bpifrance banker, November 23, 2018). Its mission was based on an analysis that argued the lack of a venture-fund industry placed France at a competitive disadvantage with respect to the US

(Bouchara, 2003). From 1998 onwards, this arm of CDC responsible for the investment into funds of funds became the anchor investor in French private equity funds (Assemblée Nationale de France, 2015).[8] Its activities were expanded in 2004 when the CDC used the proceeds from the sale of its stakes in the Caisse d'Epargne to Natixis—one of the last remnants of the Treasury circuit—in order to invest more into private equity funds. Due to these investments, this branch of CDC was able to build up financing expertise, links to private investors, and manpower, which would make it the primary contact for state officials as they were seeking to limit the negative fallout of the 2008 financial crisis (interview with former CDC Entreprises employee, now Bpifrance banker, November 23, 2018).

Their expertise was drawn upon when in December 2008, the French Presidency created the Strategic Investment Fund (*Fond Stratégique d'Investissement*, or FSI) in order to combat the ensuing recession and to supply financing to cash-strapped enterprises (Levy, 2011). The creation of the FSI, with an initial capitalization of EUR 20 billion based on EUR 14 billion of existing state assets and an additional 6 billion of debt was met with widespread political support (ibid). It was established under the auspices of CDC, which provided a slight majority of the capital and held 51 percent, with the French state holding 49 percent. And yet, the FSI clearly signaled the re-emergence of the French state itself as an active player in the allotment of large-scale financing to sectors deemed critical in the post-crisis economy (interview Bpifrance official, April 14, 2018).

Acting on this assumed new role in early 2010, the French government initiated a program for investment in the future (PIA), which was a loan taken out with a total volume of EUR 35 billion that sought to foster research and innovation in France. EUR 600 million of that program was directly entrusted to CDC Entreprises to establish the first independent state-sponsored seed fund, the *Fond National d'Amorçage*, which, in a departure from prior practice, was to directly intervene in the financing of enterprises.[9] In addition, a new EUR 5 billion state fund for investment sponsored by the FSI was set up for investment between 2012–2020, which was again entrusted to CDC Entreprises for reasons of efficiency (Fourcade, 2011, p. 48). While these new fund activities sponsored by the FSI meant an increase in the firepower of the CDC divisions active in capital markets, the state officials in charge of the FSI increasingly voiced their desire to determine the investment decisions of the CDC, which overstepped governance boundaries. In addition, these new state activities financed by the FSI also led to a duplication of governance structures, such as between regional FSI funds and CDC support for regions, which jointly with the perceived lack of expertise of the FSI by the CDC led to disgruntlement and tensions in the new structure

[8] For a critical view, see Ekeland, Landier, and Tirole (2016).
[9] https://www.caissedesdepots.fr/fonds-national-damorcage; last accessed November 5, 2019.

(interview Bpifrance, April 14th 2018; Gaston-Breton, 2015, p. 217, citing the CEO of CDC in 2010).

These perceptions of dysfunctionalities in the interplay between the FSI and the CDC in their collaboration over intervening directly in the economy, which were also voiced by a parliamentary report to the senate (Fourcade, 2011, pp. 49–57), made an institutional rearrangement seem desirable. Such a rearrangement, which would provide greater clarity of roles as well as more direct intervention capacity for the state executive, was achieved through the formation of Bpifrance.

## 7.4 The Founding of Bpifrance: From Presidential Elections in 2012 to Establishment in 2013

The combination of institutional problems and the success of the FSI (Levy, 2011; 2017) led both Sarkozy and Hollande, the two presidential candidates in the final round of the 2012 presidential election, to propose the pooling of promotional capacities dedicated to industry. The support for a state-backed financial institution for SMEs on both sides of the political spectrum demonstrated the widespread political support for a renewed strategy of direct involvement of state actors in the financing of economic sectors deemed of strategic importance. However, the two contenders offered competing visions of the structure, with Hollande's structure both more encompassing and bigger in its ambitions.[10]

The victory of Hollande's Socialist government then led to the implementation of the more ambitious plan and the establishment of Bpifrance on December 31, 2012. The act establishing Bpifrance merged the promotional bank OSEO, CDC Entreprises, and the FSI into a single entity. Through the pooled EUR 21 billion of capital in the state fund, these newly joined organizations saw their financial capacity to act and intervene in markets greatly expand. Concurrently, the new governance structure sought to overcome the frictions between the CDC and the FSI, which would both guarantee greater rights for direct intervention into industrial policy for the French state, as well as preserve CDC's influence in the overall governance architecture. The outcome of the intense negotiations in the summer of 2012 between the Ministry of Finance, the Ministry of the Economy, and the CDC itself was a governance structure that represented this equilibrium in a 50-50 ownership structure, with the CDC successfully blocking the desire of the state to gain a 51 percent stake (interview with Bpifrance banker April 14th 2018).

[10] Michel, Anne. "Banque de l'industrie : projet Sarkozy contre projet Hollande," *Le Monde*. 30 January 2012.

Organizationally, Bpifrance is owned as a 50-50 partnership between the French state through the EPIC[11] and the CDC. Critically, the EPIC provides a direct and explicit state guarantee on both bond and commercial paper issues, meaning that Bpifrance shares the French state's Aa2/AA credit rating (Bpifrance, 2019b, p. 13). Moreover, Bpifrance is legally divided into three main subsidiaries, Bpifrance Financement, Bpifrance Investissement, and Bpifrance Assurance Export (see Bpifrance's subsidiary structure in Figure 7.1). This structure reflects both the amalgamated nature of Bpifrance as a merger of prior initiatives, as well as its unique status as a de facto sovereign wealth fund with an attached development bank. In terms of its governance structure, it is headed by a board of directors of 14 people, where, in addition to the president (currently the CEO of the CDC), five government officials as well as three CDC officials are supposed to decide jointly with two employee representatives and three qualified experts from industry.

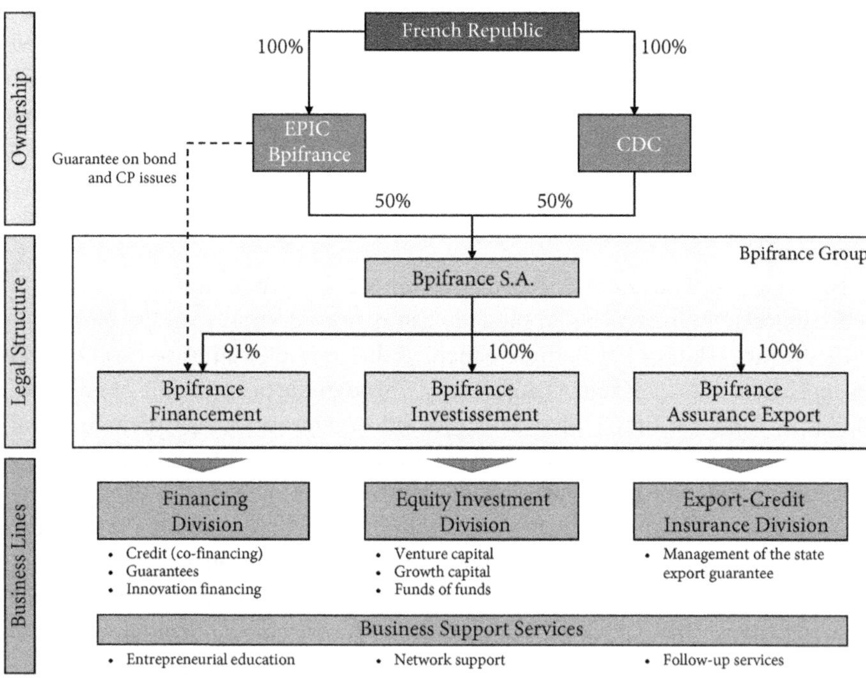


**Figure 7.1** Bpifrance's holding structure
*Source*: Bpifrance (2018b)

[11] Establissement Public Industriel et Commercial. The missions and organization of EPIC were defined by Act 2005–722 on June 29, 2005, it was modified by the decret 2015–1498 to specify the public mission of Bpifrance. In short, the decret defines the governance of Bpifrance, specifies its objective, and maintains its status as a public entity with the automatic guarantee of the French state.

The project for the formation of Bpifrance was executed by a political-economic elite that transcended the public and private sphere, involving CDC, officials from the ministries of economics and finance, as well as former state officials. The project of the merger of these different institutions itself was directed by then economic advisor to the president, Emanuel Macron (Gaston-Breton, 2015, p. 230), and Bpifrance was officially founded on July 1, 2013. Macron, who himself was pursuing a career typical of a graduate of the *Ecole National d'Administration* (ENA), convinced another ENA graduate, Nicolas Dufourcq, who was then working in the private sector, to head the new institution. Dufourcq's trajectory, which mixed government experience with stints in the private sector, reflected a common pattern. Building on this existing stock of expertise, Bpifrance in its first five years of existence would use the capital boost by the FSI to expand its activities and blend its different products into one joint offer for its clients.

## 7.5 Bpifrance's First Five Years: Growth and Diversification

Bpifrance's growth over the first five years has been remarkable, proving its capacity to act as a *dirigiste* policy tool for the French state and expanding its reach into the business community in the process. From 2013 to 2018, more than 1,000 companies have been supported through equity investments, and more than 85,000 French companies have been backed through bank guarantees or debt financing, accounting for one third of total French SMEs (Bpifrance, 2018b). In 2013, Bpifrance's first year, the bank reported a balance sheet of EUR 53.9 billion (Bpifrance, 2014, p. 36). At the end of 2018, Bpifrance maintained a balance sheet of EUR 76.8 billion, a growth of EUR 4.2 billion from the previous year and of EUR 23 billion from 2013 (a growth of 43 percent in five years). It operates a profitable business, earning roughly EUR 1.35 billion in 2018, with returns on equity (RoE) ranging from 3 to 6 percent. Interestingly, Bpifrance's rise and increasing success has also put pressure on its 50 percent shareholder, the CDC, to improve its own performance and to show its importance for France (interview Bpifrance banker April 14, 2018). Both banks now engage in techniques of market-based banking (Mertens and Thiemann, 2019), using first loss tranches to entice private investment while seeking to actively differentiate their areas of intervention.

Offering both loans and equity investments to SMEs and large cap companies, the first five years of Bpifrance were characterized by an expansion in the portfolio of services. There was a desire to merge the operations of its different forerunners into a single, one-stop institution that would be able to provide services and financing to the enterprise at all stages in the business lifecycle (interview Bpifrance official, April 14th 2018). Dufourcq followed this strategy in order to allow for an integration of the different institutions through growth of the group

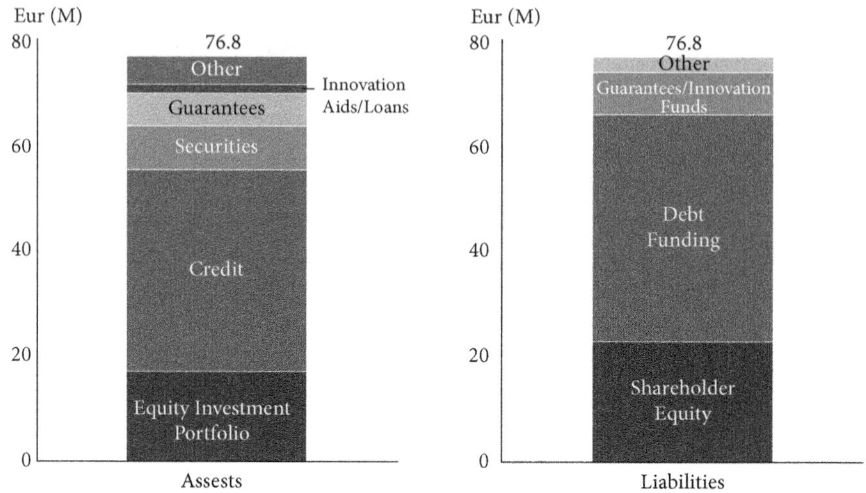


**Figure 7.2** Assets and liabilities of Bpifrance, December 2018
*Source*: Bpifrance (2018c)

rather than through cuts, as was feared in the bank. This strategy was also helped by the very limited overlap between the previously distinct organizations.[12]

As Figure 7.2 demonstrates, based on figures for 2018, the majority of the assets of Bpifrance today are in its credit portfolio (38.2 billion), equity investments (17.1 billion), and securities portfolio (8.3 billion). Guarantees (6.2 billion) and innovation assistance (1.7 billion) comprise a smaller portion of financing, though as will be analyzed later, nevertheless remain important to Bpifrance's overall strategy.

This is a marked expansion with respect to 2013, with credit provision and fund investments growing particularly strongly (59 percent and 61 percent[13] respectively), whereas equity investments, the part financed by the sovereign wealth fund, only grew by 30 percent. This indicates an increase in the promotional activities of Bpifrance, rather than its function as a shareholder/sovereign wealth fund, an expansion that was based on the continued expression of political will for the expansion of direct intervention into the lending of the economy

[12] Only a small part of the CDC team had engaged in providing loans, making their integration into the old OSEO team simple and only a limited part of the FSI team had engaged in active management of clients the fund was invested in, in turn facilitating their integration in the CDC Entreprises team (interview with Bpifrance bankers, November 23, 2018, and interview with Bpifrance bankers March 26, 2019).

[13] This is a conservative estimate, assuming that 100% of Assets Under Management in 2013 belong to Bpifrance, an aspect not disclosed in the 2013 report, but given the role of the program for investment into the future certainly not entirely true. In contrast, the 2019 report used discloses this percentage. A less conservative estimate, assuming equal third party participation would put the growth at 108%.

(interview Bpifrance, March 26, 2019, Assemblée nationale de France 2015). This direct intervention in fact was largely facilitated by the equity participations, both due to the annual income they provide in the form of dividends, but also in their capacity to pledge participations as collateral to secure cheaper financing.

Based on this capital stock and in order to finance these expanding operations, Bpifrance has turned decisively to financial markets. As Figure 7.2 above illustrates, shareholder equity accounts for EUR 22.9 billion, and medium- and long-term financing EUR 43 billion. Both of these are drawn from Bpifrance's own financial accounts, although the bank's loans are subjected to an automatic and implicit guarantee from the French state. Only the guarantee and innovation funds—valued at EUR 8 billion—directly come from the French state. Refinancing has grown from EUR 14.7 billion in 2011 to EUR 45 billion in 2018; Euro Medium Term Notes (EMTM) are the primary instrument of refinancing, reaching over EUR 35 billion in 2018, and account for the lion's share of growth. Bpifrance uses this funding to finance the activities of its three main subsidiaries of Bpifrance: Financement (formerly OSEO); Investissement (which merged FSI and CDC Entreprises); and Export (the formerly independent Coface).

Below we detail the different activities of these as well as those of the most recent arrival, Bpifrance Accompagnement, to provide a better understanding of the different parts of Bpifrance and how they interact. Together, they allow Bpifrance to become the agent of the start-up initiatives envisioned by the French state to transform the French economy. In particular, what we will show is how Bpifrance not only has sought to streamline its offer, combining debt and equity instruments, guarantees, as well as start-up investments, but has also sought to bolster the fate of these supported companies through human capital formation and entrepreneurial support. It is this new, holistic approach to the intervention of Bpifrance in the French economy that differentiates it not only from the more traditional CDC in France, but also most other development banks in the European field, including the KfW, which currently seeks to ally with Bpifrance in areas such as venture funds. Its basis is the financial prowess generated by the high profitability of both the loans and the equity holdings of Bpifrance.

### 7.5.1 Bpifrance Activities and Sectors of Intervention

**(1) Bpifrance Financement** primarily serves as the financing division for three business activities in SMEs (credit, guarantees, and innovation), which is a legacy of OSEO. In 2018, EUR 7.9 billion in loans and EUR 5.3 billion in short term financing were extended (Bpifrance 2019b, 20), which means that credits comprise the largest component of Bpifrance Financement. Loans are given pari-passu with co-financing agreements with commercial banks. For these credit activities, no direct French state funding is given; rather, the support comes only in the form of guarantees for Bpifrance Financement generally. Guarantees provided in 2018 comprise EUR 8.9 billion in loans and EUR 4 billion in risks, which receive public support from the state budget. Innovation is the smallest segment (EUR 0.9 billion in innovation aids and EUR 0.3 billion in loans allocated in 2018), which also operate with public support. While all of the bonds and commercial paper are backed by a state guarantee, French commercial banks own 9 percent of the subsidiary, expression of the continued close connection Bpifrance Financement entertains with the private sector, which helps to mobilize the latter for business targeted by Bpifrance (interview Bpifrance 14th of April 2018). In other words, Bpifrance uses its close connection to the large banks to convince them to enter into risk-taking endeavors when dealing with SMEs, which these otherwise liquidity rich but rather risk-averse banking conglomerates tend to avoid (interview Bpifrance officials, November 23, 2018).

**(2) Bpifrance Investissement** concentrates on equity investments.[14] It is effectively the outcome of the merger between the sovereign wealth fund FSI and the CDC Entreprises, itself a major investor in the funds and the fund of funds industry in France since the late 1990s. In 2018, Bpifrance Investissement managed EUR 32 billion, with EUR 18.2 billion going to a portfolio of 142 mid- and large-cap firms. Current investments include large firms in the automobile, telecommunications, and technology sectors, where Bpifrance acts as a major blockholding shareholder. Bpifrance Investissement also manages three specialized funds dedicated to the automotive industry, international expansion, and special purpose vehicles (SPVs), where it provides direct financing and advisory services to these specific sectors deemed strategic by the state. In many ways, these activities reflect the old FSI functions of behaving like a private investor according to the principle of shareholder value maximization, which allows it to avoid the complications of State Aid. Concurrently, it is also instructed to keep the French economy and public interest in mind (Bpifrance, 2018b). In the meantime, there are about EUR 2.1 billion invested in the equity of SMEs and 11.9 billion invested in funds and funds of funds,[15] which aim to foster innovation and the creation of medium-sized tech enterprises through seed capital (Dufourcq, 2019). In particular, through the latter function Bpifrance plays an important role in the innovation ecology of the French economy, seeking to move innovative enterprises from the smallest phase all the way up to the IPO, generating both growth for the French economy and business for Bpifrance.

[14] Legally, Bpifrance S. A. owns 100% of Bpifrance Participations (formerly called FSI), which in turn owns 100% of Bpifrance Investissement.

[15] Of these, EUR 2.714 billion are on behalf of third parties, which includes government programs.

**(3) Bpifrance Assurance Export** is the newest addition to the group, added in January 2017 after Bpifrance entirely absorbed COFACE as a subsidiary. Its primary task is to manage the state export guarantee for French firms. While Bpifrance had already offered services including export credit, international growth loans, and cross border investment funds, the incorporation of COFACE, formerly directly subordinated to the Treasury, enables a one-stop shop for French firms. These expanded services include multiple types of insurances (credit, prospecting, exchange risk, and investment), as well as security and pre-financing guarantees. Therefore, the centralization of all services has allowed Bpifrance to serve as the primary contact for French businesses at all stages of the enterprises' life. There has been a particular affinity to help SMEs, so that Bpifrance can "help them conquer international markets" (Bpifrance, 2017a), in a strategy that seeks to replicate in France the successes of the German Mittelstand. In 2018, the division provided EUR 19 billion in credits and guarantees (ibid).

**(4) Bpifrance Accompagnement:** Since its inception, Bpifrance has bolstered its business support services across all three subsidiaries, which led in 2019 to the creation of a fourth directorate in its organizational structure now wholly dedicated to "l'accompagnement" of SMEs and mid-caps. Bpifrance houses a dedicated team of 20 professionals and 140 external consultants to advise companies in management and digital transformations, M&A processes, and international expansion. For start-ups, Bpifrance has sponsored Le Hub, a start-up incubator space in Paris, and for SMEs, has created the Accelerator to work with firms to quickly scale-up operations (Bpifrance, 2018b). Based on its regional network of offices, Bpifrance seeks to train SME entrepreneurs with the necessary skills as well as connecting them to potential business partners. These services, training 1,000 SMEs per year are to quadruple its activities until 2021 and reach 4,000 trained firms per year. These interventions focus on growing the ambitions of entrepreneurs and SMEs to transform into mid-sized firms as well as seek to facilitate the opening of family-owned SMEs towards financial markets, especially in case of transitions in family leadership (Bpifrance, 2017b, e.g. 2016). The directorate "Accompagnement" thereby seeks to employ the insights generated by the internal research unit which is drawing on its network of more than 2000 entrepreneurs which are regularly surveyed on their most prominent problems as well as particular themes, such as the use of digital technologies and so on. The goal of the *Direction Accompagnement* is to provide enterprises with good ideas access to larger companies and investors, which might help the company grow. It is also about the build-up of human capital in terms of concrete entrepreneurial skills, such as the creation of a business plan. The underlying idea is that companies supported in this way are a much lower credit risk and have a much higher chance of delivering profits, where Bpifrance has invested in equity. It is a model that builds on the local infrastructure

Bpifrance has and is supposed to benefit not only Bpifrance, but also the larger French economy, providing a positive externality to the society as a whole. This goal, generating both a viable business model for the bank, but also positive externalities for the French economy by pursuing a focus on entrepreneurial activities of start-ups and SMEs is also visible in the three sectors of Bpifrance involvement.

## 7.5.2 Three Sectors of Bpifrance Involvement

Despite the complex legal structure of Bpifrance, its sectoral activities can be broadly divided into three target sectors: large-cap firms, SMEs, and innovation and start-ups. Each of the three subsidiaries focuses in some capacity on all three sectors, though each with a different set of tools. In each, Bpifrance provides a mix of equity finance, loans, and non-financial support, but is always designed with the broader French economy in mind. Our interviews emphasized this capacity to provide a wider array of options to potentially interested companies (as well as government actors) as possibly the biggest positive effects of the merger of the different entities (interview Bpifrance bankers, formerly CDC Entreprises November 23, 2018, interview Bpifrance bankers, formerly OSEO March 26, 2019). Often, these synergy effects are also incorporated in the generation of future programs of Bpifrance to provide future business opportunities for the bank itself (interview November 23, 2018, Bpifrance, see for example the initiative for Deeptech below).

### 7.5.2.1 Large- and Mid-Cap Firms

One of the largest business activities for Bpifrance is large-cap firms. Since 2009, Bpifrance (until 2012 FSI) has supported 25 large-caps, with currently EUR 11.9 billion invested in 21 firms. Echoing past *dirigiste* policies, Bpifrance targets firms in strategic industries in order to stabilize the shareholding structure and support their operations, whether it be an internal restructuring, market consolidation, or international expansion. Most notably, in March 2017, Bpifrance invested EUR 1.9 billion in Peugeot to replace the French state's holding, as well as to support its ambitious growth strategy and navigate the integration with a newly acquired GM unit (Opel S.A.)[16]. Bpifrance has also noted that its experience with the automotive fund provided additional insights for Peugeot's strategic planning.[17] In

[16] Bpifrance became, together with the Chinese Dongfeng Motor Group, the largest single shareholder in 2017, holding 12.2% each, thereby making Chinese investment less dangerous in terms of the risk of take-over.

[17] "France digs in as Peugeot shareholder with stake shift," *Reuters*. 27 March 2017.

addition, Bpifrance has assisted large French companies like Ingenico (payment services; EUR 364 million), Idemia (smart card and security; EUR 110 million), and Verallia (glass; 10 percent stake) to develop growth strategies and either maintain or expand market shares. As part of the strategy, Bpifrance serves as a long-term capital investor to provide shareholder stability. Critically, Bpifrance makes a point of taking an active approach in the management of each firm. This involvement in governance also extends to providing external board members,[18] though as a matter of policy Bpifrance only maintains a minority stake (Bpifrance, 2018b).

#### 7.5.2.2 SMEs

Bpifrance has the most wide-ranging support for SMEs among NDBs in the European Union, as it has developed programs from innovation assistance to financing to providing growth capital. Financing serves as the central pillar of Bpifrance's SME support. As such, in 2017, Bpifrance has provided EUR 1.5 billion in equity and mezzanine finance for SMEs, and since 2013 has supported some 85,000 SMEs, or approximately one third of France's total (Bpifrance, 2018a). As noted previously, the Juncker Plan has increased its support for innovative SMEs by EUR 600 million, providing a stable stream of financing to Bpifrance for SME projects. Additionally, Bpifrance invests in investment funds that then invest in SMEs, of which more than half of the EUR 7.7 billion of Bpifrance's investments in funds go to SMEs. However, beyond financing, Bpifrance has also provided a range of non-financial services. For instance, Bpifrance established in 2015 an SME accelerator program, which over two years nurtured around 100 SMEs annually to grow into a mid-cap company through premium support services not only from Bpifrance, but also access to Business France (for export strategy), the *Institut du Mentorat Entrepreneurial* (for business mentoring), and Pacte PME (for relations with major firms).[19]

#### 7.5.2.3 Innovation and Start-Ups

Many NDBs have emphasized innovation and start-ups as key to sustainable economic growth, but Bpifrance has undoubtedly served a leadership role in this sector (interview Bpifrance France November 23, 2018, interview KfW official August 1, 2016), a fact which is vindicated by the joint venture funds by Bpifrance and KfW, initiated more than a decade after Bpifrance funds (see Mertens, this volume). Both the Financement and Investissement divisions support these small

[18] For instance, in 2017 Nicolas Dufourcq was installed on Orange's Board of Directors.

[19] https://www.caissedesdepots.fr/en/bpifrances-accelerateur-de-pme-smes-become-tomorrow-etis: published March 5, 2015, last accessed November 5, 2019.

firms through both equity participations and loan issuance. Importantly, these activities have been the target of French politicians who deem it critical that France become the leading technological player in Europe. President Macron's strong support has enabled Bpifrance to administer a large amount of financing, but also drive France's start-up scene.[20] Between 2013 and 2016, Bpifrance invested EUR 1.6 billion in France's tech industry, and in 2016 announced that it had secured EUR 6.5 billion for investments over the next three years.[21] Moreover, Bpifrance was the most active venture capital investor in Europe in both 2016 and 2017. In 2017, Bpifrance supported 92 rounds with a total value of USD 584 million across 13 industries[22], committing in addition funds of about EUR 1 billion in both 2017 and 2018 to funds of funds (Bpifrance, 2019a). Bpifrance has further expanded tools for specific sectors in innovation. In 2017, Bpifrance began Hub HealthTech, an accelerator specifically for startups in the biotechnology sector and in 2018, following up on demands by the French state, it has installed a program to help academic research transition into profitable ventures called Deeptech, once more showing the degree to which Bpifrance has become a tool for neo-*dirigiste* policies by the state, aiming at rejuvenating the industrial sector of France through fostering technological innovation.

## 7.6 Bpifrance's Interventionist Stance and the EU Level

Today, Bpifrance's activities have a distinctly *dirigiste* flavor. First, Bpifrance is tasked with strengthening French companies through supporting their development in France and abroad, and providing both financial and non-financial services throughout the lifecycle of a business. Here the history of Bpifrance's predecessors is apparent, as Bpifrance has strong abilities in the financing of innovation (originating with ANVAR), in fund of funds management (CDI Entreprises), in a network of regional offices (OSEO), and in a mechanism for providing guarantees (Sofaris). Second, Bpifrance aims to contribute to French enterprises that "are of strategic importance to the economy" by becoming a reference shareholder, facilitating carve-outs for large firms, supporting growth, and encouraging exports (Bpifrance, 2018b, p. 4). This intimately echoes the traditional *dirigiste* approach of past French industrial policy.

[20] Rosemain, Mathieu and Gwenaelle Barzic. "France's startup scene gains traction, led by state investment bank," *Reuters*. June 15, 2017.

[21] Agnew, Harriet. "Emmanuel Macron thinks big in vision for French tech unicorns," *Financial Times*, August 20, 2017.

[22] Wijngarde, Yoram. "Europe's most active venture capital investors: Bpifrance leads." published February 4, 2018 at https://blog.dealroom.co/europes-active-venture-capital-investors-bpifrance-leads/; last accessed November 5, 2019.

The creation and rapid expansion of Bpifrance's *dirigiste* mission is made even more remarkable because European State Aid regulation has largely eliminated the possibility of traditional *dirigiste* tools. Direct state ownership of companies and directly subsidized financing would constitute an anti-competitive behavior, and the strengthening European regulatory environment precludes these interventions (Blauberger, 2009; see Volberding, this volume). Instead, Bpifrance has mitigated the impact of European integration through three avenues. First, Bpifrance cooperates closely with commercial banks to provide co-financing and investment funds according to market investor principles. Even though the EPIC still guarantees any bond or commercial paper issuance, since the financing is provided on commercial terms without public funds, these operations do not violate EU regulation because they do not distort the private market (c.f. Cattrysse, 2014). For this reason, numerous financial observers have cited Bpifrance's resemblance to a private equity or venture capital fund.[23]

Second, Bpifrance adheres to the regulations set forth by State Aid, but in interaction with DG Competition has shaped the implementation of these rules (interview with Bpifrance bankers, March 26, 2019)[24] and certainly pushed them to their practical limits. For instance, Bpifrance Financement is subjected to the laws of European State Aid, which specifically prohibits providing guarantees, R&D and innovation funds, and subsidized loans to distressed companies or those that have not fully paid their social or fiscal contributions. The case of Peugeot, however, demonstrates the limitations of State Aid control (Bpifrance, 2013, p. 61). In 2013, France won approval to provide EUR 571.9 million in guarantees and repayable advances to the PSA Peugeot Citroën group, as DG Comp found it was in accordance with EU guidelines on rescuing and restructuring firms in difficulty (European Commission, 2013).[25] In 2017, Bpifrance took over EUR 1.92 billion from the *Agence des Participations de l'Etat* (APE), a holding institution for the French state, but since Bpifrance was classified as another central government body, it did not trigger a State Aid action (European Commission, 2017, p. 62). Therefore, since Bpifrance adheres to the market investor principle, as well as abides by State Aid guidance on block exemptions and firm rescue, it remains squarely within the confines of the regulation.

[23] "The French government experiments with venture capitalism," *The Economist*, 18 January 2018.

[24] For example, OSEO, the forerunner of Bpifrance also had a big role in elaborating jointly with DG Competition on how state aid rules for R&D should be calculated, their proposed method in 2008 winning approval from the Commission (Interview Bpifrance bankers, March 26, 2019).

[25] http://europa.eu/rapid/press-release_MEMO-04-172_en.htm, published 7th of July 2004, last accessed November 5, 2019.

Third, Bpifrance has closely cooperated with the EIB to establish funds and credit lines, another avenue which exempts the operations from EU regulations. In 2006, under OSEO already, the EIB provided EUR 80 million in loans for SMEs and business start-ups.[26] In the ensuing years, the cooperation has expanded strongly, particularly in innovation for SMEs. For instance, Bpifrance has utilized the European Investment Fund's (EIF) loan and guarantee schemes to increase its lending capacity in innovation (Bpifrance, 2018a). From 2015 to 2017, the EIF provided EUR 800 million in guarantees under Bpifrance's Innovation Loan and Seed Capital Loan programs. These programs initially were difficult to bring to fruition, as the EIF had difficulties in approving the projects proposed by Bpifrance (interview Bpifrance April 2018), but over the years the collaboration has improved and in particular the collaboration with respect to the project COSME was mentioned several times as successful (interview Bpifrance bankers November 2018, March 2019).

In 2017, in conjunction with the Juncker Plan, an additional EUR 600 million was made available for investment in innovative firms over the ensuing two years.[27] The EIF also raised its support from a 40 percent to 50 percent guarantee, further strengthening the risk-sharing financial instrument.[28] The cooperation has also expanded to new sectors. For example, in January 2017, the EIF signed a guarantee agreement to allow Bpifrance to create a portfolio of EUR 30 million of loans to SMEs in the cultural and creative sectors under the EU's Creative Europe program.[29] Taken together, this three-part strategy enables Bpifrance to maintain public financing without violating existing European regulations. How exactly these different activities play out and what it means for the question of the return of state *dirigisme* will be analyzed in the following section.

## 7.7 A Return to *Dirigisme*?

Even though Bpifrance itself has only existed since 2013, we contend that, in practice, the institution brings together the remnants of French *dirigisme* into a new form of state intervention in the economy. Through a concerted attempt of consolidating public financing tools now at the behest of the state, as well as an adept understanding of European regulations and the harnessing of private financial actors' resources, Bpifrance has managed to establish itself at the center of an

[26] http://www.bpifrance.com/Our-partners/European-Institutions-and-Networks/European-Investment-Bank, last accessed 5th of November 2019.

[27] http://www.eif.org/what_we_do/guarantees/news/2017/efsi_innovfin_bpifrance_innovative_businesses.htm, published October 12, 2017, last accessed November 5, 2019.

[28] http://www.eif.org/what_we_do/guarantees/RSI/news/2013/bpifrance.htm, published September 25, 2013, last accessed November 5, 2019.

[29] https://ec.europa.eu/digital-single-market/en/news/30-million-eur-loans-cultural-and-creative-smes-france; published January 30, 2017, last accessed November 5, 2019.

attempt to reorganize the French economy towards high-tech start-ups and SMEs and to stabilize and reorient large-cap firms that generate significant employment and tax revenues. Bpifrance's intimate connection with French political objectives in the economy also demonstrates a much closer interaction between the state and the economy that is reminiscent of top-down *dirigisme*. However, unlike its predecessors, Bpifrance has integrated a wide range of financial and non-financial tools, giving the institution greater flexibility—and more importantly, control—to serve as the central institution in this endeavor. This has allowed Bpifrance to contribute to a coherent French strategy for the acceleration of R&D and the growth of these firms.

To reiterate, we agree that the old *dirigiste* policies of direct state ownership and government-led industrial policy have fallen victim to European integration, State Aid regulation, and economic globalization. However, at the same time, the characteristics of Bpifrance suggest that the French state has reinserted itself into the economy in ways that extend beyond just "market supporting" means, such as altering labor regulation and promoting competition (Levy, 2006). In our estimation, the French state has once again taken on an interventionist role in the economy, though rather than through a traditional direct intervention for a "picking winners" industrial policy, it has been steered through instruments that preserve and co-evolve with markets. This strategy of generating "winners jointly with market actors" is complemented by the institutional strength of Bpifrance in terms of human capital formation as well as institutionalized links to industrial corporations, which itself is magnified by its centralized function at the center of this new French interventionism.

This centralization enables Bpifrance to implement a comprehensive strategy on behalf of the French government, which draws on the expertise of Bpifrance to design new programs aimed at developing this sector. One program that illustrates this dynamic is Deeptech, a program launched in 2018 to increase the capacity of French academia to generate successful start-ups. Bpifrance committed EUR 300 million to the fund, which aims to leverage the capital through private equity to as much as EUR 5 billion. In addition, Bpifrance will contribute EUR 550 million over the next five years to host research incubators, in order to develop France into a "Deeptech nation" able to compete with the US, Israel, and others. In both this project as well as FrenchTech, Bpifrance played a major role in designing the program together with the ministries, identifying the best venues to generate the desired results (interview Bpifrance; November 2018).

However, this comprehensive support is just one of the distinguishing aspects of Bpifrance when compared to other European NDBs. Of particular note is Bpifrance's emphasis on the entire business cycle; it provides financial and non-financial services from incubation to expansion, and its centralized function enables Bpifrance to better coordinate French state involvement in the economy. In addition, Bpifrance maintains a network of 48 regional branches across France, helping Bpifrance better target and engage with local SMEs (Bpifrance, 2019b). Finally, its active participation in management and strategic planning is also noteworthy, as most other NDBs take a passive role towards support, limiting their services to financing and guarantees. Bpifrance has opted to involve itself directly not only in financing and management, but also the education and training of entrepreneurs and SMEs, suggesting a greater interest in guiding the strategic direction of French firms.

Naturally, revived *dirigisme* has numerous parallels to previous French programs. First, Bpifrance is, by definition, the consolidation of an existing French business promotion agency and of credit lines. The three-part objective (to favor French economic development, to promote French industrial renewal, and to support future champions) intimately reflects a *dirigiste* spirit.[30] The consolidation has made Bpifrance a strong force in centralizing disparate strains of state support. Second, Bpifrance has been charged specifically with supporting French businesses in strategic sectors to promote the French economy and exports. These objectives have not been lost on either Bpifrance's management or on French politics, both of which see Bpifrance as a potent tool to guide French economic growth and channel EU funds to priority investments. Bpifrance's continued support of large-cap firms, most notably Peugeot and Orange, deeply reflects state guidance under *dirigisme*. As Fitch Ratings has succinctly stated, Bpifrance "is a strategic tool for implementing [French] economic support policy" and is "subject to strong administrative, legal and financial oversight by the French state, which defines its missions" (Fitch Ratings, 2017, p. 1).

However, there are important differences from traditional *dirigisme*. First, Bpifrance has relied heavily on financial markets and financial instruments to distribute funding, rather than using the traditional tools of state ownership. In particular, Bpifrance has sought to integrate itself with financial markets on both the side of fundraising and the side of distribution. For instance, Bpifrance has turned heavily towards capital markets to raise funds—in 2017, Bpifrance Financement issued EUR 6.5 billion in bonds, raising the total outstanding amount to EUR 20 billion (Bpifrance, 2018a, p. 22). On the distribution side, Bpifrance has preferred to find co-investors from the private sphere or invest in funds that then invest in the target industries, usually not doing so all on its own. For start-ups, Bpifrance has preferred providing a mix of shared risk guarantees. Bpifrance will match angel investors one-for-one with low-interest rate loans or grants, further emphasizing the notion that private markets should determine the winners.[31]

[30] http://aecm.eu/bpi-france/, last accessed November 5th 2019.

[31] Liam Boogar. "BPIFrance & the blurred lines between support &competition." September 13. 2013. Blog Rudebaguette available at http://www.rudebaguette.com/2013/11/20/vc-politics-public-funds-the-blurred-lines-between-support-competition/, last accessed November 5, 2019.

Second, while Bpifrance explicitly utilizes managerial positions to share the strategic direction of firms, it has also emphasized providing supporting services for existing management to solve problems on its own. The basic insight is that by supplying not only finance, but also know-how and connections to other entrepreneurs and businesses, the probability of firm success vastly improves. Therefore, Bpifrance seeks to upgrade the human capital of the entrepreneurs and provide them with the connections and support network of businesses and consultants that are conducive to success. In 2017, 7,500 French companies received consulting services, a 36 percent increase from the previous year (Bpifrance, 2018a). Bpifrance's expanding portfolio of accelerators and incubators like Le Hub further reinforces the notion that organic growth needs to be nurtured rather than determined from the top. Bpifrance has supported a start-up cluster in Paris, called French FAB, that teaches thousands of entrepreneurs and supports their development of business plans. Another area is the Bpifrance Inno Génération (BIG), an annual conference to connect entrepreneurs and share information regarding challenges and solutions. The fourth occurrence on October 11, 2018, attracted 40,000 participants, which makes BIG the largest economic event organized in France.[32] This support has recently extended internationally, with Bpifrance seeking to promote French start-ups abroad.

Finally, Bpifrance has employed strategies similar to that of a private venture capital firm.[33] In large-cap companies, Bpifrance has certainly not shied away from high-level positions in management, and has been actively involved in strategic planning, but also maintains minority shares and lets private actors determine the course of action. When assets have become sustainable and profitable, Bpifrance has also divested. Recent large-scale divestments include Valeo (EUR 200 million, automotive spare parts manufacturer), Eiffage (EUR 932 million, concessions and public works), and Gemalto (EUR 382 million, smart card and security) (Bpifrance, 2018b). Outside of large-caps, Bpifrance has emphasized scaling-up start-ups as a key to growth, much like a venture capital firm. This has reflected the opinions of the French technocratic elite, who have argued that a stumbling block for the French economy is the lack of innovation, as well as the lack of start-ups and SMEs that transform into larger, export-oriented ones (interview with bankers Bpifrance, November 2018). In that sense, Bpifrance represents a reorientation of French bureaucratic elite towards taking a more active industrial policy role.

[32] Cesar, Nicolas. "Bpifrance va rassembler 40 000 entrepreneurs à Paris". 13.09.2018 Sudouest. Available at https://www.sudouest.fr/2018/09/13/bpifrance-va-rassembler-40-000-entrepreneurs-5386230-705.php. last accessed November 5, 2019.

[33] Reuters. "France's startup scene gains traction, led by state investment bank." June 15, 2017. Available at https://www.reuters.com/article/france-tech-conference/frances-startup-scene-gains-traction-led-by-state-investment-bank-idUSL8N1JB5L6; last accessed November 5, 2019.

## 7.8 Conclusion

Bpifrance's experiences are instructive for other NDBs, as well as the larger development banking field. For one, Bpifrance has demonstrated the power of development banking as a tool not only for industrial policy, but also structural transformation. Today, the French elite is seeking to emulate the Anglo-American model of innovation, which includes productive start-ups that are hoped to become global leaders, or at least generate sizeable employment and tax revenue in France. In this way, the French elite is seeking to generate a corporate sector—with a vibrant SME community—that resembles the strength of Germany (interview Bpifrance November 2018). In addition, Bpifrance's adept maneuvering in the field of European development banking highlights the new opportunities that have emerged after the financial crisis. Bpifrance has charted a course that has avoided the pitfalls of State Aid regulation, but also, by virtue of its strong political support from the French state and the regions, has secured financing streams above and beyond those from the EIB or other EU-level investment platforms.

Yet there are cautionary elements to this *dirigiste* move as well. First, Bpifrance as a tool for the French state for active economic nationalism (Clift and Woll, 2012, Clift, 2013) could foster national champions that threaten to undermine the European single market project and, in the process, overstretch its own financial resources. Bpifrance has already been instrumental in the strategy of the French state to push for mergers of German and French industry conglomerates to form European champions (including Peugeot-Opel, Alstom-Siemens, and the Fond Croissance Rail), projects that could jeopardize its own financial health. Bpifrance has also come under criticism for favoritism in the selection of its projects, emphasizing profits over its role of supporting the French economy, and driving out commercial actors in the process.[34] At the same time, it faces repeated pressures from the executive and parliament to aid ailing companies or to support risky technological flagship projects in ways that might not always be in line with its goals of generating profits (interview bankers Bpifrance, November 2018). Hence, Bpifrance is potentially subject to pressure from both private and public sources, and it is arguably due to its nimble and highly skilled CEO, Dufourcq, at its helm since its inception, that these tensions have not led to excessive interferences in the business of Bpifrance.

The long-term implications of Bpifrance are therefore unknown, especially due to its young age. It is unclear whether the success of Bpifrance is reproducible in the future and in other European countries. After all, Bpifrance is the outcome of a long legacy of French institutions and programs, which established an ecosystem

[34] Poullennec, Solenn. "Le rôle de bpifrance remis en question," *Les Echos*. 21 December 2017. Available at https://www.lesechos.fr/2017/12/le-role-de-bpifrance-remis-en-question-190375; last accessed 5th of November 2019.

for development banking prior to the strengthening of EU State Aid rules. Moreover, whether other NDBs, especially in Eastern Europe, could replicate innovation labs or SME networks on the same scale as Bpifrance is questionable, particularly given that Bpifrance generates revenue through its sovereign wealth fund activities. Nevertheless, regardless of the critiques and shortcomings Bpifrance may have, one thing is apparent—the French state has actively sought to reinvigorate *dirigisme*, and Bpifrance has been instrumental in this revival.

## References

Assemblée Nationale de France, 2015. No 3097: Rapport D'information déposé en application de l'article 145 du Règlement par la mission d'information commune en conclusion des travaux de la mission sur la Banque publique d'investissement Bpifrance. Assemblée Nationale de France; Paris.

Berger, S., 1981. Lame Ducks and National Champions: Industrial Policy in the Fifth Republic, in Andrews, W.G., Hoffmann, S. (eds), The Fifth Republic at Twenty. SUNY Press.

Blauberger, M., 2009. Of "Good" and "Bad" Subsidies: European State Aid Control through Soft and Hard Law. West European Politics 32, 719–37.

Bouchara, P., 2003. Le Capital-Amorçage, Chaînon Manquant du Financement des Entreprises? École de Paris, Paris.

Bpifrance, 2019a. Bilan d'activité 2018: L'année de toutes les accélérations pour Bpifrance. Bpifrance, Paris.

Bpifrance, 2019b. Debt Investors Presentation: Bpifrance Financement, Bond Issuer.

Bpifrance, 2018a. Annual Financial Report: Bpifrance Financement 2017. Bpifrance Financement, Paris.

Bpifrance, 2018b. Bpifrance Investissement Mid & Large Cap. Bpifrance, Paris

Bpifrance, 2018c. Debt Investors Presentation: Bpifrance Financement, Bond Issuer. Bpifrance, Paris.

Bpifrance, 2017a. Bpifrance Assurance Export, the new French export credit agency on behalf of, for and under the control of the State. Bpifrance, Paris.

Bpifrance, 2017b. Histoire d'incompréhension: les dirigeants de PME et ETI face au digital. Bpifrance, Paris.

Bpifrance, 2016. Vaincre les solitudes du dirigeant. Bpifrance, Paris.

Bpifrance, 2014. Rapport Annuel. Bpifrance, Paris.

Bpifrance, 2013. The Doctrine. Bpifrance, Paris

Braun, B., Gabor, D., Hübner, M., 2018. Governing through Financial Markets: Towards a Critical Political Economy of Capital Markets Union. Competition & Change 22, 101–16. https://doi.org/10.1177/1024529418759476

Cattrysse, B., 2014. The Newly Adopted Risk Finance State Aid Rules. European State Aid Law Quarterly 689–97. European Commission, Brussels

Clift, B., Woll, C., 2012. Economic Patriotism: Reinventing Control over Open Markets. Journal of European Public Policy 19, 307–23.

Clift, B. 2013. Economic Patriotism, The Clash of Capitalisms, and State Aid in the European Union. Journal of Industry, Competition and Trade, Volume 13 (1). pp. 101–17.

Culpepper, P.D., 2010. Quiet Politics and Business Power: Corporate Control in Europe and Japan. Cambridge University Press.

Dufourcq, N., 2019. Bilan d'activité 2018 Bpifrance—Conférence de presse. Bpifrance, Paris.

Ekeland, M., Landier, A., Tirole, J., 2016. Renforcer le capital-risque français. Conseil d'analyse économique 33. Bpifrance, Paris.

European Commission, 2017. Final Findings: EDP Dialogue Visit to France. European Commission and Eurostat, Luxembourg.

European Commission, 2013. Aide d'État SA.35611 (2013/C) (2013/N)—France Aide à la restructuration en faveur du groupe PSA Peugeot Citroën S.A.

Fitch Ratings, 2017. Fitch Affirms EPIC Bpifrance at "AA"; Outlook Stable. Fitch Ratings, Paris/London.

Fourcade, J.-P., 2011. Participations transférées au Fonds stratégique d'investissement (FSI) (Rapport d'information n. 588). Paris.

Gaston-Breton, T., 2015. Servir l'avenir : Un siècle de banque publique. Editions Tallandier, Paris.

Granier, C., Bedu, N., 2019. The Role of Banks and the State in the Shaping of the French Fund Industry. Review of International Political Economy 26, 573–603.

Hall, P.A., 1986. Governing the Economy: The Politics of State Intervention in Britain and France. Oxford University Press.

Levy, J.D., 2017. The Return of the State? France's Response to the Financial and Economic Crisis. Comparative European Politics 15, 604–27.

Levy, J.D., 2011. The Return of the State? French Economic Policy Under Nicolas Sarkozy. Presented at the APSA.

Levy, J.D., 2006. The State After Statism: New State Activities in the Age of Liberalization. Harvard University Press.

Loriaux, M.M., 1991. France After Hegemony: International Change and Financial Reform. Cornell University Press.

Loriaux, M.M., Woo-Cumings, M., Calder, K., Maxfield, S., Pérez, S., 1997. Capital Ungoverned: Liberalizing Finance in Interventionist States. Cornell University Press.

Mertens, D., Thiemann, M., 2019. Building a Hidden Investment State? The European Investment Bank, National Development Banks and European Economic Governance. Journal of European Public Policy 26, 23–43.

Monnet, E., 2018. Controlling Credit: Central Banking and the Planned Economy in Postwar France, 1948–1973. Cambridge University Press.

OECD, 2014. OECD Reviews of Innovation Policy: France 2014. OECD, Paris.

OSEO, 2012. Investors Presentation: May 2012.

O'Sullivan, M., 2007. Acting Out Institutional Change: Understanding the Recent Transformation of the French Financial System. Socioecon Rev 5, 389–436.

Schmidt, V., 1997. Running on Empty: The end of Dirigisme in French Economic Leadership. Modern & Contemporary France 5, 229–41.

Schmidt, V., 1996. From State to Market? The Transformation of French Business and Government. Cambridge University Press.

Zysman, J., 1984. Governments, Markets, and Growth: Financial Systems and the Politics of Industrial Change. Cornell University Press.

APPENDIX 7.1

# List of Interviews

#1 Interview KfW official, August 1, 2016, Frankfurt
#2 Interview Bpifrance officials, April, 14 2018, Paris
#3 Interview Bpifrance officials, November 23, 2018, Paris
#4 Interview Bpifrance officials, March 26, 2019

# 8

# Is a European "Hidden Investment State" Emerging in Spain? The Role of *Instituto de Crédito Oficial*

*Judith Clifton, Daniel Díaz Fuentes, Clara García, and Ana Lara Gómez*

## 8.1 Introduction

In the context of protracted low levels of investment following the 2008 Great Recession and with the launch of the European Commission's "Investment Plan for Europe" in 2014, scholars have argued a new dimension of European integration may be emerging, a "hidden Investment State" (Mertens and Thiemann, 2019) in the form of a European field of development banking (Mertens, Thiemann and Volberding, this volume). The hidden investment state refers to the idea that polities may develop a governmental infrastructure that promotes investment in specific sectors of the economy, either through direct spending, or through financial techniques that mobilize other public or private funds. The hidden investment state is said to have three main characteristics. Firstly, an intensification of network formation between European and national development banks (NDB), both vertically, between the European Investment Bank (EIB) and NDBs of the Member States, and horizontally, between NDBs of Member States. Secondly, a goal of promoting investment in specific sectors, that goes beyond counter-cyclical action and includes fostering investment in sectors determined by government. Thirdly, a significant increase in loans and equity by development banks, both by the EIB as well as NDBs, as well as a concerted effort to promote institutional innovation, as regards financial products, leveraging and revolving European funds.

Of course, NDBs and the EIB have been working in tandem for decades (Clifton et al., 2018). However, recent developments point to a quantitative and qualitative deepening of that relationship. The main driver behind the emergence of the so-called hidden investment state is the European Union's (EU) long-desired quest to better connect the fragmented landscape of European economic policy making. Scholars have long pointed out the historically weak powers enjoyed by the EU as regards traditional taxing and spending functions, as well as

Judith Clifton, Daniel Díaz Fuentes, Clara García, and Ana Lara Gómez, *Is a European "Hidden Investment State" Emerging in Spain? The Role of* Instituto de Crédito Oficial In: *The Reinvention of Development Banking in the European Union: Industrial Policy in the Single Market and the Emergence of a Field.* Edited by: Daniel Mertens, Matthias Thiemann, and Peter Volberding, Oxford University Press (2021). 
DOI: 10.1093/oso/9780198859703.003.0008

its low capacity to steer and implement fiscal policy. In addition, industrial policy has become unfashionable, whilst state aid restrictions have become increasingly stringent, all in a context of the inexorable rise of economies with more state-active approaches, most importantly, in China, as seen in the China Development Bank and the Asian Infrastructure Investment Bank. Hence, with restricted space for traditional industrial policies, the interlocking of institutions through European-level policy making is interpreted as a means of setting up a multilevel infrastructure to further investment to better "make use of Europe" (Woll and Jacquot, 2010).

As in all processes of integration, developments are shaped by institutional differences. Across Europe, the historical trajectories and institutions of national development and "promotional" banking differ. Hence, just as the European institutions offer constraints and incentives, development banks embedded in a particular economy—in this case, the Spanish economy—need to navigate these changing circumstances, whilst developing idiosyncratic relationships with government and the private sector. The particularities of the Spanish institutional landscape, in which its NDB operates, have been barely explored.[1] Nevertheless, for the purpose of this study, we build on this scant literature and highlight the mixed nature of capitalism in Spain, which leans clearly towards neoliberalism, whilst retaining a residual of statism. This mix can be seen today in the Spanish political economy's core features, including the legacy of privatization of non-financial and financial companies, a small public banking sector, and an avoidance of industrial policies. Indeed, Spain's current corporate structure (oligopolistic sectors, cross-ownership between financial and non-financial firms, power relations between big financial and non-financial corporations and the state) can all be traced back to its statist capitalist past.

This particular breed of capitalism will be used as the backdrop when we investigate if, and to what extent, a hidden investment state is becoming embedded in the Spanish context. In order to do so, we map evolving networks, evaluate the changing orientation of the public banking system, compile financial information on performance, and categorize financial instruments deployed in the search for innovation. Our study focuses particularly on Spain's NDB, the *Instituto de Crédito Oficial* (ICO). Comparatively speaking, ICO is medium sized in terms of staff and resources, and it is a relatively young NDB, emerging from 1991, after having been initially established as a state agency for public banks in 1971. We combine scrutiny of primary and secondary documentation with semi-structured, anonymized, interviews with ICO directors and chief officers to examine the extent to which we observe deeper and wider networking and, linked to it,

[1] Exceptions include Royo (2008) and Buendía and Molero-Simarro (2018).

reorientation of the purpose of Spain's NDB toward new, specific goals, increased assets and loans, and significant institutional innovations.

Our main results are as follows. First, as regards the volume of borrowing, we find the ICO reacted strongly to the financial crisis, proactively promoting countercyclical measures between 2009 and 2012. This was accompanied by significant increases in funding from both the Spanish state and the European Central Bank (ECB). However, after the crisis, overall funding liabilities dropped dramatically, returning to pre-crisis levels, with special funds becoming almost insignificant. True, funding increased sharply from the EIB—especially that associated with the EFSI—and Spain positioned itself in 2019 as one of the leading Member States to attract loans and equity (EC, 2019a). Spain was the first Member State to take advantage of the Juncker Plan. However, behind the publicized proactive position of Spain, we argue this increase replaced a sharp drop in ECB "quantitative easing" funds. A similar observation can be made for ICO loans: these increased sharply as a reaction to the Great Recession; however, shortly afterwards, they returned to pre-crisis patterns. As for evidence of institutional innovation, we discuss the main evidence here, which is the emission of social and green bonds.

Second, according to ICO's official publications, a new strategy was established for 2018–2021, whereby it is claimed loans are being made on a more selective basis than previously, according to well-defined criteria. However, on examining evidence from primary sources, it is too early to state that there has been a significant change in this regard when compared to ICO's historical patterns.

Third, as regards networks, the ICO today boasts a wide network across Europe, and beyond. However, it is difficult to uncover the extent to which these networks have had a significant impact on ICO in terms of its business activities. We find that, to date, ICO's participation in these networks is still emerging, and we have only detected a limited impact on its raison d'être, financial instruments, and performance.

In sum, we find that ICO's response post-crisis has been relatively subdued and if there is a "hidden investment state" in Spain, it is still modest to date. The next question is why. The field-theoretical lens of this volume claims NDBs in the South of Europe have been less able to influence the agenda in Europe and take advantages of loopholes created in this new scenario (see Mertens, Thiemann and Volberding, this volume). Hence, we reflect on how change at the European level filters down to the Spanish case, by looking at the ICO's historical evolution, regarding its role, approach, and instruments, as well as by its embeddedness in the economy, with its particular institutional framework and cyclical needs. While the recently launched InvestEU program (2021–27), which replaces the Juncker Plan as the European investment promotion mechanism, is perceived by ICO representatives as an opportunity for the ICO to participate more in collective institution-building, it is still too early to assess whether this will bring about a meaningful change in strategic orientation and instruments.

The rest of the chapter is organized around tracking ICO's evolution chronologically. In section 8.2, we provide a brief background on the early years of ICO from 1964 to 1991. In section 8.3, we analyze the evolution of ICO borrowing and loans from 1991 to the outbreak of the financial crisis (2007) in the context of a changing Spanish political economy; and in section 8.4, we analyze ICO from 2008 to the present. Finally, in section 8.5, we assess the extent to which ICO is part of a European "hidden investment state." Conclusions follow.

## 8.2 ICO's Background: 1964–1991

During the rule of the Franco regime (1939–1975), Spain was largely isolated from the international political scene. Funding to the domestic economy, thus, came mostly from public expenditure, pawnbroking institutions (*Montes de Piedad*), credit unions and savings banks[2]. It was only in 1964 that Spain started to receive funds from the International Bank for Reconstruction and Development (IBRD)[3] as a result of the mission to Spain in 1961 "to assist the government in working out the basis for a long-term development program" (World Bank Group, 2001). Funding from the IBRD to Spain lasted until 1978. The European Investment Bank (EIB) superseded the IBRD with the application for European Economic Community (EEC) membership and in 1981 the first EIB loan to Spain was made (Figure 8.1).

During the Franco years, Spain had tried to join the European EEC without success. As early as 1962, the Franco dictatorship started to embrace new

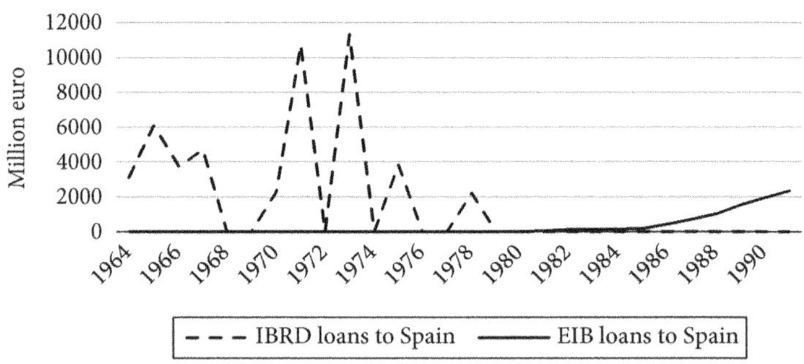


**Figure 8.1** IBRD and EIB loans to Spain 1964–1991 (EUR million)
*Source*: World Bank Group (2019), EIB (2019b)

[2] Saving banks consolidated their role within the Spanish financial system thanks to their linkage to social policies, which contributed to building cheap houses and the provision of municipal credit, among other things.

[3] The IBRD (first institution of the World Bank) was established in 1944 with the mission of financing the reconstruction of Western Europe, devastated by the War. Its mission later expanded to advancing worldwide economic development and eradicating poverty (World Bank Group, 2001).

economic policies, including the founding of ICO's predecessor, a state agency responsible for co-ordinating and controlling the public banks, and the application for association with the EEC (Crespo MacLennan, 2000). Nevertheless, the negotiations for EEC association were paralyzed as a result of the extremely complicated political context, with the dictatorship rejected by most outside Spain. It was not until 1970, in the context of a deteriorated European economic context, that the first step towards building a relationship between Spain and Europe occurred with the signing of an Association Agreement ("Spain—Common Market"). The successful application for Spanish accession to the EEC, however, did not occur until the death of Franco in 1975 and the proclamation of Juan Carlos I as King and Head of State.

The ICO was founded in 1962 under another name; however, in 1971, it was given its current name. With this change of name, ICO became a state agency in charge of Spain's public banks, regulated by Law 13/1971 (Official Credit System and Organization Act and Martín-Aceña et al., 2016). ICO, financed wholly by the Spanish Treasury, had as its main function the coordination of the funding and credit of public banks in Spain, thus directly serving government economic policy (Blasco et al., 2018). These public banks were organized in designated clusters of activities including: foreign trade (*Banco Exterior de España*); manufacturing (*Banco de Crédito Industrial*); mortgages (*Banco Hipotecario de España*); regional credit (*Banco de Crédito Local*); agriculture (*Banco de Crédito Agrícola*) and postal savings (*Caja Postal de Ahorros*).

With Franco's death, Spain moved towards a democratic transition. With democracy restored after the 1977 elections, President Adolfo Suárez, continuing with the idea of integrating Spain into Europe, started accession negotiations with the EEC (EC, 2016; Archivo Digital España-UE, 2016). This culminated eight years later, in 1985, under the Socialist government (Spanish Socialist Workers' Party, PSOE) elected in 1982, with the signature of the Accession Treaty in Madrid and the integration of Spain in the EEC on January 1, 1986.

During the accession process, Spain (under the new status of EEC candidate country) started to receive loans from the EIB from 1981, which replaced IBRD funds. Regional policy was revised and remodeled to qualify for assistance under the European Regional Development Fund (ERDF) (Salmon, 2004). Spain initiated a catching up and modernization process that allowed it to exit from isolation, putting the industrial recession of the transition behind it (Betrán et al., 2012). ICO's policy to support industrial and export activities, which had started at its origins, was reinforced in the 1980s by EIB credit lines to the public banks *Banco de Crédito Industrial* and the *Banco Hipotecario de España*, among other entities[4]. These loans were complemented by other EIB loans to private and public

[4] From 1983, the EIB provided Global loans to Spain through ICO.

companies mostly within the energy sector, including *Empresa Nacional del Gas*[5] in 1982, *Empresa Nacional de Investigación y Explotación de Petróleo S.A.*[6] in 1984, *Hidroeléctrica Española S.A.*[7] in 1985, and the transport sector, including RENFE in 1982, 1983 and 1985, Ministry of Public Works and Transports in 1985. Spain also benefitted from ERDF funds from 1986 (CEC, 1986).

For the incoming Socialist government, much of the public enterprise sector was associated with the Franco régime, hence, privatization, being undertaken in other governments in Europe at the time, was perceived in Spain as a means of modernizing the country and, therefore, embraced by the Socialist government. This influenced the trajectory of ICO. In 1988, ICO was transformed into a public bank, assuming control and ownership of all the other public banks. At the same time, it stopped receiving finance exclusively from the Treasury (Special Funds), and started to finance itself, mainly, from capital markets (Ordinary Funding). However, its new situation was short-lived: the aim of this consolidation was not to reinforce the ICO as a strong national development bank. Rather, it was a move towards privatization of most of its commercial and potentially profitable operations. In other words, privatization policies started to influence ICO's development.

In 1991, the PSOE grouped most of the commercial activities controlled by ICO into a newly created public financial holding: Argentaria. Argentaria would be managed independently from ICO and was gradually transformed into a commercial bank. Between 1993 and 1998, Argentaria was privatized. In 1999, Argentaria was merged with the private bank Banco Bilbao Vizcaya (BBV) becoming *Banco Bilbao Vizcaya Argentaria* (BBVA)—Spain's second largest commercial bank.

## 8.3 ICO's Expansion: 1991–2007

Once a member of the EEC in 1986, Spain became one of the largest recipients of EIB and EU loans. Newly organized in 1991, ICO completed EIB funding in its new phase as an NDB. From 1991, ICO also had a new legal status as an NDB, and therefore, came under the regulation of the Bank of Spain. ICO would also perform as an independent financial intermediary of the state, charging the state for its management costs in accordance with the provisions of the General State Budget Act for each year[8] (ICO, 2009). Overall, all types of funding from European institutions to Spain grew through the period. During the pre-crisis

[5] Currently known as *Enagás, S.A.*, with presence (besides Spain) in Mexico, Peru, Chile, Sweden and in the Trans Adriatic Pipeline European project.

[6] The *Empresa Nacional de Investigación y Explotación de Petróleo S.A.* or ENIEPSA merged with *Hispanoil* in 1985, to successively become a subsidiary of *Repsol S.A* (under the name of *Exploración*) in 1986, when the National Institute of Hydrocarbons (INH) reorganized the Spanish oil sector.

[7] The origin of *Iberdrola*, one of the world's five most important companies in the sector.

[8] These activities as a financial intermediary of the state are not included in the balance sheet of ICO as an NDB.

years, from 2000 to 2007, most EU funding to Spain came from agricultural and structural funds; the EIB represented under half of total EU investment.

### 8.3.1 ICO Loans: Funding

In terms of the volume and composition of ICO's borrowing (liabilities) and loans (assets), whilst the overall volume of funding did not change significantly between 1991 and 2004, the source of that funding shifted. ICO obtains funds via two main mechanisms: Special Funding and Ordinary Funding. Special Funding is mainly comprised of state loans and bonds, while Ordinary Funding is primarily raised through capital markets and bilateral loans by Multilateral Financial Institutions. Whilst, in 1991, Special Funding was still significant, this steadily decreased to virtually insignificant levels—until the outbreak of the financial crisis from 2008. Ordinary Funding grew steadily in importance and, by 1997 over 90 percent of ICO funding was from this source. Loans by the EIB were the most important source of loans from Multilateral Financial Institutions.

Figure 8.2 shows the volume and composition of ICO funding liabilities from 1991 to 2007, derived from ICO Annual Reports. Two phases can be detected overall. First, between 1991 and 1997, total Funding Liabilities declined slightly, from EUR 18bn to EUR 16bn. This change can largely be explained by a decline in Special Funding. In 1991, Special Funding totaled EUR 9.6bn (52.9 percent of overall funding), dropping to EUR 1.2bn (7.6 percent) by 1997. At the same time, Ordinary Funding increased from EUR 8.5bn (47.1 percent) to EUR 14.8bn (92.4 percent) in the same period. Loans from the EIB increased but only modestly, from EUR 1.6bn (8.9 percent) in 1991 to EUR 2.4bn (14.9 percent) in 1997.

A second phase can be seen in the decade from 1998 to the outbreak of the financial crisis from 2008. In 1999, there was another significant legal reform of ICO whereby ICO was considered as a public corporation subject to company

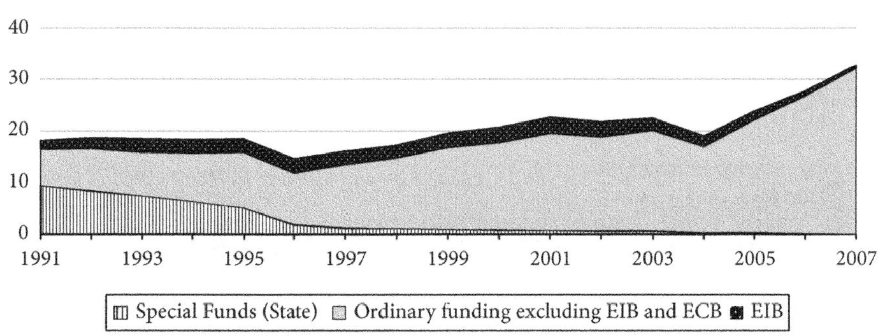


**Figure 8.2** ICO funding liabilities 1991–2007 (EUR billion)
*Source*: ICO Annual Reports (compiled by authors).

law, meaning that ICO's liabilities would be directly guaranteed by the state (Royal Decree 706/1999). Overall Funding Liabilities increased significantly, from EUR 19.6bn in 1999 to EUR 43bn in 2008. The growth in importance of Ordinary Funding was the main reason: this increased from 95 percent in 1999 to 100 percent in 2008. Hence, in this period, Treasury Special Funding became insignificant. At the same time, the importance of funding from the EIB dropped in absolute and relative terms, from EUR 2.7 (13.9 percent) in 1999 to EUR 0.5bn (1.5 percent) in 2008.

### 8.3.2 ICO Loans: Types

We examine ICO loans (assets) by type (Figure 8.3). Since its restructuring as an NDB in 1991, ICO lending activity has been classified into three main categories: Credit Institutions Loans; Mediation Loans; and Customer Loans. There was a fourth, minor category: securities, which gained importance in 2007, when the ICO resorted to the "securitization" of Mediation Loans.

In the early years, ICO's most significant loans where those supplied to Credit Institutions, in particular to Argentaria. The ratio of Credit Institutions as a proportion of total loans declined gradually from 78 percent in 1991 to 35 percent in 1997. In this category of Credit Institutions Loans, Argentaria accounted for around 89 percent of the credit from 1991 to 1997. From 1998 onwards, the category "Credit Institutions" declined in importance progressively and, as a proportion of total loans, fell to below 2 percent from 2008.

Meanwhile, ICO Mediation Loans were an instrument for supporting SMEs, which were introduced from 1993 onwards. These credit lines have gradually become diversified in order to support different objectives, including innovation and business internationalization, and features such as long repayment terms, preferential interest rates, and accessibility. These Mediation Loans increased continuously in importance as a percentage of total loans, comprising 3 percent

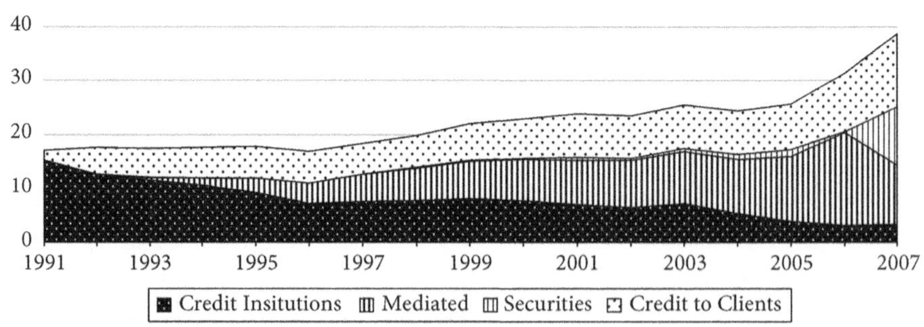


**Figure 8.3** ICO loans assets 1991–2007 (EUR billion)
*Source*: ICO Annual Reports (compiled by authors)

in 1993 to 28 percent in 1997. Until 1997, ICO assumed a part of the credit risk of the final borrowers (i.e. SME). However, from 1998, the ICO no longer assumes the risk of insolvency of borrowers (with the exception of the period during the financial crisis 2009–2012, when ICO provided liquidity lines). Nonetheless, despite the change in ICO's credit risk policy in 1997, Mediation Loans continued to increase their share as a percentage of total loans, from 20.5 percent in 1998 to 58 percent in 2007, the year before the outbreak of the Great Recession.

### 8.3.3 Sectors Addressed

Loans reflect the importance assigned to transport, energy, agriculture and SMEs. First, roads, trains, ports and airports received large EU and EIB loans (for example, EIB: *Iberia Lineas Aéreas de España S.A.*[9] from 1989; FEVE from 1990). Second, within the energy sector, wind power received significant impetus from the 1990s (Varela, 1999), which helped Spain become the producer of 20 percent of the world's wind power (Meyer, 2007). Companies such as *Hidroeléctrica de Navarra*, *Iberdrola Energías Renovables S.A.U.*, *Energías Especiales del Alto Ulla S.A*, *Parque Eólico de Padul S.L.* or *Energías Especiales Montes Castellanos S.L.* benefited during these years from Spanish legislation and EIB loans, contributing to Spain's catching-up. Third, agricultural funds traditionally constituted an important share of EU funds to Spain. Finally, SMEs were the focus of ICO from the outset, with EIB credit lines granted to the Spanish NDB, but also to *Banco de Crédito Local de España*, *Banco Central Hispanoamericano S.A.*, *Banco Bilbao Vizcaya S.A.*, *Banco de Santander S.A.*, and the *Caja de Ahorros de Valencia, Castellón y Alicante* (BANCAJA), among other entities. In particular, from 1993, one of the main strands of ICO was its program to provide credit through the commercial banking sector. The private credit entities collaborate with ICO and make credit available to companies on advantageous conditions. ICO sets the total economic endowment and the main characteristics and financial conditions, while the commercial banking sector is in charge of the analysis and the feasibility of the project, being free to decide whether to grant the loan or not. If approved, the credit entity sets out the required financial guarantees and assumes the risk of default. ICO, for its part, provides the funds to the commercial bank once the loan has been granted, so the commercial bank can, in turn, provide the funding to the company. This enables ICO funds to reach companies throughout the national territory. ICO plays an important role in the Spanish financial system by providing added value to the business sector and by supporting the activities that sustain economic growth, the creation of employment and the positioning of

[9] *Iberia* signed an agreement to merge with British Airways in 2010, becoming the third largest commercial airline in the world by revenue.

Spanish companies abroad (ICO, 2019). Indeed, coinciding with these policies, the Spanish GDP growth rate increased between 1993 and 2000 and, until 2007, it remained above 2.9 percent (World Bank, 2018), with EU and ICO funds as one of the elements encouraging its insertion into the international landscape.

## 8.4 ICO's Counter-Cyclical Role: 2008–2018

The Great Recession revealed the weaknesses of the European financial systems (Mayes, 2018; Endrejat and Thiemann, 2019): Spain in 2012 was compelled to apply for a €100 billion program for bank recapitalization, though, in the end, the final request amount was €41 billion. In an effort to enact reform, policy makers highlighted the need for a balanced and sustainable financial model able to face the new European challenges. Negotiations to change EU financial regulations, nonetheless, were difficult, due to different and sometimes conflicting national interests. Even though there was an initial consensus that the deregulated, *laissez faire,* attitude had to be reined in somewhat, ultimately, the presence of different interests and preferences prevailed. Whilst some countries, such as the UK, supported rules that would guarantee the continued advantageous position of the City of London, other countries supported tougher regulation in those financial services where their countries had limited presence, but less so in banks, which were the backbone of the continental financial system (Burns et al., 2018). Financial reform was finally only incremental.

In this context, ICO played an important counter-cyclical role from 2008 to 2014 (until the Juncker Plan was launched), seeing its loans double during the period with two peaks: one after the outbreak of the financial crisis, in 2010, and another, after the bank recapitalization package of 2012, in 2014, as seen in Figure 8.4.

### 8.4.1 ICO Loans: Funding

The outbreak of the financial crisis and the ensuing immediate years to 2012 saw a new phase: the ICO reacted substantially, expanding its Funding Liabilities from EUR 50.4bn in 2009 to EUR 106bn in 2012 (Figure 8.5). The bulk of this expansion was due to Ordinary Funding, which made up 92.9 percent and 81.1 percent of overall funding in the period. During this phase of crisis and the credit crunch, ICO acted in a counter-cyclical manner, as seen in increases in Special Funding from the Spanish State as well as Multilateral loans from the ECB (Figure 8.5).

Special Funding re-emerged, therefore, as an important source of ICO Funding Liabilities, constituting 7.1 percent in 2009, 5 percent in 2010 and 3.2 percent in 2011 of overall funds. By 2012, however, this returned to insignificant levels. As Special Funding decreased, funding from the ECB stepped up, in 2010

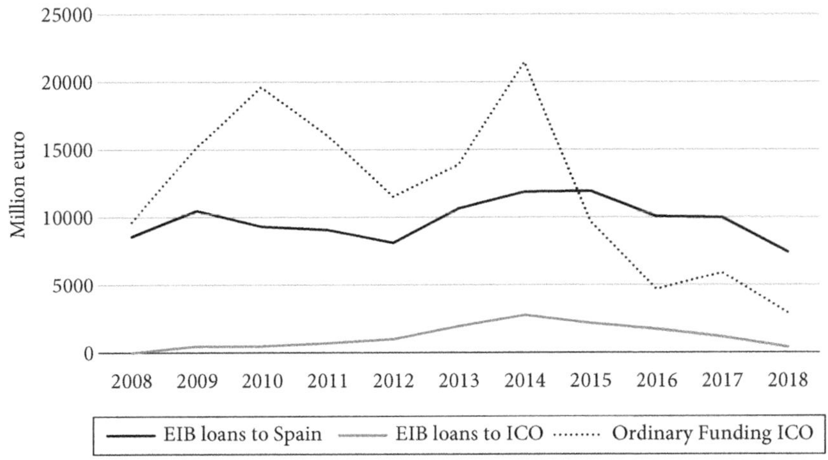


**Figure 8.4** EIB and ICO loans to Spain, 2008–2018 (EUR million)
*Source*: World Bank Group (2019), EIB (2019b)

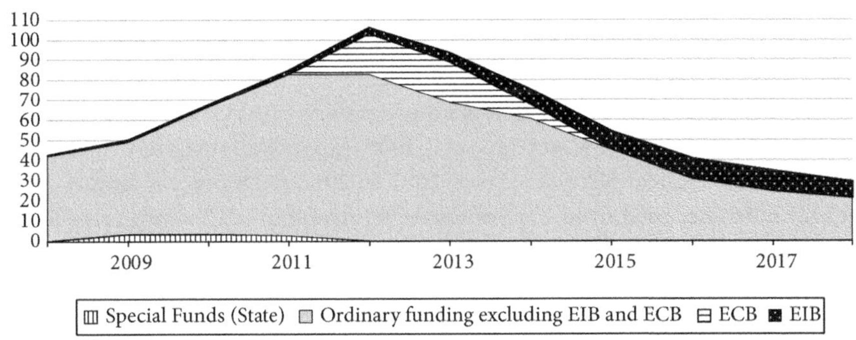


**Figure 8.5** ICO funding liabilities 2008–2018 (billion euro)
*Source*: ICO annual reports (compiled by authors)

providing EUR 0.4bn loans, growing to EUR 20bn in 2012, some 18.9 percent of ICO Funding Liabilities. The EIB loans also increased ICO loans from EUR 0.9bn (1.8 percent) in 2009 to EUR 3.2bn (3 percent) in 2012.

However, as the worst of the economic crisis passed, there was a huge drop again in ICO Funding Liabilities, from EUR 93bn in 2013 to EUR 35bn in 2017. The lion's share of this decline was due to the reduction in Ordinary Funding, from EUR 68.6bn in 2013 to EUR 24.9bn in 2017. Additionally, funding from the ECB declined from EUR 20.3bn in 2013 to insignificant levels by 2015. The major change in this period, as regards source of funding, then, is that of EIB loans. EIB loans were the only source to actually increase, expanding from EUR 4.4bn (4.7 percent) in 2013 to EUR 10 in 2016 and 2017 (28.8 percent), see Figure 8.5.

### 8.4.2 ICO Loans: Types

In 2007, given the increasing concentration of Mediation Loans as a proportion of ICO's assets and, in order to reduce its banking risk, ICO resorted to the "securitization" of Mediation Loans as a tool to manage its balance sheet (ICO, 2008, Chairman's Statement p. 5). The bonds deriving from the securitization of Mediation Loans are classified by ICO as loan accounts. From the outbreak of the Great Recession until 2013, the volume of Mediation Loans (including securitized loans) increased twofold, and the ratio of Mediation Loans as a proportion of total loans peaked at 67 percent in 2013, see Figure 8.6. With these loans, ICO was anticipating the counter-cyclical action that the ECB would take later: it was not until December 2011 that the ECB started to provide financing to banks in Spain, and then it did so only timidly. From 2014 onwards, the volume of Mediation Loans declined to pre-crisis levels (of 2006) whilst the ratio of Mediation Loans to total loans gradually declined to 52.5 percent in 2017. It could be that the worst of the crises had past, but one should also consider the more decisive action of the ECB, rendering ICO's funds less necessary for bank liquidity (the program for bank recapitalization was soon followed by funding from the ECB to commercial banks via the Targeted Longer-Term Refinancing Operations (TLTRO).

The third broad category of assets are the loans known as Credit to Clients. The volume of these loans grew steadily until 2006, expanded intensively during the first years of the Great Recession from 2007 to 2012 (26.8 percent annual average), and then declined from 2013 onwards, returning in 2017 to pre-crisis levels (2006). The ratio of Credit to Clients to total loans was around 33 percent over the period 1992–2006 and increased to 40 percent in 2012 and declined to around 30 percent in 2016–2018. This is mainly explained by the faster decline of total loans rather than an increase in Credit to Clients, see Figure 8.6.

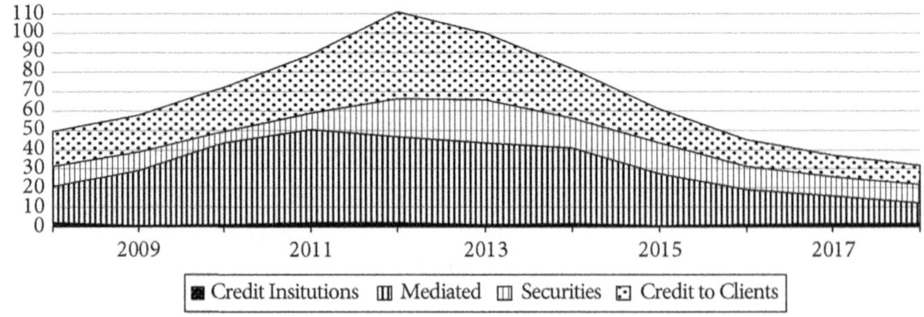


**Figure 8.6** ICO loans assets 2008–2018 (billion EUR)
*Source*: ICO Annual Reports (compiled by authors)

### 8.4.3 Sectors Addressed

In terms of sectors, after the crisis, we observe a greater emphasis on the part of ICO as regards the internationalization of companies, aid for exports, and the creation of SMEs (e.g. *Plan Avanza*). Focusing on the bulk of EIB loans to ICO, this went to credit lines, mirroring the peak of EIB loans to credit lines in Spain after the 2012 bailout. This represented 99 percent of EIB loans to ICO for the period 2009-2018, as seen in Figure 8.7, with a focus on SMEs (74 percent of EIB loans to ICO for the period 2009–2018). Internationalization and exports gained importance within credit lines. From 2014, a small increase in the diversification of the types of credit lines from the EIB to ICO can be observed, including previously unused ones within the areas of micro enterprises, SME internationalization and risk-sharing loans. EIB loans to ICO peaked in 2014, but then fell. This occurred in parallel with a drop in EIB loans to credit lines in Spain. The share of previously unused loans increased from 22 percent in 2014 to 40 percent in 2017. This could be understood as evidence of ICO seeking to imitate (following the Juncker Plan) other NDB practices under EFSI. In other words, it appears ICO was attempting to align its "product catalogue" with that of other NDB. It could be argued that the venture capital manager AXIS (completely owned by ICO since 2002) and the creation of venture capital funds such as *FOND-ICOinfrastructuras* (created in 2009; operational since 2011) or *FOND-ICO Global* (created on May 2013) constitute an influence on the type of financing granted. *FOND-ICO Global*

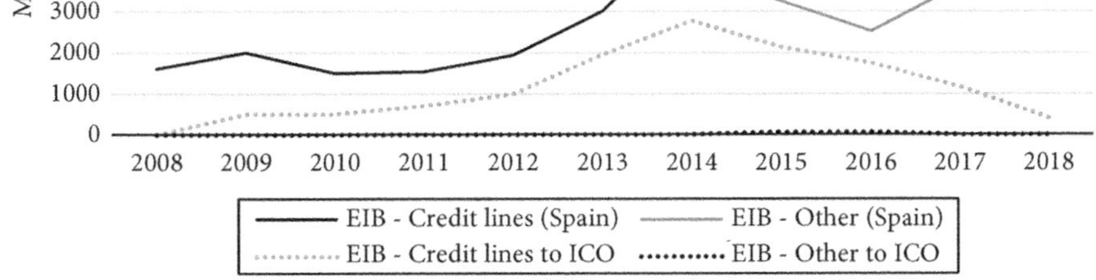


**Figure 8.7** EIB loans to Spain (as a whole) and to ICO by sector (2008–2018) (million EURO)

*Notes*: Credit lines provide greater access to credit for a wider range of clients, mainly self-employed and small and medium-sized companies, through a partnership with financial intermediaries. For EIB loans to Spain "Other" includes agriculture, fisheries, and forestry; composite infrastructure; education; energy; health; industry; services; solid waste; telecommunications; transport; urban development; and water, sewerage. For EIB loans to ICO "Other" includes energy, health, and transport.

funds are the largest of *AXIS* venture capital funds. Venture capital, however, is not new. AXIS had been established in 1986, and the ICO was its main shareholder from 1993, the same year *FOND-ICOpyme* started to operate. In sum, we observe only a minor shift in ICO policies as regards the type of EIB loans.

### 8.4.4 Juncker Plan and EFSI

Despite difficulties in reforming the financial system, Rubio (2018) argues that, among other things, the continuous lack of investment and funding led authorities to support, at least rhetorically, a shift from "grants to loans" on the part of the European financial institutions, based on the popular and often-cited idea of making "better use" of resources. This was embodied in the Investment Plan for Europe, also known as the Juncker Plan, presented in November 2014 for the period 2014–2020. In contrast to the European Structural and Investment (ESI) funds, which were based on grants, the Juncker Plan announced that it would mobilize over €315 billion investment through loans, via the creation of the EFSI. EFSI, operationalized through the EIB[10], the vertebral axis around which NDBs would work, would ostensibly allow for greater risk-taking, thus, funding projects that might otherwise go unfunded (European Parliament, 2017; see Griffith-Jones and Naqvi, this volume).

ESI funds, representing €457.6 billion for 2014–2020 (see Table 8.1), are one of the main instruments to support EU policy goals and increased significantly from 2007–2013 to 2014–2020). They are, therefore, well above EFSI finance, at €72.5 billion for 2014–2020 (see Table 8.2). Despite this, the Commission intended to place EFSI and this "renewed financial framework" at the core of the Investment Plan for Europe (European Court of Auditors, 2017).

Efforts moved in this direction with positive communication bordering on marketing, that praised the advantages of EFSI (EC, 18/07/2018). However, the implementation of ESI funds has been slower than expected (only 28 percent from the total planned amount has been spent) (EC, 19.12.2018).

Hence, as a result of the Juncker Plan and EFSI, NDBs such as ICO acquired an increasingly important position. The Commission underscored the importance of enhanced cooperation between itself, the EIB and NDBs for the Plan to work, even suggesting the convenience of setting up NDBs in Member States that did not have one (EC, 27/07/2015). Under EFSI, NDBs are said to occupy a strategic position in between the European authorities (i.e. the EIB Group and the

[10] EFSI's investment operations take place within two thematic areas: the Infrastructure and Innovation Window (IIW), managed by the EIB, which aim to provide finance to strategic projects, and the SME Window (SMEW), managed by the EIF (which is part of the EIB Group), which aims to support SMEs and enterprises with up to 3,000 employees. (European Court of Auditors, 2019).

**Table 8.1** European Structural and Investment planned funding (2014–2020) (billion euro)

| Countries | EU Amount | % | National Amount | % | Total Amount | % | % Spent (of total) |
|---|---|---|---|---|---|---|---|
| Spain | 39.95 | 9 | 16.36 | 9 | 56.31 | 9 | 22% |
| All countries | 457.60 | 100 | 181.06 | 100 | 638.66 | 100 | 28% |

*Data*: EC (2019b), EC/03/05/2019).

**Table 8.2** EFSI Finance (planned and disbursed) by EIB group and the Spanish Government via ICO (2014–2020) (billion euro)

| | | EFSI | National Amount | Total investment related to EFSI |
|---|---|---|---|---|
| **Finance (planned)** | Spain | 8.55 | 1.5 | 46.21 |
| | All countries | 72.47 | 34* | 389.77 |
| **Signed 2015–2018** | Spain | 4.44 | | 17.61 |
| | All countries | 40.23 | | 181.92 |
| **Approved 2015–2019** | Spain | 0.78 | | 2.64 |
| | All countries | 5.84 | | 27 |
| **Total disbursed (to date)** | Spain | 5.22 | | 20.24 |
| | All countries | 46.1 | | 208.92 |

*Data*: EC (2019a); EIB (2019).

*Notes*: quantities with an * are the contributions announced by the national governments (i.e. this could be subject to variation). Figures must be interpreted with caution, as EFSI financing for some signed and approved projects is not disclosed.

Commission) and national investment plans. It is stated they assume "the role of entrusted entity (like the EIB or EIF) for EU centrally-managed financial instruments" (EC, 27/07/2015; OJEU, 26/10/2012). The Commission claims this new setting will boost cooperation among all three parties, creating an integrated system of NDBs (EC, 27/07/2015). In terms of funding, ICO only receives a small percentage. The majority is channeled through other private and public financial institutions, including, in the case of Spain, the state-owned *Compañia Española de Refianzamiento* or CERSA, which is 24 percent owned by ICO.

Spain ranks third as regards the volume of EFSI resources it expects to receive in absolute terms: it is claimed €8.5 billion will generate a total investment of €46 billion out of an investment in all countries of about €72 billion, expected to help generate around €390 billion (see Table 8.2). This represents about 11 percent of all EFSI investment. Considering that the Spanish population is around 9.1 percent of the EU-28 population[11] (Eurostat, 2019), EFSI funding is

[11] The population in Spain in 2018 was 46.7 million people, while the EU28 population comprised 512.4 million people (Eurostat, 2019).

proportionate. Additionally, the Spanish Government will contribute €1.5 billion via ICO to co-finance projects since Member States are able to contribute to the EFSI in guarantees or in cash (EC, 27/07/2015). This initiative falls within the ICO "Strategic Plan" for the period 2018–2021, which, in turn, is framed under the "Internationalization Strategy of the Spanish Economy" for the period 2017–2027 (ICO, 2018). ICO staff stated they were optimistic ICO would make the most of InvestEU in Spain and better align its range of financial products in coordination with other NDBs (ICO, 2018).

Overall, therefore, we observe heightened loan volumes from the years following the Great Recession, comprised of Mediation Loans to SMEs and the self-employed to facilitate liquidity and promote internationalization, and Credit to Clients, peaking in 2012. However, with the shift from ICO funding from ECB to the Juncker Plan, from around 2014, both categories of loans decline.

### 8.4.5 The ICO Today

Today, ICO works closely with the key Ministries of Economics and Finance. The two Governing Bodies are the Executive Body (General Board and Chairman) and Management Body (Management Committee and Operations Committee). It falls to the Governing Board to exercise the main powers at ICO. The board approves ICO's annual accounts, reports and management reports, and makes the rules and decisions on economic policy measures, following the guidelines outlined by the Council of Ministers, the Government Committee for Economic Affairs or the Minister for the Economy and Business. The Governing Board also sets all internal rules of procedure, when not provided for in the articles of association, and presents amendments to the articles of association (ICO, 2017, 56–72).

The change made to the composition of the Board in 2015 to comply with European standards[12] is interesting because, not only did it introduce the position of four independent Board members, it also conferred on them a "double vote on transactions" which effectively means these four members have a majority (eight votes versus six). Of course, these independent members have been appointed by the Ministry of Economy and Business and can be removed by the same entity (ICO Integrated Report 2017, 57). As an NDB, ICO follows market banking practices, International Financial Reporting Standards (IFRS), and Basel III Capital and Liquidity (prudential) Standards.

ICO reports a number of alliances with European institutions and their programs, which it divides into being based on financial, strategic, or knowledge

[12] Communication from the European Commission to the Parliament and the European Council on 22 July 2015. The objective is to achieve greater transparency and independence in the functioning of the Board to ensure an effective allocation of the financial activity of the Institute.

management purposes (ICO, 2017, 50–52). The key relationships are with the EIB and the European Investment Fund (EIF). First, as we have seen, the ICO established a relationship with the EIB from 1981. From the financial perspective, the main aim of this relationship is to facilitate loans to Spanish SMEs. The strategic relationship is mostly associated with an agreement to regulate ICO's participation in the European Investment Advisory Hub (as part of the Juncker Plan). Second, the ICO cooperates with the EIF. From the financial perspective, the relationship is focused mainly on its venture capital subsidiary, AXIS. The ICO has been a shareholder of the EIF since it was created in 1994. From a strategic perspective, the relationship focuses on the inclusion of ICO in the EIF-NPI Equity Platform. A third dimension of this relationship is seen in the collaboration agreement for temporary exchange of staff at both institutions.

In addition to its relationships with the EIB and the EIF, ICO reports a number of bilateral relationships with other NDBs, as well as with multilateral institutions. All of these arrangements are reported by ICO to be based on cooperation, not competition. Overall, there is a marked concentration of networks linking Spain to the European region and Latin America.

Bilateral relationships promoting financial objectives to facilitate funding to Spanish companies have been established with Bulgarian Development Bank, Russian Bank for Development, Morrocan *Caisse de Dépot et de Gestion*, Argentine *Banco de Inversión y Comercio Exterior* and Mexican *Nacional Financiera*. Strategic partnerships have also been established, concentrated geographically around Europe and Latin America. These include the Swedish Export Credit Corporation, the Morrocan Finéa, BPIFrance, *Société Tunisienne de Banque*, the Portuguese *Instituição Financiera de Desenvolvimiento*, the Latin American Association of Development Financing Institutions (ALIDE), the Central American Bank for Economic Integration (BCIE), the Development Bank of Latin America (CAF), Mexico's Bancomext, and the Export-Import Bank of India. Finally, as regards knowledge management, relations have been established with KfW Germany, the Finnish Finnvera, Black Sea Trade and Development Bank, and Italy's *Cassa Depositi e Prestiti*, all for staff exchange purposes. Relationships with multilateral players include financial partnerships with the Inter-American Development Bank and the International Financial Corporation.

Just as the case of other NDBs, ICO also belongs to several organizations, such as the Network of European Financial Institutions for Small and Medium Sized Enterprises (NEFI), as well as to international networks, including the Long-Term Investors Club (ELTI); and it participates in the European Investment Advisory Hub (EIAH).

All these efforts are embedded in the process of coordinating and integrating best practices across NDBs. However, most exchanges seem to be formal (regular formal meetings of the aforementioned forums) or technical (staff exchanges, knowledge management). It was not until the build-up for InvestEU that there was a forum for the participative set-up and implementation of common goals and procedures, according to ICO interviewees. This implies that the bilateral influence between the EU's promotional banking institutions and ICO has been close to anecdotal.

## 8.5 Is ICO Part of a European "Hidden Investment State"?

ICO has become integrated into a wide horizontal and vertical network of promotional banking, both within Europe and beyond. The density of this network seems to have increased, and there is today ample opportunity for formal and technical exchanges. Despite this, evidence of the emergence of a "hidden investment state" in this context is ambiguous. Overall, we do not find strong evidence of what may be key ingredients of an investment state: the goal of promoting "investment in specific sectors"—a goal beyond counter-cyclical action, that includes public financing for specific types of investment, or changes in liabilities and assets that allow for the pursuit of those renovated goals.

Rather, the emergence of a "hidden investment state" is slow in the Spanish case. This may be explained by Spain's peripheral position in the EU, and ICO's embeddedness within a particular institutional framework characterized by more demanding cyclical needs than Spain's northern European neighbors. Since the 1980s, Spain has moved towards a more neoliberal political economy, though the path-dependency of state intervention remains significant. In addition, Spain experienced one of the most severe crises in the EU (Clifton et al., 2018).

In the pre-crisis period, Spain experienced an overall neoliberal trend towards privatization and "marketization" (under PSOE, social democratic, centre-left, and PP–conservative, center-right governments). ICO was relegated to the role of a marginal provider of additionality, and not even directly, but increasingly via the mediation of private commercial banks. ICO reflected this neoliberal mindset focusing on correcting market failures and operating as a "second floor" financial institution. The upward economic and financial cycle of 2000–07 reinforced the relative irrelevance of ICO, with commercial banks clearly leading financial intermediation in a high-liquidity environment. Furthermore, in the pre-crisis period, belonging to the EU did not imply a particularly relevant role for promotional banks, since the European "hidden investment state" had not yet emerged. Spain's direct access to agricultural and structural funds was much larger than EIB funds at that time.

Our analysis of liabilities and assets seems to confirm this "marketization" of ICO's activities during the 1990s and up until the crisis. On the liability side, Special Funding virtually disappeared in favor of Ordinary Funding, with the vast majority of the latter not stemming from EIB and Multilateral Financial Institutions. On the assets side, the share of Mediation Loans—whose purpose was mainly additionality, and whose default risk was to be borne by commercial banks from 1998—skyrocketed to close to 60 percent of the total. In any case, one should not ignore the element of continuity in relation to the more statist period, insofar as ICO kept providing direct loans for infrastructure and big corporations (retained a significant portion of all loans in this pre-crisis period).

A second stage, when the crisis hit, brought ICO's counter-cyclical nature to the fore, especially through Mediated Loans (which increased markedly in absolute terms and also reached 67 percent in 2013), as commercial banks lacked access to liquidity. ICO in effect anticipated the counter-cyclical instruments that the EU would later deploy, via the ECB or the EIB. ICO's counter-cyclical role becomes even more evident in view of the reappearance, among its liabilities, of Special Funding and of ECB funds. In any case, liquidity provision did not accompany a strategic reorientation towards specific sectors or activities.

As the economic and financial cycle shifted upwards, ICO's balance sheet shrank markedly, again demonstrating the relevance of its counter-cyclical orientation. Furthermore, considering that the more volatile type of assets are Mediation Loans (these grew and fell the most during ICO's balance-sheet expansion and contraction) we conclude not only that ICO's activities are of a counter-cyclical nature, but also they are "marketized." In times of high liquidity and low interest rates, ICO staff emphasized that Mediation Loans were less necessary, which helps explain the plummeting size of their balance sheet.

As for the goals of those shrunken Mediation Loans, whereas it is true that some changes were introduced in line with European guiding principles—for instance, since 2014, ICO has put a larger emphasis on SME internationalization (Pérez, 2018), risk-sharing, and micro enterprises—this is not entirely new. Actually, these trends may have been reinforced as part of an overall growth strategy, emerging from Spain's neoliberal political economy, consisting of offering transversal (non-selective) support to entrepreneurship and internationalization (exports and foreign direct investment)—a strategy in which the Spanish Institute for Foreign Trade (ICEX) actively helped ICO (ICO, 2013a).

Regarding the composition of liabilities, it is true that, once the worst of the crisis was over, the Juncker Plan implied access to EIB funds (ICO's only growing liabilities between 2013 and 2018), as well as joint investments. It is this growing role of EIB loans to the ICO that could be interpreted as the major evidence of the manifestation in Spain of the Juncker Plan. It is here that the "hidden investment state" may be found. However, there is little evidence that these funds substantially modified ICO's strategic goals, or aided ICO's balance sheet expansion. If anything, the Juncker Plan replaced the sharp drop in ECB "quantitative easing" funds from 2013 to 2015 (Jourdan, 2015) and facilitated continuity regarding large infrastructure and corporate investments, without significant new selectivity criteria.

Some further innovations have occurred through the interaction with the European network. We observe anecdotal evidence of the EU's influence in, for instance, the birth of AXIS in 1986, the support of new government policy goals (including energy efficiency and digitalization), the offer of social and green bonds, and the inclusion of independent members on the Governing Board. However, these do not seem sufficient to conclude that the evolving European landscape has brought about a significant difference in the size and/or composition of ICO's liabilities and assets.

## 8.6 Conclusions

In the aftermath of the crisis, the European Commission launched the "Investment Plan for Europe" (Juncker Plan) to mobilize investments in 2014. Scholars argue the "European Fund for Strategic Investments" (EFSI), established under the Juncker Plan, boosted the emergence of a European "hidden Investment state" and a European field of development banking, where NDBs would assume a prominent role. We inquired if, and to what extent, a "hidden investment state" was becoming embedded in the Spanish context. This would imply three main developments: network formation; a strategic reorientation towards the promotion of investment in specific sectors; and a boost in assets and loans together with institutional innovation. We researched this question using various sources, mapped evolving networks, compiled financial information on borrowing and loans, and categorized financial instruments deployed in the search for innovation.

First, a "hidden investment state" should reflect an intensification of network formation between European development banks and ICO, both vertically and horizontally. On the one hand, vertically, the ICO has had a relationship with the EIB since 1981 and with the European Investment Fund (EIF) since 1994. Currently, ICO participates with EIB in the EFSI Advisory Hub, with the EIF, through the EIF-NPI Equity Platform, and with both through ENSI[13]. On the other hand, at the horizontal level, ICO has bilateral agreements with other NDBs, such as KfW, but such collaboration is mainly limited to staff exchanges and information sharing, although small loan agreements were made in 2013 (ICO, 2013b). The interlocking of institutions through European-level policy making to further or strategically reorient investment has not yet occurred in Spain.

Second, a "hidden investment state" would involve a reorientation of strategic goals, particularly towards more selective financing. Evidence on this is elusive, as ICO followed the neoliberal trend during the 1980s in Spain, by putting additionality and counter-cyclical policies as its main funding principles (although coexisting with a traditional role of infrastructure and corporate financing). Even after the crisis hit, it is hard to find a strategic reorientation: the emphasis was placed

[13] ENSI is a cooperation and risk-sharing platform between the EIF, the EIB and several economic development institutions in the EU to encourage SME lending via the capital markets.

on counter-cyclicality, thanks to significant increases in funding from the Spanish State and ECB. It is true that the ICO Strategic Plan 2019–21 states the ICO intends to promote "its role as a channel for EU, EIB, EFSI Funds and other EU initiatives given that a large part of this economic policy is implemented through them" (p. 6). This certainly indicates a change in rhetoric when compared to previous plans. However, it is too early to arrive at a judgement on whether ICO has undergone meaningful strategic reorientation since the Juncker Plan was launched.

Third, the creation of such a "hidden investment state" in Spain should reflect a boost in assets and loans, particularly by the ICO and the EIB. From 2000 to 2007, most lending to Spain came from agricultural and structural funds, with the EIB representing less than half of total EU investment and ICO even less. After the financial crisis, instead, EIB efforts increased. After ICO's countercyclical role and the expansion of its balance sheet, liabilities and assets returned to pre-crisis levels. Within ICO's liabilities, the share of EIB funds increased, but only replaced the drop in ECB funds. As for institutional innovation, ICO actually declared it intended to better align its range of financial products in coordination with other NDBs, with a view to make the most of the Juncker Plan (ICO, 2018). Indeed, there has been a shift in ICO policies as regards the type of loans, towards internationalization, entrepreneurship, and specific social and environmental policy goals. Most efforts to promote institutional innovation are implemented under other entities, such as the venture capital manager AXIS or CERSA.

The chapter found that Spain, and ICO, reacted to the international context, attempting to seize opportunities to catch up with leader EU countries. The evolution of ICO and the lending provided by the EIB and the EU were marked by the political and economic objectives established by the Commission at the European level, but also by the idiosyncrasies of the Spanish institutional landscape and cyclical needs. Though ICO reacted vigorously to the Great Recession, since then, its activities have largely returned to pre-crisis normality. At best, developments around a hidden investment state in Spain are modest.

Looking into the future, there may be hints of changes towards a more active participation of ICO in an emerging European hidden investment state. From 2019, pro-forma, still unaudited, data suggest an increase in the volume of activity, especially in some areas such as "second-floor facilities," more than doubling the figures of 2018. Also, as the Juncker Plan ends and the new EU investment framework—Invest EU—emerges, it may be that a strengthened European "hidden Investment state" does alter ICO's strategic orientation towards a stronger focus in the InvestEU's policy areas: sustainable infrastructure; research; innovation and digitization; SMEs; and social investment and skills. This possible shift towards more selective funding by ICO may be traced not only to InvestEU goals, but to procedures both of design and implementation. According to interviewees, decision-making processes are more participative than they were for the Juncker

Plan, and ICO is working towards becoming an Implementing Partner of InvestEU, as reflected in the "Strategic Plan" for the period 2018–2021. All of this may entail stronger ownership and internalization of the potential benefits of coordination with the European promotional banking network.

However, it is yet to be seen whether selectivity criteria end up being concrete enough to allow for an actual implementation of goals; and if so, if funds mobilized by ICO through InvestEU reach a size that is enough to be significant. Furthermore, it is uncertain whether there will be continuity in the Governing Board of ICO, confirmed in 2018 under a provisional PSOE government. Furthermore, the decisions of ICO's governing bodies (including the implementation of its strategic plans) could be affected by the currently volatile political landscape in Spain Even with no changes in personnel, ICO's role is somewhat restrained given that it remains a small NDB when compared to other peers in the EU.

## References

Archivo Digital España—UE, (2016). Haciendo cuentas. Available online at https://archivodigitalesue.wordpress.com/tag/solicitud-de-adhesion/.

Betrán, C., Martín-Aceña, P., and Pons, M., (2012). Financial Crises in Spain: Lessons from the Last 150 Years. Revista De Historia Económica / Journal of Iberian and Latin American Economic History 30(3), pp. 417–446.

Blasco Martel, Y., Cuevas, J. and Riera i Prunera, M. C., (2018), El crédito público y el ciclo económico en España: 1971–2015. Asociación Española de Historia Económica, Madrid Documentos de trabajo nº 1801. ISSN 2174-4912.

Buendía, L. and Molero-Simarro, R., (2018). The Political Economy of Contemporary Spain. From Miracle to Mirage, UK: Routledge.

Burns, C., Clifton, J. and Quaglia, L., (2018). Explaining Policy Change in the EU: Financial Reform After the Crisis, Journal of European Public Policy, 25(5), 728–46.

CEC (Commission of the European Communities), (1986). European Regional Development Fund. Eleventh Annual Report (1985) to the Council by the Commission. COM (86) 545 final, 20 October. Brussels: CEC. Available online at: http://aei.pitt.edu/5468/1/5468.pdf

Clifton, J., Díaz-Fuentes, D. and Gómez, A.L., (2018). The European Investment Bank: Development, Integration, Investment? Journal of Common Market Studies, 56(4), 733–50.

Crespo MacLennan, J., (2000). Spain and the process of European integration, 1957–1985. Palgrave Macmillan: Houndsmills.

EC (27/07/2015) Communication from the Commission to the European Parliament and the Council. Working together for jobs and growth: The role of National Promotional Banks (NPBs) in supporting the Investment Plan for Europe. EC:

Brussels. Available online at: https://eur-lex.europa.eu/legal-content/EN/TXT/PDF/?uri=CELEX:52015DC0361&from=EN.

EC, (18/07/2018). European Commission—Press release. Juncker Plan exceeds original €315 billion investment target. EC: Brussels. Available online at: http://europa.eu/rapid/press-release_IP-18-4469_en.htm.

EC (European Commission), (2019a). Investment Plan results. Breakdown of results by country and sector from the European Fund for Strategic Investments (EFSI) [online]. EC: Brussels. Available online at https://ec.europa.eu/commission/priorities/jobs-growth-and-investment/investment-plan-europe-juncker-plan/investment-plan-results_en

EC, (2019b). ESIF 2014–2020 Finances Planned. Updated April 5, 2019 [online]. EC: Brussels. Available online at: https://cohesiondata.ec.europa.eu/2014–2020/ESIF-2014-2020-FINANCES-PLANNED-DETAILS/e4v6-qrrq.

EC (03/05/2019) European Structural and Investment Funds Data. EU Overview [online]. EC: Brussels. Available online at: https://cohesiondata.ec.europa.eu/overview.

EIB (European Investment Bank), (2019). EFSI Project List [online]. Available online at https://www.eib.org/en/efsi/efsi-projects/index.htm.

EIB, (2019b). Financed Projects [online]. Available online at: https://www.eib.org/en/projects/loans/regions/index.htm.

Endrejat, V. and Thiemann, M., (2019). Balancing Market Liquidity: Bank Structural Reform Caught Between Growth and Stability. Journal of Economic Policy Reform, 22(3), 226–41.

European Court of Auditors, (2017). The European Fund for Strategic Investments (EFSI). Audit brief, October 2017. European Court of Auditors: Luxembourg. Available online at: https://www.eca.europa.eu/Lists/ECADocuments/AB_EFSI/AB_EFSI_EN.pdf.

European Court of Auditors, (2019). European Fund for Strategic Investments: Action Needed to Make EFSI a Full Success. Special Report. European Court of Auditors: Luxembourg. Available online at: https://www.eca.europa.eu/Lists/ECADocuments/SR19_03/SR_EFSI_EN.pdf.

European Parliament, (2017). Briefing January 2017. EFSI and ESI Funds Complementarity or contradiction? European Union: Brussels. Available online at: http://www.europarl.europa.eu/RegData/etudes/BRIE/2017/595869/EPRS_BRI(2017)595869_EN.pdf.

Eurostat (2019) Database [online]. Available online at: https://ec.europa.eu/eurostat/data/database

ICO, (2008). Annual Report. ICO: Madrid.

ICO, (2009). Annual Report. ICO: Madrid.

ICO, (2016). Annual Report. ICO: Madrid.

ICO, (2017). Annual Report. ICO: Madrid.

ICO, (2018). Annual Report. ICO: Madrid.

ICO, (2019). Annual Report. ICO: Madrid.

ICO, (2013a). ICEX e ICO impulsarán líneas conjuntas de apoyo a la internacionalización de la empresa Española. 02/04/2013 [online]. ICO: Madrid. Available online at: https://www.ico.es/web/ico/notas-de-prensa/-/blogs/65615?_33_redirect=%2Fweb%2Fico%2Fnotas-de-prensa%2F-%2Fblogs.

ICO, (2013b). ICO has received funding from the German state-owned bank KfW with advantageous conditions to fund investments by SMEs. [online]. ICO: Madrid. Available online at: https://www.ico.es/gl/web/ico_en/ico-kfw-loans.

ICO, (2016). Integrated Report. ICO: Madrid.

ICO, (2017). Integrated Report. ICO: Madrid.

ICO, (2018). Integrated Report. ICO: Madrid.

ICO, (2018). Plan Estratégico 2018–2021. ICO: Madrid.

ICO, (2019). ¿Qué es la Mediación y cómo funciona? Available online at: https://www.ico.es/web/ico/funcionamiento-mediacion

Jourdan, S., (2015). Mario Draghi is Open to Considering Helicopter Money. October 6 [online]. Positive Money Europe: London. Available online at: https://positivemoney.org/2015/10/mario-draghi-is-open-to-considering-helicopter-money/.

Martín Aceña, P., Blasco, Y. and Cuevas, J., (2016). El Instituto de Crédito Oficial, 1971–2015, Fundación ICO y Dextra Editorial, Madrid.

Mayes, D. G., (2018). Banking Union: The Disadvantages of Opportunism. Journal of Economic Policy Reform, 21(2), 132–43.

Mertens, D. and Thiemann, M., (2019). Building a Hidden Investment State?—The European Investment Bank, National Development Banks and European Economic Governance. Journal of European Public Policy, 26, 23–42.

Meyer, N. I., (2007). Learning from wind energy policy in the EU: lessons from Denmark, Sweden and Spain. European Environment, 17(5), 347–62.

OJEU (Official Journal of the European Union), (26/10/2012). Regulation (EU, Euratom) No 966/2012 of the European Parliament and of the Council of 25 October 2012 on the financial rules applicable to the general budget of the Union and repealing Council Regulation (EC, Euratom) No 1605/2002. Brussels: Council of the European Community.

Pérez, R., (2018). ICO, el banco con el que el Estado ha ganado 1.200 millones en diez años. ABC Economía 05/06/2018. Available online at: https://www.abc.es/economia/abci-banco-estado-ganado-1200-millones-diez-anos-201806040425_noticia.html.

Royo, S., (2008). Varieties of Capitalism in Spain. Remaking the Spanish Economy for the New Century. New York: Palgrave Macmillan US.

Rubio, E., (2018). Making Better Use of Public Funding. The Role of National Promotional Banks and Institutions in the Next EU Budget. Report nº 115, July. Jacques Delors Institute: Paris.

Salmon, K., (2004). Adapting to a New Funding Relationship with Europe: Spain and Cohesion Policy. Working Paper (WP) 53/2004. Madrid: Real Instituto Elcano de Estudios Internacionales y Estratégicos. Available online at: http://www.realinstitutoelcano.org/wps/wcm/connect/eea432004f0187e9be22fe3170baead1/053-2004-WP.pdf?MOD=AJPERES&CACHEID=eea432004f0187e9be22fe3170baead1.

Varela, M. (1999): "El Mercado Eólico Español. BalanceyPerspectivas." Informes Técnicos Ciemat Instituto de Estudios de la Energía. Madrid: CIEMAT. Retrieved, January 10, 2018 from http://www.iaea.org/inis/collection/NCLCollectionStore/_Public/38/106/38106946.pdf

Woll, C. and Jacquot, S., (2010). Using Europe: Strategic Action in Multi-Level Politics. Comparative European Politics 8(1), 110–26.

World Bank Group, (2001). World Bank Group Historical Chronology. World Bank Group Archives. Available online at: http://siteresources.worldbank.org/EXTARCHIVES/Resources/Bank%20chronology.pdf.

World Bank Group, (2018). Databank. World Development Indicators. GDP Growth rate. World Bank Group: Washington.

World Bank Group, (2019). IBRD Statement of Loans—Latest Available Snapshot. Available online at: https://finances.worldbank.org/Loans-and-Credits/IBRD-Statement-of-Loans-Latest-Available-Snapshot/sfv5-tf7p.

# 9

# Managing the Contradictions of Development Finance in the EU's Eastern Periphery

## Development Banks in Hungary and Poland

*Dóra Piroska and Katalin Mérő*

### 9.1 Introduction

Eastern Member States of the European Union had every reason to turn to development banks in the last three decades: in the early 1990s, their economies severely contracted under the pressure of the transformational recession that followed the collapse of communism, their international trade relations, and state-owned business organizations (Kornai, 1994). At the same time, they witnessed Western business interests' advancement and the pressure of their supporting international development actors to liberalize and open up their markets, which created market access, technical upgrading, and business know-how. Nevertheless, it also contributed to the emergence of a dependent market economy (DME) structure that put constraints on the development potential of local enterprises (Nölke and Vliegenthart, 2009). Once they joined the European Union in 2004, Eastern business actors were to compete on the unleveled playing field of the EU's Single Market, which through the enforcement of liberal market regulations created favorable conditions for those business actors that were better endowed with resources (Bruszt and McDermott, 2014). Surprisingly, most Eastern periphery Member States have not, or have only recently discovered the potential of development banks to counterbalance economic constraints. Why did Eastern European governments in the last 30 years, since the collapse of communism, not turn to development banks as chief institutions for economic policy formation?

Even today, Eastern European Member States' willingness and ability to connect, contribute, and benefit from the emerging hidden investment state (Mertens and Thiemann, 2019) seems to be more limited as compared to Western Member States. Eastern development actors are less capable of linking up with the

Dóra Piroska and Katalin Mérő, *Managing the Contradictions of Development Finance in the EU's Eastern Periphery: Development Banks in Hungary and Poland* In: *The Reinvention of Development Banking in the European Union: Industrial Policy in the Single Market and the Emergence of a Field.* Edited by: Daniel Mertens, Matthias Thiemann, and Peter Volberding, Oxford University Press (2021). © Oxford University Press.
DOI: 10.1093/oso/9780198859703.003.0009

Juncker-Plan-induced development cooperation between the European Investment Bank and its new facility, the EFSI, as well as Member States' national development banks, governments, private banks, and other investors. Although an evolving EU-wide industrial policy infrastructure would be a boon to the less developed Eastern Member States, the degree to which they are willing and able to link up to it remains an open question.

In this chapter, we argue that, in order to understand why Eastern European governments have only cautiously employed development banks so far, the underlying logic of the development finance field must be uncovered. Only within the framework of the dominant and contradicting logics of their national fields, does it become clear why the "development imagination" of consecutive Eastern governments remains limited and the scope of development banking narrow.

Hungary and Poland are fascinating cases for studying Eastern Member States' approaches to development finance. Both states are outside the Eurozone and the Banking Union, but both are part of the Schengen area. Both economies are marked by the features of a DME, where western multinationals produce the most substantial part of GDP, and foreign banks own half the banking sectors' assets. Foreign ownership of banks (although substantially reduced recently) narrowed down the development potential of governments. Unlike Western governments, Hungarian and Polish governments could not rely on domestically owned banks for development policy steering in the past (Epstein, 2017). Hungary and Poland are also similar in political constellations today, with authoritarian and financial-nationalist parties' control of the government (Johnson and Barnes, 2015) and increasingly the economy.

Limited development banking evolved due to contradictions in the national fields that we trace in three periods: (1) from transition to (2) accession to (3) the rise of illiberalism and financial nationalism. We show that between 1989 and 2000, development finance was torn between the contradictory logics of neoliberalism and developmentalism. Given this paradox, although both governments founded development banks, these new banks served development only in their names; instead, they were employed in other diverse activities. It was only in the next period, from 2000 to 2008, when accession negotiations dominated the development agenda, that these banks were re-designed as development banks. However, their design reflected not only the national markets but also the legal requirements of the EU's Single Market. Finally, in the post-crisis period, political parties with a financial-nationalist agenda came to power in Hungary and Poland. Both governments value development finance but, due to their authoritarian nature, only those development institutions are promoted that are brought under firm political control, while new development actors appear on the field.

Also, a common and distinguishing feature of the national development finance fields of Hungary and Poland is the prevalence of non-domestic actors such as the World Bank, the IMF, USAID, the EBRD, the EU through its PHARE program and a large number of smaller private and public funds, especially in the

1990s. Since the 2000s, the EU's Structural and Cohesion Funds have represented an important source of development finance: these two countries are among the receivers of the largest amounts in nominal terms (see Rubio and Thiemann in this volume).

Today, we see three distinguishing features of the links between the Hungarian and Polish development banks and the European field of development finance. First, the EU played an important role in the design of these banks, but it also placed severe constraints on their functioning. Second, recently, the EIB has emerged as a key source of funding for non-government-related business enterprises in authoritarian Hungary and Poland. That is, the EU, as such, not only finances illiberal governments through the Structural and Cohesion Funds, but also provides funding for business actors that seek to operate outside the auspices of authoritarian regimes. Third, the BGK, the Polish development bank, has ambitions to become a political actor in the European development field.

Variations persist in the national development finance fields of the two countries. In the early 1990s, Polish governments deemed industrial restructuring more important and had more fiscal room to support it than their Hungarian counterparts. Polish development finance has been also more segmented between the BGK and various smaller development funds supporting regional and industry-specific objectives, while, in Hungary, development finance has been divided between a development bank (MFB) and an export-import Bank (Eximbank) both serving the whole economy. Also, the Hungarian MFB was instrumental in enterprise restructuring and served as a "bad bank" for years, a unique feature that defined its employability as a manager of permanently state-owned enterprises beyond the transition period. Besides, while Hungarian SME finance was more focused on suppliers of multinational companies, Polish SME finance was more supportive of local entrepreneurs, including agricultural and mining communities (Bluhm and Varga, 2020 ). Finally, we see a defining difference in the two central banks' approach to development finance: the Hungarian National Bank (MNB), through its Funding for Growth program, effectively took on the role of a development bank in 2013, whereas no similar mission creep has occurred in the Polish National Bank.

The organization of the chapter is as follows. The next section analyzes the fields of development finance in Hungary and Poland from the period of transition through EU accession, the impact of the financial crisis, and the post-crisis coming to power of nationalist and authoritarian governments. A separate subsection is devoted to the EU relations of the last period. The last section concludes.

## 9.2 The Evolution of the Fields of Development Finance in Hungary and Poland

Both Hungary and Poland, just like other Central and Eastern European states, (re)established state-owned development banks at the fall of communism: the

Hungarian Development Bank, the MFB (*Magyar Fejlesztési Bank*) in 1991 and the Polish Development Bank, the BGK (*Bank Gospodarstwa Krajowego*) in 1989. The main difference between the Hungarian MFB and Polish BGK is in their functions. The MFB's role is solely to finance development, while for the promotion of Hungarian export, a separate Eximbank was established in 1994, and for issuing credit guarantees to SMEs, a credit guarantee institution, the Garantiqa was established in 1992 (Figure 9.1). The Polish BGK integrates all three functions: 1) granting finance for reorganization and development; 2) export finance (since 2000); 3) issuing credit guarantees for SMEs (since 1995). Another important player in the Polish development finance field is the Industrial Development Agency (ARP), a joint-stock company established in 1991. It is a much smaller player, focusing on three strategic industries: shipbuilding, defense and iron, and the steel industry. Legally, it is regulated as a corporate business unit with a public mandate; however, it also performs some minor lending activity. In 2016, all Polish development finance institutions were centralized under a newly established umbrella organization, the PFR (Figure 9.1). Besides, in both countries, several satellite institutions are connected to the banks. In Poland, numerous development funds take part in BGK's activity that are on or off of its balance sheet. In Hungary, MFB works in a group structure, with a changing composition. Before EU accession in 2004, Hungarian and Polish development banks were little involved in the EIB's investment activities. In Hungary, the first EIB project with MFB's involvement took place in 1995, the second in 2003. In Poland, the first joint investment project of the BGK and the EIB took place in 2001, followed by three other projects before the EU accession.

### 9.2.1 The Transition Period (1990 to 2000): Managing the Paradox of Development Banking in the Era of High Liberalism

During the transition period of the 1990s, the field of development finance was grounded on a paradox that all relevant actors of the field struggled with. It derived from the contradicting logic of the first freely elected governments' motivations to advance transition driven by neoliberal ideology and to satisfy their constituents' demand for protection and economic development. Development finance was defined between the contradictions of the Washington Consensus policy scripts of International Financial Institutions (IFIs), local elites (Epstein, 2008; Johnson, 2016) and the need to attract foreign capital (Appel and Orenstein, 2018), which effectively saw no room for "traditional" development banks in public administration, on the one hand.

On the other hand, transition governments entertained diverse economic development ideas and strategies with national capital and capitalists at the central stage (Bohle and Greskovits, 2012; Myant and Drahokoupil, 2010). Although neoliberal policy prescriptions for transition governments have effectively denied

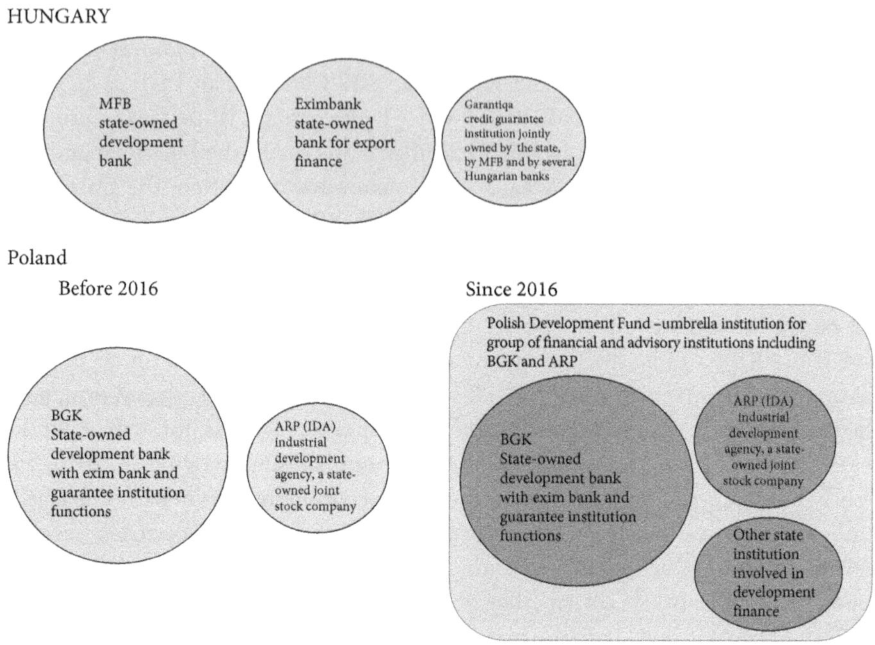


**Figure 9.1** Venn diagrams of the institutional structure of development institutions in Hungary and Poland
*Source*: Author's own

them the use of industrial policies, European countries, and the US had relied on during their development (Wade, 2003). Nevertheless, these governments also sought out the instruments of development finance and industrial policy. It is this fundamental paradox of development finance that defined the logic of the field in the 1990s.

The result was that most CEE governments founded development banks[1] early into transition but did not put them into actual development use. Slovenia was the only exception to this trend where economic nationalism dominated development policy (Lindstrom and Piroska, 2007). When founding development banks, both examined governments were inspired by the German KfW and the EBRD (Gém, 2012). However, the KfW was an outlier in the era of high liberalism and globalization: the hidden asset of the German government's industrial policy (Naqvi et al., 2018; see Mertens, this volume). Contradictions between the development bank blueprints that the KfW represented and the Washington-based IFIs' neoliberal economic policy scripts shaped the Hungarian and Polish governments' incongruous policy preferences for development finance.

[1] Such as Hungary in 1991, Poland in 1989, Czech Republic in 1992, Slovakia in 1991, and Slovenia in 1992.

In addition, three structural constraints and their particular interpretations formed the thinking of the actors in the field: (1) heavy indebtedness of the governments (perceived as an obligation to refinance in Hungary and to negotiate in Poland), (2) severe contraction of the economy due to the transitional recession (Kornai, 1994), and (3) gradually increasing foreign direct investment levels. These constraints importantly narrowed down the development policy room for maneuver for Hungarian and Polish governments and development banks.

Given the contradictions of the field and the severe economic constraints, it becomes obvious why we find the newly founded development banks being used primarily for non-development purposes. Development banks were employed in such diverse activities as asset management, bank consolidation, and even privatization in Hungary, and as Treasury agent, interbank market maker, and student loan programs manager in Poland. None of the two banks examined here engaged in the more traditional development tasks such as promoting economic development in less-developed industries or regions or resolve unemployment issues in the transition period.

There was one exception to this general trend, namely the promotion and financing of SMEs. This traditional development policy focus was embraced by governments and IFIs alike. This is because it corresponded to SMEs' perceived relevance to market building: SME financing is not opposed to the logic of privatizing market relations or building a liberal market dominated by private actors. Moreover, SMEs' promotion can also be seen as a developmental goal, and the means to support them as market correcting instruments in as much as private banks usually consider SME financing among the less attractive business opportunities. As a result, a specialized credit guarantee institution (Garantiqa) was established in 1992 in Hungary, while the National Credit Guarantee Fund was established in Poland under the BGK's management in 1995.

#### 9.2.1.1 Hungary

In more detail, in Hungary, MFB (MBFB until 1993) in the early 1990s was employed in the framework of the first bank consolidation scheme as a "bad bank," i.e., the financial asset manager of failing corporations (Karsai, 1999). Part of these corporations were successfully reorganized and then destined for privatization, and others had to be written-down as losses (Balassa, 1996; Voszka, 1994). This origin is important as subsequent governments regularly turned to MFB to permanently manage state-owned companies.

Furthermore, the MFB also suffered from several institutional weaknesses. First, no *sui generis* legislation existed for MFB; instead, the "development bank" was regulated by commercial banking law, developed with the help and the expertise of the World Bank. The only difference between MFB and regular commercial banks were a few exemptions granted to MFB under this law from capital adequacy and large exposure regulations. Second, the Hungarian governments inherited substantial foreign debt (and accumulated large public deficits) that became an essential constraint on MFB's activities. Thus, even if a Hungarian government had deemed development finance important, their room for providing funding for such purposes was severely constrained by high public debt levels. Therefore, the loans provided by MFB remained at a minimal level until 2000. In 2001 the MFB started to contribute to the financing of motorway construction, which gave impetus to the growth of its loan portfolio. Nevertheless, development banks were instrumental as a tool through which to channel development funds of multilateral banks or public donors such as Japan, Germany, or the EIB (Gém, 2012).

#### 9.2.1.2 Poland

In the early 1990s, Polish policy makers were importantly influenced by the World Bank and the IMF to formulate what was later known as the "shock therapy" policy package, which also included banking sector reforms (Epstein, 2006; Johnson, 2016). However, as King and Sznajder, (2006, p. 769.) point out, "despite the neoliberal rhetoric, the Polish state intervened early and often in the economy, in ways explicitly proscribed by neoliberals, in an effort to manage the transition." The paradox of development finance was thus established in Poland.

In 1989, as Epstein (2006) reports, it was USAID affiliates who advised Poland on how to design the structures and write the bylaws for the nine state-owned commercial banks that emerged from that legislation[2]. The same year, the Polish State Treasury put aside a part of its assets to re-establish as a state-owned development bank, the BGK, a bank with an important pre-WWII history. Its reopening had outstanding symbolic value in Polish politics. During the first half of the 1990s, the BGK had minimal activity; its main task was the issuing of Treasury bonds and management of the consolidation of public finance (Kozak, 2013). BGK's limited role resulted from several developments. The Polish financial market and the economy were in a flux where the neoliberal prescripts dictated little state involvement. However, Polish governments—more than their Hungarian counterparts of the time—deemed industrial restructuring a priority and had more extensive resources to financially support such institutions due to the government's successful reduction of the inherited public debt with the Paris Club (Kiss, 1994). Therefore, several smaller development agencies, with actual developmental mandates, including the Industrial Development Agency (ARP) as well as a small bank dedicated to development finance, the Polski Bank Rozwoju (Polish Development Bank) S.A., were established in the early 1990s[3]. At the same time, the Polish banking sector underwent a critical restructuring phase financed

[2] The law was designed to open up the Polish banking sector for foreign investors.
[3] In 1998 the bank merged with a private commercial bank and ceased to be a development bank.

by the IMF under the informal condition that Poland privatize six of its remaining state-owned banks by 1996 (Epstein, 2006).

The growth of BGK started in the second half of the 1990s when two real estate development funds, a fund for financing energy-saving investments and one for financing road constructions were established under the BGK management (Skuza, 2009). The government's increasing interest in development activity is also reflected in the establishment of the National Credit Guarantee Fund under BGK to provide credit guarantees for SMEs in 1995. The credit guarantees were granted through cooperation agreements with commercial banks to achieve nation-wide coverage. Besides, the BGK had a commercial loan portfolio, too, which increasingly became development oriented. For example, in 2000, it started to finance mining communities.

### 9.2.2 The Accession Period and Pre-GFC (2000–2008): Managing the Tensions of Building National Development Banks Fit for the EU Market

The EU accession process had a formative impact on the field of development finance in Hungary and Poland. As Bruszt and Vukov (2017) argue, in the process of Eastern enlargement, the EU played an instrumental role in building the institutions that are instrumental in creating and maintaining economic state capacity. More room for development policy and institution formation was also possible because the influence of the IFIs diminished in this period. Development banks were among the most important beneficiaries of the state-building efforts of the EU on the Eastern periphery (Bruszt, 2002). In fact, the first development bank-like regulations for both MFB and BGK were developed in view of the EU accession and were the results of extensive negotiations between EU representatives and the two states. As such, national development banks were legally defined in the Eastern periphery under very different conditions than in old Member States. Whereas in old Member States, such as Germany, Italy, or France, the purpose and profile of development banks were defined with only the national economy in mind, in the East national development banks were designed at birth with the EU Single Market in mind, and the EU was acting as mid-wife.

From the perspective of development finance, however, the EU Single Market is built upon conflicting logics. On the one hand, it is defined by liberal market regulations that aim to provide equal access to the EU market for all actors. Therefore, the EU's State Aid regulation effectively restricts government finance or government ownership in a large number of cases (Blauberger, 2009; Cini, 2001). This is true even if we consider that the scope of permitted regional state aid is higher by EU design in the East than in the West (Medve-Bálint, 2014). On the other hand, the smooth functioning of the Single Market is aided through the application of several EU level transfers and institutions that aim at market correcting, i.e., they aim at correcting for the different endowments of the differently situated actors wishing to take advantage of the Single Market. The EU's Structural and Cohesion funds are relevant financial sources of development finance in Eastern Europe (see Rubio and Thiemann in this volume). Thus, national development banks in the Eastern periphery have to navigate through these enabling and constraining conditions.

Following successful EU accession, the field of development finance in both countries started to resemble development finance in old EU Member States with two important structural caveats. First, in this period, the dependent market economy features of these economies became one of the most critical constraints on increasing the scope of development finance (Nölke and Vliegenthart, 2009). This is because, due to the foreign capital domination of the economy, Eastern governments were constrained in using development finance to help advance national champions (Myant and Drahokoupil, 2010). Most of the "national" champions, if defined in terms of their contribution to GDP and employment, were foreign-owned. Moreover, foreign multinationals mainly finance their activities through intra-firm transfers. It is their mother company that seeks out finance (including development finance), either in its home country or on international markets.

This fact is further reflected in the relative shallowness of banking finance in Eastern Europe. At the time of EU accession, the percentage of private credit granted by domestic banks as a share of GDP was 42 percent in Hungary and 27 percent in Poland, while the same figure for the Eurozone was 67 percent. By 2008 the Hungarian ratio had increased to 64 percent and the Polish to 43 percent while that of the Eurozone to 90 percent.[4] That is, the difference between the depth of banking intermediation in the Eurozone and the two countries remained unchanged during the period.

Moreover, Eastern Member States' banking sector also became dominated by foreign-owned banks (Epstein, 2017). By 2002 out of the 33 Hungarian commercial banks only seven and out of the 59 Polish banks, only 11 remained domestic-owned. Expressed as a percentage of registered capital, the relevant proportions were 78 percent in Hungary and 60.5 percent in Poland (Mérő and Valentinyi, 2003). High foreign ownership of banking sets limits to governments' efforts to use the local financial market to stimulate the economy, i.e., it curbs its development potential (Epstein, 2017). As a consequence of the DME structure, foreign-owned enterprises and banks became the main actors of development finance. This fact also meant that large corporations, the "national" champions, expressed little interest in publicly funded development banking finance.

[4] Source: Global Financial Development Database, https://www.worldbank.org/en/publication/gfdr/data/global-financial-development-database, accessed at 19.05.2019.

Second, Eastern Member States received significant funding from the EU through cohesion funds as well as preferential credits from the EBRD and the EIB. These external funds were regarded as relevant sources of development finance. After the EU accession, the relation between the EIB and the national development banks also became more complex. On the one hand, national development banks became more active in the allocation of EIB funds, with BGK playing a more significant allocation role than MFB. On the other hand, the EIB and national development banks became competitors in the domestic markets.

However, often, the EU funds facilitated the privatization of Eastern assets to Western companies, financed infrastructure development that better connected Western and Eastern markets, or were used to build state institutions that were more capable of managing a liberal market economy. As such, these two impacts of the EU (large FDI flow and EU funds combined with state-building) were not independent of each other (Medve-Bálint, 2014).

#### 9.2.2.1 Hungary

In the year 2000, and in preparation for accession, the first Fidesz government separated the MFB's strategic activities serving economic policy priorities from the activities performed at the bank's own business risk. In the next year in 2001, in preparation for EU accession, the first *sui generis* law for MFB was accepted. The Hungarian accession negotiators held out the German KfW as an example. During EU accession, Eastern Member States were in a position to negotiate derogations from EU regulations for their development banks. The Hungarian negotiating team put the MFB and the Eximbank on the list of exemptions from the Banking Directive, as following the standard in old EU Member States. However, unlike the German authorities, which granted a large range of exemptions to KfW from domestic banking law, Hungarian authorities did not exempt the MFB from several other, possibly restricting, regulations. Instead, they aimed at achieving as commercial bank-like features in terms of prudential regulation as possible. They pursued the path set by existing legislation that applied for MFB, written in the era of high liberalism under the influence of the World Bank.

Hungarian policy makers and the MFB officials held commercial bank-like prudential requirements valuable even if it meant diminishing the MFB's competitiveness vis-à-vis commercial banks as well as government-sponsored development projects. This is true even if we take into consideration that both MFB and Eximbank have an essential competitive advantage in comparison to commercial banks, namely that all their liabilities are backed with 100 percent government guarantees. Their capital also comes 100 percent from the central government budget.

Why did the governments not grant more considerable discretion to their development banks? The first reason is that as long as MFB conformed to commercial banks' lending practices and provisioning, external creditors could be presented with a commercial bank-like balance sheet that facilitated MFB's bond issuance on international markets. With such a balance sheet, MFB could also seek a rating from rating agencies such as Moody's and Standard and Poors, which further facilitated its ability to raise funding on international markets. Second, the European Union's State Aid regulation has been very strictly applied by the Commission in the case of Eastern Member States (Personal communication with former MFB officer, August 9, 2018). Therefore, the commercial bank-like balance sheet of MFB and its inclusion under the Hungarian commercial bank regulatory framework made its functioning a lot easier under European State Aid regulation. This is because MFB could credibly claim that its loans do not represent a form of State Aid, i.e., MFB's lending activities are not crowding out commercial banks from the domestic financial market. Third, the applicability of commercial bank standards was also instrumental in the bank's leadership vis-à-vis the government's "special" requests. Pointing out that MFB is required by law to satisfy specific capital requirements, its management could refuse to finance such government projects that it deemed unsustainable. As such, these regulations increased the autonomy of MFB from the government.

In the heyday of MFB, post-accession, and pre-Orban, the EIB-provided funding played a more critical role for MFB, although never really a defining one (see Figure 9.4 in section 9.2.3). The EIB-provided loans were denominated in Euros, and the interest rate differential between HUF and Euro interest rates provided MFB with a profit-making opportunity. MFB's management has been keen on ensuring the best possible funding arrangements from EIB. For this purpose, the management made sure that it was MFB, which nominated the Hungarian director to EIB.

In the 2000s, the MFB finally started operating as a "traditional" development bank. In 2002, for the first time, the MFB was asked to design a development strategy in line with traditional development bank business lines. Upon the acceptance of the new strategy in 2003, the government also increased the MFB's capital with HUF 40 billion destined to invest in Hungarian domestically owned enterprises in the next five years (Karsai, 2007). Under the strong leadership of János Erős (president between 2002 and 2010), MFB increased its autonomy vis-à-vis the government to define development projects' content.

In line with its new strategy, the main task of MFB was to grant medium- and long-term investment loans and equity finance to SMEs and finance the state's and local governments' investment projects. At the same time, the banks' organization structure was also re-shaped. The MFB Banking group was reorganized into two lines: 1) the financial subsidiaries, such as the Eximbank, the Export Credit Insurance Company, an asset management company and a venture capital fund; and 2) the state aid intermediation subsidiaries.

The new strategy and its extension in 2006 were the basis for the MFB's involvement in the allocation of the EU funds for 2004–2006 and especially for the

2007–2013 Program Period in the form of financing the New Hungary Development Plan of the government (Gém, 2012). Also, several development finance programs were launched. A new municipality infrastructure development loan program was initiated, which also covered loans for the reconstruction of panel buildings. In the corporate sector, SME finance remained the MFB's primary focus, which was supplemented with more development credit products for agricultural companies. Besides, within the New Hungary Enterprise Development Loan Program, the target group was determined in very general terms, so the selection of companies for finance allowed for a wide range of priorities. Households also became a new target group for MFB in the form of loans for residential buildings' energy conservation. Parallel to the loans financed in the different programs' framework, the MFB also granted loans on its own initiative to finance individual companies' development projects. These included several different investment finance projects, for example, road construction, industrial investments, hotels, spas and shopping, and leisure centers, etc.[5] All in all, the 2000s saw the birth of development banking in Hungary, with the EU accession playing an essential role in the design of an active national development bank.

#### 9.2.2.2 Poland

In 2003, in preparation for EU accession, a *sui generis* law for the BGK was accepted. It defined more clearly the public mission of the bank. Just like the MFB, the BGK was also exempted from EU banking regulation. The concrete legal reliefs, granted by the Polish authorities to the BGK, were significantly narrower than those of MFB's. However, BGK's regulation was more flexible since the new law granted discretional rights to the Polish Financial Supervisory Authority to—on request of the BGK—exempt it from compliance with specific prudential requirements for activities that either relate to servicing funds transferred to the BGK under different laws or implement government programs (Skuza, 2014). However, the BGK has very rarely asked for exemptions.

Although the development banking activity of the BGK had started evolving since the mid-1990s, it gained an impetus during the EU pre-accession and accession period. In the 2000s, the BGK's activity developed in two directions. First, it continued to finance its own-initiated lending programs as a commercial bank with a more-and-more clear development profile. Second, the government commissioned the BGK to manage different public funds, through which the EU pre-accession funds and later the EU structural funds were channeled to the economy, including managing the EU Guarantee Fund that granted credit guarantees for EU co-financed projects. In addition, the BGK remained actively involved in public finance management and the financial consolidation of public institutions.

[5] See the Annual Reports of MFB at https://www.mfb.hu/en/reports-s2012 accessed at 28.10.2019.

As regards the government-commissioned activities, in the wake of EU accession the main areas of developmental activity of the BGK were the following: 1) financing the housing construction industry; 2) financing the road construction industry; 3) grant credit guarantees to SMEs; 4) grant finance to venture capital funds that invest in new innovative enterprises; and 5) carry out different state-initiated programs. Besides, the state-commissioned activity of the BGK also covered two programs for private persons: the student loan program and an interest subsidy program for the establishment of private medical practice. Financing these activities took place in the form of managing funds created for specific purposes. The funds managed by the BGK can be classified into three groups: credit funds with credit risk taking (recognized in BGK's balance sheet); flow funds (managed funds not recognized in BGK's balance sheet); and guarantee funds.

As regards their own-initiated commercial banking business activity, local governments remained the central counterparties of BGK. Besides lending to them, the BGK was active in organizing their bond issues and market-making for these issues as well. Financing the housing and property construction industry also was among the market segments where the BGK was active; in the pre-crisis era, it was the most dynamic lending area in Poland. On its own initiative, the BGK also took part in enterprise restructuring of selected industries, with particular regard to the shipyard industry. It provided loans for the otherwise highly underbanked SME sector as well. Mortgage loans were granted to retail customers, too, for residential real estate development. In sum, by the end of the 2000s—similar to Hungarian developments—the BGK's activities significantly expanded, its loan size increased, and its importance for governments' development policy increased.

### 9.2.3 Post-GFC period (2008–2018): Under Nationalist, Illiberal Governments: Tightening Control of Development Banks and the Emergence of New Development Actors

In the post-GFC period, from 2010 in Hungary and 2015 in Poland, structuring logics of the field of development finance are defined by the financial nationalist governments' rhetoric on the necessity of the breaking out of the dependent market economy structure (dominated by foreign banks and enterprises) and the same governments' preference for centralized institutions. As a result, we observe the emergence of a weak form of developmentalism, including a diminished democratic oversight of these state institutions.

In concrete terms, we detect, in Hungary, decentralization of the field manifested 1) in increased government control of the development banks, 2) new development actors such as private domestically owned banks and the central bank entering the field, and 3) cooperation among domestic, public, and private development actors. In Poland, the field becomes centralized, and the BGK emerges as a winner from the increased political focus on development. However, it is an open question whether the new umbrella organization for development finance (the PFR) will take center stage in Polish development finance.

In this period, the two national development fields' trajectories differed in important terms. In 2008, the global financial crisis hit Hungary more severely than Poland. Hungary experienced a public debt crisis, a banking crisis, and a foreign exchange currency crisis in October 2008 and turned to the IMF and the EU for financial assistance (Piroska, 2017). The Polish banking sector weathered the crisis relatively well; its western multinational-dominated economy only suffered moderately under the prolonged recession that followed. In Hungary, during crisis management, we see governments turn to development banks as countercyclical financiers and their balance sheet increased. Thus, by 2017, the two Hungarian development banks' combined total assets to GDP became almost twice as high as that of the BGK's (Figure 9.2).

Compared to the banking sector's activity, the two Hungarian development banks are also more dominant in lending to the national economy than their Polish counterpart (Figure 9.3).

In the post-crisis period, the priorities of development policies also differed in the two countries. In Hungary, the nationalist rhetoric hides, in concrete terms, a mixture of Eastern opening, financial nationalism in the banking sector, full-scale corruption to nurture domestic capitalists, social spending directed towards the middle and higher classes, and the introduction of neoliberal labor and tax policies favoring foreign multinationals. In Poland, the Tusk government's Polish Investment Program had already marked a shift in development thinking that was embraced by the successor PiS' government whose development policy focuses on a "re-Polonization" of the economy to break out of the middle-income trap and an emphasis on social and welfare spending (Toplišek, 2019). Nevertheless, so far, the financial-nationalist governments' development policy mix has not resulted in a break out or lessening of domestic dependence of foreign dominance of the economy (Bohle and Greskovits, 2018), or the upgrading of the position of the two economies on global value chains (Éltető and Antalóczy, 2017; Szent-Iványi, 2017). The only exception to this general trend is the financial sector, where an essential proportion of banking came under domestic ownership in both countries (Mérő and Piroska, 2016).

#### 9.2.3.1 Hungary

In 2010, the coming to power of the Fidesz-KDNP government marked a shift in the Hungarian governments' development policy broadly understood. The Fidesz-KDNP government's development policy employs aggressive rhetoric on the imperative of breaking out of dependent market status. Shortly after coming to power, it levied high taxes on a few foreign-owned strategic companies, while granted tax exemptions to German car producers, and announced a new strategy

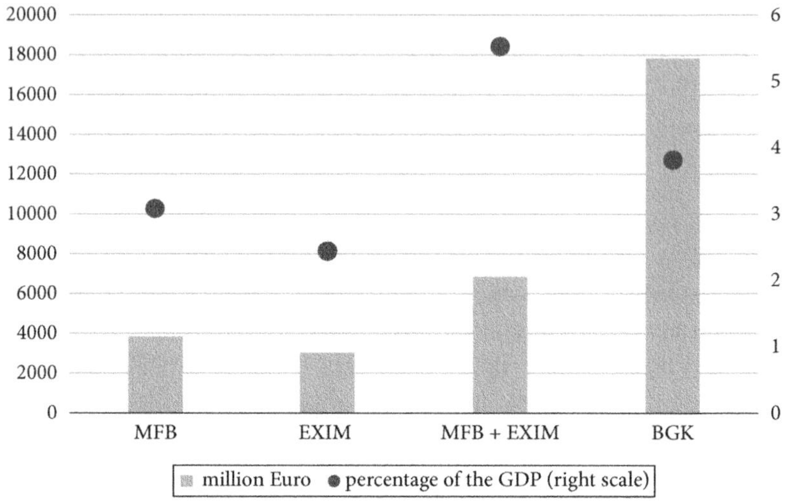


**Figure 9.2** Total assets of development banks in 2017
*Source*: Annual reports of MFB, Eximbank and BGK

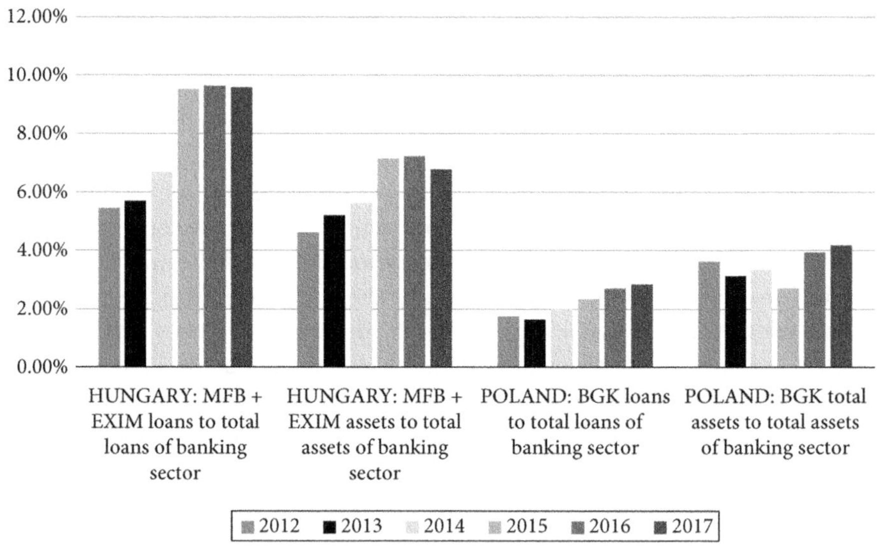


**Figure 9.3** The relative size of development banks (2012–2017)
*Source*: MNB (Central Bank of Hungry), NBP (Central Bank of Poland) and annual reports of the MFB, Eximbank, and BGK

to promote an Eastern opening, especially towards China (Jacoby and Korkut, 2015) and Russia. The new government embraced financial nationalism in the banking sector (Johnson and Barnes, 2015), nurtured corruption to enrich domestic capitalists (Magyar, 2016), and promoted neoliberal labor and tax policies. This particular policy mix accompanied by heightened authoritarianism had important repercussions on the field of development finance. On the one hand, the nationalist rhetoric increases the political value of state-controlled financial institutions and therefore reinforces the government's interest in development finance. However, and on the other hand, development institutions are employed according to their quality of subordination to the control of the ruling political elite. Development funds are increasingly distributed according to clientelist and not developmental priorities.

Hence, 2010 and the coming to power of the Fidesz-KDNP coalition marked the beginning of a new era for development banks in Hungary. The turn was marked by a change of management not only at MFB but also at the companies it owned. At the same time, the state property management function of the MFB was strengthened; the property rights of several significant companies were relocated to the MFB.[6] Besides this, the MFB's group was also enlarged. In the summer of 2010, the Student Loan Centre (established in 2001) and the Garantiqa became members of the MFB group. It seemed that the government's goal was to increase the scope of MFB's activities as it was now allowed to finance a broader range of activities, with its capital base increased in 2010 and again in 2011.

A change in the opposite direction, towards weakening MFB's roles in development finance appeared in 2012 (Figure 9.4). This year, the government decided to reallocate Eximbank from MFB's control to the National Economic Ministry. Subsequently, Eximbank's lending portfolio was enlarged. The favored position of Eximbank was also promoted by amending the *sui generis* law on Eximbank in 2014 that allowed it to grant credit and invest in non-export related activities as well. In the following years, the government made regular and large-scale capital increases in Eximbank to promote its non-export related finance to well-connected businesses[7]. As shown in Figure 9.6, the shift of interest from MFB to Eximbank has also taken place in relation to EIB finance. Since 2013, there have only been Eximbank-related EIB projects in Hungary, whereas the MFB has not signed an EIB project from 2013 to 2018.

Nevertheless, the MFB remained instrumental in the Orban government's financial nationalist goals to increase domestic ownership in banking and large strategic enterprises. The MFB—with substantially decreased autonomy under the new management—was the instrument through which the Orban government approached German DZ Bank to purchase Takarékbank in 2012.[8] After a significant capital increase in 2015, it funded the government's purchase of Budapest

[6] https://index.hu/gazdasag/magyar/2010/05/18/megosztjak_az_allami_vagyont_az_mnv_es_az_mfb_kozott/ accessed at 28.10.2019.

[7] https://444.hu/2016/11/30/kikoltekezett-az-andy-vajnat-a-tv2-megszerzesehez-segito-allamibank accessed at 28.10.2019.

[8] https://index.hu/gazdasag/magyar/2012/11/15/eltitkoljak_a_takarekbank_arat/ accessed at 28.10.2019.

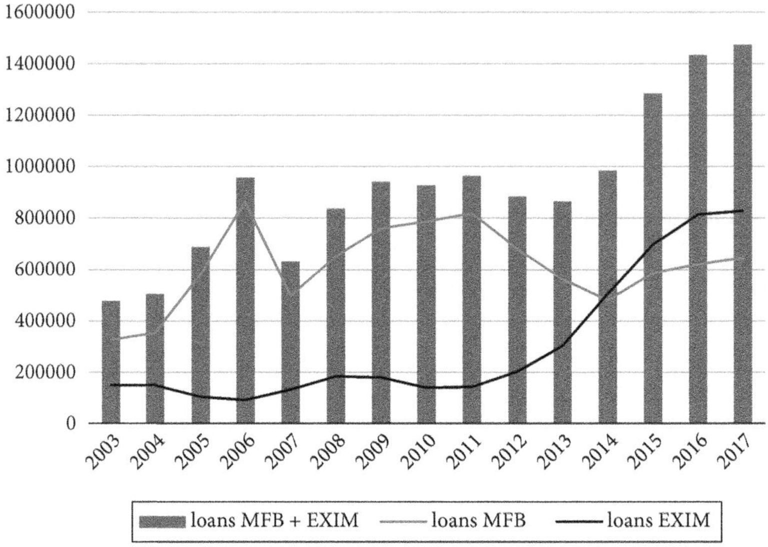


**Figure 9.4** Total loans provided by MFB and Eximbank in Hungary (HUF million)
*Source*: annual reports of MFB and Eximbank

Bank from its foreign owner (General Electric Capital).[9] Furthermore, the MFB was the instrument through which the Orban government achieved its objective of increasing national control of strategic sectors, which also supported its political campaign of "Utility Reduction." The MFB was instructed to found a natural gas trading company in 2014[10] and became the owner of the capital city's gas provider.[11] In the meantime, the MFB also became central in distributing EU transfers.[12] However, because the disbursement of these funds does not generate significant income for the MFB, their increasing importance in its balance sheet reduces the ability of MFB's management to initiate programs in a further decrease in its autonomy.

We identified four reasons for the general decline of MFB as an instrument of the government's development policy. First, due to both political motivations as well as economic constraints since 2010, the government did not engage in major government-financed infrastructural upgrading, and the number of development projects decreased in general. Railway development and motorway constructions

[9] https://index.hu/gazdasag/bankesbiztositas/2015/06/29/orult_dragan_allamositottuk_a_budapest_bankot/ accessed at 28.10.2019.

[10] https://index.hu/gazdasag/energia/2014/09/12/uj_gazkereskedo_ceget_csinal_maganak_az_allam/ accessed at 28.10.2019.

[11] https://index.hu/gazdasag/2014/10/22/hopp_megint_szerzett_valamit_az_mfb/ accessed at 28.10.2019.

[12] https://index.hu/gazdasag/2015/09/21/igy_osztja_majd_az_eu-s_hiteleket_az_mfb/ accessed at 28.10.2019.

were the primary targets of MFB in the past, under the Socialist governments. Second, several new competitors appeared. Most importantly, the central bank, with its Funding for Growth Scheme (FGS), represents significant competition. In the framework of FGS, the central bank has provided zero interest rate loans to SME's through the commercial banking sector since 2013. As such, with FGS, the central bank effectively acquired a new function as a development bank. Third, the political preference for Eximbank against the MFB also contributed to MFB losing importance. Finally, since 2014, dramatic changes have taken place in banking sector ownership: foreign ownership declined from 85 percent to 50 percent. The new domestic owners are well-connected businesspersons. Since 2014, the new domestically controlled banks have been targeted by the government and the central bank's FGS to realize development policy goals (e.g., SME financing).

Since 2016, there has been an increase in the MFB's balance sheet, but not in its development profile or autonomy. In 2016, the MFB introduced micro and SME finance products based on the EU instruments of GINOP and VEKOP. The new products are combinations of loans and non-refundable finances, and due to their favorable conditions, they are competitive with the central bank-sponsored SME loans within the FGS. At the same time, the MFB has changed the distributional method for these products: instead of granting loans through refinancing commercial banks, it built up its country-wide sales network in the form of MFB Points. The MFB Points were established in cooperation with some selected commercial banks using their branch networks. The participating banks are exclusively domestically owned banks with good relations with the government. Even the extended branch network was not a requirement for selection: two small domestically owned banks with excellent government connections[13] and both having only one branch in the capital city, also became members of the scheme.

In sum, we see the decentralization of development finance, with increased government control of both banks, a shift towards Eximbank, and the entry of new development actors, such as the central bank and domestically owned bank. There is also increased cooperation among the various actors.

### 9.2.3.2 Poland

In contrast, the crisis did not hit Poland severely, so there was no credit crunch and commercial banks' profitability decreased only slightly (Strojwas, 2010). In the post-crisis period, between 2008 and 2013, the BGK's lending activity remained at the same level (Figure 9.5), while it increased its involvement in granting guarantees and sureties, and in the distribution of EU funds. Besides, the structure of funds managed by the BGK was consolidated, and the size of those funds that are not accounted in BGK's balance sheet increased significantly.

[13] One of them, the Növekedési Hitelbank, has since become bankrupt.

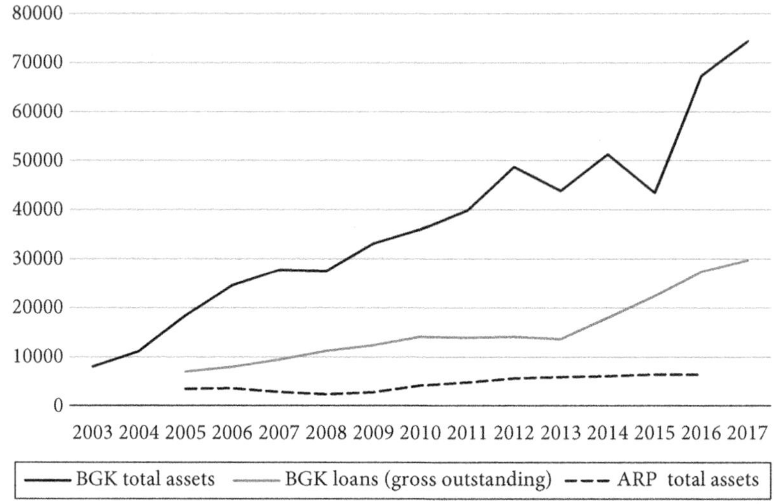


**Figure 9.5** The size of BGK and ARP (PLN million)
*Source*: annual reports of BGK and ARP

In 2012, the Polish Investment Program was announced by Donald Tusk, the then prime minister. This is an essential shift in the Polish development policy (Naczyk, 2014). Consequently, the BGK's main goal became financing the Polish Investment Program and extending *de minimis* sureties and guarantees. The BGK's own programs' foci were infrastructure projects and providing banking services to the government sector. To promote the Polish Investment Program, a state-owned special purpose vehicle (SPV) was also established in 2012, the Polskie Inwestycje Rozwojowe (PIR). Its owners were the State Treasury (50 percent) and the BGK (50 percent). To be able to grant capital to PIR, the BGK's capital was significantly increased. The BGK and the PIR together served as the two pillars of the Investment Program. Even during this time, the government's preference for increased domestic control in the corporate sector in general and in the banking sector, in particular, could be observed (Naczyk, 2014).

In October 2015, the PiS came to power with an absolute majority and launched an economic policy aiming at reversing the course of the foreign-led development (Kozarzewski and Bałtowski, 2017). PiS' rhetoric is nationalist, anti-immigrant, and Eurosceptic, while PiS's economic policy is motivated by a need to break out of the "middle-income trap" that it sees as the result of excessive dependence on foreign capital. Therefore, PiS's economic policy promises a halt to privatization and the "re-Polonization" of the economy (Toplišek, 2019). Importantly from the perspective of development finance, the PiS government engaged in the "re-Polonization" of the domestic banking sector and increased (direct or indirect) state control from 30 percent to over 50 percent (Rohac and Miszerak, 2017). Unlike the Fidesz government economic policy, which favors neoliberal measures to attract foreign investment, the PiS government, with a higher state-owned share in more capital-intensive production, has followed a national actors-based developmental strategy (Toplišek, 2019).

In November 2015, just after PiS came to power, essential changes occurred to the BGK's legal status, which reduced its commercial bank-like legal profile. The new regulation gives several exceptions and reliefs for the BGK from the EU's CRD/CRR framework. It is important to see here that the PiS is following on the development path set by its predecessor; indeed, no new law could have been designed and implemented in a month.

In terms of its development policy, the BGK started a pilot program (*Mieszkanie Plus*) for apartments for rent as an alternative to homeownership for middle-income people in 2016. Since its launch in 2015, it also became the core institution of the Investment Plan for Europe in Poland; it distributes EFSI funds and grants credit portfolio guarantees within the COSME program.

In 2016, all the state development functions were integrated into a newly established development company, the Polish Development Fund (PFR), and the PIR discontinued its operations. Since then, both the BGK and the ARP, together with some other institutions (for example, the KUKE, the Export Credit Insurance Company) became part of PFR Group. The governance structure of PFR was constructed in a very controversial way; namely, it is 50-50 percent owned by the State Treasury and the BGK, while, as an umbrella organization it covers the group of development institutions, including the BGK (for a similar development in the French case, see Thiemann and Volberding, this volume). However, according to personal communications of two different sources, as of the Fall of 2018, the PFR is not acting as an umbrella organization, it is more "a marketing name" than an operating institution. Accordingly, *de facto*, the BGK remained the key development institution in the Polish field; however, the organization structure allows for the strengthening of the PFR against the BGK. In other words, the decision-making autonomy of BGK is intended to be curtailed by the government.

## 9.3 Interactions Between European and National Fields of Development Finance

In this time period, understanding the evolutions of the two national development fields must take the context of the European development finance field into account. Concerning the EU's role, our findings correct previous accounts on the EU's overall impact on supporting authoritarian governments in the Eastern periphery:

The role of the EU's Structural and Cohesion funds clearly plays an enabling role for these financial nationalist and authoritarian governments, as argued by Johnson and Barnes (2015). Rubio and Thiemann found in this volume that these two countries are the largest recipients of EU Funds on nominal terms. However, turning our attention to the role of the EIB, we see that the lion share of EIB funding is, actually, directly targeted to domestic corporate actors, not the development financial institutions. That is, the EIB emerges as an alternative source of finance for those business enterprises, which seek a level of autonomy from the ruling government. This is true even if a vital share of EIB financing goes to state-controlled enterprises, that are under the authoritarian governments' control.

In more detail, in the period of the 2010s, the two countries' shares of total EIB finance varied between 8–10 percent in Poland and 1-3.5 percent in Hungary. Taking into account that Poland's share in the EU population is 7 percent and that within the EU its GDP is 3 percent while the respective values for Hungary are 2 percent and 0.8 percent, it can be stated that the EIB was active in both countries. Moreover, Figures 9.6 and 9.7 show clearly that the amount of EIB-provided finance that went directly to local actors was more significant than that provided through the government-controlled development banks in both countries.

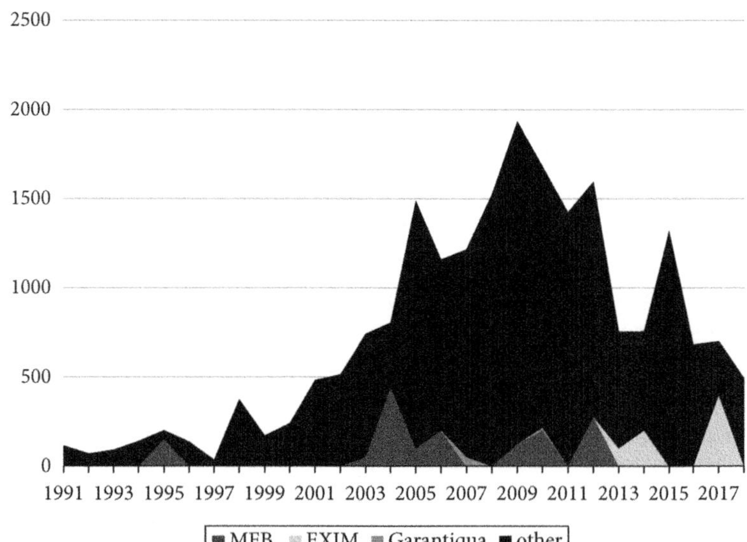


**Figure 9.6** EIB finance to Hungary 1991–2018 (signed amounts, EUR million)
*Source*: EIB database and EIB communication

In the case of Hungary, the EIB finance shows a clear pro-cyclical pattern with a significant increase before the crisis and a marked decrease in the wake of it. In Poland, the importance of EIB-provided finance remained at the same level or even increased a bit during the post-crisis period.

A similar effect, enhancing business actors' autonomy, cannot be said to be found in the European Fund for Strategic Investment (EFSI) for two reasons linked to the design of EFSI: first, the new EU Member States had only limited

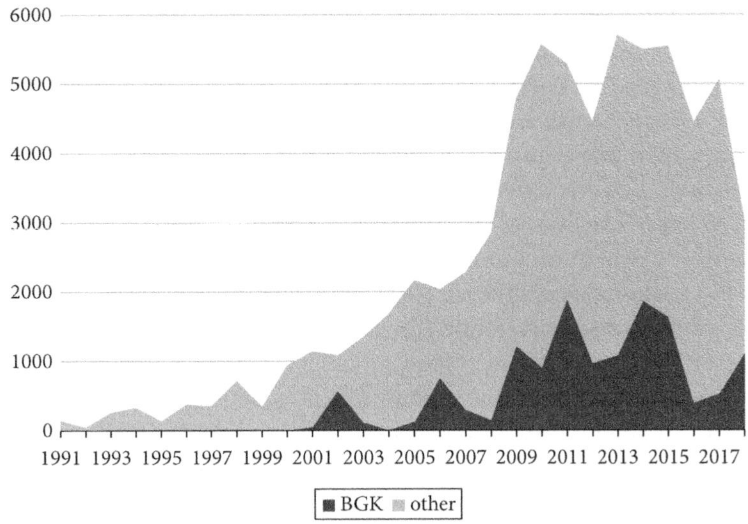


**Figure 9.7** EIB finance to Poland 1991–2018 (signed amounts, million euro)
*Source*: EIB database and EIB communication

access in general to EFSI funding as compared to western core countries. The EFSI funds' spread shows a marked gap between core and periphery EU Member States. In 2017, 82 percent of all signed EFSI financing went to the 15 "old" Member States. As the EFSI's audit report pointed out, "countries with the highest EFSI uptake were those with the most developed and active National Promotional Banks and Institutions" (European Court of Auditors, 2019 p. 6.). Hungary and Poland, as we have seen, are among the countries with better developed national development banks; however, these countries also suffer from the lack of additional private capital and therefore also find it very hard to meet the 5x external multiplier that EFSI requires (Nyikos, 2018; see Griffith-Jones and Naqvi, this volume). Accordingly, at the end of 2017, EFSI finance to Hungary measured by the signed financing per capita was the lowest within the EU while that to Poland was 19th out of 28. Ranking of countries in their access to EFSI finance measured by signed financing per GDP places Hungary on 16th and Poland on 7th among the EU28.

Second, development banks' involvement in EFSI finance has been very limited in both countries as most of the signed projects are financed either through commercial banks or directly. Out of the 42 Polish projects signed within the infrastructure window of EFSI, only three were financed through the BGK, while none of the five Hungarian EFSI financed projects within the infrastructure window were financed by MFB[14]. As regards the SME window of EFSI, neither the MFB

[14] https://www.eib.org/en/efsi/efsi-projects/index.htm?c=HU&se= accessed at 13.10.2019.

nor the BGK took part in its operations. The only success story within EFSI is the SME-window-granted guarantee programs, above all, the COSME. In Hungary, the Garantiqa, and in Poland, the BGK provide COSME guarantees for SMEs under the EIF counter-guarantee scheme, and both countries actively utilize its possibilities. BGK grants guarantees within the Creative Europe Guarantee facility (CCS), as well. Besides, several commercial banks also participated in COSME and—to a lesser extent—other guarantee programs (i.e., CCS, InnovFin, and EaSI[15]) directly in both countries (European Court of Auditors, 2019).

This also means that only the simplest, most traditional guarantee products are available to these countries, while the more sophisticated and riskier products with higher risk-sharing requirements are difficult to access for Hungarian and Polish entrepreneurs. Also, these countries also perform less well in project management and administration that makes their access to EFSI funding more difficult. Nevertheless, it also must be pointed out that the nationalist, authoritarian leaders of these countries prefer to have access to such EU funds that came under direct governmental control, i.e., Cohesion and Structural funds). Therefore, the EFSI-provided business-oriented framework is less attractive to the ruling governments (personal communication with former MFB official).

As regards the European commitment of the development banks, the MFB, the Eximbank and the BGK are members of the most important EU level professional association. MFB opened its representation office in Brussels in 1997, while the BGK do so in 2018. However, nowadays, BGK is more active on the European level than the MFB. BGK was one out of the five large European national development banks that—together with the EIB—signed a letter to the Commission on the need for further development of EU Investment Plan in 2015 (Mertens and Thiemann, 2019). The same group of development banks are the core sponsors of the Marguerite I and II funds that make capital-intensive infrastructure investments in the EU. BGK has committed to grant 100 Million EUR to back Marguerite II investment projects[16].

## 9.4 Conclusions

This chapter has reviewed the evolution of the field of development finance in Hungary and Poland from the time of transition up until 2018. The argument put forward here conceptualized development finance as a field populated by several actors such as governments, EU institutions, and development finance institutions that structure the field and set the rules of the game, which further constraints and enables actors' choices. With an aim of understanding the limited

[15] Employment and Social Innovation Programme.
[16] See: http://www.marguerite.com/about-us/background/ accessed at 13.11.2019.

scope of Eastern Member States' development policy in general and the restricted use of development banks in particular, the chapter placed the structuring logic of the field of development finance at the center and analyzed three periods characterized by three different contradictions in this logic that the actors of the field were compelled to manage.

In the transition period, development finance was managed among the contradicting ideologies of the Washington Consensus and industrial policy and the national development fields populated by international development actors. In the accession period and into the early years of EU membership, the EU not only helped in bringing development financial institutions alive, but its Single Market rules also constrained their activities. Finally, post-GFC, nationalist and authoritarian parties came to power in both countries, which are in favor of national economic promotion, but prioritize institutions that are under their political networks' control and promote the strengthening of new development actors such as central banks and domestically-owned commercial banks. Within these constraints, the Hungarian and Polish development fields are on diverging paths: 1) the Hungarian MFB's importance is declining while that of the BGK seems to increase, 2) the Hungarian development field is more decentralized, the Polish more centralized, 3) there is a marked difference in the role of the two central banks where the Hungarian central bank has entered development finance, but the Polish bank did not.

With regard to the role of the EU, this chapter concludes that the EU has played a crucial enabling role in the functioning of development banks in Hungary and Poland, however, it also sets essential constraints on how these banks may function. In line with Bruszt and Vukov's, (2017) argument, we see that the EU was instrumental in building development banks, providing funding through Structural and Cohesion Funds, and through the EIB. We also detect that development banks in these countries were built for the Single Market, and not solely for their national economy. This is crucial, as development banks are *per definition* essential instruments in the hand of EU Member States to manage the disparities of economic integration. However, in the case of Hungary and Poland, these banks function under severe domestic as well as EU-wide regulatory constraints and, therefore, only have limited capacity to fulfill their development purposes. Since the coming to power of nationalist and authoritarian leaders, through Structural and Cohesion Funds, the EU effectively finances and thus legitimizes these governments' operations (Johnson and Barnes, 2015). However, we also find that through EIB loans, the EU is also capable of reaching out to non-government related corporate actors and thus finance businesses that seek to operate outside the grip of nationalist, authoritarian governments in Eastern Europe.

Finally, this chapter concludes that today, Eastern development banks' ability to connect, contribute, and benefit from the emerging hidden investment state of the EU shows a marked difference from core Member States. Because economic development in the East is a prerequisite for the proper functioning of the Single Market, and because the evolving EU-wide industrial policy infrastructure could be a boon to the less developed Eastern Member States, it is in the interest of European integration, and therefore of all actors, to work out such EU-wide development structures as can cater for the historically defined needs and interests of all member states.

## References


Appel, H., Orenstein, M.A., 2018. From Triumph to Crisis: Neoliberal Economic Reform in Postcommunist Countries. Cambridge University Press, Cambridge.

Balassa, A., 1996. Restructuring and Recent Situation of the Hungarian Banking Sector. NBH Workshop Studies, 4.

Blauberger, M., 2009. "Compliance with Rules of Negative Integration: European State Aid Control in the New Member States." Journal of European Public Policy 16.7: 1030–46.

Bluhm, K., Varga M., 2020. "Conservative Developmental Statism in East Central Europe and Russia" New Political Economy 25.4: 642–659.

Bohle, D., Greskovits, B., 2018. "Politicising Embedded Neoliberalism: Continuity and Change In Hungary's Development Model." West European Politics 42.5: 1069–93.

Bohle, D., Greskovits, B, 2012. Capitalist Diversity on Europe's Periphery, Cornell Studies in Political Economy. Cornell University Press.

Bruszt, L., 2002. "Making Markets and Eastern Enlargement: Diverging Convergence?" West European Politics 25.2: 121–40.

Bruszt, L., McDermott, G. A. (eds), 2014. Leveling the Playing Field: Transnational Regulatory Integration and Development. Oxford, New York: Oxford University Press.

Bruszt, L., Vukov, V., 2017. "Making States for the Single Market: European Integration and the Reshaping of Economic States in The Southern and Eastern Peripheries of Europe." West European Politics 40.4: 663–87.

Cini, M., 2001. "The Soft Law Approach: Commission Rule-Making in the EU's State Aid Regime." Journal of European Public Policy 8.2: 192–207.

Éltető, A., Antalóczy, K., 2017. "Export- És Befektetésösztönzési Rendszerek a Visegrádi Országokban—Tapasztalatok és Kihívások." Külgazdaság 51.11–12: 32–57.

Epstein, R.A., 2017. "East European Exceptionalism: Foreign Domination in Finance," in Adam Fagan, Petr Kopecky (eds), Routledge Handbook of East European Politics. London: Routledge.

Epstein, R.A., 2008. "The Social Context in Conditionality: Internationalizing Finance in Postcommunist Europe." Journal of European Public Policy 15.6: 880–98.

Epstein, R.A., 2006. "Cultivating Consensus and Creating Conflict: International Institutions and the (De)Politicization of Economic Policy in Postcommunist Europe." Comparative Political Studies 39.8: 1019–42.

European Court of Auditors, (2019). European Fund for Strategic Investments: Action Needed to Make EFSI a Full Success, Special Report No. 03.

Gém, E., 2012. "A Magyar Fejlesztési Bank 20 éve: változó fejlesztési banki szerepkör", in Levente Kovács (ed.), Negyedszázados a Magyar Bankrekdszer, 187–202. Budapest, Magyar Bankszövetség.

Jacoby, W., Korkut, U., 2015. "Vulnerability and Economic Re-orientation: Rhetoric and in Reality in Hungary's 'Chinese Opening.'" East European Politics and Societies 30.3: 496–518.

Johnson, J., 2016. Priests of Prosperity: How Central Bankers Transformed the Postcommunist World. Cornell University Press, Ithaca.

Johnson, J., Barnes, A., 2015. "Financial Nationalism and Its International Enablers: The Hungarian Experience." Review of International Political Economy 22.3: 535–69.

Karsai, Judit, 1999. "A megfontoltan kockáztató tőkések. Kockázatitőke-befektetések Magyarországon [Capitalists taking considered risks. Venture-capital investments in Hungary]," Közgazdasági Szemle (Economic Review - monthly of the Hungarian Academy of Sciences), Közgazdasági Szemle Alapítvány (Economic Review Foundation), vol. 0(9), pages 789–812.

Karsai, Judit, 2007. "Kifelé a zsákutcából. Állami kockázati tőke és innováció [Out of the blind alley. State venture capital and innovation]," Közgazdasági Szemle (Economic Review - monthly of the Hungarian Academy of Sciences), Közgazdasági Szemle Alapítvány (Economic Review Foundation), vol. 0(12), pages 1085-1102.

King, l, Sznajder, A., 2006. "The State-Led Transition to Liberal Capitalism: Neoliberal, Organizational, World System, and Social Structural Explanations of Poland's Economic Success." American Journal of Sociology 112.3: 751–801.

Kiss, J, 1994. "Debt Management in Eastern Europe." Eastern European Economics, 32.3: 52–75.

Kornai, J, 1994. "Transformational Recession: The Main Causes." Journal of Comparative Economics 19.1: 39–63.

Kozak, S., 2013. Consolidation of the Banking Sector in Poland in 1989–2013 in Comparison with the Structural Changes of the Banking Sector in the USA and the EU, NBP Working Paper No. 166.

Kozarzewski, P., Bałtowski, M., 2017. "Change in the Ownership Policy Paradigm in Poland: State Control vs. Privatisation." Acta Oeconomica 67.1: 1–20.

Lindstrom, N., Piroska, D., 2007. "The Politics of Privatization and Europeanization in Europe's Periphery: Slovenian Banks and Breweries for Sale?" Competition & Change 11.2: 117–35.

Magyar, B., 2016. "The Post-Communist Maffia State." CEU Press, Budapest.

Medve-Bálint, G., 2014. "The Role of the EU in Shaping FDI Flows to East Central Europe." JCMS: Journal of Common Market Studies 52.1: 35–51.

Mérő, K., Valentinyi M., 2003. The Role of Foreign Banks in Five Central and Eastern European Countries, MNB Working Paper, 2003/10.

Mérő, K., Piroska, D., 2016. "Banking Union and Banking Nationalism—Explaining Opt-Out Choices of Hungary, Poland and the Czech Republic." Policy and Society, 35.3: 215–26.

Mertens, D., Thiemann, M., 2019. "Building a Hidden Investment State? The European Investment Bank, National Development Banks and European Economic governance." Journal of European Public Policy, 26.1: 23–43.

Myant, M., Drahokoupil, J., 2010. Transition Economies: Political Economy in Russia, Eastern Europe, and Central Asia (1st edition). Hoboken, NJ: Wiley.

Naczyk, M., 2014. Budapest in Warsaw: Central European Business Elites and the Rise of Economic Patriotism Since the Crisis (SSRN Scholarly Paper No. ID 2550496). Social Science Research Network, Rochester, NY.

Naqvi, N., Henow, A., Chang, H.-J., 2018. "Kicking Away the Financial Ladder? German Development Banking Under Economic Globalisation." Review of International Political Economy 25.5: 672–98.

Nölke, A., Vliegenthart, A., 2009. "Enlarging the Varieties of Capitalism: The Emergence of Dependent Market Economies in East Central Europe." World Politics, 61.4: 670–702.

Nyikos, G., 2018. "Comments on the Functioning of the European Fund for Strategic Investment." Európai Tükör 21 (Special Edition), 107–110.

Piroska, D., 2017. "Funding Hungary: Competing Crisis Management Priorities of Troika Institutions." Third World Thematics: A TWQ Journal 2.6: 805–24.

Rohac, D, Miszerak, M., 2017. "Poland's Rush to Banking Sector Socialism" Financial Times, June 30, accessed 5.31.2019, https://www.ft.com/content/f7283548-5cd1-11e7-b553-e2df1b0c3220.

Skuza, S., 2009. "Bank Gospodarstwa Krajowego (Domestic Management Bank) as a Financial Institution in the State Public Finance System." Bialostockie Studia Prawnicze, 5: 98–106.

Skuza, S., 2014. "The Issues of Regulatory Environment of Bank Gospodartswa Krajowego Operation with Reference to European Standards for Public Development Banks. Current Situation and Own Proposal for Changes." Problemy Zarzadzania, 12.4: 169–85.

Strojwas, M, 2010. The Polish Banking System: Hit by the Crisis or Merely by a Cool Breeze? ECFIN Country Focus, Volume 7 Issue 2.

Szent-Iványi, B, 2017. "Investment Promotion in the Visegrad Four Countries: Post-FDI.Challenges," in Béla Galgóczi, Jan Drahokoupil (eds), Condemned to Be Left behind? Can Central and Eastern Europe Emerge from Its Low-Wage Model? Brussels: ETUI.

Toplišek, A., 2019. "The Political Economy of Populist Rule in Post-Crisis Europe: Hungary and Poland." New Political Economy 25.3: 388–403.

Voszka, E., 1994. Centralization, Renationalization, Redistribution: The Role of the Government in Changing the Ownership Structure in Hungary. Centre for Economic Policy Research (Great Britain).

Wade, R.H., 2003. "The Invisible Hand of the American Empire." Ethics & International Affairs 17.2: 77–88.

APPENDIX 9.1

# List of interviews

1. Former MFB mid-level officer, August 9, 2018 and April 17, 2019, Budapest
2. Former MFB high-level officer September, 12018, Budapest
3. Four expert interviews in October 2018, Budapest and Warsaw
4. Former BGK officer, October 9. 2018, Warsaw
5. Two representatives of Polish professional associations, October, 10. 2018, Warsaw

# 10

# Development Finance in the Baltic States and the Process of Europeanization

*Olga Mikheeva and Egert Juuse*

## 10.1 Introduction

After the fall of the Berlin Wall, many countries of the former socialist bloc established development banks in the early 1990s and in some cases they resumed operations from pre-WWII times, as was the case in Poland (Piroska and Merö, this volume). The Baltic countries, however, differed from other Central and Eastern European (CEE) countries with a clear U-turn from any notion of industrial policy, including industrial financing. *Gradual* transition towards a capitalist financial system as elsewhere did not seem to be an option for political reasons. As the economist Hyman Minsky (1991, 1) noted: "...there [was] a great deal of public impatience. It is understandable that there [was] little tolerance for delayed real results in societies in which so much has been sacrificed for so long to no avail." In all three countries there was an immediate and sharp focus on European integration—the very choice of becoming part of political Europe has never been questioned or faced any opposition from business and political elites (Furman, 2002), implying a significant EU influence on these economies (Bauer et al., 2007, see also Suurna and Kattel, 2010).

Within the context of rapid European integration, the old industrial structures were not upgraded but were rapidly replaced with foreign-owned factories operating within Western European value-chains. Their productivity remains the lowest in the EU (Reinert, 2006; Reinert and Kattel, 2014; Kattel and Reinert, 2018). At the same time, the financial structures needed for economic development based on foreign direct investments (FDI) consisted of increasingly foreign-owned financial institutions and very small capital markets. In particular, Estonia's development path is one of the starkest instances of applying a liberal market economy model. However, some properties such as nearly full foreign ownership of the banking industry and a heavy reliance on foreign public and private financing of capital development make not only Estonia, but also Latvia, quite extreme cases. This is important in the context of our analysis that looks at the national

Olga Mikheeva and Egert Juuse, *Development Finance in the Baltic States and the Process of Europeanization* In: *The Reinvention of Development Banking in the European Union: Industrial Policy in the Single Market and the Emergence of a Field.* Edited by: Daniel Mertens, Matthias Thiemann, and Peter Volberding, Oxford University Press (2021).
 DOI: 10.1093/oso/9780198859703.003.0010

development finance institutions[1] (DFIs) and the challenges in development financing, stemming from the countries' historical background, policy choices, and patterns of European integration.

In particular, we place the analysis of the creation of DFIs in the Baltics in a broader policy landscape, existing on national and supranational levels, since DFIs never function in isolation but are integral to economic policies. Hence, for understanding the role of DFIs in the peculiar economic and financial context of the Baltic States, we adhere to Nurkse's ([1953] 2009, 120) notion of a "circular constellation of forces" for presenting a broader picture. In other words, the analysis focuses not only on institutional, but also on economic and political interrelationships that operate through feedback mechanisms. And, given that newly created DFIs have been the result of EU-led external policies, we are interested in the process of "Europeanization"[2] in relation to development financing. As noted by Suurna and Kattel (2010), EU funding could be considered as the main vehicle for Brussels to exercise strong influence over national innovation and economic policy decisions. In the financial policy domain, the process of Europeanization in CEE countries has been previously studied but through the lenses of financial integration (Juuse, 2016a; Juuse, 2016b; Quaglia, 2007), banking regulation and supervision (Juuse, 2015; Kattel, 2010; Juuse et al., 2019), and European Monetary Union (EMU) and monetary policy (Dyson, 2000).

Our comparative study focuses on three Baltic countries—Estonia, Latvia and Lithuania—where Estonia serves as the primary case of analysis while Latvia and Lithuania act as "shadow" or supporting cases. The three republics represent a homogeneous sample in terms of key characteristics, that is, economic structures, socio-political history, over-dependency on EU external funding, monetary regimes, and a continuous prevalence of neoliberal political discourses. The time frame for our study spans the period of roughly ten years, 2007–2018, i.e. from the time of the first programing period (2007–2013), which involved the first significant injection of structural funds, until the most recent data. When

[1] There is a re-emerging interest in the strategic roles that national development banks can play, both from the academic community (Mazzucato and Penna, 2016; Griffith-Jones and Ocampo, 2018) as well as policy makers (European Commission, 2015). Within the EU, it has been acknowledged that innovation-led development policies should have an innovation-oriented financing component because various types of finance (e.g. internal vs. external; short- vs. longer-term) result in various types of investments. In the context of this article, "development bank" seems to be a less appropriate term to use due to the nature of these financial institutions operating in the three Baltic states, which are in most cases oriented towards provision of guarantees and/or soft loans rather than development-oriented investment activities. The term Development Finance Institution seems to be more appropriate and will be used instead.

[2] Following Börzel and Risse (2000, 2–4), the term Europeanization is used to describe the domestic change resulting from the interplay of EU and national policies, institutions and policy making processes, where the design and implementation of general policy approaches and policy measures are dependent on the administrative structures and patterns of interest intermediation. Here, either a "top-down" and a "bottom-up" dimension in the concept of Europeanization can be distinguished.

structuring the case studies, we were guided by the three main aspects of financing of development in the Baltic region:

- The transition of post-Soviet industrial structures towards integration into foreign-controlled value chains and respective financing patterns with the supportive contextual factors of transformation.
- The importance of EU structural funds in national budgets and public investments.
- The role of Development Finance Institutions, their capacities in implementing respective policy mandates, and the types of policy instruments that have been used. Among all DFIs existing in each country we focus on those that provide support to businesses through various financial instruments; namely, KredEx in Estonia, ALTUM in Latvia and INVEGA in Lithuania.

In terms of data collection, we relied on previously conducted studies IN the case of Estonia, largely because the Estonian financial system was extensively analyzed as part of the FESSUD project[3]. In addition, inputs from academia, industry representatives, and policy makers were gained through four focus group interviews conducted in late-2018. We relied on descriptive statistics and (scarce) secondary sources in order to show fundamental similarities in structural dynamics in the three small Baltic economies. In addition, a total of six interviews were conducted in the three countries with top managers of selected DFIs and supervising ministries (Ministries of Economy and Ministries of Finance) during May–July 2019. Interviews were essential to gain a more nuanced understanding of how DFIs were conceived or recently restructured, how they coordinate their work with supervising ministries and to what extent they have operational discretion (e.g. designing financial instruments, defining terms of financing, helping identify priority sectors and financing needs, etc.) By doing so, we aim to emphasize differences in design that nevertheless largely remain differences in degree and, thus, support our overall hypothesis: in close coordination with the EU, DFIs in the Baltics perform managerial roles within a supranational state-aid framework by acting as efficient managers of state-aid programs rather than development-oriented investment bankers.

The structure of the paper is as follows: (1) first, we briefly introduce the context of the transition economies of the three Baltic countries, including an overview of economic structures, main economic policy trajectories and governance mechanisms in terms of implementing an EU-led policy agenda; (2) subsequently, we elaborate on the financing of development and the case of national DFIs in

[3] Financialisation, Economy, Society and Sustainable Development (FESSUD), http://fessud.eu, last accessed 19 November 2019.

Estonia; (3) next, two supporting cases of DFIs in Latvia and Lithuania are presented, largely building on interview materials; (4) we then provide a comparative summary with the focus on the process of Europeanization and its effects on the capacities of DFIs; and (5) we conclude by outlining the limitations of the study and provide suggestions for future research.

## 10.2 Eastern Enlargement and the Three Baltic Republics

The three Baltic republics (Estonia, Latvia and Lithuania) have been characterized by a strictly neoliberal policy agenda since the 1990s (Bohle and Greskovits, 2012), which has been reinforced by very rapid integration into the EU common market (for a comparison with the more gradual integration of Spain and Greece see Reinert and Kattel, 2007). This can also be observed from similar policy responses to the Global Recession after 2007–2008 in the three countries: austerity policies resulted in low government deficits combined with sharp contractions of GDP and high unemployment rates. Estonia differed in substantially lower government indebtedness and entered into the Euro Zone in 2011, that is, in the middle of the recession. Table 10.1 lists selected economic and policy indicators.

While higher rates of Foreign Direct Investments (FDI) have been present in Estonia and Latvia, considering the net balance of FDI flows, all three countries represent small open economies. FDI has been particularly strong in the financial sector (banking) and all three countries demonstrate a high share of foreign ownership. The Baltic republics also share similar structural characteristics: knowledge intensity has been growing as more complex economic structures developed but this has not always translated into similar dynamics in productivity. Karo et al. (2017) point out the close proximity of Estonia to Scandinavian production networks and markets is one of the reasons why it outperforms Latvia and Lithuania. Nevertheless, productivity has been stagnating: despite an increasing trend in industrial value added, production of new knowledge (as measured in charges for IP) has been stagnating, especially in the last decade[4]. Such dynamics largely reveal an asymmetrical integration of the Baltics into the EU[5] (also see Reinert and Kattel, 2014).

[4] See, for example, World Bank's World Development Indicators Database.

[5] Asymmetrical integration refers to the main characteristic of the Eastern Enlargement whereby a block of CEE countries with lower levels of development were included in the common market and many of them, subsequently, into the common currency union. This is in contrast with more symmetrical integration of South European countries into the EU before the Eastern Enlargement. Asymmetrical integration resulted in significant structural imbalances within the common market, which have persisted ever since. (Reinert and Kattel, 2014)

**Table 10.1** Economic and policy indicators in Estonia, Latvia and Lithuania (2007–2018)

| | 2007 | 2008 | 2009 | 2010 | 2011 | 2012 | 2013 | 2014 | 2015 | 2016 | 2017 | 2018 |
|---|---|---|---|---|---|---|---|---|---|---|---|---|
| **Real GDP growth (%)** | | | | | | | | | | | | |
| Estonia | 7.7 | −5.4 | −14.7 | 2.3 | 7.6 | 4.3 | 1.9 | 2.9 | 1.9 | 3.5 | 4.9 | 3.9 |
| Latvia | 10 | −3.5 | −14.4 | −3.9 | 6.4 | 4 | 2.4 | 1.9 | 3 | 2.1 | 4.6 | 4.8 |
| Lithuania | 11.1 | 2.6 | −14.8 | 1.6 | 6 | 3.8 | 3.5 | 3.5 | 2 | 2.4 | 4.1 | 3.5 |
| **Unemployment rate (% of active population, annual average)** | | | | | | | | | | | | |
| Estonia | 4.6 | 5.5 | 13.5 | 16.7 | 12.3 | 10.0 | 8.6 | 7.4 | 6.2 | 6.8 | 5.8 | 5.4 |
| Latvia | 6.1 | 7.7 | 17.5 | 19.5 | 16.2 | 15.0 | 11.9 | 10.8 | 9.9 | 9.6 | 8.7 | 7.4 |
| Lithuania | 4.3 | 5.8 | 13.8 | 17.8 | 15.4 | 13.4 | 11.8 | 10.7 | 9,.1 | 7.9 | 7.1 | 6.2 |
| **General government deficit (% of GDP)** | | | | | | | | | | | | |
| Estonia | – | −2.7 | −2.2 | 0.2 | 1,2 | −0,3 | −0,2 | 0,7 | 0,1 | −0,3 | −0.4 | −0.6 |
| Latvia | −0.5 | −4.2 | −9.5 | −8.6 | −4.3 | −1.2 | −1.2 | −1.4 | −1.4 | 0.1 | −0.6 | −1 |
| Lithuania | −0.8 | −3.1 | −9.1 | −6.9 | −8.9 | −3.1 | −2.6 | −0.6 | −0.3 | 0.2 | 0.5 | 0.7 |
| **General government gross consolidated debt (% of GDP)** | | | | | | | | | | | | |
| Estonia | 3.7 | 4.5 | 7.0 | 6.6 | 6.1 | 9.7 | 10.2 | 10.5 | 9.9 | 9.2 | 9.2 | 8.4 |
| Latvia | 8.0 | 18.2 | 36.3 | 47.3 | 43.1 | 41.6 | 39.4 | 40.9 | 36.8 | 40.3 | 40.0 | 35.9 |
| Lithuania | 15.9 | 14.6 | 28.0 | 36.2 | 37.2 | 39.8 | 38.8 | 40.5 | 42.6 | 40.0 | 39.4 | 34.2 |
| **FDI inward stock (% of GDP)** | | | | | | | | | | | | |
| Estonia | 70.5 | 63.9 | 80.6 | 79.7 | 70.6 | 82.2 | 87.8 | 80.0 | 84.0 | 84.6 | 92.2 | 82.5 |
| Latvia | 35.6 | 31.8 | 44.4 | 46.0 | 42.5 | 48.1 | 52.7 | 48.1 | 54.7 | 51.4 | 57.5 | 49.7 |
| Lithuania | 37.1 | 26.7 | 35.4 | 36.1 | 32.8 | 37.2 | 37.8 | 31.9 | 35.4 | 34.2 | 37.4 | 33.3 |
| **Balance of FDI flows (inward minus outward; % of GDP)** | | | | | | | | | | | | |
| Estonia | 2.8 | 2.8 | 2.4 | 6.9 | 10.6 | 2.2 | 1.0 | 2.4 | −0.7 | 2.4 | 3.7 | 4.5 |
| Latvia | 6.3 | 2.9 | 0.6 | 1.5 | 4.9 | 3.3 | 1.6 | 1.3 | 2.4 | 0.1 | 1.9 | 2.1 |
| Lithuania | 3.5 | 3.4 | −0.6 | 2.2 | 3.2 | 0.7 | 0.6 | 0.0 | 1.9 | 0.4 | 1.3 | 0.1 |
| **Foreign ownership of the banking sector (% of total assets)** | | | | | | | | | | | | |
| Estonia | – | 98.9 | 98.9 | 98.5 | 94.2 | 96.4 | 95.7 | 95.1 | 94.2 | 93.4 | 74.1 | 72.7 |
| Latvia | – | 65.9 | 66.7 | 65.9 | 62.3 | 61.3 | 59.0 | 52.5 | 47.4 | 49.7 | 51.6 | 67.1 |
| Lithuania | 83.1 | 85.1 | 82.8 | 78.4 | 90.0 | 94.4 | 91.5 | 92.0 | 91.8 | 91.9 | 91.6 | 91.1 |

*Source*: authors' calculations based on Eurostat, OECD, UNCTAD and ECB statistics

### 10.2.1 Cohesion Policy Funds

Accession to the EU implied an inflow of EU financial assistance, following the Cohesion Policy priorities in terms of convergence of productivity and economic activities across the EU. National governments in the CEE region got acquainted with the Cohesion Policy funds during pre-access negotiations in early 2000s through the PHARE, ISPA (Instrument for Structural Policies for Pre-Accession, infrastructure and environment) and SAPARD (agricultural and rural development) programmes. Creating financial management capacities in national governments was one of the explicit priorities of pre-accession financial support, which would increase exponentially after the accession in 2004. Table 10.2 illustrates the amount of structural funds as a share of average expenditures for development in Central and Eastern European (CEE) countries during 2000–2006.

In all three republics, EU support forms more than 10 percent of their state budget revenues and the lion share of all public investments (Varblane, 2016, 121). Although immediate post-crisis figures should be treated with care (due to a considerable decline in budgetary revenues and spending), during 2010–2012 the share of EU funds was 79 percent of Lithuanian, 70 percent of Estonian, and 61 percent of all Latvian public sector investments (European Commission, 2013). Indeed, as one of the interviewees commented, most investments in Latvia are being financed from structural funds. Table 10.3 presents the amount of structural and cohesion policy support in comparison to investments by the government sector during the first programing period. In all cases the share has been steadily growing and in 2013 reached 50 percent, 68 percent and 78 percent for Estonia, Latvia and Lithuania, respectively. Given almost the same allocations for the ongoing programing period (2014–2020[6]) in nominal terms to all three

**Table 10.2** Relevance of Cohesion Policy on National Expenditure for Development in selected CEE countries (annual average 2000–2006)

| Country | Structural and Cohesion Funds as % of expenditure for development |
|---|---|
| **Latvia** | **81.8** |
| **Lithuania** | **80.9** |
| Slovakia | 58.9 |
| **Estonia** | **55.3** |
| Poland | 50.3 |
| Hungary | 29.7 |
| Slovenia | 21.7 |
| Czech Republic | 13.5 |

*Source*: Ferry and McMaster (2013)

*Note*: Estimate calculated based on total allocation and in relation to the period 2004–2006 for new Member Countries and EU25. ESF is not included in coherence with EfD calculation.

[6] https://cohesiondata.ec.europa.eu/dataset/Available-Budget-per-MS-2014-2020_chart/7rq3-5nxf Last accessed 19 November 2019.

**Table 10.3** Structural and Cohesion Policy funds as a share of investments by the government sector in Estonia, Latvia, Lithuania (2007–2013)

| | 2007 | 2008 | 2009 | 2010 | 2011 | 2012 | 2013 |
|---|---|---|---|---|---|---|---|
| **Estimated structural and cohesion funds interventions (EUR million)*** | | | | | | | |
| Estonia | 356 | 380 | 405 | 433 | 463 | 494 | 527 |
| Latvia | 480 | 513 | 549 | 584 | 619 | 655 | 691 |
| Lithuania | 725 | 772 | 820 | 868 | 918 | 971 | 1023 |
| **Gross fixed capital formation - government sector (EUR million)** | | | | | | | |
| Estonia | 977 | 1025 | 882 | 713 | 819 | 1134 | 1055 |
| Latvia | 1340 | 1256 | 913 | 841 | 1009 | 1072 | 1012 |
| Lithuania | 1572 | 1759 | 1189 | 1391 | 1479 | 1326 | 1309 |
| **Structural and cohesion funds as a share of gross fixed capital formation by the government sector** | | | | | | | |
| Estonia | 36.5% | 37.1% | 45.9% | 60.8% | 56.5% | 43.6% | 50.0% |
| Latvia | 35.8% | 40.8% | 60.1% | 69.5% | 61.4% | 61.1% | 68.3% |
| Lithuania | 46.1% | 43.9% | 69.0% | 62.4% | 62.1% | 73.2% | 78.1% |

*Source*: authors' calculations based on AMECO database; * Veld 2007 based on DG REGIO

countries, we may conclude that structural funds continue to form the major share in government investments in the Baltics.

Such dependency on external financing and its conditionality, which comes as a set of policy priorities (e.g. "Smart Specialisation"), has several implications for nation states and the governance of development financing. First, a significant inflow of funds has implied a strain on domestic administrative capacities. Even the bigger countries of the CEE region, such as Poland, faced significant challenges in terms of management and implementation of funded programs, exacerbated by existing weaknesses and fragmentation in domestic innovation systems and related public agencies (Breznitz and Ornston, 2017). Second, the co-financing requirement has affected Member States (MS) differently. The burden of substantial increase in the national contribution particularly affected the newer Member States where, both, the nominal amount of cohesion funds and respective national contributions, have been higher than elsewhere (Ferry and McMaster, 2013).

At the same time, as one of the interviewees has noted, co-financing can come from private sources and not necessarily from the public sector, but smaller countries tend to have greater difficulties in finding matching resources in the private sector. Third, dependency on, and the conditionality of, EU funds have produced an institutional environment where "absorptive capacity" and financial prudence have been prioritized. For example, respective Ministries of Finance report on the rate of absorption of EU structural funds by different ministries to the EC on a monthly basis (Varblane, 2016). Likewise, an explicit emphasis on spending ("we have to spend it all and quickly") associated with "absorption capacity" incentivizes adherence to more short-term policy horizons while also strengthening managerial competences. The latter were needed following the creation of regional and local agencies—"agencification"—to administer EU funds as one of the EU conditionalities (arguments in favor of agencification included decentralization and accountability, professionalization of agencies and their (more) active engagement with the clients and real-life circumstances) (Suurna and Kattel, 2010).

In the following sections, we will show how such a context de-incentivizes and hinders the development of a more strategic and long-term take on public investments and on using DFIs as policy tools. We shed a light on the establishment of agencies as government-backed Venture Capital Funds in line with the overall innovation/industrial policy discourse that rested on a high-technology bias (industrial parks, incubators) and short-term plans, resulting in a decontextualized formulation of innovation/industrial policies in almost all CEE countries. By "decontextualization" we refer to the mismatch between policy objectives and actual socio-economic and technological structural problems[7]. And here, the EU's impact cannot be overestimated, in particular on innovation/industrial policies in CEE countries. In the Baltics, innovation policy formulation is an extreme example of policy import: the policy mix has strongly reflected the priorities of and objectives defined in the EU programs for R&D and innovation (see for example INNO-Policy TrendChart 2006–2007; INNO-Policy TrendChart 2008; Suurna and Kattel, 2010, 653). Under such conditions, there is little space left for DFIs in terms of developing capacities and competences as strategic investors or active financing agents of development.

## 10.3 The Case of Estonia

### 10.3.1 Institutional Landscape, Policies and Economic Structures

After re-gaining independence in 1991, Estonia has not practiced extensive intervention in the economy beyond fiscal reforms for the purpose of macroeconomic stability. In the early years of independence in the 1990s, there was already a clear tendency towards a "regulatory state" model in socio-economic reforms, as public institutions were not supposed to intervene in the economy other than regulate (see Bohle and Greskovits, 2012). As one of the key reformers at that time, Siim Kallas, who was in charge of the central bank then, has argued, such choice was a conscious one, as there was low trust in government's ability to get interventions right (Kallas, 2003, 511). At the same time, political rhetoric since the early years has reinstated the need to fill the savings gap with foreign capital because

[7] There is an extensive literature based on empirical studies on how EU-led innovation policy priorities were not aligned to the actual structural problems of former Socialist economies: emphasis on commercialization, R&D funding and clustering/networking was at odds with the prevalent absence of university-industry linkages, lack of collective action, and a dismantled Soviet R&D system. (see, for example, Radosevic, 1998, 1999, 2004)

development has been conceived as savings-constrained (Juuse, 2015). In Estonia, FDI was seen as a supplement to internal resources for financing the growth and restructuring of the economy (Juuse, 2016d; Bank of Estonia, 1995).

Subject to this mainstream economics approach, Estonia has sympathized with monetarist principles by relying on market-based self-adjustment mechanisms (Juuse, 2015). For instance, the Central Bank of Estonia imposed upon itself a lender-of-last-resort constraint, implying an inability to provide reserves without limits, when needed. In this regard, the risks associated with the speculative financing or Schumpeterian financing of innovative activities have not been socialized (see Minsky [1986] 2008, 48–49). Under the currency board system, the central bank was deprived of the right to credit commercial banks or governments with either advances or purchases of government securities, respectively (see Godley and Lavoie, 2012, 214 on the currency board system in general). Cooperation between the central bank and other financial institutions regarding the provision of industrial finance was never on the agenda in order to overcome long-term financing bottlenecks, typical for a transition economy (see Singleton, 2011, 139; Juuse, 2016b). Essentially, such a conservative monetary regime entailed a commitment to fiscal prudence (Hansson, 1994 cited in Feldmann, 2013, 361), implying a meager government role for providing economic security to private entities. In that respect, countercyclical demand management and active industrial policies as the inherent elements of Keynesianism (see Soskice, 2007; Davies and Green, 2010) have been eschewed in Estonia and replaced by an emphasis on the improvement of supply-side conditions such as labor market and business environment.

In principle, the stabilization of aggregate demand has been to a great extent outsourced to external actors, i.e. EU funding in the form of transfer payments for capital formation, and the provision of liquidity from foreign public institutions (Scandinavian central banks) to support the banking reserves (Juuse, 2016d), since domestic banking structures have been largely foreign-owned. Such liberalism and exposure to external factors have been accompanied by the Europeanization process, i.e. the transposition of EU legislation as the major force affecting and directing developments in regulation and policy making. However, the anchoring to EU directives and policies has detached local financial market regulations from real-life business practices (Juuse, 2016a). The same could be seen in the EU-funded policy measures for economic and industrial development that have been detached from business needs and real economic problems.

By and large, the peculiarities of the Estonian economy are related to the dual structure of a productive economy whereby medium-sized and large businesses—as a rule, foreign-owned, who have access to foreign credit and know-how—are able to undertake innovation activities and thereby affect prices with their market power. These entities tend to have heightened (export) sales as well as profit expectations, while the financing of growth is undertaken with external (foreign) funds, which partially explains the disembeddedness of Multinational Enterprises (MNEs) from local productive conditions (Juuse, 2015; Juuse 2016d; Kilicaslan and Taymaz 2006). Likewise, the reality of FDI-led growth with a modular production profile has resulted in a number of MNEs having essentially no contacts with locally created, but EU-funded, R&D competence centers. This, in turn, created another dual structure: local high-tech small enclaves with no linkages to MNEs operating in the region (Radosevic and Reid, 2006; Karo and Kattel, 2015). Locally owned micro- and small enterprises, on the other hand, which predominantly operate in the services sector, target the volatile local market and rely on internal funds and when possible, loans from domestic banks (Juuse, 2016d; Kaarna et al., 2012, 15–16). Thus, one can observe power imbalances in both market concentrations, i.e. oligopolistic market features, and the increasing control of foreign owners over some of the industries, such as banking and electronics.

### 10.3.2 The Importance of Structural Funds

As stated above, state budget revenues and public investments for capital development purposes (in particular entrepreneurship, R&D and innovation) have been largely comprised of EU structural funds. For instance, the share of EU structural funds in public investments was 70 percent in Estonia in 2010–2012 (European Commission, 2013, see also Figure 10.1 and Tables 10.2 and 10.3). This implies that strategic plans for EU structural funding have become more important tools

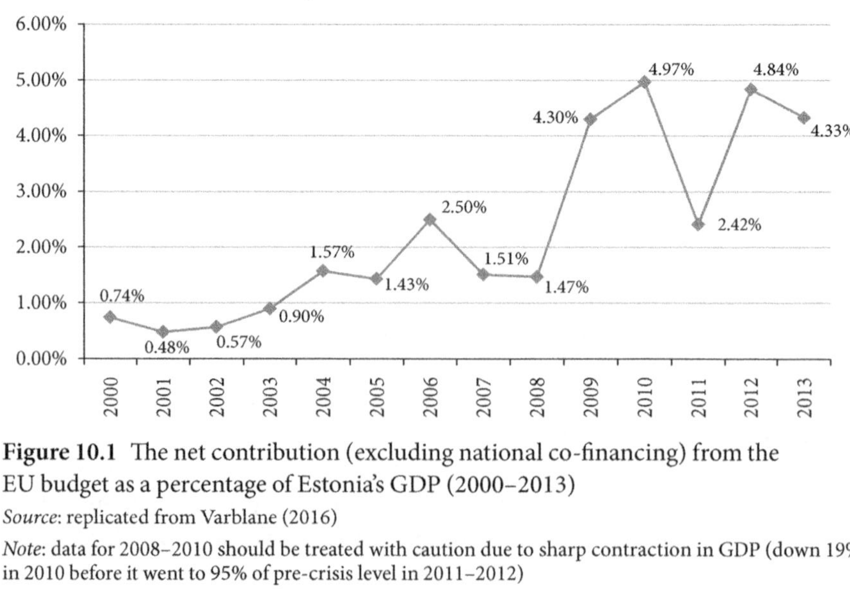


**Figure 10.1** The net contribution (excluding national co-financing) from the EU budget as a percentage of Estonia's GDP (2000–2013)

*Source*: replicated from Varblane (2016)

*Note*: data for 2008–2010 should be treated with caution due to sharp contraction in GDP (down 19% in 2010 before it went to 95% of pre-crisis level in 2011–2012)

for providing substantive innovation policy priorities than national innovation policy and budgetary strategies (Karo, 2011, 522). In that respect, one can observe a form of external anchoring and embeddedness in institutional structures that increase the country's vulnerability to external developments. Even though the EU-funded socialization of investment has kept up aggregate demand and employment, such a fiscal framework presents hazards to tranquil progress and leads to further dependence on foreign financial assistance. This is especially apparent when most government expenditures have been consumption supporting transfer payments, which are not self-sustaining (Juuse, 2016c).

In the 1990s there were already public support schemes that targeted small and medium-sized enterprises (SME) and were funded by external actors, such as the EBRD, while during the pre-accession period, Estonia used the PHARE fund of the EU to finance entrepreneurship and employment growth (Kinks, 2000; OECD, 2000; European Commission, 2007). Since the accession to the EU in 2004, several development programs have targeted new technologies in prioritized key areas as well as encouraging innovation in companies. In order to improve the competitiveness of businesses in the international arena, due to insufficient private investments in R&D, innovation, product development and export marketing (see Kalvet, 2006; Reid, 2011), several EU-funded public financing schemes have been established and mainly operated by *Enterprise Estonia* and *KredEx,* since the early 2000s. The priority in allocating public grants and loans has been given to growing enterprises in prioritized technology fields, which have the potential to produce products with higher value-added and export potential, and thus pay higher than average salaries (Traks, 2012). Hence, in a catching-up process, access to EU financing (structural funds) has become an alternative source of financing for SMEs in different economic sectors (see e.g. Madureira et al., 2007, 36–37).

### 10.3.3 Financing Patterns

By and large, the preferred source of financing of Estonian enterprises has been internal equity capital, while bank loans or funds from intra-group foreign parent companies have been used in case of dire necessity or when internal resources are insufficient (Kõomägi and Sander, 2006; Sander and Kõomägi, 2007; Raudsepp et al., 2003, 61–67). Here, the nature of the privatization of state-owned business, which in essence dismantled large production complexes in the manufacturing and agriculture sectors (see Purju, 2000), had a significant impact on bank-industry relations. As the privatization policy targeted strategic (foreign) investors, the result was a high concentration of ownership with control over financial decisions (OECD, 2000), which explains why businesses have been reluctant to be influenced by external actors, such as foreign banks

(Juuse, 2015). Moreover, the tax reform of 2000 incentivized the accumulation of retained earnings[8].

At the same time, foreign takeovers led to the centralization and concentration of the banking market, which drifted the banking practices away from the locally embedded *relationship-oriented banking* (see Levy Economics Institute, 2012, 19–20). This was manifested in the shift of banks' focus from local businesses to FDI-led companies—the result of the internationalization of production, which explains the *follow-the-client* approach taken by foreign banks—and to households in the 2000s (Juuse, 2016c). At the same time, the restructuring of the economy, which has entailed the emergence of small businesses, delinking processes, decreased capitalization, and primitivizing of the productive base, has suppressed the demand for bank or market-based financing (Raudsepp et al., 2003; Karo et al., 2018; Sander and Kõomägi, 2007). Recently, the main obstacle for local businesses in accessing bank loans has been insufficient collateral or guarantees, as foreign-owned banks operating in Estonia have taken a uniform stance to their credit policy at the regional level (Bank of Estonia, 2019, 12). Overall, in light of the heavy reliance on foreign savings in both financial and nonfinancial sectors the links between the Estonian financial sector and the productive part of the economy were gradually and substantially weakened.

The financing structure of Estonian businesses in terms of reliance on internal funds and occasional use of government support is predicated on some stylized characteristics of companies. Namely, a profile of an average Estonian business unit is a non-listed, owner-managed SME, which is active in low-technology sectors (Juuse, 2015; Juuse, 2016d; Polt, 2007). It is precisely low and medium-low technology sectors, where business expenditures on R&D account for 90.62 percent of total manufacturing business expenditures on R&D, and where the vast majority of firms (89.10 percent in 2011) report having received government support in the form of loans, grants or procurement contracts to undertake R&D activities (OECD 2013).

### 10.3.4 Development Finance Institutions

The Estonian Development Fund (EDF), which is sometimes listed as a DFI, never played the role of a financial institution with the exception of its managerial role in a state-owned fund of funds "SmartCap". EDF was established in 2006 and operated under the supervision of the Estonian Parliament until its reorganization and liquidation in 2017. During 10 years of operations, it played a substantial role in the development of the Smart Specialisation strategy for Estonia and acted

[8] For instance, accumulated retained earnings of the non-financial corporate sector increased from 7% of GDP in 2000 to 113.5% of GDP in 2009 (authors' calculations based on Statistics Estonia 2018).

as a national foresight think-tank as well as a Venture Capital (VC) fund (seed and start-up phases), thereby facilitating the development of a national VC industry and related ecosystem. The case of EDF is an illustrative example of a high-tech bias—by channeling EU support to targeted high-tech sectors, EDF was holding a portfolio of 15 high-tech companies (own investment around EUR 7m) by 2011 and had produced a number of foresight exercises in selected industries (EDF, 2011).

After the liquidation of EDF, its investment activities were transferred to KredEx, which has been envisioned as a national development bank with the mission to deal with market failures in the financial services' market on a reactive basis[9] without taking excessive risks (Majandus- ja kommunikatsiooniministeerium, 2017; KredEx, 2012). Established in the form of a foundation in 2001, KredEx provides access to capital (for SMEs primarily) through various market-correcting and supplementing financial instruments such as loan guarantees, for the most part, but also industry loans, start-up loans, export loans, and credit insurance solutions. In essence, KredEx has become a link between Estonian financial institutions and borrowers (KredEx, 2019a) and, in principle, it has been functioning as a bridge-financing provider or arm's length extension of commercial banks.

Since 2001, KredEx has guaranteed bank loans, bank guarantees and leasing transactions for 3735 companies for a total amount of EUR 1.4 billion, which has made it possible for enterprises to raise additional funding from banks (KredEx, 2019b). In addition, KredEx has continued to act as a venture capital investor, mainly through funds of funds such as SmartCap, the Baltic Innovation Fund I (and II), and the EstFund, whose capital has been used by subsidiary funds for investments in the Baltic region and beyond. At the same time, there has been a shift towards more passive state interventions in investment activities: e.g. SmartCap, a subsidiary of KredEx, has not invested directly in enterprises since 2017 but instead invests in accelerator funds managed by private companies (KredEx, 2018). Cooperation with EIF resulted in EstFund (est. 2016), a dedicated initiative to provide equity investments to high growth SMEs and financed under EU structural funds. The initiative was believed to catalyze further development of early-stage equity investments in Estonia.

In the case of KredEx, shifting the emphasis towards second-tier development banking, i.e. allocating public funds to financial institutions to make credit and investment decisions, implies a greater risk of bypassing projects with higher social returns and making lending programs (e.g. via the creation of funds of funds)

[9] For instance, this is reflected in the recent decision of the Ministry of Economic Affairs and Communications in cooperation with the Ministry of Finance to design a policy instrument—an industrial loan guarantee for businesses—that would solve the problem of SME's lacking collateral for getting a bank loan in rural areas (see Sutt, 2019).

ineffective (see Fernández-Arias et al. 2014, 197). In this case, it is also hard to identify market gaps[10] or gain knowledge of systemic failures to be able to propose or formulate policy solutions, instead of mere implementation, due to the lack of contact with productive firms (ibid, 199–200).

The same supply-based approach is reflected in KredEx' activities in the start-up field, where the focus is on building a strong ecosystem and designing friendly regulations. At the same time, corresponding to the above-mentioned shift of credit policy by commercial banks, a large component of the KredEx portfolio consists of various instruments and support measures such as grants directed towards the housing sector. As of 2018, eight different grant and loan instruments were on offer for the purposes of increasing energy efficiency, rejuvenating housing stock or real estate purchases (KredEx, 2019b). In its activities, KredEx uses both internal and external funds, including EU structural funds, but raises capital from other external sources, such as the European Investment Fund and the Council of Europe Development Bank (ibid).

Aside from KredEx, one can mention the foundation Enterprise Estonia that offers various grants and public services to businesses. Both institutions have been established in response to EU integration with clearly defined equity and state-aid rules as well as limitations on (investment) activities for the purpose of absorbing EU structural funds. Likewise, both institutions have been closely associated with and supervised by the Ministry of Economic Affairs and Communication. Most of the policy instruments have been designed by the latter in cooperation with KredEx and Enterprise Estonia. In that regard, neither Enterprise Estonia nor KredEx possess strategic policy autonomy, as they do not decide on activities, policy instruments, outputs, or outcomes and effects. The agencies are primarily policy implementers and hence, the goal has been efficiency in delivery, de-politization, and responsiveness (Tavits and Annus, 2006). Even though there are bi-directional consultations between the ministries and KredEx (or Enterprise Estonia) on designing and implementing policy instruments, any discretionary actions or leeway for adjustments are hampered by national development strategies and operational programs that are coordinated with and, in principle, mandated and approved by the EU[11].

## 10.4 Development Finance Institutions in Latvia and Lithuania

As with Estonia, the policy discourse in Latvia has been dominated by neoliberal policies while the production sector has a high share of foreign ownership among

[10] It is not uncommon for *ex ante* and impact analyses to be outsourced to private sector contractors—consultancies—who bring the knowledge of existing market failures and potential solutions.

[11] See operational programs for the 2014–2020 period in Estonia, https://www.struktuurifondid.ee/et/oigusaktid/rakenduskava-2014-2020, last accessed November 22, 2019.

large industrial firms, lower wages, and lower productivity. In March 2016, the Innovation Department was established within the Ministry of the Economy to enhance synergies between the policy planning functions and the EU support instruments as well as to insure more effective implementation of the state administration functions. In the same year the Ministry of Economy started to develop sectoral development strategies with the aim of encouraging companies to move towards more knowledge-intensive products and to increase labor productivity. While there is still little visible progress, the focus of the current policies is placed on productivity (Kulikovskis et al., 2018).

Lithuania has also placed productivity at the top of industrial and innovation policies. In both countries, productivity levels and wages are among the lowest in the EU while increasing labor costs further undermine the competitiveness of Lithuania's industrial exports. As was mentioned earlier, all three Baltic republics represent small open economies that have been historically relying on FDI. Similar to Estonia, the dual structure of Latvia's and Lithuania's national productive bases is made up of large foreign-owned MNEs and low-tech domestically owned SMEs with very few linkages between these two sectors. On the other hand, Lithuania and Latvia have recently taken a more active policy approach to industrial strategy as compared to Estonia. This is reflected in policy documents such as Latvia's "National Development Plan 2014–2020" and "National Industrial Policy Guidelines 2014–2020" and Lithuania's "Industry Digitalisation Roadmap 2013–2019". Nevertheless, the dependence on EU external financial assistance in the two countries is only slightly less than in Estonia (Table 10.3). Further, both countries exhibit high foreign ownership of the banking sector, which makes the availability of finance for capital investments similarly limited, as in Estonia.

### 10.4.1 Latvia

The main agencies in charge of the financing of development in Latvia are ALTUM, which is a non-banking development finance institution and Latvia's Investment and Development Agency (LIDA), which mostly administers grants. Both agencies are supervised by the Ministry of Economy (MoE) while ALTUM has two additional shareholders: the Ministry of Finance (MoF) and Ministry of Agriculture. ALTUM is tasked to provide SMEs with access to finance and non-financial professional support services (consulting, training, monitoring). The range of financial instruments it provides includes loans, guarantees, export credit, investments in risk capital funds, as well as alternative risk capital funding for businesses in the event of insufficient collateral. ALTUM also administers EU-funded targeted funds such as Loan Guarantees and Mezzanine Loans (target: all enterprises), Seed Capital Funds (target: start-ups, SMEs), Business Angel Co-Investment (target: SMEs), and Technology Accelerator (target: start-ups, SMEs).

The establishment of the new ALTUM in 2015 was closely coordinated with the European Commission (EC) in a consensual manner[12]. The design of the new institution's mandate, scope, and operations was proposed in line with all key EU regulations, particularly state aid rules, the overall eligibility criteria of structural funding, and EC guidelines on financial engineering. The overall policy framework proposed by Latvia to the EC implied that ALTUM would be operating as a non-commercial institution providing state aid through various financial instruments. The plan suggested by the government was also based on an overview of demand for financing programs and did not include any commercial activities, although the EC does allow some room for commercial activities. The government did not see the need for, or any potential areas of expansion of, ALTUM's mandate and scope: closing market gaps by supporting agriculture, SMEs, micro firms and MidCaps, providing acceleration funds, Venture Capital and guarantees. In other words, the establishment of ALTUM involved "playing by the [EC] rules" from the very start, as suggested by one of our interviewees. As demonstrated by ALTUM's annual reports, its *raison d'être* is promoting economic development through efficient state aid (e.g. ALTUM 2015).

The implementation of financing programs implies *ex ante* appraisals by both MoF and MoE, as well as the approval of the Cabinet. Every financing program is designed by the MoE (ALTUM has a strong say in the regulatory side of the program), for which ALTUM must design a business plan. The financing program typically defines eligibility criteria, maximum size of a loan, or other type of financial instrument and remains rather broad as it is meant for the entire programing period. The substance of every program is checked by the line ministries while there is a group of sector-specific managers in the MoE who oversee the implementation of every program.

ALTUM has embarked on a strategy to minimize the share of EU structural funds in its funding portfolio and instead to raise funds from multilateral banks such as the EIB/EIF and the EBRD. Minimizing the share of structural funds was a strategic decision due to demanding reporting and less flexible guidelines for spending the funds. Further, a lot of reporting and regulatory requirements connected to the EU funds were designed for grants and reporting on other financial instruments (even just loans) is quite cumbersome given the grant-dominated logic of financial reporting. Borrowing from multilateral financial institutions involves much less reporting and at the same time helps build a stronger image of ALTUM on capital markets.

[12] A successor of a mortgage bank ALTUM, the newly established Development Finance Institution, ALTUM, resulted from a merger of the old Development Finance Institution (a state-owned mortgage bank, which had a development finance and a commercial division; the former was liquidated during reorganization in 2015), Latvian Rural Development Fund and Latvian Guarantee Agency.

ALTUM directly interacts with the borrowers and only a very modest share of financing facilities is provided through other financial intermediaries. In terms of sector-specific expertise, ALTUM has the leading competences in financing agriculture and in energy efficiency financing. In addition, the potential to provide financing to local municipalities for implementing programs in energy efficiency is currently being discussed within the Ministry of Economy. ALTUM is confined to the domain of SMEs and describes this as one of major limitations to diversifying its operations. Interestingly, the National Association of Commercial Banks equally supports the vision of ALTUM to work with large companies too as they refer to the "signaling effect" whereby ALTUM successfully finances projects in new sectors. Yet, this is not possible since the DFI has a clear-cut SME-related mandate. Further, ALTUM does not see itself venturing into the financing of innovation-oriented economic activities since, in their view, financing of innovation involves grants since "it is all about projects" as business companies reported to ALTUM. Repayable assistance is considered an area where ALTUM could contribute with its appraisal and evaluation skills: evaluating a company's competitiveness and performance targets (defined by MoE). Further, should MoE decide to be part of InvestEU, ALTUM would be well positioned to become an implementing agency and it is planning to apply for the verification procedure to the EC. The MoE also sees regional initiatives in the Baltic countries as an opportunity for collaborative development of regional infrastructure, energy and transport sectors.[13]

### 10.4.2 Lithuania

There are two major DFIs in Lithuania with quite distinct mandates. VIPA (Public Investment Development Agency) was established in 2012 in order to provide various financing facilities for urban development, infrastructure, and energy efficiency programs. Its financing portfolio is smaller than that of INVEGA and VIPA tends to be involved in the financing of public entities to a large extent. Currently VIPA also features prominently on an emerging green financing policy landscape in Lithuania.

INVEGA was established in 2001 as a guarantee institution to assist the development of SMEs and is now fully owned by the Ministry of Economics and Innovation (MEI). In 2018 it was granted the status of a "development finance institution". The new status implies that the agency is now supervised by the Central Bank, in line with the general supervisory requirements for financial

[13] The Baltic Innovation Fund (BIF), started in 2014, and established by the three Baltic countries together with EIF is an illustrative example of such a cooperation. In 2019, the BIF 2 Agreement was signed in order to extend the activities of BIF to investing in local investment funds (mezzanine, growth capital, venture capital).

intermediary institutions. Further, INVEGA sees the change of status as a very positive development: it has now become the single implementing agency of programs financed by EU structural funds. In terms of governance structure, INVEGA is supervised by the Board, which is independent from the government and consists of only business representatives.

In essence, INVEGA acts as the Fund of Funds while managing two types of financial pools. Two of them represent EU structural funds, and the other two Funds are made of national/repaid loans from the previous programming period (2007–2013). The proportion of national/EU funds is roughly 50/50 in the total portfolio and each of the Funds used to be supervised by a dedicated committee formed by representatives from MoF and MEI. The overall portfolio of funds managed by INVEGA is around EUR 700 m (as of May 2019) and includes some 30 financial instruments. The funds are channeled through the MEI, which designs financing programs for prioritized sectors and according to development targets (e.g. increase in productivity, support to SMEs). INVEGA designs financial instruments for these programs as well as advises the Ministry on market gaps. INVEGA is a second-tier financial institution and implements financial instruments mainly through commercial banks and credit unions. Intermediary organizations are selected as a result of the bidding process conducted by INVEGA. This is launched for each financial instrument and there might be a few financial intermediaries selected to work with one type of instrument. The duration of cooperation with financial intermediaries is usually defined by the amount of funding available for each financial instrument.

INVEGA sees itself primarily as the manager of both EU and national finances and does not see any need to diversify its funding sources, unlike ALTUM in Latvia. In that regard, structural funds require extensive reporting and are more rigid in terms of allowing for new types of financing facilities. For example, co-financing provided to individuals who obtained initial financing from crowdfunded platforms was implemented from the national funds (re-paid structural funds from the 2007–2013 period) as it would not qualify for support from EU funds. Interaction with MEI and implementation of the funding programs happens in a similar way as described for Latvia: programs and financial instruments are designed according to pre-defined market gaps as part of *ex ante* evaluation conducted prior to a seven-year programing period. In the meantime, when financing programs involve national funds, the government is keener to review *ex ante* evaluations, which adds to the flexibility INVEGA has in designing new financial instruments.

To conclude, while drawing some parallels with the Estonian KredEx, ALTUM is actively seeking to lessen its dependency on EU structural funds and to have some key non-financial competences such as project appraisal, in particular in energy efficiency and agriculture. They nevertheless remain constrained by their mandates: financing of SMEs provided within the state aid framework with no commercial activities allowed. INVEGA does have similarities with KredEx in its emphasis on structural funds (as the main implementing agency) and in operating through financial intermediaries. In that respect, there are differences in the operations of covered DFIs in the Baltics in terms of first-tier vs. second-tier banking (see Fernández-Arias et al., 2014). ALTUM adheres to the first-tier banking approach, INVEGA takes the second-tier banking stance and KredEx has a hybrid structure of both forms[14]. Despite the differences, ALTUM, INVEGA and KredEx are all subordinated to ministerial oversight (MoE/MEI, MoF) and have to face constraints stemming from the absorption of EU funds, while at the same time, are required to be self-sustainable. Further, all three DFIs operate in a highly limited policy space and adhere to the market failure logic of intervention by primarily addressing the market gaps identified through *ex ante* evaluations. All this makes the three cases comparable only in degree with no substantive differences in how little operational discretion DFIs have been given.

## 10.5 Europeanization Tendencies: Missing Capacities and De-Contextualization of Policy Measures

As already claimed (see Suurna and Kattel, 2010), the EU is the key actor in having an impact on the evolution of industrial/innovation policy, i.e. ideas and models[15], and the related structures since the late 1990s, as the EU had the means and tools to demand rather specific changes in policy plans. At the same time, the Europeanization process has also brought to the fore specific problems, such as a weak administrative environment lacking policy skills for networking and long-term policies. These challenges were reinforced by the prolonged adherence to the Washington Consensus policies that were considered as implicit innovation and industrial policy measures (see Karo, 2011, 529; also see Piroska and Mérö, this volume). Hence, the capacity building in economic policies was directed at macro-economic competencies with no proper innovation policies and related institution-building, as indicated above.

Efforts were mainly made in the creation of regional and local institutions—a system of implementation agencies—and being prepared to administer EU's structural funds (European Commission, 2003a; European Council, 1999; European Commission, 2003b; Grabbe, 2006, 82). This explains the meager public attention to and discussion of policy strategies (Tiits et al., 2008; also Tavits and Annus, 2006). Hence, it is not a surprise that the newly established implementation

[14] KredEx has been considering enlarging direct financing to companies, which up to now has been very modest. Yet, the lack of capacities (human capital, competences) and other related factors make this uncertain.

[15] The Action Plan for Growth and Jobs 2008–2011 and the National Strategic Reference Framework 2007–2013 both served as examples of European-type innovation policy (Kalvet, 2010).

agencies were mostly for managing external (EU) funding, as policy creation and respective capacity-building played almost no role there (Suurna and Kattel, 2010, 652; Karo and Kattel, 2010, 183).

Within such a context, the DFIs act as implementers of structural funds within quite rigid guidelines that are related to "typical" policy priority areas such as support for entrepreneurship, start-ups and midcaps, and SMEs. As the interviews conducted for this study revealed, the capacities of DFIs have been mostly related to the management of EU funds rather than making strategic decisions related to public investments or to act as active investing agents while leveraging on government funds. Management and reporting on the use of EU funds also require complex coordination competences but due to specific incentives (absorption, short-termism), the existing policy discourse and financing conditions have not been conducive to a more strategic and long-term take on the financing of development and innovation-led growth in the Baltics.

The Europeanization of industrial/innovation policy tends to substitute national perspectives with EU-based models, while the rigidity and path-dependency of the fragmented industrial/innovation policy model undermines any potential to develop policy capacities, all of which reinforce the de-contextualization tendencies in development financing (Karo, 2011, 530–531). For instance, the interviewed stakeholders[16] have recognized a meager or no effect of various Smart Specialization measures on the selected priority fields of economic activity, which reflects the growing mismatch between R&D system, high-tech biased innovation policy and actual industry circumstances. Likewise, SMEs have been given preference by DFIs due to both EU stipulations and market-failure logic, but this approach has been heavily criticized, e.g. in Estonia by industry representatives on the grounds of capture and rent-seeking. In this light, there are expectations for expanding policy instruments for supporting large businesses, which seem to have more export and R&D cooperation potential, which implies adopting more selective policies (see Espenberg et al., 2018). By and large, the industry representatives have acknowledged the need for flexible and agile innovation and industrial policies with sector-specific tailor-made (export and R&D supporting) measures that respond to the development needs of companies in different industries, including in the Smart Specialization areas. However, these issues have not been addressed by policy makers in the core activities of Smart Specialization strategies or various policy instruments (Karo et al., 2018; Espenberg et al., 2018).

Overall, the building of new institutions has not managed to respond to specific local needs (see Suurna and Kattel, 2010, 654). Almost all policy implementation

[16] We conducted focus group interviews with representatives of businesses, associations and academic experts in Smart Specialization areas in Estonia—ICT, health technologies (biotechnology and food), knowledge-based construction, and material technologies.

problems go back to weak or non-organized actors, capacity shortages and the fragmented policy-making system[17], resulting in considerable coordination problems in policy design and implementation together with accountability problems and insufficient policy appraisal, evaluation, monitoring and policy-learning systems (INNO-Policy Trend Chart 2006–2007; OECD, 2005; also Radosevic, 2002, 355). At the same time, enterprises have been deterred from submitting project-proposals for governmental support due to prejudices, fears and high bureaucratic burden as well as rigidity, e.g. in terms of qualification terms (Karo et al., 2018; Espenberg et al., 2018)—elements that are associated with the administration of EU structural funds.

## 10.6 Conclusion and Further Research

In the longitudinal perspective, as the Baltic economies have evolved after regaining their independence, economic and financial policies have not been altered accordingly, but instead have either been left to stagnate or have been driven by external sources—mainly EU policies. Accordingly, little attention has been paid to assuring the coherence of EU-anchored industrial and financial policies and their relevance to local circumstances, which to some extent has been outside the scope of local policy makers (Juuse, 2016a; Juuse, 2016b). Moreover, a simplistic approach to running the economy, where monetary, banking or innovation policies are outsourced to external actors—either the EU or foreign countries—has resulted in poorly coordinated and fragmented policies, typical of transition economies.

One could argue that the Baltic states have ended up in a situation that can be denoted as "foregone autonomy" (i.e. an ineffective institutional structure reflecting a bureaucracy without a holistic insight into and understanding of evolving finance, banking, and productive economy), following Evans' perspective on the autonomy of states (Evans 1992, 141). Moreover, the recent financial crisis and a series of fiscal crises across Europe has resulted in empowered EU institutions, especially in financial and fiscal governance, thereby substantially reducing national capacities in respective policy domains (Juuse et al., 2019).

One of the recurring themes in current literature on national development banks is the heterogeneity of its roles and setups. There is a growing consensus

[17] While policy plannning is done at the "core executive" level in Estonia, coordination between the Ministry of Economic Affairs, the Ministry of Education and Research and the Ministry of Finance has been complicated in the current innovation policy governance model—all parties are driven by their own visions on R&D, innovation development and support, which has created a need for higher coordination mechanisms, i.e. the establishment of R&D and innovation councils and other bodies to support coordination, priority setting, and decision making (Suurna and Kattel, 2010). In addition, for a comparative view of policy and administrative capacities in the Baltic countries see Karo (2011); for Central and Eastern Europe see Reinert and Kattel (2014); also Breznitz and Ornston (2017).

over strategic roles that government-backed financial institutions can play in facilitating more inclusive, innovation-led growth: there are many examples of strategic development banks or financing agencies (e.g. SBIR or DARPA in the US, BNDES in Brazil, BDC in Canada, or FINNVERA in Finland) which played precisely that role. Yet, there are many instances when despite a "strategic rhetoric," development banks are confined to more managerial roles whereby they are not able to exercise the role of active investment agents (Mikheeva, 2018, 2019). In addition, the three Baltic cases demonstrate that what constitutes "strategic" should necessarily be considered within a broader economic policy discourse, the processes of policy priority setting and coordination thereof. A combination of national policy choices and the EU agenda (accession and rapid integration, Smart Specialization) makes the experience of Baltic and other CEE countries particularly worth noting due to the inability of these states to benefit from post-WWII protectionist industrial policies and a significant pressure from the EU just some years after regaining political and economic independence. Further, external financing in the form of EU structural funds resulted in a set of incentives that reinforced managerial competences: financial instruments are provided by DFIs within a very narrow space of an allegedly efficient state aid framework.

There are some differences between the three DFIs, however: INVEGA sees its mandate as being the manager of EU funds and its design (fund of funds) suggests carrying out mainly managerial functions, while ALTUM has decided to develop another avenue of interaction with the EU through financing agencies such as the EIB/EIF, and KredEx is operating on both spectrums (although its direct financing operations are currently very limited). It is too early to say whether there will be a shift in their financing competences but ALTUM and KredEx resemble agencies operating with the latest policy initiatives at the EU level, particularly, to switch from grants towards financial instruments, which arguably implies a greater role for DFIs/promotional banks (European Commission, 2015). At the same time, the overall policy discourse(s) and a very limited attention to the actual financing and policy-support needs of domestic productive structures, act as inhibiting factors to developing stronger and more strategic competences in development financing by DFIs in the Baltics.

Further research should be done in other CEE countries where dependency on EU financial assistance is combined with a stronger legacy of national industrial strategies, larger domestic industrial structures, and, in some cases, more protectionist economic and financial (such as in Poland or Hungary) policies (see Piroska and Mérö, this volume). Following the "convergence hypothesis"—which states that despite an initial variety of capitalisms, CEE countries have been moving towards the neoliberal type (Bohle and Greskovits, 2012)—it would be useful to test it against recent developments in national policy financing agencies, which in some cases have been substantially empowered (in Poland and Slovenia). Further, the literature on development banks and financing of development would benefit from more thorough and nuanced conceptualization of what strategic development banking entails in various national policy and ideational contexts/discourses. Synthesizing the literature on varieties of capitalism with empirical studies on the political economy of EU financing in CEE countries would enable a better differentiation between the types of DFIs operating in the EU as well as to emphasize various institutional contexts and capacities that should be part of the discussion on national development banks.

## References

ALTUM. 2015. Annual Report. Available at: https://www.nasdaqbaltic.com/market/upload/reports/altm/2015_ar_en_eur_con_ias.pdf

ALTUM. 2016. Annual Report. Available at: https://www.nasdaqbaltic.com/market/upload/reports/altm/2016_ar_en_eur_com_ias.pdf

Bank of Estonia. 1995. Eesti Pank Annual Report 1994, Tallinn: Bank of Estonia. Available at: http://www.eestipank.ee/en/publication/annual-report/1994/eesti-pank-annual-report-1994.

Bank of Estonia. 2019. Financing of the Economy, February, 2019. Tallinn: Bank of Estonia. Available at: https://www.eestipank.ee/en/publication/financing-economy/2019/financing-economy-february-2019.

Bauer, Michael, Christoph Knill, and Diana Pitschel. 2007. "Differential Europeanization in Eastern Europe: The Impact of Diverse EU Regulatory Governance Patterns." Journal of European Integration 29 (4), pp. 405–23.

Bohle, Dorothe, and Bella Greskovits. 2012. *Capitalist Diversity on Europe's Periphery.* Ithaca, NY: Cornell University Press.

Breznitz, Dan, and Darius Ornston. 2017. "EU Financing and Innovation in Poland." *EBRD Working Paper no 198.* Available at: https://www.ebrd.com/publications/working-papers/eu-financing-and-innovation-in-poland.

Börzel, Tanja, and Thomas Risse. 2000. "When Europe Hits Home: Europeanization and Domestic Change." *European Integration online Papers (EIoP)*, 4(15), pp. 1–24.

Davies, Howard, and David Green. 2010. *Banking on the Future. The Fall and Rise of Central Banking.* Princeton, NJ; Woodstock, UK: Princeton University Press.

Dyson, Kenneth. 2000. "EMU as Europeanization: Convergence, Diversity and Contingency." *JCMS: Journal of Common Market Studies*, *38*(4), pp. 645–66.

European Commission. 2003a. Decision (C) No 4906/2003 of 23 December 2003 on the Review of the Guidelines for Implementation of the Phare Programme in Candidate Countries for the Period 2000–2006, Application of Article 8 of Regulation 3906/89. Available at: https://eur-lex.europa.eu/legal-content/ET/ALL/?uri=URISERV:e50004

European Commission. 2003b. "Report from the Commission – The Phare Programme Annual Report 2001. COM(2003)97." Available at: http://aei.pitt.edu/48023/.

European Commission. 2007. "Supporting Enlargement – What Does Evaluation Show? Ex-post Evaluation of Phare Support Allocated between 1991–2001, with Brief Review of Post-2001 Allocations, Consolidated Summary Report 2007." Available at: https://ec.europa.eu/neighbourhood-enlargement/sites/near/files/pdf/financial_assistance/phare/evaluation/consolidated_summary_report_phare_ex_post_eval.pdf

European Commission. 2013. "EU Cohesion Policy Contributing to Employment and Growth in Europe." Available at: https://ec.europa.eu/regional_policy/sources/docgener/studies/pdf/cp_employ_growth_en.pdf

European Commission. 2015. Communication from the Commission to the European Parliament and the Council. Working together for jobs and growth: The role of National Promotional Banks (NPBs) in supporting the Investment Plan for Europe. Available at: https://eur-lex.europa.eu/legal-content/EN/TXT/?uri=CELEX:52015DC0361

Espenberg, Siim, Kaidi Nõmmela, Erkki Karo, Egert Juuse, Kadri Lees, Veiko Sepp, Sille Vahaste-Pruul, and Jari Romanainen. 2018. "Kasvualade edenemise uuring." [Progress Study of the Growth Areas] Tartu Ülikool, Tallinna Tehnikaülikool ja Technopolis Group Eesti OÜ. Available at: https://www.mkm.ee/sites/default/files/kasvualade_edenemise_uuring_lopparuanne_20190111.pdf

Estonian Development Fund (EDF). 2011. Report to the Parliament of Estonia.

European Council. 1999. Regulation (EC) No 1266/1999 of 21 June 1999 on Coordinating Aid to the Applicant Countries in the Framework of the Pre-accession Strategy and Amending Regulation (EEC) No 3906/89. Available at: https://op.europa.eu/en/publication-detail/-/publication/24ba93e2-6f1b-4fb0-8457-c9e2a552c2c3/language-en

Evans, Peter. 1992. "The State as Problem and Solution: Predation, Embedded Autonomy, and Structural Change." In *The Politics of Economic Adjustment. International Constraints, Distributive Conflicts, and the State,* edited by Stephan Haggard and Robert Kaufmann, pp. 139–81. Princeton, NJ: Princeton University Press.

Feldmann, Magnus. 2013. "From the Ruble Zone to the Euro Zone: The Political Economy of Estonian Macroeconomic Policy." *Post-Soviet Affairs*, 29 (4), pp. 354–70.

Fernández-Arias, Eduardo, Ugo Panizza, and Fernando de Olloqui. 2014. "Giving Credit to Productivity," in Gustavo Crespi, Eduardo Fernández-Arias and Ernesto Stein (eds), *Rethinking Productive Development. Sound Policies and Institutions for Economic Transformation*. Inter-American Development Bank, New York, NY: Palgrave Macmillan.

Ferry, Martin, and Irene McMaster. 2013. "Cohesion Policy and the Evolution of Regional Policy in Central and Eastern Europe". *Europe-Asia Studies*, 65 (8), pp. 1502–28.

Furman, Dmitri. 2002. "Опыт Балтийских стран и его значение для России," in Страны Балтии и Россия: Общества и государства. [*The experience of the Baltic countries and its relevance to Russia. In Baltic countries and Russia: Societies and States.]*. Publications of Andrei Sakharov's museum and public center, vol. 5, pp. 3–27.

Godley, Wynne, and Marc Lavoie. 2012. *Monetary Economics. An Integrated Approach to Credit, Money, Income, Production and Wealth.* Basingstoke, UK: Palgrave Macmillan.

Grabbe, Heather. 2006. *The EU's Transformative Power: Europeanization through Conditionality in Central and Eastern Europe.* Basingstoke: Palgrave Macmillan.

Griffith-Jones, Stephany, and Jose Ocampo (eds). 2018. *The Future of National Development Banks.* Oxford: Oxford University Press.

Hansson, Ardo. 1994. "The Political-Economy of Macroeconomic and Foreign Trade Policy in Estonia," in Constantine Michalopoulos and David, G. Tarr (eds), *Trade in the New Independent States*, Washington, DC: World Bank.

INNO-Policy TrendChart. 2006–2007. 'INNO-Policy TrendChart Annual Country Reports for Czech Republic, Estonia, Hungary, Latvia, Lithuania, Poland, Slovakia, Slovenia, Bulgaria and Romania. Reports for the years of 2006 and 2007. European Communities. Available at: http://www.proinno-europe.eu/index.cfm?fuseaction=page.display&topicID=263&parentID=52.

INNO-Policy TrendChart. 2008. European Innovation Progress Report 2008. European Commission. Available at: http://www.proinno-europe.eu/page/european-innovation-progress-report.

Juuse, Egert. 2015. "'Latin Americanization' of the Estonian Economy – Institutional Analysis of Financial Fragility and the Financialization Process." *Journal of Post-Keynesian Economics*, 38 (3), pp. 399–425.

Juuse, Egert. 2016a. "Financial Regulation in Estonia – a World of 'Dead Letters': The Interplay of Europeanization Process and National Idiosyncrasies," in Rainer Kattel, Jan Kregel and Mario Tonveronachi (eds), *Financial Regulation in the European Union, pp. 132–62.* Routledge.

Juuse, Egert. 2016b. "Regulatory Convergence, Financialization and Hollowing Out of the State: The Case of Financial System in Estonia." *Halduskultuur—Administrative Culture*, 17 (1), pp. 19–46.

Juuse, Egert. 2016c. "Financial Fragility and Economic Instability in the Context of Transition Economies: The Case of Estonia." Tallinn University of Technology Doctoral Theses, Series I: Social Sciences, No. 28, TUT Press.

Juuse, Egert. 2016d. "The Real Sector Developments in Estonia: Financialisation Effects Behind the Transition Process," in E. Hein, D. Detzer and N. Dodig (eds), *Financialisation and the Financial and Economic Crises: Country Studies.* Cheltenham, UK; Northampton, MA: Edward Elgar Publishing, 137–62.

Juuse, Egert, Ringa Raudla, Aleksandrs Cepilovs, and Olga Mikheeva. 2019. "The Europeanization of Financial Regulation and Supervision on the Baltic-Nordic Axis – National Bureaucracies' Perspective." *Journal of Baltic Studies*. https://doi.org/10.1080/01629778.2019.1678495

Kaarna, R., M. Masso and M. Rell. 2012. *Väikese ja keskmise suurusega ettevõtete Arengusuundumused. [Developments of small and medium-sized enterprise]* Tallinn: Praxis Center for Policy Studies.

Kallas, Siim. 2003. Reminiscing with the "Father of the Kroon": Interview with Siim Kallas. *Demokratizatsiya*, 11(4), pp. 509–16.

Kalvet, Tarmo. 2006. "Private Sector R&D in the New Member States: The Case of Estonia." Brussels: European Techno-Economic Policy Support Network.

Kalvet, Tarmo. 2010. "Policy Paper on Innovation: Estonia." Expert Evaluation Network Delivering Policy Analysis on the Performance of Cohesion Policy 2007–2013 Final Draft. A Report to the European Commission Directorate.

Karo, Erkki. 2011. "The Evolution of Innovation Policy Governance Systems and Policy Capacities in the Baltic States." *Journal of Baltic Studies*, 42 (4), pp. 511–36.

Karo, Erkki, and Rainer Kattel. 2010. "The Copying Paradox: Why Converging Policies but Diverging Capacities in Eastern European Innovation Systems?" *International Journal of Institutions and Economies*, 2(2), pp. 167–206.

Karo, Erkki, and Rainer Kattel. 2015. "Economic Development and Evolving State Capacities in Central and Eastern Europe: Can 'Smart Specialization' Make a difference?" *Journal of Economic Policy Reform* 18, pp. 172–87.

Karo, Erkki, Rainer Kattel, and Ringa Raudla. 2017. "Searching for Exits from the Great Recession: Coordination of Fiscal Consolidation and Growth Enhancing Innovation Policies in Central and Eastern Europe.' "*Europe-Asia Studies* 69(7), pp. 1009–26.

Karo, Erkki, Jaanus Müür, Margit Kirs, Egert Juuse, Kadri Ukrainski, Youjun Shin, Nino Kokashvili, Tõnus Tänav, Jaan Masso, and Erik Terk. 2018. *Eesti ettevõtete osalemine rahvusvahelistes väärtusahelates ja poliitikameetmed kõrgemat lisandväärtust andvate tootmisprotsesside toetamiseks*. [Participation of Estonian enterprises in international value chains and policy measures for increasing the value added in manufacturing.] Tallinn: Tallinna Tehnikaülikool, Tartu Ülikool ja Tallinna Ülikool.

Kattel, Rainer. 2010. "Financial and Economic Crisis in Eastern Europe." *Journal of Post-Keynesian Economics*, 33 (1), pp. 41–60.

Kattel, Rainer, and Erik Reinert. 2018. "Friedrich List and the Present Problems of the European Union," in H. Hagemann, S. Seiter, and E. Wendler (eds). *"Through Wealth to Freedom" - 225th Anniversary of Friedrich List*, Routledge.

Kilicaslan, Y., and E. Taymaz. 2006. "The Structure of Structural Change." Paper presented at DRUID Summer Conference: Knowledge, Innovation and Competitiveness: Dynamics of Firms, Networks, Regions and Institutions, Copenhagen, Denmark, June, 2006.

Kinks, R. 2000. "Small and Medium Enterprises in the Economy of Estonia," in B. Lesser (ed.), *Baltic Economic Case Studies*, Vol. 5. Baltic Economic Management Training Program.

KredEx. 2012. "KredEx Annual Report 2011." Available at: http://kredex.ee/sites/default/files/2019-04/Kredex_aastaraamat_2011.pdf.

KredEx. 2018. "KredEx Annual Report 2017." Available at: https://issuu.com/sihtasutus_kredex/docs/fund_kredex_annual_report_2017.

KredEx. 2019a. "KredEx. Who We Are." Available at: https://www.kredex.ee/en/who-we-are/sa-kredex.

KredEx. 2019b. "KredEx Annual Report 2018." Available at: https://issuu.com/sihtasutus_kredex/docs/fund_kredex_annual_report_2018.

Kulikovskis, Gundars, Diana Petraitytė, and Blagoy Stamenov. 2018. Research and Innovation Observatory Country Report Series. RIO Country Report 2017: Latvia. Available at: https://rio.jrc.ec.europa.eu/en/country-analysis/Latvia/country-report

Kõomägi, Margus, and Priit, Sander. 2006. *Venture Capital Investments and Financing in Estonia: A Case Study Approach*. Tartu: Tartu University Press.

Levy Economics Institute. 2012. "Beyond the Minsky Moment. Where We've Been, Why We Can't Go Back, and the Road Ahead for Financial Reform." Annandale-on-Hudson, NY: Levy Economics Institute of Bard College.

Madureira, Ana Mafalda, Jan-Evert Nilsson, and Victor Gheorghe. 2007. *Structural Funds as Instrument to Promote Innovation—Theories and Practices*. VINNOVA Report VR 2007:02. Stockholm, Sweden: VINNOVA — Swedish Governmental Agency for Innovation Systems.

Majandus- ja kommunikatsiooniministeerium. 2017. "Tööstuspoliitika roheline raamat." [Industrial Policy Green Book] Available at: https://www.mkm.ee/sites/default/files/toostuspoliitika_roheline_raamat_.pdf

Mikheeva, Olga. 2019. "Financing of Innovation: National Development Banks in Newly Industrialised Countries". *Journal of Post-Keynesian Economics*. https://doi.org/10.1080/01603477.2019.1640065.

Mikheeva, Olga. 2018. "Institutional Context and the Typology of Functions of National Development Banks. The Case of Development Finance Institutions (DFIs) in Malaysia." *Working Papers in Technology Governance and Economic Dynamics No 82*. Tallinn University of Technology. Available at: http://technology-governance.eu/files/main//2018121211430101.pdf.

Minsky, Hyman. [1986] 2008. *Stabilizing an Unstable Economy*. New Haven: Yale University Press.

Minsky, Hyman. 1991. "The Transition to a Market Economy: Financial Options". *Jerome Levy Economics Institute Working Paper No. 66*. Available at SSRN: https://ssrn.com/abstract=179455.

Nurkse, Ragnar. [1953] 2009. "Problems of Capital Formation in Underdeveloped Countries," in Rainer Kattel, Jan Kregel and Erik Reinert (eds), *Ragnar Nurkse: Trade and Development*, pp. 99–212. London, UK; New York, NY: Anthem Press.

OECD. 2000. *OECD Majandusuurimused. Balti Riigid: Regiooni Majandusülevaade* [OECD Economic Surveys. Baltic States: A Regional Economic Assessment]. Tallinn: Välisministeerium.

OECD. 2005. *Governance of Innovation Systems*. Vol. 1: Synthesis Report.' Paris: OECD Publications.

Mazzucato, Mariana, and Caetano Penna. 2016. "Beyond Market Failures: The Market Creating and Shaping Roles Of State Investment Banks." Journal of Economic Policy Reform, 19(4), pp. 305–26.

Polt, Wolfgang. 2007. *OMC Policy Mix Review Report: Country Report Estonia*. M. Turco (EC Observer). Available at: https://ec.europa.eu/invest-in-research/pdf/download_en/omc_ee_review_report.pdf.

Purju Alari. 2000. "Eight Years of Economic Reform in Estonia: A Review of Accomplishments," in Barry Lesser (ed.), *Economic Policy and Reform in Estonia, Latvia and Lithuania, 1992 to 2000 and Beyond*, pp. 6–16. Halifax: Baltic Economic Management Training Program.

Quaglia, Lucia. 2007. 'The Politics of Financial Services Regulation and Supervision Reform in the European Union. *European Journal of Political Research*, 46(2), pp. 269–90.

Radosevic, Slavo. 1998. "The Transformation of National Systems of Innovation in Eastern Europe: Between Restructuring and Erosion." *Industrial and Corporate Change* 7(1), pp. 77–108.

Radosevic, Slavo. 1999. "Transformation of Science and Technology Systems into Systems of Innovation in Central and Eastern Europe: The Emerging Patterns and Determinants." *Structural Change and Economic Dynamics* 10 (3–4), pp. 277–320.

Radosevic, Slavo. 2002. "Introduction: Building the Basis for Future Growth – Innovation Policy as a Solution." *Journal of International Relations and Development*, 5(4), pp. 352–6.

Radosevic, Slavo. 2004. "A Two-Tier or Multi-Tier Europe? Assessing the Innovation Capacities of Central and Eastern European Countries in the Enlarged EU." *Journal of Common Market Studies* 42 (3), pp. 641–66.

Radosevic, Slavo, and Alastair Reid. 2006. "Innovation Policy for a Knowledge-Based Economy in Central and Eastern Europe: Driver of Growth or New Layer of Bureaucracy?" in Krzysztof Piech and Slavo Radosevic (eds), *The Knowledge-Based Economy in Central and East European Countries: Countries and Industries in a Process of Change*, pp. 295–311. London: Palgrave Macmillan.

Raudsepp, Vambola, Priit Sander, and Kaia Kask. 2003. "Financing Problems in Estonian Firms." *Current Politics and Economics of Russia, Eastern and Central Europe*, 18 (1), pp. 55–73.

Reid, Alastair. 2011. "Eesti innovatsioonipoliitika rahvusvahelises võrdluses." [Estonian Innovation Policy From an International Comparative Perspective]. Innovaatiline tegevus ettevõtetes aastatel 2006–2008. [Innovative activities in enterprises during 2006–2008] EAS, Innovation Studies, 16, pp. 83–4.

Reinert, Erik. 2006. "European Integration, Innovations and Uneven Economic Growth: Challenges and Problems of EU 2005". *Working Papers in Technology Governance and Economic Dynamics No 5*. Tallinn University of Technology. Available at: http://technologygovernance.eu/files/main//2006042407120202.pdf.

Reinert, Erik, and Rainer Kattel, 2007. "European Eastern Enlargement as Europe's Attempted Economic Suicide?" *Working Papers in Technology Governance and Economic Dynamics No 14*. Tallinn University of Technology. Available at: http://technologygovernance.eu/files/main//2007070309122525.pdf.

Reinert, Erik, and Rainer Kattel. 2014. "Failed and Asymmetrical Integration: The Baltics and the Non-financial Origins of the European Crisis," in Jeffrey Sommers and Charles Woolfson (eds), *The Contradictions of Austerity. The Socio-Economic Costs of the Neoliberal Baltic Model*, pp. 64–86. Oxon, UK: Routledge.

Sander, Priit, and Margus Kõomägi. 2007. "The Allocation of Control Rights in Financing Private Companies: Views of Estonian Private Equity and Venture Capitalists." TRAMES, 11 (61/56), no. 2, pp.189–205.

Singleton, John. 2011. *Central Banking in the Twentieth Century*. Cambridge, UK: Cambridge University Press.

Soskice, David. 2007. "Macroeconomics and Varieties of Capitalism," in Bob Hancke, Martin Rhodes and Mark Thatcher (eds), *Beyond Varieties of Capitalism. Conflict, Contradictions, and Complementarities in the European Economy*, pp. 89–121. New York, NY: Oxford University Press.

Suurna, Margit, and Rainer Kattel. 2010. "Europeanization of Innovation Policy in Central and Eastern Europe", *Science and Public Policy*, 37 (9), pp. 646–64.

Sutt, Kadi-Ann. 2019. Kagu-Eesti välitööd jätkuvad kokkulepete elluviimisega. Tallinn: Ministry of Finance. Available at: https://www.rahandusministeerium.ee/et/uudised/kagu-eesti-valitood-jatkuvad-kokkulepete-elluviimisega.

Tavits, Margit and Taavi Annus. 2006. "Agencification in Estonia." *Public Administration and Development*, 26, pp. 3–14.

Tiits, Marek, Rainer Kattel, Tarmo Kalvet, and Doris Tamm. 2008. "Catching Up, Forging Ahead or Falling Behind? Central and Eastern European Development 1990–2005." *Innovation: the European Journal of Social Science Research*, 21(1), pp. 65–85.

Traks, Kristina. 2012. "EAS tuunib uuest nädalast stardiabi andmise tingimusi." Postimees, 3.07.2012. Available at: http://www.juhtimine.ee/895278/eas-tuunib-uuest-nadalast-stardiabi-andmise-tingimusi/.

Varblane, Urmas. 2016. "EU Structural Funds in the Baltic Countries—Useful or Harmful?" *Estonian Discussions on Economic Policy* 24 (2), pp. 1–17.

APPENDIX 10.1

# List of interviews

| | |
|---|---|
| Int 1 | Latvia, Ministry of Economy (2.05.2019) |
| Int 2 | Latvia, ALTUM (6.05.2019) |
| Int 3 | Lithuania, INVEGA (7.05.2019) |
| Int 4 | Latvia, Ministry of Finance (19.06.2019) |
| Int 5 | Lithuania, VIPA (26.06.2019) |
| Int 6 | Estonia, KredEx (10.07.2019) |

# 11
# The Rise, Fall, and Return of Promotional Banking in Greece

*Jens Bastian*

## 11.1 Introduction

Development banking is a growth industry across most EU Member States; all the more in the context of the European Commission rolling out its InvestEU program (2021–2027). But in our comparative sample of countries comprising this volume there is an exception to this observation. Greece is distinct in various respects.[1] For one, Greece established a state-sponsored development bank in 1964, namely the Hellenic Industrial Development Bank (ETBA). But for reasons that will be elaborated below, this lender was privatized in 2002. Since then different domestic and foreign lending institutions with developmental mandates have emerged in Greece. Further, in the course of 2019, government-sponsored legislation created the Hellenic Development Bank (HDB). This initiative took place against a twofold background. In August 2018, Greece successfully concluded its third multi-year financial rescue program with its international creditors[2]. Other euro area countries such as Ireland, Cyprus, Spain and Portugal—all of which also had similar rescue programs during the past decade—had previously engaged in building a state-owned development institution. In that respect, Greece represents a catch-up initiative vis-à-vis its European peers.

The advocacy in favor of creating the HDB is anchored in the expectation that the lending institution can contribute to overcoming a multi-year economic crisis and re-charge the credit supply to targeted sectors of the real economy. In other words, the rationale guiding the establishment of the HDB is defined by the objective to support a sustainable economic recovery in a post-program political economy in Greece. The institutional void left by the absence of a state-sponsored

[1] This line of argument applies to the comparative sample of countries included in this volume. When compared in a wider European context, then Greece is not such an outlier. Romania also does not have a development bank. Cyprus, similar to events in Greece, used to have a development bank, but privatized it in 2008. For the case of Cyprus, see Kavvadia and Savvides (2019).

[2] The creditors are the European Central Bank (ECB), the European Stability Mechanism (ESM), the European Commission and the International Monetary Fund (IMF).

Jens Bastian, *The Rise, Fall, and Return of Promotional Banking in Greece* In: *The Reinvention of Development Banking in the European Union: Industrial Policy in the Single Market and the Emergence of a Field.* Edited by: Daniel Mertens, Matthias Thiemann, and Peter Volberding, Oxford University Press (2021). 
DOI: 10.1093/oso/9780198859703.003.0011

promotional bank in Greece was filled by a plethora of funding institutions that included a development mandate. Large international lenders such as the European Investment Bank (EIB), the European Bank for Reconstruction and Development (EBRD) and the Black Sea Trade and Development Bank (BSTDB) have all operated as development banks in Greece. Even Beijing's state-owned China Development Bank (CDB) has recently expanded its footprint in Greece. Smaller domestic initiatives such as the Institution for Growth (IfG) briefly saw the light of day but had to close for lack of political support after a change of government in 2015.

Even during the crisis years (2009–2018), with three macro-economic adjustment programs financed by a troika[3] of international creditors, Greece did not lack funding resources in the realm of promotional financing. Rather, its political economy was characterized by two inter-related factors. For one, public investment capacity became increasingly dependent on the availability of EU funding programs and EIB-linked financial engineering instruments, in particular after the onset of the crisis in 2009. Secondly, the example of the Institution for Growth (IfG, see section 11.3.4) is a telling illustration of how financial sector innovation with a development mandate can be captured in Greece by a lack of political will between government and opposition in a highly polarized parliament during the crisis years.

This overview does not seek to advocate the establishment of a development bank as a panacea, one-size fits all solution to Greece's political economy. Such a financing institution should not be idealized—although attempts are being made—as progressive (public) solutions to major economic challenges. The creation of a promotional bank can contribute to mitigate pressing issues in the public-private nexus of the domestic financial system. Such a lender can also provide sovereign guarantees for lending initiatives, advance mechanisms such as funds of funds and develop risk-sharing arrangements between public-private partnerships.

It remains to be seen if the newly established development bank will contribute to overcoming Greece's outlier status in "the emergent European field of development banking" (see Mertens, Thiemann and Volbering, this volume). It will take time until tangible results will be identified and measurable. The organizational architecture, legal framework, and funding conditions will need to be tested in practice, e.g. to see how resistant they are to the possibility of interventions by political parties and operating in competition with other financial institutions operating in Greece.

[3] The troika consisted of the International Monetary Fund (IMF), the European Central Bank (ECB) and the European Commission. At a later stage during the third program (2015–2018) the European Stability Mechanism (ESM) joined the troika as an international creditor, thus turning it into a quartet.

In the following section we first establish the historical background of development banking in Greece. Just as the creation of the Hellenic Industrial Development Bank marked a watershed moment in 1964, its privatization and sale to a domestic private sector competitor in 2002 signaled a gradual withdrawal of the Greek state from a policy of promotional banking. Section 11.3 illustrates how the ecosystem of development banking in Greece was recalibrated with international and special-purpose domestic lenders. Some of these institutions have a multi-decade presence in the country, while others are newcomers following the twin fiscal and economic crisis in 2009.

Section 11.4 then discusses the international context, i.e. financial institutions operating in Greece that carry in their official title the term "development". What distinguishes these international development banks is the fact that they do not carry the prefix "Hellenic" in their respective names. Section 11.5 highlights the resurgence of a state-sponsored development bank institution that was adopted by the Greek parliament in April 2019. The former government of Prime Minister Alexis Tsipras (from January 2015 until July 2019) advocated the establishment of a public development bank as part of its exit strategy following the conclusion of the third macro-economic adjustment program in August 2018.

## 11.2 Historical Background: The Hellenic Industrial Development Bank

A state-sponsored promotional or investment bank did not exist in Greece after World War II[4]. This institutional void was the result of a more general deficit, i.e. the absence of a defined industrial policy. Only the state-owned *National Bank of Greece* (NBG) catered to companies, in particular in the industrial sector, which sought funding for development purposes at the corporate level. Various Greek governments during the period 1945–1963 attempted to cover the institutional lacunae with targeted sectoral development policies. During these two decades a number of organizational steps were undertaken to create specialized funding institutions such as the Organization for Tourism Credit (Greek acronym *OTP* in 1946), the Organization for the Financing of Economic Development (Greek acronym OXOA in 1954), and the Organization for Industrial Development (Greek acronym OBA in 1960).

In 1964, these three organizations were merged by Legislative Decree No. 4366 into the Hellenic Industrial Development Bank (ETBA, in Greek: *Ελληνική Τράπεζα Βιομηχανικής Ανάπτυξης*). The mandate of the public entity ETBA was

[4] Since 1929 Agricultural Credit Bank operated as a subsidiary of Agricultural Bank of Greece. But its sector-specific mandate did not include any explicit reference to development and promotional objectives. It rather served as a provider of micro-finance in rural areas and on Greek islands.

to promote industrial, shipping, and tourism development. It was also tasked with supporting the implementation of the government's program of creating industrial zones, particularly in shipping construction. As a public institution ETBA did not have a banking license for commercial operation. That limitation was changed in 1973 when ETBA was transformed into a commercial bank with a mission to provide long-term lending to private and state-owned companies[5].

In parallel to the establishment of ETBA at the state level, domestic lending institutions created their own commercial subsidiaries with a development mandate. In 1963 the National Investment Bank for Industrial Development (ETEBA) was established. ETEBA was majority-owned by the National Bank of Greece (55 percent) and included 14 foreign banks as minority shareholders[6]. ETEBA sought to promote industrial and related activities and was registered as a bank with limited liability. A year earlier the Investment Bank was created by the Commercial Bank of Greece, Ionian and Popular Bank (its two majority shareholders) and ten foreign banks (with a total shareholding of 11 percent).

In 1973, ETBA received a fully-fledged banking license and established its subsidiary ETBA Bank. It thus became possible to attract deposits and offer wide-ranging banking services, including letters of credit, lease financing, underwriting equity and bond offers, and advising on mergers and acquisitions. ETBA was even given the operational mandate to take equity stakes in Greek companies. Between its founding in 1964 and prior to its privatization in 2002 (see below), ETBA provided financing for more than 2,000 companies, participated in the management of numerous European programs (e.g. Mentor, Retex, Jopp-Phare, Prisma) and held equity positions in 142 enterprises, 12 of which were majority-owned by ETBA (To Bima 2008).

ETBA had a country-wide network of branches in Greece and established its first subsidiary in 1972 with the creation of Greek Exports *S.A.* (in Greek: *Ελληνικές Εξαγωγές AE*). The financing of Greek companies' export capacity became an ever-larger part of ETBA's *portfolio of activities after being converted into a commercial bank.* In 1990, Greek Exports S.A. was renamed ETBA Finance, a 100 percent subsidiary of ETBA Bank.

The following year ETBA created the Hellenic Portfolio Investment Company (in Greek: *Ελληνική Εταιρεία Επενδύσεων Χαρτοφυλακίου* (*EEEX*). Fifteen years later, in 1987, ETBA branched out further into the leasing business with the registration of *ETBA* Leasing *AE.* Both subsidiaries, EEEX and ETBA Leasing were subsequently listed on the Athens Stock Exchange. In 1996, ETBA entered into a

[5] The Greek state remained the majority shareholder, but through the new share capital structure public and private institutions were able to invest in ETBA, e.g. the Bank of Greece and the National Bank of Greece.

[6] The largest foreign shareholder was Chase International Investment Corporation (7,04 percent).

cooperation agreement with Natwest Bank Plc. to create *ETBA* Natwest *AEΔAK*, focusing on the management of mutual fund investments.

What does this brief overview tell us about development banking institutions in Greece? Over the course of more than 30 years of operation, ETBA grew from a single-mandate development bank into a financial behemoth with a complex architecture of subsidiaries in different sectors of the Greek financial and real economy. The culmination of this expansion was the listing of ETBA's banking subsidiary—ETBA Bank—on the Athens Stock Exchange in 2000. ETBA thus transformed into a complex financial intermediary whose initial development mandate became increasingly secondary or was obscured by the web of activities ranging from mutual bond management over M&A to export promotion and leasing.

With the extension of ETBA's activities and growing corporate investments, the state-owned funding institution increasingly became the subject of allegations of cronyism, corruption and above all, operational inefficiency due to regular political intervention in the institution's governance. Funding scandals, lack of accounting standards, and dubious lending practices, in particular at ETBA Finance[7], created the public perception of a banking institution that was politically captured by the government of the day (Cleopatra Kontonika, 2002).

The reputational capital of ETBA suffered as a result of such allegations, recurring judicial investigations, and frequent turnover of personnel following changes in the government or ministries. Furthermore, the operational environment around development banking in Greece also changed in the course of the 1990s. Privatization, mandated deregulation (e.g. by the European Commission), market liberalization and political challenges to industrial policy making in general became the order of the day; not only in Greece. Thus, when an opening presented itself in 2002, Piraeus Bank took control of the controversial ETBA conglomerate. It paid 510 million euros for a 57.8 percent stake in ETBA. The full absorption of ETBA by Piraeus Bank was finalized in December 2003 (Naftemporiki, 2001).

The privatization of ETBA has to be seen in context. Starting in the mid-1990s, the Greek banking sector underwent gradual change through a plethora of mergers and acquisitions. This concentration process included numerous commercial banks, domestic and foreign. M&A activity concerned state-owned commercial banks, foreign subsidiaries and private funding institutions. Moreover, the sale of ETBA to a private Greek bank sent out a twofold signal: for one, the end of an era of state intervention in the banking sector. Second, the gradual withdrawal of

[7] ETBA Finance became the subject of a widespread scandal and subsequent investigation concerning the misuse of roughly 11 billion Greek drachma (approximately 3.2 billion euros) between 1996 and 2001.

government-led entities from industrial policy making implemented during the period 1960 to 1980.

But the sale of ETBA also reshaped for almost two decades the idea of development banking in Greece. The reputational damage to this policy concept from the ETBA Finance scandal made the idea politically toxic. Until 2018, no Greek government would consider re-launching such a policy initiative. Against this background we can argue that Greece became an outlier in Europe at a point in time when other countries were increasingly prepared to embrace the concept of state-sponsored development banking.

While the Greek state gradually withdrew from this policy field, other international and some special-purpose domestic lenders with a development mandate filled the void. The next section considers the ecosystem of development banking in Greece through the prism of such lenders; some of which have a multi-decade presence in the country, while others are newcomers following the twin fiscal and economic crisis in 2009. As shall be illustrated, it was primarily European institutions that provided funding arrangements and policy instruments, thereby—unintentionally—contributing to the resurgence of promotional banking in Greece.

## 11.3 Filling the Void After ETBA's Privatization

After the privatization of ETBA, development banking did not fully disappear from the landscape of policy making in Greece. Rather, an institutional realignment emerged which placed greater emphasis on smaller public entities that primarily managed European Union funding instruments. This emerging ecosystem was not only state-driven. Private sector commercial banks were motivated to co-invest in such instruments. Put otherwise, in order to leverage and multiply public funding, the collaboration with private lenders was welcome. Thus, public-private partnerships (PPPs) emerged in Greek development banking that can be interpreted as complementary. This section addresses a number of development financing initiatives emerging after the sale of ETBA.

This plethora of funding initiatives in Greece was primarily supported through European programs. They included Greek stakeholders from the private and public sector that targeted specific constituencies, had multi-year funding schemes and were renewable through revolving funding arrangements. Specifically, the European Investment Bank (EIB) and the European Investment Fund (EIF) combined with the Hellenic Fund for Entrepreneurship and Development (*ETEAN*) to either co-finance or guarantee loans to SMEs (Small and Medium-sized Enterprises) and private households. These funding instruments were subsequently channeled through domestic commercial banks to the recipient constituency.

But this plethora also illustrates the splintering of the field of development financing in Greece after the privatization of ETBA. Moreover, as will become apparent in the sections that follow, the new domestic actors that emerged after 2003 exhibited a large resource dependency from EU funding instruments and programs. Thus, the reshaping of the institutional space of promotional financing in Greece post-ETBA is characterized by a high degree of reliance on external funding. Moreover, it could even be argued that this new path dependency illustrated a transformational shift from a previous reliance on the Greek state towards primarily European institutions.

### 11.3.1 The Hellenic Fund for Entrepreneurship and Development (ETEAN SA)

The Hellenic Fund for Entrepreneurship and Development (*Εθνικό Ταμείο Επιχειρηματικότητας και Ανάπτυξης* ETEAN SA) is a public funding agency. ETEAN was formerly known as the Guarantee Fund for Small and Very Small Businesses (*Ταμείο Εγγυοδοσίας Μικρών και Πολύ Μικρών Επιχειρήσεων* (*ΤΕΜΠΜΕ Α.Ε*), which was established by the government in 2003, one year after the sale of ETBA. This SME guarantee fund was not explicitly linked with a development mandate. Rather, it reflected the government's determination to support a specific constituency of Greece's real economy which frequently lacked access to affordable credit resources from commercial banks. Moreover, the adoption of a guarantee fund based on co-financed resources from the EU's Structural Funds signaled that grants and loan guarantees were the new policy instruments, not outright promotional banking. *ΤΕΜΠΜΕ*'s name was changed in February 2011, thereby becoming ETEAN. The name change entailed a revised and larger mandate, including "entrepreneurship." Put otherwise, firms addressing ETEAN for loan guarantees could henceforth include medium-sized companies.

ETEAN is based in Athens, Greece. It is a 100 percent state-backed financial intermediary under the supervision of the Bank of Greece. ETEAN links EU financial engineering instruments with local banking institutions for the benefit of medium and small sized enterprises. It provides low-cost financing solutions through guarantees and repayable credit enhancement facilities for business entities with limited access to customary bank financing. Its budget is a combination of diverse EU funding programs and co-financing instruments provided (or guaranteed) by the Greek government, among which is:

- The SMEs global loans (Guarantee Fund),
- The Business Restart—Working Capital Fund,
- The Entrepreneurship Fund,
- The Fund for Business Restructuring,

- The Energy Efficiency for Households Fund,
- The Fund for Digital Economy,
- The Fund for Industry 4.0,
- The Tourism on the Islands Fund.

The diversity of these funding programs, most of which were financed by EU structural funds, with the Greek co-financing share ranging between 10 and 25 percent, underline the degree to which various instruments geared towards development financing continued to exist in Greece in the absence of a state-sponsored promotional bank. Moreover, it can be argued that, following the sale of ETBA in 2002, the role of *TEMPME* and ETEAN grew in terms of the administration of funding volumes and flag-bearer for development financing in Greece. In short, *TEMPME* replaced ETBA without having to confront the legacies and reputational costs of its *de facto*, but not *de jure* predecessor. ETEAN continued this process and expanded the conceptual focus as well as financing volumes available for development purposes in Greece. As will be discussed in section 11.5, in April 2019 ETEAN AE was transformed through legislative act (4608/2019) into the *Hellenic Development Bank* (*Ελληνική Αναπτυξιακή Τράπεζα*, EAT).

### 11.3.2 The New Economy Development Fund (TANEO)

In addition to ETEAN, other state-backed financing organizations emerged in Greece during the past decade. The New Economy Development Fund S.A. (TANEO) was established in 2001 by a combination of ETEAN (its parent organization) and the Greek Ministry of Economy and Development. TANEO was the first "fund of funds" aiming at the competitive development of venture capital funds oriented towards supporting SMEs. TANEO participates in venture capital arrangements with an investment focus on Greek SMEs that have previously implemented financial and structural adaptations. These investments are implemented via equity participations and/or quasi-equity financial instruments originating from the Strategic Investment Plan 2018 on behalf of the Hellenic Republic.

To illustrate TANEO's operational capacity and funding diversity, consider the following development. Abu Dhabi-based Mubadala Investment Company signed in March 2018 a deal with Greece's TANEO to create a euro 400 million co-investment platform (Gulf Business 2018). Under the agreement, TANEO and Mubadala each contribute euro 200 million to invest in businesses with growth potential across key sectors of Greece's economy, in particular telecommunications, information technology, e-commerce and biotechnology.

This joint venture underlines two striking aspects. For one, TANEO managed to attract funding *outside* the EU while the country was still subject to implementing the third macro-economic adjustment program (which it concluded in

August 2018). Secondly, TANEO illustrates the determination of certain funding institutions to reach out, to internationalize their funding resources beyond European lenders. This could only have been achieved based on the reputational capital established by TANEO in the years before, despite the crisis in Greece. In this approach we can therefore identify a strategic reorientation, i.e. a geographic expansion of funding resources by specific Greek development financing institutions. It cannot therefore come as a surprise that such an expansion was undertaken by a venture capital fund towards a Gulf state.

### 11.3.3 The EquiFund Greece

A third example in the ecosystem of Greek-based development financing institutions is the EquiFund Greece. EquiFund is an initiative of the Hellenic Republic in cooperation with various EU funding institutions, showing once more the importance of EU level actors for development banking activity in Greece. EquiFund is co-financed by the EU and national funds. Its so-called "cornerstone investors" include the European Investment Fund (EIF), the European Investment Bank (EIB) and the European Fund for Strategic Investments (EFSI). In order to underline the PPP structure of EquiFund private "strategic partners" such as the Onassis Foundation and the National Bank of Greece (not to be confused with the Central Bank of Greece) have also committed to invest in the initiative. Finally, apart from EU funding institutions, the EquiFund is also receiving financial support from the Black Sea Trade and Development Bank (BSTDB) located in Thessaloniki, Greece (see section 11.4).

The Fund was established in 2018 and focuses on equity financing to build and develop SME businesses and start-ups. As Greece has one of the lowest levels of venture capital and private equity activity in the EU, the need for such a funding institution is self-evident (Invest Europe, 2018). EquiFund's initial capital was 300 million euro with a mandate to invest in "entrepreneurship." A total of nine sub-funds are geared towards specific constituencies such as the "Innovation Window," the "Growth Stage Window" or equity investments in start-ups as well as "scale-ups" (Konti, 2019a) Since its inception in 2018 EquiFund has invested 60 million euros (until August 2019) in more than forty companies, mainly in the innovation window and early stage sub-funds. The companies are primarily start-ups in the technology and tourism sectors, the Internet of Things and Big Data (Konti, 2019b).

This brief—but for reasons of space necessarily incomplete—overview of the post-2002 Greek ecosystem of funding institutions with a development mandate underlines that after the privatization of ETBA, other financing providers emerged in the public and private sector. These lenders can be seen as providing a certain degree of continuity in the field of promotional banking. But this sense of continuity was also characterized by scaling-down the individual institutions, redefining their mandates and opening them up to private sector participation. Put otherwise, instead of an over-extended financial behemoth that ETBA had gradually morphed into, the various newly established smaller players signaled a fragmentation of the market with different development mandates catering to different constituencies and with diverging funding instruments at their disposal.

In addition, the European dimension of this development cannot be underlined enough. As a result of numerous programs geared towards development financing, this policy mechanism managed to establish a new lease of life after the privatization of ETBA. To illustrate this expanding ecosystem, consider some additional examples from the aforementioned domestic players which were implemented during the past decade. These financial arrangements were particularly important during Greece's execution of three macro-economic adjustment programs between 2010 and mid-2018 when access to affordable credit and working capital became increasingly difficult, e.g. for SMEs. It is to the credit of European lending programs and their cooperation with domestic players in Greece that they kept the loan pipeline open when the Greek government was hardly in a position to provide the required levels of funding because of fiscal constraints and compliance requirements vis-à-vis its international creditors.

Approximately €1 billion in loan agreements between the EIF and Greek banks were adopted under the European Commission's COSME initiative (Competitiveness of Small and Medium-Sized Enterprises). In 2014, National Bank of Greece signed the first COSME agreement with the EIF, totaling €100,000,000 for the implementation of the COSME Loan Guarantee Facility, with the support of the EFSI. In 2016, the "Entrepreneurship Fund II" was founded as an independent unit inside ETEAN SA. The aim of the Fund was to enhance the competitiveness of enterprises, through the facilitation of access to finance. The initial budget reached €400 million.

For its part, the EIB established the "Trade Finance Facility II." The new program totaled 400 million euro of trade finance to be provided by local banks in cooperation with international financial partners to export-oriented Greek companies. Between 2015–2019, more than €2 billion in credit lines were signed between the EIB and Greek banks to support lending to SMEs and Midcaps across the country. Finally, in September 2019 a joint cooperation agreement was signed between Greek private Banks (Alpha Bank and Eurobank) and the EIB to implement the Infrastructure Fund of Funds (InfraFoF) created by the Development Ministry and the EIB. InfraFoF is expected to mobilize investments of at least 650 million euros for sustainable economy projects.

Table 11.1 below highlights different European support programs and initiatives with a development financing objective integrated to their operational guidelines. The volumes involved underscore that it is not primarily a lack of funding instruments that characterizes promotional banking arrangements in

**Table 11.1** Greece: European Fund for Strategic Investments (EFSI SME Window, Signatures as of 31.08.2019 in euros)

| Financial Intermediary | EU Initiative | Type of Support | Portfolio Volume |
|---|---|---|---|
| Alpha Bank | COSME | Portfolio Guarantee | 500 million |
| Alpha Bank | InnovFin | Portfolio Guarantee | 100 million |
| Cooperative Bank Epirus | EaSI* | Portfolio Guarantee | 5 million |
| Cooperative Bank of Thessaly EaSI | EaSI | Portfolio Guarantee | 7.5 million |
| Eurobank Ergasias | InnovFin | Portfolio Guarantee | 100 million |
| Eurobank Ergasias S.A. | COSME | Portfolio Guarantee | 650 million |
| Eurobank Ergasias | EaSI | Portfolio Guarantee | 10 million |
| National Bank of Greece | InnovFin | Portfolio Guarantee | 100 million |
| National Bank of Greece | COSME | Portfolio Guarantee | 800 million |
| National Bank of Greece | EaSI | Portfolio Guarantee | 40 million |
| Pancretan Cooperative Bank Ltd. | COSME | Portfolio Guarantee | 50 million |
| Piraeus Bank | InnovFin | Portfolio Guarantee | 100 million |
| Piraeus Bank | COSME | Portfolio Guarantee | 900 million |

*Source*: EIF (2019): https://www.eif.org/what_we_do/efsi/guarantee-deals.pdf.* EaSI: Employment and Social Innovation (Programme of the European Commission)

Greece. Through co-financing instruments and widespread EU participation Greece does not lack funding resources in the realm of promotional financing. What it frequently lacks are two inter-related factors. For one, public investment, including institutional development financing, became increasingly dependent on the availability of EU funding programs and EIB-linked financial engineering instruments, in particular after the onset of the crisis in 2009. Secondly, the example of the Institution for Growth (IfG) is a telling illustration of how financial sector innovation can be captured by a lack of political will between government and opposition in a highly polarized parliament during the crisis years.

### 11.3.4 The Institution for Growth (IfG)

As illustrated by the existence of ETEAN, TANEO and the EquiFund, there exists a plethora of smaller public and private funding institutions that have a development mandate in the Greek financial sector. The institutional vacuum emerging after the privatization of ETBA gradually gave rise to innovation and experimentation in this sector. Adding to this development is the observation that during the crisis years. and subject to the macro-economic adjustment programs, Greek governments experimented with the creation of a development institution at the micro level. In doing so extensive technical assistance was provided by international partners.

In May 2012, a European working party was appointed by the then Greek Minister of Development and Competitiveness, Kostis Hatzidakis, to prepare a concept for the foundation of an institute to promote the development of the Greek real economy. The working party included representatives of the EIB, the European Commission, the French Ministry for Finance and the German promotional bank *Kreditanstalt für Wiederaufbau* (KfW). Such international outreach activity in favor of capacity building was unprecedented in Greece.

The conceptual result of this endeavor was the Institution for Growth (IfG)[8]. The IfG operated as a non-bank finance institute addressing the need to overcome existing structural funding gaps in the Greek economy. It included an umbrella fund with three different sub-funds based on specific promotional objectives: (i) one sub-fund would lend to Greek SMEs, (ii) a second sub-fund focused on equity capital to Greek SMEs, and (iii) a third sub-fund targeted financing infrastructure projects. The Greek parliament adopted the law for the IfG in December 2013.

The short history of this institution can serve as a cautionary tale when establishing a micro-lending institution in the context of the highly polarized political environment in Greece. More specifically, the coalition government of then Prime Minister, Antonis Samaras (2012–2015), established the IfG in the course of 2014, only to see the incoming coalition government of Prime Minister Tsipras (from January 2015 until July 2019) rejecting such a micro lender as German-driven and thus letting it pass away on the heap of failed institutions in Greece.

The IfG was jointly financed by Greek sources and the German KfW[9]. The Greek authorities committed €350 million in funding. The government's contribution came in the form of an equity participation. For the initial capitalization of €200 million, the government reallocated NSRF (National Strategic Reference Framework) funds from the 2007–13 programing period and €150 million from the central budget's Public Investment Program. The German promotional bank KfW invested (through equity) an additional €100 million in seed financing. The Athens-based *Onassis Foundation* pledged €30 million to the IfG.

What set the IfG apart from other micro-lending institutions in Greece (e.g. ETEAN or TANEO) was its legal structure, institutional membership and location of registration. The first of its three sub-funds was established in Luxembourg in May 2014 where the IfG was officially registered as a legal entity (Task Force for Greece 2014). The location in Luxembourg was an explicit recognition by the Greek government and its international lenders that the IfG should be shielded from the risk of state capture. Moreover, the lack of institutional trust inherent in such a move on the part of Greece's creditors is apparent. What is all the more

[8] The author of this contribution was a member of the European Commission Task Force for Greece (TFGR) from September 2011 to September 2013. He assisted in the consultation process establishing the IfG.

[9] The KfW provided these financial resources on behalf of the German Federal Ministry of Finance (see Mertens, this volume).

significant is that the then government of Prime Minister Antonis Samaras accepted such a legal relocation.

The commencement of business activities by the IfG took place in the third quarter of 2014. By the end of the year four loans had been provided to Greek SMEs. The private Piraeus Bank provided the first loans in partnership with the IfG. The funds included working capital and investment loans with preferential terms up to €5 million. They were used to cover expenses for equipment, research & development, trade activities and raw materials. The interest rate was based on Euribor + margin, which was lower when compared to the margin if the company was financed with a loan from Piraeus Bank only.

Once the coalition government of Prime Minister Tsipras took office end-January 2015 the lack of political will expressed by the incoming administration to continue supporting the IfG relegated the initiative to a slow death. As was often the case in Greece during the three bailout programs, any new government would seek to distance itself from numerous initiatives and commitments of its predecessors, claiming that these projects did not correspond with its own political priorities. These multi-annual macro-economic adjustment programs provided the most important—and controversial—context condition for Greece during the period 2010–2018. While Greece was not the only euro area country to have such a program—Cyprus, Portugal, Ireland and Spain also were subject to such fiscal conditionality frameworks—only Greece needed three such programs and only exited these after almost a decade of macro-economic adjustment requirements.

What we see here is a key fault line of Greek politics. The absence of a consensus on certain policies and their institutional representation constitutes a major point of difference with other former program countries in the euro area such as Ireland, Portugal, Cyprus and Spain. This renders many initiatives obsolete the moment a new government or cabinet reshuffle takes place in Athens.

## 11.4 The International Context of Development Financing in Greece

Prior to and frequently in parallel with the emergence of development financing institutions in Greece a number of European public lenders also operate in the country. Together with domestic peers they provide for what one may call a rather crowded field of development banking institutions. Some of these have had residence offices in Athens for decades while others are newcomers, e.g. from China or the United Kingdom. It can be argued that there is no shortage of international financial institutions in Greece that carry in their official title the term "development".

What distinguishes these international development banks from their operational environment in Greece is the fact that they do not carry the pre-fix

*Hellenic* in their respective names. This is an additional, not only symbolic reason why the Greek authorities undertook to establish a genuine Hellenic Development Bank (see next section). These international lenders—in particular the EIB, the BSTDB and the EBRD—established different levels of cooperation with their Hellenic peers as regards joint ventures in supporting development financing. In order to understand the operational environment further, it is therefore useful to briefly shed some light on the international development lenders that are currently present in Greece.

The European Investment Bank (EIB), despite not carrying development in its name, clearly has such a mandate, including in Greece. It has the longest presence in the country—since 1963—and the highest volume of financial exposure, namely 35 billion euros (between 1963 and end-2017). Flagship projects include the loan financing of the Athens Metro, the provision of "framework loans" for schools, museums, tourism and the environment. In November 2019, the EIB provided a euro 140 million loan to support the expansion and upgrading of the Port of Piraeus, the principal port of Greece. This represented the largest ever loan for port investment in the country by the EIB.

The Black Sea Trade and Development Bank (BSTDB), based in the northern city of Thessaloniki, started its operations two decades ago in June 1999.[10] In 2018, the lender invested three million euros in the so-called EOS Hellenic Renaissance Fund of EquiFund. The purpose of the investment is to support Greek SMEs that are active in sectors such as food & beverage, hospitality services, energy efficiency. Similarly, since February 2017 the BSTDB has been engaged in a consortium with the private Alpha Bank (Greece), the EBRD representative office in Athens (see below), the EIB and the World Bank's subsidiary, the International Finance Corporation (IFC) in providing long-term project financing of euro 1.6 billion for the modernization of 14 regional airports to Fraport Greece, a consortium of Fraport AG Frankfurt Airport Services Worldwide and the Greek industrial holding company Copelouzos Group. BSTDB's share of lending in the consortium is 62.5 million euro with a duration of 17 years. The project represents the largest investment BSTDB has made in any Member Country since its inception in 1999.

The European Bank for Reconstruction and Development (EBRD) has had a representative office in Athens since 2016 which has been extended through 2025. After four years of operations, 49 projects have been approved for financing by the EBRD in Greece. The cumulative investment reached EUR 2.8 billion (mid-2019). The EBRD portfolio is 100 percent private sector. The composition of its investment portfolio in Greece comprises a share of 32 percent in financial

[10] It was established by Albania, Armenia, Azerbaijan, Bulgaria, Georgia, Greece, Moldova, Romania, Russia, Turkey, and Ukraine who are the 11 founding members of the *Black Sea Economic Cooperation* (BSEC).

institutions, 33 percent in industry, commerce & agribusiness as well as 35 percent in sustainable infrastructure (EBRD, 2019).

The newest international development bank to arrive in Greece comes from China. In July 2016 the China Development Bank (CDB) signed an MoU (Memorandum of Understanding) with the Bank of Greece. CDB's activities focus on financing infrastructure projects, in particular in the energy sector. In September 2017, CDB signed a Memorandum of Cooperation (MoC) with Greece's state-run power utility, the Public Power Corp. (PPC). Furthermore, ADMIE, Greece's Independent Power Transmission Operator and CDB signed a MoC for the funding of ADMIE in November 2017.[11] In January 2018, the world's biggest bank by assets, the Industrial and Commercial Bank of China (ICBC) became the second Beijing-based bank to arrive in Greece.

This brief overview illustrates that the ecosystem of international development banks in Greece has significantly evolved in the course of the past two decades. What emerges from these examples is the following: next to domestic initiatives in the public and private sector, international lenders with a development mandate established representation and sought cooperation with selected Greek peers. Some of these lenders have a long-term presence in Greece, i.e. the EIB with its auxiliary funds (e.g. the EIF) and the BSTDB, based in Thessaloniki. The latter interacts with the former in a variety of infrastructure projects in Greece. This ecosystem of domestic and international institutions raises a twofold question. Are they either competing with each other or contributing to project overlap? What such a crowded field of active players suggests is that the domestic players compete for the attention and financial resources of the international institutions.

The recent arrival of the EBRD and the growing presence of Chinese banks in Greece is a result of two related factors. The London-based lender was invited by the Greek government to provide capacity building expertise, trade facilitation funding and targeted investments in companies of the private sector. This cooperation between Athens and London is equally the result of the EBRD's multi-decade experience in transition economies of Central and Eastern Europe. By contrast, the growing footprint of Chinese banks in Greece follows on the heels of COSCO's (China Ocean Shipping Company) anchor investment in the Port of Piraeus in 2008. This initial investment in maritime infrastructure has subsequently created clusters of Chinese investment in the energy sector, tourism and real estate.

[11] ADMIE is a fully owned subsidiary of Greece's state-owned power utility PPC. In June 2016 State Grid of China purchased a 24 percent stake in ADMIE's equity capital for 320 million euros, the largest Chinese investment in Greece after the Chinese state-owned shipping company COSCO acquired a 51 percent stake in Piraeus Port Authority in August 2016 for 280.5 million euros.

## 11.5 Establishing a New Development Bank in Greece

In the previous sections we have elaborated on historical predecessors of development banking institutions in Greece. That discussion included highlighting domestic and international lenders that, in name and substance, had the characteristics of promotional banking. We now turn our attention to the resurgence of a state-sponsored development bank institution that was adopted by the Greek parliament in April 2019. The former Syriza-led government of Prime Minister Alexis Tsipras (from January 2015 until July 2019) advocated the establishment of a public development bank as part of its exit strategy following the conclusion of the third macro-economic adjustment program in August 2018.

This initiative was integrated in the government's "Holistic Plan," presented to the public in May 2018. The economic master plan (Hellenic Ministry of Finance, 2018) detailed how to restore economic growth after Greece emerges from eight years of three successive bailout programs. The new growth strategy emphasizes a more productive, export-focused Greek economy by recalibrating its structural characteristics in the next decades. The economic blueprint mandated a Hellenic Development Bank (HDB, in Greek *Ελληνική Αναπτυξιακή Τράπεζα*) to assist in the financing of SMEs and start-ups, cooperatives and social enterprises as well as public entities. It will not focus on retail banking but may act as a wholesale intermediary for commercial banks, private investors and other financial intermediaries. The proposed HDB will not be a deposit-taking bank.

The legal draft for a Hellenic Development Bank was submitted to parliament at end-February 2019. Following a public consultation process the draft was adopted by parliament in March. The Greek state's shareholding in the HDB cannot exceed 50 percent plus one share. The Board of Governors comprises seven members with a five-year mandate. The HDB will have two branches, with headquarters in Athens and an office in Thessaloniki. The latter branch is to support companies in Northern Greece and serve as an ambassador for joint initiatives in neighboring countries.

The manner in which the Tsipras government argued in favor of a promotional bank (a.k.a. development banks) is based on coordinated efforts to direct public investments into specific sectors of the domestic economy. Such a national policy institution seeks to mitigate a multi-year credit crunch to the real economy, e.g. in sectors where access to loans from Greek commercial banks is constrained by complex collateral requirements, high interest rates, and short maturities, in particular for SMEs and start-ups. To illustrate, in July 2019 the average interest rate for a business loan of 250,000 euro reached 4.90 percent in Greece against 2.06 percent in the Euro area average (Tsortzi, 2019).[12] This disparity in interest

[12] The average interest rate for the same amount reached 6.88 percent in December 2011 (see CEIC 2019).

rates for business loans between Greece and other member states of the euro area would even be higher if European programs such as COSME and development lenders such as the EIB and the EBRD did not provide various funding options that operate as a subsidy to lower the interest rates for investment loans and working capital!

### 11.5.1 The Modus Operandi of the Hellenic Development Bank

The adoption of the HDB cannot be seen in isolation from the wider financial sector challenges in Greece. The Greek private banking sector during the three bailout programs from 2010 to mid-2018 has been characterized by a number of structural features that also impact as legacy issues on the operational environment of a new HDB. These features can be summarized as follows:

- The four systemic banks (*National Bank of Greece*, *Alpha Bank*, *Piraeus Bank* and *Eurobank*) have had to be recapitalized three times during the past eight years. In order for these four domestic lenders to return to long-term sustainability, the clean-up of their balance sheets is an arduous work in progress.
- Until September 2019 the Greek banking sector was subject to capital controls which were adopted July 2015.
- Greece's banking sector is the most concentrated in the euro area, as the four systemic banks hold around 96 percent of total financial assets.
- The loan portfolios of the four systemic banks and their capacity to lend to the real economy continue to be adversely affected by high ratios of Non-Performing Loans (NPLs). While a comprehensive reduction plan has been agreed and is being implemented, the resolution of NPLs is expected to take until at least 2021.
- Aggregate credit growth in the Greek real economy has been negative since 2012. Not a single (!) month during the past seven years has registered a positive aggregate supply of lending to private households and businesses in Greece.

It is against the background of this highly challenging operational environment that the start of the new HDB must be placed. When issuing loans to SMEs the HDB will not (!) operate as a direct lending institution. The provision of credit will be arranged in cooperation with Greek commercial banks, investment funds and other public as well as private funding entities. Put otherwise, the HDB would be serving as an intermediary institution in the Greek financial sector. The rationale behind this construction is the following: the HDB should not operate in competition with other commercial banks, the latter thereby retaining the prerogative of lender of first resort. Furthermore, the HDB has a mandate to provide consultancy and advisory capacity-building services to companies in order to "further the development policies of the country." The promotional bank will issue bond finance and "collect financing," albeit without "taking in deposits" from private or corporate constituencies.

It is worth highlighting that the mandate and rationale for the new Greek development bank has been anchored on the principles of the French promotional bank *BPI France*. In September 2017, the then Greek Ministry of Economy and Development (Yiannis Dragasakis) established a roadmap with BPI France, the latter providing technical assistance and advisory services in the creation of a development bank in Hellas. One of the key results of this cooperation was the inclusion in the HDB's mandate that it will not operate as a lending competitor to the four systemic banks in Greece. Put otherwise, this provision places the HDB as engaging in on-lending, including in cooperation with domestic commercial banks, but not in competition to them. In that respect, the HDB follows the prevailing on-lending model of other national development banks in Europe.

In terms of financial capacity, the new development bank is to initially have at its disposal between four to five billion euros (Kathimerini, 2019 and Naftemporiki, 2018). The basis for these financial resources are a mixture of structural funds available to Greece from the current (2014–2020) and forthcoming (2021–2027) National Strategic Reference Framework (NSRF) funding programs of the European Commission, the transfer of assets provided by the former ETEAN, other Greek public agencies such as TANEO, and private capital resources.

The integration of ETEAN's activities and the use of TANEO's funding instruments by the new development bank represents a formidable administrative, legal, and institutional task. The interplay of such diverse institutions is an operational challenge and requires deft political management. Moreover, the politics involved in this integration process will take time. Put otherwise, the potential for politicizing this formidable integration process is real and could adversely impact on the initial operational capacity of the HDB. Furthermore, potential conflicts (of interest) between the development bank and private commercial institutions cannot be excluded. They have the same target constituency, i.e. small and medium-sized enterprises, compete for similar funding sources in the venture capital market of Greece, and all engage with EU funding institutions such as the EIB, EIF and European Social Fund (ESF).[13]

Finally, re-introducing a financial development institution requires astute attention to its governance mechanisms, risk management capacity, the specifics

[13] Targeting credit supply to SMEs is becoming a crowded sector and competitive field in the Greek banking sector. *Praxia Bank* whose business model is focused on lending to SMEs concluded a capital raising initiative totaling euros 200 million in May 2018. Its self-definition describes Praxia Bank as an "alternative bank" in the domestic market.

of the banks' lending mandate, sectoral focus, origin of financial resources and transparent accountability. The definition of these preconditions is all the more necessary as the legacy of past development bank initiatives in Greece has been that they frequently served as vehicles for rent-seeking politicians, included allegations of corruption and provided political lending while ignoring the viability of applicants' business plans. Addressing these legacy issues by establishing governance principles and adequate risk controls will be key to enhancing the reputational capital of any new HDB.

## 11.6 Conclusions

Compared to other countries in our comparative sample, it could not be taken for granted that in the Greek case following the change of government in July 2019[14] the new administration of Prime Minister Kyriakos Mitsotakis would emphasize institutional continuity in the field of development banking. However, his new Minister for Development and Investment, Andonis Georgiadis, pledged five billion euro in leveraged financing within two to three years for the HDB (Naftemporiki, 2019).

The newly created HDB changes the institutional architecture of promotional banking in Greece. The HDB will have to navigate a network of EU programs and a crowded field of domestic as well as international stakeholders in Greece. Finding its place and rationale, providing additionality and creating synergies instead of funding overlap and project duplication will be a policy-making challenge for the HDB, particularly in its initial phase of operation. Neither can the HDB be expected to deliver "quick fixes," i.e. solutions that enhance liquidity provision for the real economy in the short run.

On a more conceptual level, the empirical evidence presented begs the question how much of an outlier Greece is? Is it an outlier in our sample of countries because of the duration and depth of its economic crisis? On that count the answer is positive. But can it also be argued that Greece is an outlier given the fact that it is a late comer to the table of state-sponsored development financing in Europe? In light of the recent creation (April 2019) of the state-sponsored Hellenic Development Bank this part of the outlier argument also has empirical merit.

The re-emergence of a national development bank in Greece faces various policy constraints. After the conclusion of its third macro-economic adjustment program the Greek government is subject to a so-called "enhanced" monitoring process. This supervision chiefly concerns multi-year fiscal policy compliance as

[14] The general elections resulted in a landslide victory for the largest opposition party New Democracy which was able to form a single-party government with an absolute majority.

agreed between the previous government and its European creditors. Put otherwise, the government's fiscal autonomy is restricted. This constraint can have an impact on the portfolio of financial instruments available to the HDB. The execution of its operational mandate is limited by the government's requirement to deliver a primary budget surplus of 3.5 percent of GDP until at least 2022.[15] No other country in the comparative sample of this volume faces such supervision and fiscal compliance requirements. These constraints de facto impact on the operational capacity of the HDB. This set of limitations further confirms the outlier argument.

Does the HDB fulfill a need to narrow an investment gap that is not covered by the plethora of other institutions active in the country? Put otherwise, what is its practical additionality? The regulatory environment in which it will operate continues to require a process of economic and financial normalization. This process is far from complete. Section 11.5.1 highlighted a set of legacy issues which impact on the practical additionality of a Hellenic Development Bank. As a national policy vehicle, the HDB's mandate is to mitigate credit crunches for specific constituencies in the real economy, particularly SMEs, business start-ups and social enterprises. Such a mandate positions the HDB at the intersection of public and private as well as domestic and European financial service providers in Greece. But there is a challenge here: expectations are created for the HDB to assist in solving structural issues of current credit supply impasses in Greece's real economy. Managing these expectations will be as challenging as managing the financial resources and operational environment of the HDB.

As the previous sections have shown, the absence of a public development bank did not imply that Greece fully abandoned financing institutions with a promotional mandate. On the contrary, the empirical evidence of domestic and international lenders present in Greece after the sale of ETBA suggests that the vacated policy space for development financing reconstituted itself after 2002 and became a rather crowded arena. One could pointedly argue, that Greece increasingly appeared "overbanked" in terms of development finance. To what degree the new HDB can recalibrate this policy space remains to be seen. It is still early days for a comprehensive evaluation as the bank has only operated since April 2019. Furthermore, the Covid-19 pandemic and the lockdown during March and April 2020 have impacted on the bank's operational capacity. The first indications of the HDB's lending performance are summarized by two initiatives:

- In cooperation with commercial banks the HDB has provided 3.6 EUR billion in loans to businesses through two programs, *Business Financing* and the *Warranty Fund*. Both facilities were designed by the HDB.

[15] Because of the Covid-19 pandemic, in Mai 2020 the euro group of finance minister granted Greece a temporary suspension of the primary budget surplus requirement for 2020.

- More specifically, the HDB provided €1.6 billion through Business Financing (out of €1.8 billion available). The loan program was launched in April 2020 to counter the economic effects of the pandemic. The Warranty Fund was launched in May 2020 and has dispersed €2 billion of capital guarantee loans (out of €3.6 billion available, see Kathimerini 2020).

Finally, an open question remains. Is Greece a rule maker or rule taker in the arena of promotional banking in Europe? The process of setting up the new HDB would suggest that *rule taking* was in play, in particular through on-demand technical support provided by French consultants (e.g. from Caisse des Dépôts et Consignations (Deposits and Consignments Fund) and the European Structural Reform Support Service (SRSS). Other external actors can also be considered as impacting on the rules Greece can set. The European Commission services, the European Central Bank's supervisory arm, the European Stability Mechanism (ESM) and the IMF in Washington continue to hold sway by different means and ways over Greece's future. These stakeholders will closely monitor the rational for and financing of a Hellenic Development Bank.

But rule making by Greece is equally in play. First and foremost, by regaining a measure of policy sovereignty that is not anymore explicitly defined by a macroeconomic adjustment program. While the policy space faces constraints, it is nevertheless a different point of departure than during the three programs lasting from 2010 until mid-2018. Furthermore, despite a crowded field of smaller domestic and large foreign institutions, the government of former PM Tsipras used considerable political capital to pass legislation for the establishment of a national development bank. In other words, it not only defined politics but also created the rules.

With the establishment of a national development bank in 2019, Greece caught-up to its European peers. In the Greek case, during the past decades, development banking was primarily based on the provision of European funding instruments and programs. In other EU Member States national trajectories in development banking were supplemented and re-enforced by European initiatives and institutions. In Greece, it was rather the other way around: European institutions such as the EIB, the Juncker Plan, international lenders such as the EBRD, the BSTDB and the China Development Bank shaped the field of domestic development, past and present. In a word, belatedly Greek development banking is switching from a rule taker to a rule maker in 2019.

It will take time to evaluate the spectrum of empirical outcomes in Greek development banking. It will continue to be a work in progress until the HDB is fully operational and has established its proper place in the architecture of financial intermediation in the Greek political economy. Thus, one of the inspiring outcomes of this comparative project is the observation that in the Greek case we were and continue to be witnesses to an institutional experiment in real time.

## Acknowledgement

I am thankful to Prof. Kostas Kostis, National and Kapodistrian University of Athens, for valuable assistance concerning the history of the Hellenic Industrial Development Bank.

## References

CEIC, (2019). "Greece Lending Rate: NB: NF: Up to 1 Year or Floating: Over Euro 0.25 MN and up to Euro 1 MN," [online available] https://www.ceicdata.com/en/greece/lending-rates/lending-rate-nb-nf-up-to-1-year-or-floating-over-euro-025-mn-and-up-to-euro-1-mn.

EBRD, (2019). "Greece Data," [online available] https://www.ebrd.com/greece-data.html.

EIF, (2019): https://www.eif.org/what_we_do/efsi/guarantee-deals.pdf.

Gulf Business, "UAE's Mubadala, Greece's Taneo to Invest EUR 400 million in Greece," 28th March 2018, [online available] http://gulfbusiness.com/uaes-mubadala-greeces-taneo-invest-eur400m-greece/.

Helen Kavvadia and Savvakis C. Savvides, (2019). "Funding Economic Development and the Role of National Development Banks-The Case of Cyprus," Development Discussion Papers 2019–09, JDI Executive Programs.

Hellenic Ministry of Finance, (2018). *Greece: A Growth Strategy for the Future*, May 2018, Athens.

Kathimerini, (2019). «*Με «προίκα» 5 δις. Ξεκινάει η Αναπτυξιακή Τράπεζα*» (With a "dowry" of 5 billion starts the Development Bank), Kathimerini, 28. February 2019.

Kathimerini, (2020): "Help for businesses from the Hellenic Development Bank", 12. August 2020, [online available] https://www.ekathimerini.com/255793/article/ekathimerini/business/help-for-businesses-from-the-hellenic-development-bank.

Konti, Despina, (2019a). "*Σε 8 μήνες το* EquiFund *επένδυσε* 45 *εκατ. Ευρώ σε* 34 *ελληνικές* startups" (In Eight Months the EquiFund invested 45 million euros in 34 Greek Start-ups), Kathimerini, 30. August 2019, [online available] https://www.kathimerini.gr/1040382/article/oikonomia/ellhnikh-oikonomia/se-8-mhnes-to-equifund-ependyse-45-ekat-eyrw-se-34-ellhnikes-startups.

Konti, Despina, (2019b). "Ten startups absorbed most of the capital from funds", Kathimerini (English edition), 13. December 2019, [online available] https://www.ekathimerini.com/247567/article/ekathimerini/business/ten-startups-absorbed-most-of-the-capital-from-funds.

Kontonika, Cleopatra, (2002). "*Πώς στήθηκε το «μεγάλο κόλπο» στην* ETBA' (How the 'Big Trick" Was Set Up inside ETBA), Kathimerini, 03. February 2002, [online available] https://www.kathimerini.gr/110297/article/epikairothta/politikh/pws-sth8hke-to-megalo-kolpo-sthn-etba.

Naftemporiki, (2001). "*Οι όροι ιδιωτικοποίησης της ETBA*" (The Framework for the Privatization of ETBA), 30. October 2001, [online available] https://www.naftemporiki.gr/finance/story/3536/oi-oroi-idiotikopoiisis-tis-etba.

Naftemporiki. (2018). «*Βόμβα ρευστότητας*» 4 *δισ. ευρώ μέσω της Αναπτυξιακής Τράπεζας* (Liquidity Bomb 4 Billion Euro From the Development Bank), Naftemporiki, 12. July 2018, [online available] https://www.naftemporiki.gr/finance/story/1370623/bomba-reustotitas-4-dis-euro-meso-tis-anaptuksiakis-trapezas.

Naftemporiki, (2019). "*Αδ. Γεωργιάδης*: 5 *δις. από την Αναπτυξιακή Τράπεζα*" (Five Billion Euro for the Development Bank), Naftemporiki, 08. September 2019, [online available] https://www.naftemporiki.gr/finance/story/1512762/ad-georgiadis-5-dis-apo-tin-anaptuksiaki-trapeza.

Task Force for Greece, (2014). *Sixth Activity Report* (March 2014), Brussels.

To Bima, (2008). "*Η προίκα της τράπεζας*" (The Dowry of the Bank), 24. November 2008, [online available] https://www.tovima.gr/2008/11/24/finance/i-proika-tis-trapezas/.

Tsortzi, Evgenia, (2019). "*Λίγα και ακριβά τα νέα δάνεια προς επιχειρήσεις και νοικοκυριά*" (Few and Expensive the New Loans for Businesses and Households), Naftemporiki, 04. September 2019.

# 12
# Conclusion
## Development Banking and the Future of European Capitalism

*Daniel Mertens, Matthias Thiemann, and Peter Volberding*

Development banks have returned (Griffith Jones et al, 2018), and surprisingly nowhere more prominently than in the EU. At the time of writing, tens of thousands of development bankers go to work in Europe every day to advance "promotional" projects. Over the past decade, these activities have expanded outside the traditional realm of national industrial champions to encompass everything from SMEs to innovation. Moreover, not only is this done with other NDBs, but also in ever greater cooperation with the European Investment Bank and the European Commission, the latter of whose DGs increasingly involve NDBs in European-wide policy objectives. As a high level banker at the Bpifrance involved in these deliberations puts it in one interview, "we begin to have common visions, common economic visions... And then we each have our own specificities, that's clear. Voilà." (November 23, 2018).

Operationally, these banks today not only invest in traditional loan and subsidy business, but they are also more involved in venture capital and fund-of-funds investment vehicles, financial risk-sharing arrangements, and human resource formation, a phenomenon mirroring the development in the private financial sector. Drawing upon EU and national funds—together with the EIB, the EIF, or other national development banks—NDBs are now a financial and political force to be reckoned with. This current intensity of NDBs' strategic involvement in the European economy has reached a level that would have been outright impossible to any European observer prior to the 2007 global financial crisis.

In this volume, we have endeavored to capture this phenomenon through the concept of field formation. Within this new development banking field, NDBs and the various European institutions share a common, mutually identified space in which they interact. This new development-banking field has emerged as each actor has increasingly taken relevant others into account when acting and coordinating their actions around common goals, namely the expansion of development banking activities within the EU. Moreover, this new field of development

Daniel Mertens, Matthias Thiemann, and Peter Volberding, *Conclusion: Development Banking and the Future of European Capitalism* In: *The Reinvention of Development Banking in the European Union: Industrial Policy in the Single Market and the Emergence of a Field.* Edited by: Daniel Mertens, Matthias Thiemann, and Peter Volberding, Oxford University Press (2021). © Oxford University Press. DOI: 10.1093/oso/9780198859703.003.0012

banking has grown precipitously within the last decade and has become intimately intertwined with policy at all levels. Yet the specific trajectory of the field has been guided by constraints and incentives particular to the EU. In terms of constraints, we have focused on the budgetary constraints imposed from the Maastricht treaty in 1992 onwards, as well as EU State Aid rules that regulate Member State support for domestic industries (Volberding, this volume). On the incentive side, we have pointed to the increasing creation of financial instruments funded by the EC, which desperately seeks to increase its impact despite its limited budget (Rubio and Thiemann, this volume). Responding to these financial incentives, Member States have found an opportunity to push their existing NDBs to take advantage of these funds and, for those who did not have an NDB, have been incentivized to create new ones. Explicit political support during the Juncker period further signaled that NDBs were not only tolerated by the EU, but actively supported. The EIB spearheaded this process, as it was exempted from the beginning from any State Aid considerations and was thought of as the natural ally by the Council and the Commission.

In January 2020, the Commission President Von der Leyen took the next step in the political use of NDBs at the European level by proposing a "Green Deal" to mobilize one trillion Euros to help the EU economy transition onto a sustainable path.[1] As the evolution of the European field would have suggested, NDBs and the EIB are to function as important policy levers, set to mobilize private and public funds through leveraging the EU budget. This latest guidance to transform development banking into a (financial) market-oriented system to invest in key policy priorities of the EU is the pinnacle of a development of at least 25 years—both conscious and accidental—that this book has sought to document. Currently no specific policy proposals have identified NDBs as *the* mechanism to achieve transformative investment, but if our book is any guidance, the same forces that have ushered in a European field of development banking are likely to be at work here again, and will most likely even intensify as the European fiscal and regulatory constraints will bring together the same coalition of the EC, the EIB, and NDBs.

Whether this configuration and the policy tools chosen are the appropriate ones to achieve their goals is a question for future research. Nevertheless, the chapters in this book enable us to capture, for the first time, the properties of what we have called a European field of development banking, to summarize, and to urge us to further reflect in this conclusion on the potential for an EU-wide industrial policy, including cohesion and transition policies, but also the pitfalls in terms of the political-economic costs and benefits.

[1] See https://ec.europa.eu/commission/presscorner/detail/en/qanda_20_24, last accessed 14 January 2020.

## 12.1 The History of the Field and its Implications

As this volume has shown, it was the establishment of the EIF in 1994, and the concomitant expansion of the EU budget for financial instruments channeled through that fund, that served as the starting point for the development-banking field. Critically, these sources of funding and financial instruments generated a collaborative thrust between NDBs and the EIB so that each could serve as a potential partner, rather than merely as a competitor. Just as field theory would predict (DiMaggio and Powell, 1983; Fligstein, 1996; 2001), NDBs increasingly started to take each other and the EIF into account, and incumbent NDBs adopted a leadership role to help guide the fledgling field in ways that served their interests. New NDBs emerged that expanded the field to new geographies and industries. In this process, the very understanding of development banking itself changed. Critically, this involved an emerging understanding of these institutions as legitimate tools for policy makers to tackle not only cyclical, but also structural economic problems in the single market. As we have shown, immediately following its creation, the field of development banking came to be characterized by the priorities and interactions of a few established incumbents, such as the KfW and the EIB, imprinting their understanding of what development banking is onto the field as a whole.

The economic crises of the 2000s further empowered both the EIB and NDBs. The EIB gained greater authority to implement EU-wide financial instruments and NDBs themselves gained political backing and financing prerogatives. These institutions expanded their financing as counter-cyclical tools during a banking crisis characterized by liquidity freezes and a halt of credit. The assets on the balance sheets of NDBs and the EIB exploded from EUR 1.27 trillion in 2007 to EUR 1.98 trillion in 2013, an increase of more than 30 percent in just six years. But as we show, the 2007 financial crisis and the Euro-zone crises were more than just a short-term fire-fighting exercise; instead, they were critical junctures for states to regain command over financial and human resources and, over time, actually increase the scope and size of NDBs even after the dual crises had subsided (for the deviating case of ICO, s. Clifton et al, this volume). In 2017, the then 26 NDBs and the EIB group together had more than 2.14 trillion Euros in assets on their balance sheets and employed a work force of more than 24,000 employees. The EIB is symptomatic for this expansion, having almost doubled its balance sheet in the course of these ten years and more than doubled its personnel, from 1,569 to 3,204 employees.

All this growth came with both increasing collaboration and new instances of competition between NDBs and EIB over the resources in the field. The question over who shapes the rules of the game, both in terms of the reinterpretation of existing EU rules that limited development banking activities, as well as in terms of the use of EU budgetary funds for such activities, led to intense contestation not only between NDBs and external actors, but also between development banks themselves. For instance, NDBs and the EIB both had an interest in legitimizing and expanding their operations, yet they struggled over who should lead these activities in the field and under which conditions. A particularly persistent source of conflict has been the joint push for financial instruments between NDBs and European institutions, including broader access to the EU budget for leverage and the use of the EIF as the host. Aware of these pressures, NDBs have become increasingly concerned about the EIB encroaching on their local business—and have organized in Brussels to ensure their views are heard[2]—whereas the EIB has seen its status as the sole administrator of EU budgetary funds challenged by NDBs. Consequently, NDBs and the EIB have proposed various solutions to political actors to raise investment levels, lobbied for changes to State Aid regulations, and promoted new financial instruments as innovative solutions. In this sense, field theory enables us to see how these relations emerge from the awareness of a common stake in the expansion of development banking activities within the EU.

The evolution of development banking as a practice in Europe, however, does not chart its course autonomously. Instead, the evolution occurs path-dependently within a regime—and a network of adjacent fields—built by successive steps in European integration. State Aid rules, financial regulation, and Eurostat governance today serve as—potentially flexible—constraints and guidance to what development banks (ought to) do, while the practices of channeling European funds molded by each episode of crisis management—such as ESIF and EFSI—has contributed to the Europeanization of funding national development finance. In addition, the case studies in this volume have shown that field formation is strongly influenced by the state of European integration at large. Importantly, the historical conjuncture at which a country enters the EU also shapes how NDBs are inserted into the field, conditioning their position as incumbents or challengers. This consequently means that the field of European development banking is also characterized by very strong power asymmetries, which intimately shape how the field of European development banking affects these national political economies.

[2] For instance, NDBs have organized in Brussels through the European Association of Long-Term Investors (ELTI) in order to help structure future financial instruments. They also meet with the EIB semi-annually in the EIB-NDB taskforce and there are more frequent informal exchanges between the large NDBs and the EIB. There is also intensified exchange between the European Commission, NDBs, and EIB on how to design financial instruments to make them effective as policy tools, as has been the case with European Structural and Investment Funds (ESIF) or the European Fund for Strategic Investment (EFSI) and its advisory and project pillars.

## 12.2 Power Asymmetries and the Uneven Distribution of Development Banking Capacities in the EU

Many Western NDBs have historically pre-dated EU regulations and EU-led funding initiatives. This early presence in the EU has meant that they were not only able to exert a greater ability to shape policies and regulations, but also had a more established set of administrative and strategic capacities than many younger and peripheral counterparts. This further sets aside the extensive history of development banking experience in infrastructure and SME financing. Germany, France, and—to a certain extent—Italy were able to chart a more powerful course for their banks within European constraints and command development banks who have often taken the initiative in instances of field formation. For example, the widespread focus on SME financing within the field of European development banking is also an outcome of the engagement of the KfW in Eastern Europe once the iron curtain fell, spreading its focus of activity there (Mertens, this volume). Bpifrance, jointly with the EIF, has spread more innovative methods of SME financing such as venture capital in the field within the last decade. Its parent company, CDC, together with the CDP and EIB further engaged in the set-up of investment funds for the purpose of promoting particular developmental goals, such as the Marguerite Fund, which finances projects that expand renewable energy projects in Europe.

Other banks in Western Europe have been less influential in setting the rules, experimented less with financial instruments, and have been less savvy in taking advantage—and occasionally exploiting—the loopholes within European regulation. A lack of extensive political backing, such as in the case of the Spanish ICO, seems to account partially for such timidity. Other banks, such as the large development banks in the Netherlands, based on a long tradition of public infrastructure construction seem to not have needed any external funds and hence have not engaged visibly in the political game in Brussels. Banks and investment funds in Scandinavia or in Belgium have seen their activities expand, sometimes more than double or even triple, as in the case of Vaekstfonden in Denmark and Finnvera in Finland, without entering into conflict with European rules or overtly engaging with the policy making apparatus in Brussels. Further research is necessary, however, in order to detail the particularities of each banks' trajectory, both domestically and supranationally.

The picture is very different in Eastern Europe, where banks are much smaller, often younger, and more under the influence of the EIB, which provides with cheap financing based on global loans. All the national development banks in Eastern Europe combined command less than 2 percent of the assets in the European field of development banking (EUR 30 billion Euros). While this number might be slightly misleading due to the emphasis on guarantee rather than loan business in Eastern Europe, business which is recorded not as loans, it already clarifies the difference in statute and power. Accordingly, in the largely neoliberal Baltics (Bohle and Greskovits, 2012), development-finance institutions seem less able to influence policy and State Aid regulations. They have struggled to scale up and obtain political support for strategic autonomy, rather becoming mere tools for policies whose priority were set in Brussels rather than their national capitals, in part because their mandate has been limited to serving as a passive distribution channel for European funds (Mikheeva and Juuse, this volume). On the other hand, the increasingly financial-nationalist cases of Hungary and Poland have recently reorganized their financial institutions to become more "developmentalist". But as Piroska and Mero (this volume) show, this might imply different fates for NDBs. Whereas the Polish BGK, the oldest and most powerful NDB in Eastern Europe, finds itself at the center of the developmentalist state in Poland (c.f. Naczyk, 2019), the MFB increasingly finds itself marginalized by the Orban regime, as it is disadvantaged with respect to the Eximbank, the domestic bank that is favored by the Hungarian government.

Finally, Southeastern Europe is the most underdeveloped region for NDBs, with by far the weakest presence of NDBs. However, while NDBs might be limited, there is a strong presence of multilateral and non-EU development banks, such as the EBRD, the China Development Bank, and the Black Sea Development Bank. While Bulgaria's development bank has a constant rate of expansion, it is reliant on bilateral loans such as from the China Development Bank. The case of Greece (Bastian, this volume) furthermore demonstrates the crowded field of development banking in the area, with competition between national, European, and multilateral banks for business and influence in Greece. This, and the lack of cross-party support for the establishment of a development bank, independent of the party affiliation of the bank management, have led to a convoluted and arduous process to (re-)establish a core development financing institution, with very limited success so far. Romania (Ban, 2019) and Cyprus (Kavvadia and Savvides, 2019) similarly have currently no functioning national development bank, as political elites wrangle over the proper institutional form of such institutions, which are seen as important elements of possible political patronage. Other peripheral countries hit by the Eurozone crisis, namely Ireland (SBCI, set up in 2014) and Portugal (IFD, in 2014), today have national development banks largely set up based on initiatives of the European Commission and in consultations with other NDBs, and with the primary goal of mobilizing EU funds for national development and SMEs. The effect of EU resources is, thus, very unevenly distributed, as are the consequences of Europeanization.

This is because, in most of the cases in this volume, we clearly see the dominance of domestic politics, historical legacies, and institutional settings regarding the shape, size and activities of NDBs over European forces—similar to what early

Europeanization research has highlighted (Héritier and Knill, 2001). As each NDB is endowed with different characteristics in terms of political power, financial autonomy, operational focus, and organizational governance, the field is characterized by disparities concerning the capacity of NDBs to tap into EU budgetary means and engage in financial engineering jointly with the EIF. These asymmetrically distributed capacities have the effect that in Eastern Europe we can observe the fear that financial instruments and InvestEU may deepen a two-speed Europe, thus affecting the extent to which actors are able to "make use of Europe" (Woll and Jacquot, 2010). To address these asymmetries in terms of development banking capacities, the European Commission has mandated the Structural Reform Support Service, for which they mobilize both private consultancy firms and development banks from the core countries. Further research will be necessary to examine whether the organizational and distributional consequences of the field's properties, including its politics, can be equalized by such remedial actions on the EU level.

## 12.3 Prospects for Industrial Policy in the European Union

Reflecting on these asymmetries is crucial, not only to evaluate the capacity of development banking to reduce or aggravate regional inequality and uneven development within the EU, but also to understand the broader transformation of the European political economy of which the development-banking field formation is but a subset. For one, scholars of political economy have highlighted a change in the instruments of state intervention from overt subsidies and public ownership to state management of industrial organization and the use of state-owned entities as a more indirect means of shaping markets. These means enabled the continuity of public power in the capitalist economy as opposed to images of the retreated state (Clift, 2013; Thatcher, 2017). Here, we believe development banks should be understood as key actors in this broader shift, however variegated their particular manifestations are. Furthermore, it has become fashionable again—academically and politically—to discuss industrial policy and its revival in the context of more open rivalries in the global economy and fears of secular stagnation (Wade, 2012; Eder and Schneider, 2018; Bulfone, 2019). State banking has historically been instrumental to the implementation of industrial policies (Zysman, 1983; Epstein, 2017), which is no less true for contemporary development banks, both in Europe (Naqvi et al., 2018) and beyond (Griffith-Jones et al., 2018; Chen, 2020).

The case studies in this volume confirm the continuous role of development banks in achieving national industrial policy goals, but it seems useful to relate our field's properties to existing visions of an EU-wide industrial policy. Research on industrial policy in the European Union has long acknowledged the limits of a "national" industrial policy in the single market under the condition of increasing transnationalization of production and investment (Hayward, 1995). Yet while "national identities of state capitalism (for example, the idea of 'national champions' within the context of protectionist and nationalist developmental policy) have changed and become more transnational" through cross-investments and strategic alliances (Gill, 1998, p. 7), European institutions have lacked both power and legitimacy—not to speak of a developmental mindset (Thurbon, 2016)—to take on the task of active industrial policy. The "clash of capitalisms" in the European Union and the supranational prerogative of a liberal, rule-based order in the spirit of competitive markets prevented an overt market-steering stance, dismissing—at least discursively—the use of "vertical" policies (Cowling, 1999; Fioretos, 2001). Today, the observation of an industrial policy revival in the EU that may enable public institutions to subordinate the accumulation process to specific developmental targets, is anything but clear-cut and needs to resist an overly linear view on the "pendulum swinging back" towards organized capitalism (Wigger and Horn, 2019). Rather, it needs to reflect on the marketized, financialized nature of contemporary capitalism, however state-led (c.f. Alami and Dixon, 2019).

The European field of development banking documented in this volume arguably entails such a quasi-public financial infrastructure for a revival of industrial policy in the EU. This is, first, because NDBs seem both able to remain locally anchored and yet at the same time equipped to build transnational networks and investment relations, all the while being under (mostly national) political control.[3] Second, the field bears the imprint of financialized capitalism in the EU today and "promotional banks and institutions" have become agents to deepen and partly steer it as its practices become more and more aligned with marketized practices based on risk-sharing mechanisms (Mertens and Thiemann, 2018; see Griffith-Jones and Naqvi, this volume) and often reflect second-tier development banking based upon on-lending. NDBs have been instrumental in the expansion of the venture funds industry in Europe, with more than 25 percent of capital in that industry stemming from public sources. Furthermore, they have focused on providing capital market instruments such as guarantees and sought to revive securitization alongside the more traditional instruments of subsidized and risk-sharing loans. This "reinvention of development banking" began in the late 1990s with the EIFs strategic repositioning—based on demands from the Amsterdam summit to step up risk financing for a sluggish economy—and a move by leading NDBs into this realm—mainly the French CDC and the German KfW.

[3] Furthermore, several of the NDBs have in-house engineering departments, capable of assessing the viability of innovations and their potential profitability (see Moslener et al., 2018, also Thiemann and Volberding, this volume).

Since this volume has shown that this "reinvention" is highly variegated and the involvement of national development banks in the guarantee-based European investment policies such as EFSI and InvestEU is uneven at best, little of this quasi-public engagement in financial innovation suggests it is meaningfully tackling the regional inequalities within the European Union or any key transformative goal of "mission-oriented finance". The European Court of Auditors, (2019) in its evaluation of EFSI has pointed out how the skewed distribution of EU funds for investment purposes relates to the uneven capacities of NDBs; few of which fully represent what development economists have recently coined "smart development banks" (Fernández-Arias, Hausmann and Panizza, 2020). Thus, the emergence of a European development banking field, with both its power asymmetries and its unfulfilled potential for a comprehensive investment financing that pursues other goals than (short-term) profit poses new questions about the political economy of development banking, on which we want to conclude this volume.

## 12.4 The Political Economy of European Development Banking: Towards a Critical Research Agenda

Against the background of this volume's studies and its aforementioned implications, a number of themes appear that a critical research agenda for European development banking should attempt to address, particularly as NDBs continue to become large players in the European political economy. These concern (1) the agency of NDBs and the relationship between the NDB's principles and the private financial sector; (2) the consequences of these for transformative and distributional politics; (3) the democratic accountability of NDB activity; and (4) the future politics of a fragmented field and the threat of disintegration.

(1) The conventional political economy perspective on development banks is tilted towards the dangers of political capture and the resulting lending inefficiencies. In contrast, this volume suggests one conceives of NDBs as agents who also pursue their own goals and are not assumed to be simply "captured" by political forces. In fact, this volume has contended that NDBs may manage the incentives and constraints from *both* their political owners and the financial markets they engage with. While certain banks such as in Greece have succumbed to domestic and international political pressures, the assumption that *all* national development banks do so is unfounded. Instead, researchers should endeavor to uncover the forces that enable, constrain, and guide NDBs to achieve autonomy, and to understand the reasons for such variation.

We believe that field theory is a good first step into analyzing these dynamics. This volume has treated NDBs as equipped with agency and, critically, embedded within a system of relationships that guide how they behave. Within this framework, NDBs naturally need to be seen as legitimate in their national environment to justify their existence and, as such, they need to serve certain political needs. But NDB officials may also be able to manage political demands in a way that allows them to act according to their professional norms as bankers.[4] They are willing to foster employment and even regional development, but request to be able to do so in a way that does not violate the long-term profitability of their bank nor the principles of sound banking. In this sense, NDBs have gained autonomy vis-à-vis their governments by refinancing their operations via capital markets, which in turn become justification devices to fend off riskier missions on the banks' accounts.

At the same time, as NDBs have become reliant on other financial intermediaries—particularly when operating as second-tier banks—they have also shrunk their room to maneuver. The reason is that the missions they pursue, may it be subsidized lending for innovation, budget-constrained SMEs, or social housing, need the consent—i.e. incentives—of pass-through commercial banks, investors, or rating agencies. Relying on risk-sharing arrangements and public-private partnerships in contemporary development banking, however, also has an advantage to policy makers, particularly when under fiscal constraint. By basing their investment policies on the leverage effect of development banks that are supposed to mobilize private capital, they can employ higher headline numbers, which allow them to project action in the face of mediated crises and has the possibility of delaying real transformation. The reader is well advised to take the political headline figures, such as the "Green Deal" 1 trillion EUR, with a grain of salt, as the total investment is achieved through financial leverage rather than as budgeted line items, reflecting the interests of specific sectors and social groups.

In this respect, the European Commission and its direct engagement with these NDBs through providing access to EU budgetary funds might be a factor that further complicates the principal-agent relationships around contemporary NDBs. Conventionally, making access to EU funds contingent upon meeting certain standards of governance might limit opportunities for national policy makers to use NDBs for ulterior motives. But it may also enable NDBs to navigate a course between the two levels of

[4] On the professional background of development bankers see Ban and Tillerkeratne, 2019.

government, providing leeway for agency. Here we may encounter a tendency diametrically opposite to political capture, namely the risk of mission drift through which the dependency on specific resources and the organizational tendency to expand may infringe the core objectives of a given NDB. In the EU, this would mean securing additional resources in terms of headcount and budgetary instruments, while not engaging in the increased risk-taking demanded by the political principal.

(2) These sets of social relations provoke a number of questions over the distributional and transformative politics implicated. What is the rationale for investment projects being financed through a public-private partnership, and how has the project been made attractive to private investors?[5] Is it more than a means to provide large financial actors, such as pension funds, with a secure form of income? Does it provide the risk capital that brings about the desired changes in the direction of a more sustainable economy? And if it does so, who actually gets to accumulate the profits, when start-ups are brought to the initial public offering? And if it does not, who bears the costs?

As suggested above, coming up with large headline numbers based on financial risk-sharing agreements might promise business for NDBs, projects for yield-searching investors and less pressure to tackle more difficult public policy objectives. For instance, if NDBs are able to raise money through financial markets, it may reduce the political appetite to raise public money through taxation or other public policy actions.

In addition, NDBs might be overselling their ability to impact change, and, with such ambitious headline investment numbers, might distract from other public policies that would have a similar, long-term impact. First, NDBs—that are protected by their parastatal status—face a trade-off between pursuing safer investments with guaranteed returns or investing in higher-risk, but perhaps more transformative, projects. The EIB in particular is a case of a bank which has sought to leverage its status as a multilateral lending institution to generate low-risk arbitrage returns emerging from its AAA credit rating (cf. Toplensky and Barker, 2019). As a result of this government backing, both NDBs and the EIB could end up prioritizing a profitable business model over other investment because of their objective to still be "bankable" and manage financial risks.

The intersections of distributional and transformational politics also appear within the context of European integration more generally. The variation among European NDBs in terms of strategic capacities, financial resources, and political backing—analogous to the heterogeneity of

[5] For a critical view on PPPs and the EIB, see Liebe and Howarth 2020.

European capitalisms—is a further obstacle to a coordinated effort for socio-ecological transformation. It is not surprising, then, that much of the praise for creating a sustainable infrastructure is reserved for KfW (Mazzucato and Penna, 2016; Griffith-Jones, 2016)—but it is unlikely this experience can be easily reproduced in the face of all the difficulties of institutional transplantation and despite new possibilities for European NDBs to collaborate and forge joint projects. The crucial question will be whether the funds provided at the EU level for such initiatives and the administrative burden erected to access these funds will be balanced out and matched by Member States. The political choices how to arrange cross-national and public-private coordination in this European investment infrastructure to be just and effective are thus far from trivial and require greater attention from across the social sciences.

(3) Certainly, these issues raise the question whether the European public sphere is properly equipped to evaluate the effects of this new investment infrastructure as it unfolds. The report of the European Court of Auditors on EFSI in 2019 is a first step in this direction, but a stronger civil society that takes up these findings and contributes to public awareness regarding the effects of these risk-sharing arrangements may be warranted. Recent reports by NGOs like Counter Balance (2019) and Transparency International (2017) on the activities of the EIB are important in providing a countering view to the trends in development banking, particularly as more investment decisions are moved away from traditional public policy fora. However, is there enough sensitivity for these issues in the media and amid the broader European public sphere to demand and provide sufficient critical scrutiny? Or is the arcane technical detail of contractual risk-sharing arrangements depoliticizing these manners to such a degree that it is effectively shielded from such a public debate? This is even more important as the typical mechanism, which evaluates companies' effectiveness and scrutinizes their behavior, an interested financial public, is not present with respect to NDBs, and only slowly emerging with the EIB. The question the European public needs to answer is: What is the equivalent of the maximization of shareholder value these public banks are supposed to follow and how are we going to hold them accountable?[6]

In addition, it is important for academics and public policy practitioners to better understand how these changes to development banking compare with its prior incarnations. A persistent question in this area has been, How are we as a public supposed to gauge the social return on these investments? This is a very hard exercise indeed, as there is no

[6] On the issue of the political determination of the goals to be pursued by the World Bank see Babb 2009.

alternative universe to observe a different course of action. Much more engagement with this form of banking is needed also from economists, to have proper ways of doing impact assessment. The questions of what the rate of return on these investments is, both for private and for public actors should be the product of input from all actors—from NDBs to politicians to everyday citizens.[7]

Development finance institutions, and first and foremost the EIB, have built up economic departments and economic publications, which make the case for public-development banking. The quality of these publications is outstanding and it is only fair that these institutions develop their own in-house expertise to evaluate the impact of their activities. Yet there is a need for counter-expertise that can feed diverging interpretations to a critical public, for which transparent data and greater scrutiny is required. Currently, there is little regarding the capabilities that can assess the effects of the field of development banking, a void which in the long-term poses democratic accountability issues.

(4) Finally, what does this all tell us about the future of the field and European integration more broadly? Current trends suggest that the European development-banking field will continue to expand. The European financial instrument-based investment agenda has strengthened with every contested multiannual financial framework and every new "grand investment project" from EFSI (EUR 315 bn) to EFSI 2.0 (EUR 500 bn) to InvestEU (EUR 650 bn) to the latest "Green Deal" proposal (EUR 1000 bn). Incumbents such as the EIB and the KfW have started to present themselves as "climate banks", linking up to what may emerge as a future "grand narrative" of European integration: tackling climate change as a truly transnational challenge and purposeful endeavor that requires the pooling of resources and the solving of collective action problems in an environment of competition states. Even development finance institutions in the periphery have devoted more attention to issues such as energy efficiency, sustainable infrastructure, and "green finance". In this sense, the transformation of European capitalism in the face of climate change awareness might be a process that further consolidates the field around a shared understanding of what is at stake and how development banking should work to address it. This might also open up new venues for challengers to destabilize the present understanding of development banking. Fields, after all, are characterized by "constant jockeying…as a result of their contentious nature" (Fligstein and McAdam, 2012, p. 12), implying it

[7] For a broader discussion on the democratization of public finance see the contributions in Transnational Institute, 2019.

always carries the possibility of destabilization. This is even more true because the field is dependent upon the preferences of multiple principles, first and foremost EU governments, that are themselves struggling over the economic and political future of the Union. Especially the Euro area is ridden by persistent processes of "structural polarization" between and within core and periphery countries, which requires nothing less than a fundamental political compromise between Member States to address, going beyond the impasses of structural reform and emphasizing public investment and redistributive policies (Gräbner et al. 2020).

The European way of tackling polarization, in combination with financial instability and sluggish growth since the Great Financial Crisis, mainly rested on a technocratic arrangement of "governing through financial markets" (Braun, Gabor, and Hübner 2018), which provokes some further questions about how development banking is intertwined with the larger ecosystem of public financial institutions—central banks, sovereign wealth funds, state-owned banks, multilateral banks—that may deliver greater output, if not input, legitimacy in contemporary capitalist democracies. How is development banking embedded in this ecosystem, as one instrument among many, and how does it coordinate and—potentially—compete with those actors arguably crucial for the trajectories of the European and global political economy?

These, we believe, are a host of questions an interdisciplinary research agenda should take up, starting from the proposition that NDBs are inherently ambivalent institutions. This book's purpose is to draw attention to a rarely studied actor in the domestic, regional, and global political economy by employing a field theoretical lens. NDBs are resource dependent, reflexive actors, with both their own agendas and an institutional linkage to the broader relations of social forces. The German KfW, for instance, was instrumental in assisting the German government in large-scale privatization and financial liberalization as it was in financing the turn to renewable energy; it has an internationally renowned pool of own resources, but is still dependent on international (dollar-denominated) capital markets and respective ratings. Such ambivalences and tensions are no less in play when it comes to development banking in increasingly illiberal Hungary or crisis-torn Greece, even if for different reasons. Hence, advocates of public financial institutions (e.g. Block, 2014; Mazzucato and Penna, 2016) should take note that nowhere in the EU do NDBs represent significant and progressive counterforces to reigning in financialized capitalism, even if some of them are capable of being important providers of patient, mission-oriented finance. To change this is not solely an issue for the governance of public banks, but of political economy at large.

## References

Alami, I., Dixon, A., 2019. State Capitalism(S) Redux? Theories, Tensions, Controversies. Competition & Change 24, 70–94.

Babb, S. 2009. Behind the Development Banks. Washington Politics, World Poverty, and the Wealth of Nations. Chicago: University of Chicago Press.

Ban, C., 2019. Dependent Development at a Crossroads? Romanian Capitalism and Its Contradictions. West European Politics 42, 1041–68.

Ban, C., Tillerkeratne, S., 2019. The Managerial Elite of Development Banks. GEGI Working Paper 28, Global Development Policy Center.

Block, F., 2014. Democratizing Finance. Politics & Society 42, 3–28.

Bohle, D., Greskovits, B., 2012. Capitalist Diversity on Europe's Periphery. Ithaca: Cornell University Press.

Braun, B., Gabor, D., Hübner, M. 2018. Governing through financial markets: Towards a critical political economy of Capital Markets Union. Competition & Change 22 (2), 101–116.

Bulfone, F., 2019. The Political Economy of Industrial Policy in the EU: Insights from the State-Centered Literature. Conference paper presented July 2019 at SASE annual conference, New York.

Clift, B., 2013. Economic Patriotism, the Clash of Capitalisms, and State Aid in the European Union. Journal of Industry, Competition and Trade 13, 101–17.

Chen, M. 2020. State Actors, Market Games: Credit Guarantees and the Funding of China Development Bank. New Political Economy 25 (3), 453–468.

Cowling, K. (ed.), 1999. Industrial policy in Europe. Theoretical Perspectives and Practical Proposals. London: Routledge.

DiMaggio, P.J., Powell, W.W., 1983. The Iron Cage Revisited: Institutional Isomorphism and Collective Rationality in Organizational Fields. American Sociological Review 48, 147–60.

Eder, J., Schneider, E., 2018. Progressive Industrial Policy—A Remedy for Europe?! Journal für Entwicklungspolitik 34, 108–42.

Epstein, R., 2017. Banking on Markets. The Transformation of Bank-State Ties in Europe and Beyond. Oxford: Oxford University Press.

European Court of Auditors, 2019. European Fund for Strategic Investments: Action needed to Make EFSI a Full Success. Special Report 03. European Union, Luxembourg.

Fernández-Arias, E., Hausmann, R., Panizza, U. 2020. Smart Development Banks. Journal of Industry, Competition and Trade 20 (2), 395–420.

Fioretos, O., 2001. The Domestic Sources of Multilateral Preferences: Varieties of Capitalism in the European Community, in Hall, P., Soskice, D. (eds), Varieties of Capitalism. The Institutional Foundations of Comparative Advantage. Oxford: Oxford University Press, 213–46.

Fligstein, N., 1996. Markets as Politics: A Political-Cultural Approach to Market Institutions. American Sociological Review 61, 656–73.

Fligstein, N., 2001. The Architecture of Markets: An Economic Sociology of Twenty-First-Century Capitalist Societies. Princeton: Princeton University Press.

Fligstein, N., McAdam, D., 2012. A Theory of Fields. Oxford: Oxford University Press.

Gill, S., 1998. European governance and new constitutionalism: Economic and Monetary Union and alternatives to disciplinary Neoliberalism in Europe. New Political Economy 3 (1), 5–26.

Griffith-Jones, S. 2016. National Development Banks and Sustainable Infrastructure: The Case of KfW. GEGI Working Paper 006.

Gräbner, C., Heimberger, P., Kapeller, J., Schütz, B., 2020. Is the Eurozone disintegrating? Macroeconomic Divergence, Structural Polarisation, Trade and Fragility. Cambridge Journal of Economics 44 (3), 647–669.

Griffith-Jones, S., Ocampo, J.A. (eds), 2018. The Future of National Development Banks. Oxford: Oxford University Press.

Héritier, A., Knill, C., 2001. Differential Responses to European Policies: A Comparison, in Héritier, A., Kerwer, D., Knill, C., Lehmkuhl, D., Teutsch, M., Douillet, A.C. (eds), Differential Europe. The European Union Impact on National Policymaking. Lanham: Rowman & Littlefield, 257–94.

Hayward, J. (ed.), 1995. Industrial enterprise and European integration. From national to international champions in Western Europe. Oxford: Oxford University Press.

Kavvadia, H. and S. Savvides, 2019. Funding Economic Development and the Role of National Development Banks—The Case of Cyprus. Conference paper presented September 2019 at the EAEPE conference, Warsaw.

Liebe, M., Howarth, D., 2020. The European Investment Bank as Policy Entrepreneur and the Promotion of Public-Private Partnerships. New Political Economy 25 (2), 195–212.

Mazzucato, M., Penna, C.C.R., 2016. Beyond Market Failures: The Market Creating and Shaping Roles of State Investment Banks. Journal of Economic Policy Reform 19, 305–26.

Mertens, D., Thiemann, M., 2018. Market-Based but State-Led: The Role of Public Development Banks in Shaping Market-Based Finance in the European Union. Competition & Change 22, 184–204.

Moslener, U., Thiemann, M., Volberding, P., 2018. National Development Banks as Active Financiers: The Case of KfW, in Griffith-Jones, S., Ocampo, J.A. (eds), The Future of National Development Banks. Oxford: Oxford University Press, 63–85.

Naczyk, M. 2019. Taking back control: Indigenous managerial elites' push for state-led developmentalism in Poland's dependent market economy. Conference paper presented at the 31st Annual EAEPE Conference, Warsaw.

Naqvi, N., Henow, A., Chang, H.-J., 2018. Kicking Away the Financial Ladder? German Development Banking Under Economic Globalisation. Review of International Political Economy 25, 672–98.

Thatcher, M., 2017. The Reshaping of Economic Markets and the State. Economic Crisis and State Changes, in King, D., Le Galès, P. (eds): Reconfiguring European States in Crisis. Oxford: Oxford University Press, 179–200.

Thurbon, E., 2016. Developmental Mindset. The Revival of Financial Activism in South Korea. Ithaca: Cornell University Press.

Toplensky, R. and Barker, A., 2019. European Investment Bank: the EU's hidden giant. Financial Times, 15 July 2019.

Transnational Institute, 2019. L. Steinfort and S. Kishimoto (ed.) Public Finance for the Future We Want, Amsterdam: TNI.

Wade, R.H., 2012. Return of Industrial Policy? International Review of Applied Economics 26, 223–39.

Wigger, A., Horn, L., 2019. The Bed You Made. Social Democracy and Industrial Policy in the EU, in Hay, C., Bailey, D. (eds), Diverging Capitalisms. Britain, the City of London and Europe. Palgrave Macmillan, 171–93.

Zysman, J., 1983. Governments, Markets, and Growth. Ithaca: Cornell University Press.

# Index

*Note*: Tables and figures are indicated by italic '*t*' and '*f*' following the page number; 'n' after a page number indicates the footnote number.